DIARY OF A
PHILOSOPHY STUDENT

Simone de Beauvoir

DIARY OF A PHILOSOPHY STUDENT

VOLUME 2, 1928–29

Edited by Barbara Klaw,
Sylvie Le Bon de Beauvoir,
Margaret A. Simons,
and Marybeth Timmermann

Foreword by Sylvie Le Bon de Beauvoir

Translations, Notes, and Annotations by Barbara Klaw

Transcription by Barbara Klaw and Sylvie Le Bon de Beauvoir

UNIVERSITY OF
ILLINOIS PRESS
Urbana, Chicago, and Springfield

English language translation of Notebook Six in *Cahiers de jeunesse, 1926–1930*, by
    Simone de Beauvoir

First Illinois paperback, 2021
This edition © 2019 by the Board of Trustees
of the University of Illinois
1 2 3 4 5 C P 5 4 3 2 1
♾ This book is printed on acid-free paper.

The Library of Congress cataloged the cloth edition as follows:
Beauvoir, Simone de, 1908–1986
[Carnets de jeunesse. English]
Diary of a philosophy student / Simone de Beauvoir; edited by Barbara Klaw, Sylvie Le
    Bon de Beauvoir, and Margaret A. Simons, with Marybeth Timmermann; foreword
    by Sylvie Le Bon de Beauvoir; translation, notes, and annotations by Barbara Klaw;
    transcribed by Barbara Klaw and Sylvie Le Bon de Beauvoir.
p. cm.—(The Beauvoir series)
Includes bibliographical references and index.
ISBN 978-0-252-04254-6 (cloth : alk. paper)
ISBN 978-0-252-05138-8 (ebook)
1. Beauvoir, Simone de, 1908–1986.
I. Klaw, Barbara.
II. Le Bon de Beauvoir, Sylvie.
III. Simons, Margaret A.
IV. Title.
B2430.
B344A313   2006
194—dc22[b]   2006021222

PAPERBACK ISBN 978-0-252-08591-8

IN MEMORY OF CHRISTINE PIERCE AND CATHERINE NAJI

Contents

Foreword to the Beauvoir Series   *ix*
   Sylvie Le Bon de Beauvoir

Acknowledgments   *xi*

Introduction   *1*
   Margaret A. Simons

On Reading Beauvoir's Early Writings, 1926–1930,
as a Philosophy of Self-Help   *5*
   Barbara Klaw

Sixth Notebook: September 27, 1928–September 12, 1929   *23*
   Simone de Beauvoir

Bibliography   *337*

Index   *343*

Errata for the Hardcover Edition of *Diary of a Philosophy Student,*
Volume 1, 1926–27   *371*

Foreword to the Beauvoir Series

Sylvie Le Bon de Beauvoir

TRANSLATED BY MARYBETH TIMMERMANN

It is my pleasure to take this opportunity to honor the monumental work of research and publication that the Beauvoir Series represents, which was undertaken and brought to fruition by Margaret A. Simons and the ensemble of her team. These volumes of Simone de Beauvoir's writings, concerning literature as well as philosophy and feminism, stretch from 1926 to 1979— that is to say throughout almost her entire life. Some of them have been published before, and are known, but remain dispersed throughout time and space, in diverse editions, diverse newspapers, or reviews. Others were read during conferences or radio programs and then lost from view. Some had been left completely unpublished. What gives them force and meaning is precisely having them gathered together, closely, as a whole. Nothing of the sort has yet been realized, except, on a much smaller scale, *Les écrits de Simone de Beauvoir* (The writings of Simone de Beauvoir), published in France in 1979. Here, the aim is an exhaustive corpus, as much as that is possible.

Because they cover more than 50 years, these volumes faithfully reflect the thoughts of their author, the early manifestation and permanence of certain of her preoccupations as a writer and philosopher, as a woman and feminist. What will be immediately striking, I think, is their extraordinary *coherence*. Obviously, from this point of view, *Les cahiers de jeunesse* (*Diaries of a Philosophy Student*), previously unpublished, constitutes the star document. The very young eighteen, nineteen, twenty-year-old Simone de Beauvoir who writes them is clearly already the future great Simone de Beauvoir, author of *L'invitée*, (*She Came to Stay*), *Pour une morale de l'ambiguïté* (*The Ethics of Ambiguity*), *Le deuxième sexe* (*The Second Sex*), *Les Mandarins* (*The Mandarins*), and *Mémoires* (*Memoirs*). Not only is her vocation as a writer energetically affirmed in these diaries, but one also discovers in them the roots of her later reflections. It is particularly touching to see the birth, often with hesitations, doubt, and anguish, of the fundamental choices of thought and existence that would have such an impact on so many future readers, women and men. Torments, doubt, and anguish are expressed, but also exultation and confidence in her strength and in the future—the foresight of certain passages is impressive. Take the one from June 25, 1929, for example: "Strange certitude that these riches will be welcomed, that some words will be said and heard, that this life will be a fountainhead from which many others will draw. Certitude of a vocation."

These precious *Cahiers* will cut short the unproductive and recurrent debate about the "influence" that Sartre supposedly had on Simone de Beauvoir, since they incontestably reveal to us Simone de Beauvoir *before* Sartre. Thus, their relationship will take on its true sense, and one will understand to what point Simone de Beauvoir was even more herself when she agreed with some of Sartre's themes, because all those lonely years of apprenticeship and training were leading her to a definite path and not just any path. Therefore, it is not a matter of influence but an encounter in the strong sense of the term. They each *recognized themselves* in the other because each one already existed independently and intensely. One can discern all the better the originality of Simone de Beauvoir in her ethical preoccupations, her own conception of concrete freedom, and her dramatic consciousness of the essential role of the Other, for example, because they are prefigured in the feverish meditations, pen in hand, which occupied her youth. *Les cahiers* constitute a priceless testimony.

I conclude by thanking Margaret A. Simons and her team again for their magnificent series, which constitutes an irreplaceable contribution to the study and the true understanding of the thoughts and works of Simone de Beauvoir.

Acknowledgments

Barbara Klaw writes: I applaud the numerous individuals who helped in the production of this annotated translation. First, I thank Sylvie Le Bon de Beauvoir for her kind encouragement in my continued work on Beauvoir's 1927–1930 diary. I am grateful to the staff in the Manuscript Room of the Bibliothèque Nationale in Paris and especially to Mauricette Berne for facilitating my study of the manuscripts. To Margaret Simons and Marybeth Timmermann, I am indebted for comments on earlier versions of my translation and annotation. For their help in finding references for the works or places that Beauvoir cited, I acknowledge Madeleine Leveau-Fernandez, Tamara F. O'Callaghan, and Richard Shryock. The Interlibrary Loan Department of Northern Kentucky University deserves praise for its success in making requested translations available for use. I am beholden to Annlaug Bjørsnøs, Alan Hutchison, Nadia Ibrahim, Katherine C. Kurk, Tove Pettersen, and Gerald Prince for their moral support. For the funding of my continued work on this manuscript for many years, I express gratitude to the American Philosophical Society, the National Endowment for the Humanities, Northern Kentucky University, and the Southern Regional Education Board.

Margaret Simons writes: I would like to congratulate Barbara Klaw on her tremendous achievement and to thank her once again for so generously sharing her draft transcription of Beauvoir's 1927 diary back in 1994, effectively launching the collaborative project of the Beauvoir Series. I would like to extend my warmest thanks to Sylvie Le Bon de Beauvoir, coeditor of the Beauvoir Series, for her unwavering support and encouragement, and to our longtime editor, Joan Catapano, without whom we would not have dared begin. I am very grateful to Anne-Solange Noble, at Editions Gallimard, for her invaluable advice and assistance; to Laurie Matheson, at the University of Illinois Press, for her continued guidance and encouragement; to Mauricette Berne, for her guidance in accessing the manuscripts at the Bibliothèque Nationale; to Marybeth Timmermann, for her assistance in preparing the completed volume for publication; and to Pam Decoteau and Cindi Pearlman, for their helpful suggestions as I was working on my introduction. This volume would not have been possible without the generous support of a Collaborative Research Grant from the National Endowment for the Humanities, an independent federal agency; a Matching Funds grant from the Illinois Board of Higher Education allocated by the Graduate School of Southern Illinois University Edwardsville; and a translation grant from the French Ministry of Culture.

DIARY OF A
PHILOSOPHY STUDENT

Introduction

Margaret A. Simons

"That's when everything started," Simone de Beauvoir wrote in an entry dated July 8, 1929, in her 1928–1929 diary. Her relationship with Jean-Paul Sartre that started on that day is a highlight of this volume, the second of three projected volumes of Beauvoir's *Diary of a Philosophy Student*. The first volume, published in 2006, includes notebooks two and four of her 1926–1927 diary (notebook one is missing).[1] The forthcoming third volume will include notebook three from her 1926–1927 diary, along with her 1927–1928 and 1929–1930 diaries.

Fans of Beauvoir's *Memoirs of a Dutiful Daughter* (1958) will recognize episodes from that story, beginning with Beauvoir's shock at entering Sartre's smoke-filled dorm room and the timidity she felt in lecturing Sartre (who was three years older) and his *petits camarades* on Leibniz's philosophy as they prepared for the oral exams of the *agrégation* in philosophy.[2]

But her *Diary* and *Memoirs* differ in important ways. The story told in *Memoirs* fills in gaps in Beauvoir's *Diary*, providing background (some of which we have included in endnotes), while the account recorded in her *Diary* reveals experiences missing from her *Memoirs*, including paradoxically, Beauvoir's early commitment to doing philosophy.

1

Understanding Beauvoir's decision to erase philosophy from her life story requires a closer look at her goals in writing her autobiography. Beauvoir wrote *Memoirs*, she tells a 1960 interviewer, in order to defend her 1949 essay in feminist theory, *The Second Sex*, against the charge that it was a product of "resentment," the work of an "embittered" woman.[3] And *Memoirs* is, in a sense, a literary version of *The Second Sex*, written, as Beauvoir remarks in *Force of Circumstance*, for girls like Beauvoir's childhood friend, Zaza, "who are in need of family and religion, and who do not yet dare to dare."[4]

By 1958 when *Memoirs* appeared, Beauvoir was known worldwide as Sartre's companion and philosophical follower. Her writings, including her 1943 metaphysical novel, *She Came to Stay* and *The Second Sex*, were seen as applying Sartre's philosophy from his 1943 essay, *Being and Nothingness*. But the reality was very different, as we learned after the deaths of Sartre in 1980 and Beauvoir in 1986. Their posthumously published wartime diaries and correspondence reveal that in February of 1940 Sartre drew upon a final draft of *She Came to Stay*, including Beauvoir's theory of the Other, as he began writing *Being and Nothingness*. Her novel, long assumed to be its application, was instead a source of Sartre's philosophy.[5]

Telling the story of the failure of her original philosophical work to win recognition would have been a dangerous gift to critics eager to disparage *The Second Sex* as the work of an "embittered" woman. In order to protect her feminist message and bring it to more readers, Beauvoir would have to erase her life story as a philosopher, whatever the personal costs.

The rewrite of her life begins in *Memoirs* with the story of Sartre forcing Beauvoir to recognize her intellectual limitations: "I sometimes attempted to argue with him, . . . but Sartre always succeeded in turning the tables on me." "Day after day, and all day long I set myself up against Sartre, and in our discussions I was simply not in his class."[6] *Diary* gives a different account full of intellectual sparring, as on July 11, 1929: "it seems that I angered Sartre quite a bit when for fun I compared him to Gandillac. What's more, I let loose this afternoon. . . . [I]n fact I am getting the better of Sartre today; I am having great fun, but how well we are working too!"

The famous story from *Memoirs* of Sartre defeating Beauvoir in an argument near the Medici Fountain in Luxembourg Gardens is confirmed, in part, by a diary entry for July 21, 1929: "I go to Luxembourg Gardens with Sartre where we discuss good and evil for two hours. He interests me enormously, but destroys me; I am no longer sure of what I think or even of thinking." According to *Memoirs*, the argument forced Beauvoir "to take a more modest view of myself."[7] But the *Diary* entry for July 21, 1929, instead shows the argument firing Beauvoir's ambition: "Revelation of . . . a strength of thought that demands the most serious work for me to attain it, and a maturity that I envy and promise myself to attain." The argument also ignited her intellectual aggression, unfortunately for Beauvoir's kid sister: "In the evening I take a walk with Poupette, very exalted with such prospects of a fervent life. I demolish her Catholicism for her in a few words. . . . I feel within me something tumultuous that frightens me, an intensity that exhausts me. But I accept the great adventure of being me." No sign of modesty here.

Nor did the argument in Luxembourg Gardens damage Beauvoir's academic performance. "My Latin explication went well," she reports the following day, July 22, 1929, after the second oral. Indeed, *Diary* shows Sartre supporting Beauvoir's achievement from the first day of the orals, July 19, 1929: "Good Greek explication, after the nervousness of the morning when seeing the *agrégation* students gathered before a paternal jury made me feel nauseated. Merleau-Ponty and Zaza kindly tried to help me shake it off, but in vain, until Sartre authoritatively took me to Luxembourg Gardens to do some Plato."

Beauvoir's decision to write her *diplôme* on Leibniz in 1928–1929, the same year as the *agrégation*, allowed her to skip a year (and catch up with Sartre who had flunked the written exam the year before). But it left her little time for her own writing. She expresses her regret, in a mechanical-sounding phrase in the November 17, 1928, diary entry, at being "the work-ing ma-chine." She did, however, continue to read outside the required program, as she notes on October 4, 1928, in her earliest known reference to Hegel: "Have read a very clear and intelligent book by Benedetto Croce on Hegel."

Diary points not to Hegel, however, but to Maurice Barrès as influencing Beauvoir's early formulation of the problem of the Other. "Oh, how Barrès has made his mark on me!" she writes in the October 25, 1928, diary entry: "[O]thers, for me, are 'adversaries,' and I construct a world that I like against this world that I do not like."[8] Beauvoir reflects on her struggles to hold onto the romantic illusions of her childhood, realizing on some level that they are in bad faith, as in the October 5, 1928, diary entry: "I have read, I have seen many, many things, but the things roll off me and because I do not consent to believe in their existence, I say that they are not." Beauvoir will address the epistemological and ethical dimensions of bad faith in *When Things of the Spirit Come First*, written in 1935–1937. But the antiblack racism evident in her July 9, 1929, diary entry will not face a serious challenge until after the war, under the guidance of the African American writer, Richard Wright, an experience recounted in *America: Day by Day* (1948).[9]

3

Readers interested in the development of Beauvoir's phenomenological method must wait for the forthcoming third volume of *Diary* where a February 10, 1928, entry contains her first reference to "lived experience." The reference appears in a discussion of her paper for a Sorbonne professor, the Catholic Husserlean Jean Baruzi, whose classes, she explains in *Memoirs*, were disdained by students at the École Normale Supérieure (including Sartre and his friends).[10] This present volume of Beauvoir's *Diary* does include tantalizing hints of phenomenology, including a November 1, 1928, conversation about Husserl and retrospective accounts in October 1928, June 25, 1929, and September 1929 of an earlier interest in her "metaphysical intuitions." The forthcoming volume of the *Diary* will show that Beauvoir does not return to her philosophical work until late in 1930, after the shock of Jacques's marriage and Zaza's death had changed forever her work in philosophy and her relationship with Sartre.

NOTES

1. Beauvoir, *Diary of a Philosophy Student*, vol. 1.

2. Simone de Beauvoir, *Memoirs of a Dutiful Daughter* (MDD), trans. James Kirkup (New York: Harper Colophon, 1974), 334; originally published as *Mémoires d'une jeune fille rangée* (MJFR), Folio ed. (Paris: Gallimard, 1989), 467; my revised translation.

3. Madeleine Chapsal, "Une interview de Simone de Beauvoir par Madeleine Chapsal," in *Les écrits de Simone de Beauvoir*, ed. Claude Francis and Fernande Gontier (Paris: Gallimard, 1979), 396.

4. Simone de Beauvoir, *Force of Circumstance II*, trans. Richard Howard (New York: Harper Colophon, 1977), 417; originally published as *La force des choses II*, Folio ed. (Paris: Gallimard, 1963), 189; my revised translation.

5. See Edward Fullbrook, "*She Came to Stay* and *Being and Nothingness*," in *The Philosophy of Simone de Beauvoir: Critical Essays*, ed. Margaret A. Simons (Bloomington: Indiana University Press, 2006), 42–64; and Margaret A. Simons, "Beauvoir, Philosophy and Autobiography," in *A Companion to Simone de Beauvoir*, ed. Laura Hengehold and Nancy Bauer (Hoboken, N.J.: Wiley Blackwell, 2017), 393–405.

6. MDD, 335; MJFR, 467.

7. MDD, 344; MJFR, 480.

8. See the reference to Barrès in *Diary* 1:103; the October 5, 1926, entry tells of Beauvoir reading Barrès's "[Sous] L'oeil des barbares," which could be translated as "Under the Gaze [or Look] of the Barbarians," the first volume of his 1888 trilogy, *Cult of the Self*.

9. See Simons, "Richard Wright, Simone de Beauvoir, and *The Second Sex*," in *Beauvoir and* The Second Sex, 167–184.

10. MDD, 262; MJFR, 363.

On Reading Beauvoir's Early Writings, 1926–1930, as a Philosophy of Self-Help

Barbara Klaw

> *I alone can have an authentic liking for myself. The time has come to realize my life. . . . I must see what I am, what I think, and try to want something, to want myself, to love myself. I must not be an illusion for myself.*
>
> —*January 28, 1928, "Fifth Notebook"*

Although this second volume of Beauvoir's *Diary of a Philosophy Student* (henceforth *Diary*) presents only the sixth notebook of Beauvoir's student diary, this study will give an overview of the way Beauvoir focuses on self-development throughout her diary, including the forthcoming third volume. One major value of reading Beauvoir's *Diary* is the discovery of pertinent self-help tips that reflect an ancient literary and philosophical tradition. The Bible is replete with parables meant to show people how to live together more successfully. The Hindu Upanishads focus on people knowing themselves in depth as individuals beyond their political and social dimensions.[1] Philosophers such as Seneca, Marcus Aurelius, and Epictetus provide maxims and anecdotes to illustrate how to live.[2] French literature classics such as Montesquieu's *Essays* and the *Maxims* of François de la Rochefoucauld portray and comment on human behavior partly to improve relationships and hasten progress in the world. The title of Samuel Smiles's

1859 book, *Self-Help*, about working-class men who rose to success, lives on to describe inspirational works.[3] In the twenty-first-century, self-help could be viewed as a melting pot of thoughts and traditions from Eastern, Western, and Native American philosophies and spiritual practices enriched by scientific discoveries. In its most basic form, it might promise everything but deliver little as some suggest.[4] But in its most comprehensive versions, much of today's self-help could be viewed as a type of popular philosophy from which one learns to nurture the development of one's ideal self.[5]

Beauvoir draws upon practices from her Catholic upbringing and her extensive studies in philosophy, literature and psychology to analyze her thoughts and feelings.[6] In *Diary*, Beauvoir cites the Bible, philosophers, scientists, novelists, and poets including Tagore, the Indian poet raised with strict Upanishadic ideals.[7] Writing helps Beauvoir to remember what she has already learned, to see how her thoughts and behaviors have progressed, and to understand how she might obtain everything she wants while making an honorable impact on society.

Building on my earlier work on Beauvoir's use of her diary for self-creation and self-support, this study will show the plan for successful goal achievement that emerges from Beauvoir's *Diary*, provide specific examples of her trials and tribulations as she put her own advice to the test, and illustrate how her plan anticipates today's self-help systems.[8] Her true tales of struggle, heartache, and success in living her plan suggest to readers that she is just like them and that her methods could work for them. In fact, she encourages this analogy by identifying herself as a universal twenty-year-old, "For I am not just one young girl, but rather within her all the youth of today, this entire soul of twenty-year-old people dreamed indefinitely within me, collective soul, closer and more tender than that of any singular individual" (February 10, 1928, "Fifth Notebook").[9]

Long before women had legal or social rights to focus on their own desires, Beauvoir already understood her own power both as a universal being and as the inventor of her own reality: "As for me, I feel so free, so much like the creator of my present" (July 24, 1927, *Diary* 1, 292). As we read *Diary*, it becomes clear that such creation of reality involves several things: consistent gratitude and optimism; unconditional self-love and self-trust; continued analysis of the self and the self's desire; and the will to remain focused on the present moment.

Beauvoir shows a reader that being thankful and joyful are viable ways to move beyond disappointments. She establishes as a given that our reactions to our experiences matter more than the experiences themselves. Therefore, one way of engendering success is to find something good in every experience. As Beauvoir suffers through her devastation at learning of her beloved Jacques's affair with another woman, she calms herself by looking for what she learned from her discovery, and she focuses on being grateful and optimistic about her discovery:

> Besides, this ordeal allows me to better measure my strength; I now know ... that one must joyously affront reality without demanding *anything* from it: and demand only of oneself to measure up to what is proposed. . . . one must know how to transform even an apparent defeat into a much more magnificent victory. (May 4, 1929, "Sixth Notebook")[10]

In this way, Beauvoir's *Diary* is years ahead of its time in teaching a self-help technique based on the popular idea of a "Law of Attraction." This means that unless we make a conscious effort to choose a positive focus for our thoughts, we will unwittingly attract to ourselves whatever we most often contemplate, be it good or bad.[11]

Beauvoir's diary also illustrates how one might rise to greatness through self-love and self-analysis, for example, in her repeated reminders to herself that she has the ability to accomplish great feats. Because she believes in herself and her own uniqueness so much, she questions herself until she understands precisely what she wants. Thus, when she desperately seeks how to reconcile the desire to be alone struggling with ideas and sublime goals and the desire to let herself go and simply enjoy life, she writes an entire dialogue with herself. Readers can identify with her indecision and explanations and learn from her to persevere and affirm their own potential greatness: "You've said what you wanted one hundred times: not to give yourself up to things, but rather to take them with you; take up your burden again, my girl, you've been resting and living beneath yourself for too long" (August 28, 1928, "Fifth Notebook"). In this way, too, Beauvoir anticipates today's self-help programs: to attract good things, we must repeatedly answer the following questions, "What do I want? Why do I want it? How do I want to feel?"[12]

Yet Beauvoir's process of analysis goes beyond simple self-examination. It also involves contemplating what each of her desires means and doesn't mean in its relationship to her plans for the future. It includes looking back to measure her progress and studying what needs to be changed to move forward more quickly.

> But to do what one wants does not mean that one wants everything. "Give me inner beauty . . ." But this gets back to the evolution of an entire year: to want only joy. I have to beware of recreating these states of joy

"blissfully in the rapture of emptiness"—or at least to make these states only elements of the synthesis. Finally constructive judgment alone permits the attainment of what did not exist before it. (April 27, 1929, "Sixth Notebook")

Beauvoir also shows how to love and honor oneself by affirming that she is truly the only person who can know what is best for her. Beauvoir, the philosophy student, leaves a legacy of examples that remind us that we must trust ourselves to recognize the path that we wish to follow at each turn of the road. Almost a century later, today's life coaches lead clients to their own truths by asking pertinent thought-provoking questions and telling them that they alone hold the solutions to their own problems.[13] Beauvoir uses her diary to move beyond moments of doubt by repeating to herself that she is the only one who can truly know what is best for her own self-development and self-fulfillment:

As in your despair, you possess yourself now in a magnificent serenity. Ah! here you are at the height of yourself, you can have confidence, and you ask yourself: what shall I do with this self, grown up like this? Eternal question, the answer is only in this self. (March 1928, "Fifth Notebook")

She is also successful because she understands that part of being self-loving means to continually celebrate her strengths, develop a concrete plan, and envision herself becoming the true answer to all her dreams. Even at age eighteen, she shows tremendous self-confidence and belief in her projects. As self-help programs and books promulgate today, she creates affirmations and recites them to herself.[14] Part of the power of her affirmations comes from her repeated efforts to take stock of her strengths, to visualize a powerful and reliable future self, and in so doing, to personalize her affirmations and lead herself to greater achievements:

My own strength: I know that, for all of my existence, I will be able to count on myself; that I will need neither advice nor energy, but rather and always this great power of recovery. This love and this ardent interest and this desire for perfection for myself. I know that I will be faithful to myself . . . that I will always know how to find myself in all of my integrity in the midst of necessary banalities. I walk with confidence towards this self of tomorrow, who will not betray me. (December 23, 1926, "Third Notebook")

She is also effective because she has clearly stated goals and a process for accomplishing them just as today's self-help industry encourages everyone to do.[15] She consistently writes them down, establishes a time frame for their achievement, and focuses on what the achievement of those goals will bring her:

> It will suffice that by 22 years of age I will have taken the *agrégation* and written a book. Then, released from my youth and enriched with a rare culture, I will start to *realize* my life. To do something. Yes, me too . . . For perhaps it is through the act alone that the self is posited; and I want *myself*. I no longer want to lose my freedom. But to save it and myself with it; and freely choose; to be. (Monday, October 31, 1927, "Fifth Notebook")[16]

To advance in weaker moments, she illustrates how to be self-loving by reminding herself that she is valuable enough to accomplish whatever she desires even without the validation of anyone else. She needs only to pursue her own careful plan with the certitude that her own approval of herself and her plans suffice to leave a legacy to the world:

> If I am worth more than they, I have only to make a name for myself without asking their permission. This program that I sketched out a week ago is beautiful and I will hold on to it. I know where I am, I am finding myself. I am known. I will write to Baruzi, and I will write my book. (February 19, 1928, "Fifth Notebook")

Parts of her planning include meditation, writing, learning to control the focus of her thoughts, and to plan for what is wanted: "Meditation. Every day write for myself, as in the past. Work: prepare my work that I will write later at leisure. Leave the doors open; don't confuse the issues; control my life" (August 28, 1928 "Fifth Notebook"). These are all habits that one must adopt for success according to today's self-help plans.[17] Yet, her *Diary* demonstrates how one might put these habits into practice. In "Third Notebook," her meditations sometimes take the form of a written dialogue (January 4, 1927). Her "Fifth Notebook" provides an in-depth look at the impatience one feels when faced with desires and how one vacillates between pursuing one's careful planning, which requires study and thought, and charging ahead impulsively in the moment (January 28, 1928). Her "Sixth Notebook" includes the elation one feels at being accepted and admired by many others and the temptation to abandon all serious work and goals when in love or other close relationships (May 10, 1929). Her "Seventh Notebook" shares yet another version of her realization that no matter how much she is in love, she must pursue her own path (June 9, 1930). Such written meditations later

9

develop into the philosophical, autobiographical, and fictional works that became her legacy to the world. The success that resulted from her early writings shows readers how to pursue their own paths to greatness. It may also comfort readers torn by similar conflicting ideas and desires to know that they are not alone, and that such moments of doubt are an integral part of the human experience that could lead to creating a work or carving a new path as a legacy to future generations.

Another way that a reader learns from *Diary* how self-love and self-trust function is in observing the evolution in Beauvoir's attitude toward others. The more Beauvoir loves, accepts, and trusts herself, the more kindly she views other people, the more easily she accepts them, and the more readily she expects that they will like and accept her too. In moments of self-doubt, however, as when a friend walking with Sartre failed to greet her in a garden, she wrongly assumes it means that she is less liked:

> Over these last ten days when, without admitting it to myself, I was hurt to believe that he was so far away and that with Sartre he must be looking at me as a stranger. . . . How silly I am! Why believe in the slightly hostile indifference of people—even when they are full of solicitude and smiling welcome for me? But also what sweetness each time to see this phantom of defiance evaporate and to become aware that I am installed in the bosom of a friendship that I don't dare by far even hope to approach. (May 24, 1929, "Sixth Notebook")

Weeks later when Beauvoir is feeling quite secure about herself, she clarifies the lesson by analyzing what someone else is doing wrong. To be accepted as a friend, one must decide to look for the goodness in other people, to approach all others as though they loved her:

> Thereupon along comes G. Lévy who does not understand what we are doing there and who makes a speech while everyone is making fun of her. We hate her: isn't it simply because she approaches others as if it were given that they were enemies whereas I am immediately aware of them as brothers? (June 4, 1929, "Sixth Notebook")

Beauvoir also sets an example that inadvertently presents how to love someone. We must allow them to be as they are. If we wish to remain with them, it is not our responsibility to make them change to please us. She first contemplates this notion when she is in love with Jacques and initially wishing that his behavior were different: "I am like his grandmother. Thus one can't leave him alone. I must desire him as this or that; 'If only he were this! If only he thought that!' people say; that is not what must be said. What must be said is: 'I will always love you' (January 15, 1927, "Third Notebook"). She drives this point fully home to herself and to her readers when she recounts her love for Sartre almost three years later: "There he told me about himself: that there were *ugly and vile things in him and that if* we ever have to renew the lease, he will show them to me, but already I knew that he could be anything, do anything, and I would accept it with the same fervor (October 10, 1929, "Seventh Notebook")"[18]

Another part of Beauvoir's legacy of self-love to all who aspire to be in a relationship with a significant other is her awareness that she must continue to honor her own dreams and aspirations even when she is in a couple. Each individual in a couple has to remain at the center of an individual universe that will, in the ideal relationship, happily intersect with their partner's. Without this, the love relationship fails. This becomes one of her most important lessons for herself and her future readers. *Diary* reveals that she struggles with two opposing desires that will nourish all her later writings: to become one and the same with the object of her love and, in contrast, to remain true to herself and her own projects first and foremost and live side by side with her love. This struggle is most apparent with her first love, Jacques: "In this way I had to become a complete being, center of my universe, and not a satellite in yours. But now that this conquest is achieved, join this world to yours, and ah, be happy together! . . . I know that you love me; I know who you are. This is the desire for you to be near me and to see what is mine become truer as it passes through your eyes; to be exhilarated by what is yours (May 1, 1929, "Sixth Notebook").

But Beauvoir also illustrates that there are layers of learning to every lesson and that we may have to repeat new versions of the most difficult lessons until we have fully understood the message. Thus, one of her greatest legacies is to show that even when she thinks she has learned how to be in love and still remain the center of her own universe, she will be challenged repeatedly until she entirely comprehends this principle of successful love relationships. Observing the trajectory of her thought and her ongoing analysis may help a reader to be realistic about the conflicting thoughts that each member of a couple may experience and have to work through to have a loving relationship. Beauvoir vacillates between knowing what she wants for her life in the long term and feeling that she must squeeze every drop of enjoyment out of the present moment without worrying about her future:

> I want to read regularly at least three hours a day. I want to write. I want to give myself the desire to write: . . . if by chance I succeeded, what a refuge,

what wonderful strength I would be securing within myself. I already have the strength of seeking beauty and splendor in my life, and loving myself, but it can often fail me. . . . This year and for two or three years I want only to live, to live and forget vain books and let all novelties settle within me. It is not a question of gaining self-confidence; I'm in love. I am insanely happy in this love. (November 3, 1929, "Seventh Notebook")

Her later observation of how little living only for happiness and being in love can advance her toward her goals and dreams helps readers to put their own choices and future decisions into perspective. Remembering her dreams, she analyzes who she is and what she wants in order to continue on her own path of self-realization:

Others gave me everything that they could give me, and now I alone will be able to find peace for myself forever. I learned . . . I learned, but I alone can put it to use. . . . And yet, more than anything, I must take into account this passion that I have for my life and my solitude. I love myself, and not another. I want to save myself, and not another. It is only alone that I will save myself. (September 6, 1930, "Seventh Notebook")

Once she is fully aware of what she wants, she comes up with a concrete plan including a schedule to accomplish her goals and a reiteration of her belief in herself:

I could have a splendid year if I write every day like today. Today I took up the outline for my novel again and started the second chapter with so much joy! If only I could force myself to write *four hours per day*! I will read very little if necessary. . . . I would like to finish the first part by January and the entire book within a year. Tonight I believe with all my might that I can, and I want to do it; I cannot live without this thing of my own, I cannot live only to receive everything from him. (September 7, 1930, "Seventh Notebook")[19]

Another key to success found in Beauvoir's *Diary* is her insistence on focusing on the present moment. Already in the 1920s Beauvoir seems to understand what science has just recently proven—that the human brain continuously changes its own structure and function through thought and activity.[20] Almost a century before the self-help specialists who now promulgate multiple methods for helping people to focus on the present, Beauvoir provides numerous examples of her own struggles with reliving the past and her solutions for remembering that only the present counts.[21] The essential rationale underlying the advice to remain focused on the present is as follows: the past is useful only if we can access the knowledge gained that will allow us to create a brighter present and visualize the brilliant future that we desire. To be fully cognizant of our abundance we must stay grounded (fully aware of ourselves as physical beings in a physical world), centered (perfectly balanced between our emotions and our rational mind), and focused on the present moment (as opposed to reliving memories of the past or projecting oneself continuously into the future).

Readers of *Diary* witness Beauvoir's construction of her own system for living in the present. Her system, as it shines out of *Diary*, contemplates what are now commonplace maxims and go beyond them by exploring their possible meanings as they relate to her lived experience. In this way, she offers readers a new understanding of how to access living in the present.

Already as a teen diarist, Beauvoir is aware that she has the power to control her mood and to focus on the present or the past and thus to change her perception of reality. It is tempting to review the most beautiful moments of the past, but mourning what is over can keep us from creating new wonderful experiences in the here and now: "No, no pity for my vanished past. Live in the present. It is beautiful enough if I know how to make it so" (December 27, 1927 "Third Notebook").

Reading her analysis leads a reader to understand that living in the present may be a different experience for each individual. It is a matter of asking the right questions, such as "What makes me feel as though I am completely experiencing the present moment?" Beauvoir's answer is that to access her purest and most unified state of being she needs a disregard for the past or future and connection to nature and to her health:

> I feel that my mind is pure (the completely physical voluptuousness of a sun beam, of perfect health is necessary to this charming state). . . .
> I coincide with my thought. I coincide with myself. Neither the future nor the past exist, nor the "selves" that I have been or will be tomorrow: there is only the present; I am with intensity. (April 12, 1927, "Third Notebook")

Another question evoked by her thoughts might be, "If I am living in the present moment, how does that affect my perception of reality and truth?" She suggests that her self is multifaceted even in her purest state; for that reason, by focusing on the present she can more easily assume a different dimension of that self: "The truth can never be anything but my truth of the moment" (February 23, 1927, "Third Notebook").

Her tendency to challenge and analyze herself when her thoughts dive toward negativity encourages a reader to ask, "What gloomy predictions do I tend to make and how can I correct them?" Anticipating Don Miguel Ruiz's 1997 best seller, *The Four Agreements*, Beauvoir advises herself that every forward step is important, that she can only do her best each day and have faith in tomorrow.[22] Looking at past failures is pointless. She reminds herself of the need for patience:

> Don't think about later. Don't say that if this existence were over, you would fall into a rut again. Make today as great as you must; tomorrow will keep this grandeur. We have surpassed many things. We must learn to live at the level of ourselves. To love, so passionately, to take hold of oneself, to remain calm with oneself. (February 10, 1928, "Fifth Notebook")

Similarly, her repeated assertion that every decision, every action is only one tiny piece of a huge project reminds a reader to keep moving ahead toward a brighter future. No mistake is too big to correct; no moment of glory or happiness predicts a lesser future. Future success always remains a possibility: "I must beware of regrets—beware of putting my entire destiny into every moment; every moment is on the line of a destiny that embraces years. Adieu, beautiful yesterday; adieu tragic yesterday when I so tortured myself" (April 27, 1929, "Sixth Notebook").

For Beauvoir, to fully live in the present moment also requires understanding the experience of presence, which is comprised of the existence of oneself, the bodily existence of another person, or the imagined presence of another.

Discovering one's own presence means, first of all, rejecting the popular criticism of solitude as the antisocial behavior of a misfit and recognizing the benefit and necessity of being alone, "How savagely I like . . . material solitude, which alone permits you to rediscover the company of real or imaginary cherished beings, and the presence of oneself. To talk to others is to become similar to them, to give oneself up" (*Diary* 1, 69).[23] In other words, one can only fully focus on one's own existence if other beings are not physically present. The implicit danger in conversing with others is the pressure to accept their worldviews or needs as superior to your own.

A second step in discovering one's own presence is to fully experience all of one's emotions. In reading that Beauvoir, one of the great thinkers and philosophers of the twentieth century, values emotion so highly, readers may be encouraged to honor previously suppressed feelings of their own. This is important for even today certain ongoing views hold that emotions, especially negative ones, are to be ignored, hidden, or dominated.[24] Back in the 1920s Beauvoir already knew that her health depended on the expression of all of her emotions. In addition, she understood that rational thinking and clarity about her life were closely associated with the awareness of her feelings:

> But on days of calm lucidity, what healthy relaxation! Finally to be able to exhaust all of my feelings without being hurried by work or annoyed by inopportune presence, not to stifle anything any longer, but to abandon oneself to emotions' caprices. (August 21, 1926, *Diary* 1, 75)

She also suggests that being fully present in thought and emotion is necessary to appreciating any experience:

> I felt this, for example, during our return from Uzerche when we remained silent for a quarter hour at night: first I smiled while I looked at his bodiless arm, then I thought: don't smile anymore; try to think and feel his presence as completely as possible. And only then did I begin to be moved. (October 8, 1929, "Seventh Notebook")

Beauvoir warns herself to beware of memories; if you wish to have a productive relationship with anyone, it must be continually renewed and lived in the present. This warning occurs in her differentiation between the material and imagined presence of individuals (*Diary* 1, 156). Material presence requires that the other person actually be physically present in the here and now with you. Imagined presence requires only a very strong sense that the other is with you: "Raspail Boulevard at 7:00 in the evening next to invisible Jacques whose presence I did not desire" (*Diary* 1, 152). Such a feeling might be based on memories, which Beauvoir understands as much different from reality: "The past sometimes becomes so present that it is almost hallucinatory . . . and the memory is more poignant than the reality itself was" (*Diary* 1, 62). She repeatedly comments that when the objects of her affections are absent, her ideas of these same people are inaccurate. For example, on April 18, 1927, she writes, "If you [Jacques] were present, I would not be so scrupulously seeking how I love you" (*Diary* 1, 229). Similarly, her August 2, 1927, entry includes the following advice to herself: "Don't get carried away by absent Ponti when his presence is not there to modify the idea I have of him" (*Diary* 1, 300).

The imagined presence and physical presence of another person produce different emotions, a finding that might comfort a reader faced with similar challenges in relationships with others. "But I can never manage not to feel this jolt that destroys my peace of mind, each time that his presence replaces my image of him. How easily I do without him, I who filled every minute of this winter with his name!" (*Diary* 1, 231). This observation about the difference between how she imagines someone who is momentarily absent and that same person's physical presence appears in relationships with most of the important people in her life, inviting readers to consider their own tendency to project false images onto others, potentially harming their relationships.

Beauvoir's diary offers subtle warnings that may help readers to maintain balance in their own lives. For example, she notes how easily she cuts herself off from the real world and from relationships with others by overthinking her experience and by failing to fully express her thoughts and emotions:

> And people really don't know how to make the most of the presence of those with whom they could speak soul to soul; the best of oneself does not dare express itself. . . . So many sentences lovingly prepared that I did not dare let out, and I knew however that they would reverberate, so many others that come to mind afterwards, and that one is irritated for not having said. (August 17, 1926, *Diary* 1, 69)

As a reader, I understand this to mean that if, in the presence of others, I am reliving past moments or projecting myself into an imagined future, I am not living in the present moment and not allowing others to benefit from who I really am.

Beauvoir also warns readers that philosophy and imagination may impede living fully in the present if balance is not sought. Individuals who love to look for the deeper meaning in behaviors, events, thoughts, and words, might cut themselves off from feelings and awareness of the present moment and lean solely toward a life of the mind. As she notes on May 6, 1927, "Naturally one can demonstrate the vanity of all things in terms of intelligence, but what if this [philosophy] becomes as important as a living presence?" (*Diary* 1, 247).

Similarly, she contemplates the difficulties of expressing the self or other presences that existed in the past, are currently in existence, or might exist in the future. She comments again, "I carry within me the infinite, the worlds of fiction that exist only in my brain (those created by me or recreated with a Proust) are more *present* than the outer world!" (April 12, 1927, "Third Notebook").[25] In short, one must be very careful to differentiate between what one imagines or thinks and what is actually taking place in the world. In addition, she suggests that being fully present governs the realization of inner beauty. Beauvoir advises herself to "have the will to be always present to myself, not to flee from myself, not to stifle my voice" (*Diary* 1, 233). A reader thus learns that inner beauty depends on the self-nurturing skills previously mentioned. One must not only stay focused on the present moment, but also embrace one's true feelings, thoughts, and desires, all of which demand the ability to speak one's truth and express the uniqueness of one's voice in the moment.

In coming to the end of *Diary* as its reader, I have come full circle. I have seen exactly how I could be more successful in the world and leave a note-worthy legacy of my own. What would it take? Young Beauvoir has taught me that I must be unswervingly self-confident and self-loving, willing to embrace and express my every emotion until it dissipates, and willing to pursue my dreams without fail. I must keep in mind that I am the only one who can truly know want I want, which path to follow, and how to make myself feel happy and loved. Solitude, sunlight, and nature are all recom-mended for good health. Meditation, writing, work, and planning will help me with all of this. Focusing on the present moment is key, and this entails frequent social contact with others, for the real presence of others is much different from my memories or imagined images of them. If I approach all others as friends, they are more likely to embrace me as a friend as well. No matter how much I love, I must remember that the only way to be able to love anyone else is to nurture myself first and remain the center of my own universe. Finally, reliving either past tragedies or past golden moments serves only to escape from oneself and the happiness of the present moment, unless one is writing a narrative or remembering a past lesson that will help one to move forward.

NOTES

1. Das. "What Are the Upanishads?"

2. Lamb Shapiro, *Promise Land*, 17, 18.

3. Ibid., 19, 20.

4. Jessica Lamb Shapiro questions the existence of the entire industry and what it actually offers in her memoir describing her self-help experiences.

5. It is popular today even in the best of the self-help industry, to tell one's personal story, with all of one's defects, defeats, and trials in triumphing over adversity. For example, Hay House Writer's Workshop of Fall 2017 featured numerous such authors including Louise Hay; Caroline Myss; Mike Dooley; Jessica Ainscough; Gabrielle Bernstein; Gregg Braden; Kris Carr; Deepak Chopra, M.D.; Nick Ortner; Marianne Williamson; Lynne Mctaggart; and Dr. Wayne W. Dyer. Similarly, Christy Whitman's forthcoming book, *Quantum Success*, presents in easily understandable form, techniques, meditations, and her own experiences to help

her readers explore, realize, and enhance the impact of their thoughts on their speech and actions.

6. For example, Beauvoir wrote as early as April 30, 1927, "Psychological analysis will always be my passion" (*Diary* 1, 243). For other instances where Beauvoir mentions psychology, see *Diary* 1, 123, 232, 243, 274.

7. "Rabindranath Tagore—Biographical." For references to Tagore, see *Diary* 1, 14, 54, 66, 67, 70, 71, 113, 130, 147, 200.

8. In "Simone de Beauvoir and Nelson Algren," Klaw shows evidence from the handwritten manuscript of Beauvoir's *Diary* that depicts her relationships as evoking conflicting desires for separation and unity; her struggle to reconcile physical presence and intellect; her commitment to optimism and gratitude, and her self-reliance (120, 125–127, 129, 134, 136). In "Simone de Beauvoir: du journal intime aux *Mémoires*," Klaw shows how Beauvoir transforms elements of *Diary* to construct a public presentation of her life in her first autobiographical volume, *Mémoires*. In "Simone de Beauvoir, Cousin Jacques du journal intime à l'autobiographie," Klaw analyzes the way Beauvoir re-creates herself by altering her depictions of her relationships with Jacques and Sartre from *Diary* to *Mémoires*. See also "The Literary and Historical Context," where Klaw discusses self-help, Beauvoir's fascination with psychology and its relationship to philosophy, writing as therapy, and Beauvoir's use of her diary to develop and love herself more fully (9, 10, 12, 13, 19).

9. I hold that any reader older than twenty still has many of the emotions and aspirations of themselves at twenty roaming in their psyche, and for this reason, the self-help plan offered by *Diary* will be pertinent to all.

10. In Beauvoir's handwritten diary, the French equivalent of "anything" is underlined. See also Beauvoir's *Cahiers de jeunesse* (henceforth CJ), where Sylvie Le Bon de Beauvoir provides potential reasons that parts of Beauvoir's diary are highlighted with underlining, other markings, or comments (CJ 15).

11. For an abbreviated history of this law and its relationship to quantum physics, other philosophers, psychiatrists, and self-help promoters, see for example, Christy Whitman, *The Art of Having It All* (2041).

12. See Hicks and Hicks, *Ask and It Is Given*, for a fuller explanation of this process (155–161).

13. This information on life coaching is based on an intensive yearlong program of study that I completed in 2016 to be certified as a life coach by Christy Whitman's Quantum Success Coaching Academy (QSCA).

14. For example, Christy Whitman's 2017 Creating Money program for coaching included a list of 27 affirmations to repeat throughout the month.

15. See, for example, John Assaraf's videos, teaching "How to Set and Achieve Any Goal," on YouTube to see how self-help gurus teach this process of goal accomplishment. https://www.youtube.com/watch?v=TRHcu_tNVo4 (accessed June 19, 2017).

16. The French equivalents of "realize" and "myself" are underlined in the French edition (CJ 417).

17. Meditation, daily writing, and visualizing the future are all integral parts of the self-help promoted by Christy Whitman in the courses offered by the Quantum Success Coaching Academy and in online courses such as John Assaraf's *Winning the Game of Fear* available at https://www.myneurogym.com (accessed July 6, 2017).

18. In Beauvoir's handwritten diary, the French equivalent of "ugly and vile things in him and if" is underlined.

19. In Beauvoir's handwritten diary, the French equivalent of "four hours per day" is underlined.

20. Doidge, *Brain That Changes Itself*, xix.

21. Beauvoir's focus on the present moment is, in fact, so prominent that it has influenced my entire translation of this volume of *Diary*, in which she often intersperses the present and the past in retelling events. For an in-depth understanding of this usage, see Klaw, "Troublesome Translations," 74–83. For an example of the current popularity of marketing the concept of living in the present moment, see Tolle, *Power of Now*, 39–88. A quick search of his name on Google produces numerous YouTube videos promulgating his ideas. Teaching others to live in the present moment is also a huge moneymaker for the current self-help industry that offers Internet courses, podcasts, and more. A site hosted in the United Kingdom entitled "Live in the Present" claims to be "an education institute for the 21st century" and offers books, audio recordings and apps to teach its buyers how to live in the present. http://www.liveinthepresent.co.uk/ (accessed June 19, 2017).

22. See Ruiz, *Four Agreements*, 75–91.

23. See, for example, the first page of Brent Crane's "The Virtues of Isolation."

24. To realize the extent to which stigma against having negative emotions remains prominent, one only has to read the second sentence of articles such as Tori Rodriguez's "Negative Emotions," which states, "Surprise: negative emotions are essential for mental health."

25. The French equivalent of "present" is underlined in the French edition (CJ 299).

Diary of a Philosophy Student

Volume 2, 1928–29

Sixth Notebook

September 27, 1928–September 12, 1929

September 27, 1928—Thursday

Back to school in Paris. Not only a new year, but also, it seems to me, a new cycle is beginning. In the drawers of my desk I have stored three years of notes, mementos, and letters. And now here I am engaged in the true story of my life, the apprenticeship that I summarized in the green notebook is over.[1] Here every day I want to mark the brief passage of time for myself and for Jacques.[2] And I daresay it will no longer be tragic debates and sentimental complications that I will write down, but the simple history of each day and its joyous or burdensome gifts.

Here I am, three years older, knowing exactly what I can expect from the world and myself, desiring to live, and as new as if I had never suffered, as if I didn't know anything. Here I am, calm and ardent, with the year's task and the expectation and the promised accomplishment, so complete and so wonderful all ahead of me! Year of work and expectation, dear final year of solitude, dear first year of living certitude.

Metaphysically, I am at the same point as some months ago, believing in the mind; in its moral value, in its creative power. The universe rests upon my will to love aided by my intelligence. Moreover I know that I do not know anything, but that perhaps there is nothing to know, but to live.*

Intellectually, lots of ardor, and less curiosity than love. Consciousness of all of my strength, confidence in a "genius" that will be able to blossom into a work—but the program for the year is to continue my progress, to enrich myself even more because I do not have the time to produce. I am as interested in myself and in my life as on the day I was born.

Sentimentally . . . ah! For so long as I have loved you [*tu*], loving you as if it were yesterday when you came to me and said: "Will you regard me as your friend?"[3] These first days in Paris were only a slow pilgrimage to the places where I lived your existence so intensely—exquisite weakness at night, the same as two years ago when I used to go see you. It is neither the fever of every minute that prevents my very hand from gripping my throat suffocated with tears, nor the tranquil forgetfulness, that although not unfaithful erects a temporary solitude. It is your presence, not stifling but fraternal, a long conversation with you very close, and memories engaged in the present, giving it flavor and fragrance, without weakening it and losing it in the past. It is the two of us already living *our* life in Paris, rediscovered with all of its sweetness, and the days of the past are all around me, as alive as at the moment when they blossomed.[4]

Luxembourg Gardens in their luxurious fall flowering, framed by the gilded reddish-brown chestnut trees; boulevard Saint-Michel in the cold gray evening, when day fades without woe, you used to lead me to him . . . And now the lowered blinds of the house do not distance me from him or from the house where your room awaits you with books that smell familiar and wait as I wait. How good it is to feel this immense love in me surrounding the contours of my life, with always this same heartbeat, this funny little movement in my throat, and even this way of breathing, a bit different when I am in this love.

I think about *Zaza* with an infinite tenderness, and I also feel her presence in my heart.[5]† I offer to you, Jacques, this year, which will be beautiful, I want it that way. And I am not yet sad . . .

As usual, I left by the rue de Rennes; in the rue Bonaparte some Botticelli faces in the old shops smiled at me; across from the "Porte Étroite," a swamp odor rose from the Seine; the golden shivers of the trees brushed my joy.[6] Following me along the bridge and through the Carrousel was the

---

* From "Metaphysically" to the end of the same paragraph is highlighted in black ink in the right margin with a vertical line.

† "Zaza" is underlined in black ink in the manuscript.

triumphant certainty of my life and of yours, of our promised success, of our internal greatness and our authority over the given world; life was radiant. At the Apollo, Maurice Chevalier was saying farewell to Paris.[7] Entering the red room with the red lights and passing in front of the abandoned bar stools before a deserted counter, I understood ... understood how tenaciously this part of the world revealed tardily, clung to me. I understood how much exaltation, weeping and fatigue cling lovingly forevermore to the half-empty rows of seats in front of the first notes of an orchestra, the curtain lowered— and that this woman, with the dyed hair and makeup, was awakening some perhaps impure attraction, to things that incessantly shirk a promise that their very escape renews. The dancer in her pink feathers had a strange flexibility; and when Chevalier passed by, straw hat, lip drolly puckered, I seemed to see before me, looming up and ephemeral, the image of an elusive dream, the salvation of your soul in mine, as only an outline, but rich with profound meanings and with a bit of sadness about their immediate uselessness.[8] I would like to say everything about it: the steady quivering of almost immobile legs, the gestures that appear to deliver all and yet reserve all at the same time, this perfect nonchalance ... "If I were a young lady ..." and the story of the female elephant who said, "my dear Tom ..." and the imitations, and the English song, and the slightly ironic confidence of his smiles. Perfection. Once again you yourself revealed it to me; I don't attach *too much* importance to this since these songs transform the very soul of Paris, and I rediscover you in it, as if a precious part of you that *nothing* else even comes close to expressing, had been made perceptible for me. I walked down the boulevards of Montmartre, smiling at the Morris columns.[9] In contrast, in Aunt Lili's narrow apartment, I tossed handfuls of gaiety and kisses on the heads of graceless children. And as always, seeing place St. Augustin in the light of the cars along the rue du général Foy, caused a shivering and solitary happiness to rise towards me. On boulevard Malesherbes, I am carried away by a radiant and lilting enthusiasm—Parisian couples cross my path as I, the living incarnation of this hour, watch without envy but with tenderness. A small dwarf at the corner of the rue Royale is selling violets, "It is too expensive for you," he says shyly to my schoolbag, then he calls me back, and for a small sum I carry away the mauve perfume of my insolent gaiety.* Singing, I pass by the rich people of chez Weber and Maxim's, uplifted by a richness of life unknown to them.[10] In the invisible sky over the Tuileries, the moon, rejoicing under its beige veil watches the place de la Concorde where cars zoom by and pass each

---

* From "Parisian couples" to "calls me back" is highlighted in the right margin.

25

other. The black Seine has shimmering reflections of an incomparable beauty; like a light-colored muslin, the black line of trees lets the bluish light of the streetlamps and the cars' headlights shine through. Paris, with its ever similar and yet new attractions, beloved Paris where the life of others is so mysterious and powerful, and so much your domain, Jacques, that to walk there is to live in you.

Have just read *Dans les mers du Sud* [*In the South Seas*] by Stevenson, of no interest, and some admirable poems by Poe translated by Mallarmé.[11]

September 28

There will be loads of days like today. The bus brought me through the gray morning to the Bibliothèque Nationale. I am reading the book by Caird and the one by Renouvier on Kant, the first interesting one.[12] Rolls in all shapes, round, twisted, flat, long, and a cup of coffee on the counter. Return a bit dismal, a bit humid, a bit tender for being so true to itself. I copy some lines from Poe—note 1—I pick up *Tristan* by Thomas Mann, a vaguely charming book that I have moreover already read.[13] A smile, a look, and the gesture of this extended hand came back to life with more precision than they have had for weeks.

Evening similar to those of that winter—two years ago—when I loved him so. Evening of study. Without joy, I look at you, studies that I will have to take up again. There is almost a sweetness in this semi-melancholia.

September 29

Same as yesterday. Rather joyous departure in the clear morning, Kant, Renouvier (*Le système de Renouvier* [Renouvier's system] by Hamelin—*Renouvier* by Milhaud) with an interruption for the afternoon snack and another to go from the Bibliothèque Nationale to the library at Ste. Geneviève.[14] Slight stupefaction that follows nine hours of studying without a break; in the clear evening, couples, who appear touching in the contemplative mystery of this hour, pass by. A café corner and a glimpsed bar instill in me a brief and poignant desire for a hot evening in a noisy place that would envelop our solitary intimacy. My dream wanders around the delightful *Simon le pathéthique* [Simon the poignant] by Giraudoux that I read last night as I fell asleep.[15] I imagine exquisite friendships in large well-lit rooms . . . *Le reflux* [*The Ebb Tide*] by Stevenson awaits me and hardly attracts me. A note from Mademoiselle Mercier invites me over on Monday—some photos remind me of vacation.[16] I am rereading *L'enfant chargé de chaînes* [*Young Man in Chains*, Mauriac] really weak as literature and distressing; I am rereading it for one or two sentences that are, in contrast, a caress: "Like all young girls, she has the soul of a poor little housewife."—"You [*tu*] haven't read anything.—As for you [*toi*], you [*tu*] have read too much."[17] Oh! The two of us. Nothing is like the caress of this familiar form of you. "Jacques, you [*tu*] . . ."—I like this you [*tu*]. I like not being the girl with the soul of a housewife, but rather your girl friend [*amie*], your friend [*ami*]. One by one the past days when I loved you so are repeated by present days and fall away. I am not suffering. I remember you. I do not have the strength to go to you. I stop at the void within me; and to fill it I speak, without seeing him clearly, to my life's companion who is present, I know—without believing too much in what I know because one cannot really know life when one is not living.

Henriette is wallpapering our room with nude men and women.[18]

You were seated in this armchair. You said to me, with that look and that smile, "And so, how have you been?" I look at this armchair, I remain on the threshold of a regret: was this dream once reality? In bed at night, I finish rereading *Dominique*.[19]

September 30

Getting up late because some still lingering dream lulls me. I finish *La philosophie de Kant* [Kant's philosophy] by Delbos.[20] Around 11 o'clock, as it is Sunday, I go down to buy the *Nouvelles littéraires*, of no interest, and to wander through the dead leaves of the Luxembourg Gardens. I meet Poupette there and together we travel along the boulevard Montparnasse where the dear house is bored. I think about this entire family that I love, about its freedom . . . Afternoon at the Ursulines.[21] The orchestra, the eyeglasses and the shiny hair of the young people bustling around elegant young women who are laughing in a foreign language compose an atmosphere that I like. A film on "the zone" depicts the lives of ragmen; an adventure film of no interest ends the show. Between the two, Man Ray presents some photos linked together by Robert Desnos's poem, "L'étoile de mer [Starfish]."[22] Some photos are beautiful, like this nude foot on an open book near a star similar to a glass flower; and the method using frosted glass, that finally shatters after softening the lines, is felicitous. But I like intelligence to guide the juxtaposition of impressions that here do not prolong the contours of any thought. The eyes are gratified; the mind feels no joy—(I am exaggerating). Return through the Luxembourg Gardens. Here a window opens onto a slate colored sky; red reflections fade on the houses. Six o'clock goes by without a cloud; illusion of this instant of false transparency. It is rich only to a full soul; with luck the full soul could develop in a serene simplicity, welcoming like a robust smile. For those who have nothing, nothing is proposed, and on this green table in the middle of blackened pear wood furniture, the Greek books look rather sad.

There is a long gallery with a couch, a desk where this hour exquisitely darkens—there used to be someone to whom one could describe Man Ray's photos. There was rest after work, an expectation, cushions on which one could cast off fatigue and boredom while he was walking in the room. Oh! . . . I received a brief note from Zaza telling me that she will not come to play tennis and that she was upset by my letter.* She didn't know how much I love her![23] . . . But who could believe that I love in this way with so many tears, in such a passionate dream and with the poignant feeling that a casual love is not possible, that I have too much to give—do you [tu] know this, you?[24]

Monday, October 1

The Bibliothèque Nationale again this morning. I crossed through the gardens of the Palais Royal. An overturned body adrift in the rippling water in a fountain is indeed a rather touching thing by itself; but is it enough to reflect on these false appearances of mystery as the surrealists do? The true mystery is this group of women, a dwarf, a little girl holding onto a bunch of violets with all her might and jumping rope on the avenue des Champs-Elysées.[25] Only the human has value†. . . At the Institut Catholique, in the stairwell I find the smell of the books that I used to take out three years ago. The trees and the light haven't changed. Nor has the abbot who greets me gaily. Tastes of good work to be done (Aunt Marguerite, Jeanne, et Riri had lunch here).[26]

In Neuilly, at the end of a familiar path I am waiting for sad young girls to walk down a hallway still empty and sad from sad nights; more memories and Josée's dear face.[27] Mademoiselle Mercier with the calm and serious face opens the door of her blue office; her dress is blue. As in the past, as dusk falls her face is a serene spot of light. She finds me older and as though "internally sculpted." She admires my sense of security; she promises me a

---

* This entire paragraph is highlighted in black ink in the right margin.
† The previous sentence concerning the human is highlighted.

happy serenity. In leaving me, she embraced me with true tenderness. It is true; I have gotten older. I was rereading my journal from two years ago as I fell asleep yesterday. I used to study myself with such an anxious interest that I no longer have. But I cannot miss this time of searching and suffering although I do love it above all else. A little while ago in the diffuse fog bathing the posters illuminated on the avenue des Champs-Elysées, and surrounded by these objects that I love without desire, I recognized the ardor of previous return trips, all of them the same, and yet, at place de la Concorde, playing the game of the pedestrian versus death, I found a profound desire not to be run over by a car; a very real liking for life.[28] So much strength.

I think of that wild, focused, austere child I was two years ago, the girl who did not want happiness. But the girl who got drunk on life and passionately promised herself every joy is back, deeper and humanized by the somber visit of pain. I really like myself tonight.

One day, I too will tell you things, Jacques, some things that will make you smile, and others so that you will not smile. You taught me not to be the humorless and defiant intellectual I might have been—you taught me the gravity of beautiful things—you taught me the sweetness of not being alone—you taught me the grace of life. Your image slips away when I try to grasp it, but I know, I know . . .

I have just perused *La robe prétexte* [*The Stuff of Youth*] once again after dinner.[29] In it a young girl is doing some English embroidery; a delicate adolescent boy takes her silences for depth and is wrong about love; it is good that we are not like them . . .

October 2—Tuesday

Upon coming downstairs, I find a letter from Zaza, from a Zaza who loves me and to whom my tenderness brought some sweetness; emotion at finding some passages quoted from *L'offrande lyrique* [*Song Offerings*] that I also read with tears when I first discovered them. "If it is not my portion to meet thee in this my life . . ."[30] Once again life was poignant and beautiful.* Work, still Kant and Renouvier, whom I am going to leave with a sufficient knowledge of his hazy ideas; I have a cold. But it is delightful to have sandwiches for lunch in the sunny garden of Palais Royal where the last rose is blooming, in the midst of people like me for whom a meal is not a social ritual, but rather a necessity:

---

* From the beginning of the paragraph to here is highlighted in black ink with a vertical line in the left margin.

red wine and farmhouse bread on park benches. And I think of Laforgue who, melancholic and alone, used to eat melon and salami.*[31] I am not working well. Jacques is incessantly here, not as an oppression or an anxiety; my emotional state is very decent; but rather like a constant thought, a dialogue that I am prolonging, a letter that I am preparing, what is, what will be. Our serious love ... I stop by Stépha Avdicovitch's home; on rue St. Sulpice, at the hotel Riviéra, on the 6th floor in a blue room, seated on her bed, tired but joyful, she welcomes me.[32] We make plans. She tells me about Lourdes and what the priest said, and tells me about the Lacoins. Poor Zaza! "The things that I love do not love each other."[33] An anger rises in me against this tyranny of friendly appearance. Madame Lacoin "hates intellectuals," forbids Zaza to "read these stupid books" etc. As a good Christian, she submits, but she is pale, sad, and wounded.† She ought to marry someone who resembles you, Jacques, and be happy. I think of her; I am full of chagrin. I don't care if Madame Lacoin hates me, but I do indeed care that she is annoying Zaza. Sad fate of young girls; their solitude and their unemployed wealth. I see Zaza in the chapel of Carmel, praying that her mother, whom she loves too much, will let her love our dear male friend.[34]

October 3

Have read Caird's *Kant*, which is drawing to a close, and Duhamel's *La méthode dans les sciences de raisonnement* [Methods in the sciences of reasoning].[35] Of no interest. With Stépha who has a pretty gray cap and lots of gaiety in her eyes, we have lunch in a popular bar while we discuss Gagnepan and Paris. A beautiful noon sun gilds the Carrousel. In the Tuileries Gardens we speak of the museums of Belgium, the churches of France, of Chantilly where there are, so it seems, admirable paintings by Clouet. I meet her again at 6 o'clock at her place, bring her to "L'Ami des Livres," where she recommends some interesting German books to me, then I go back home.[36] Tonight I've read Ungar's *Enfants et meurtriers* [*Boys and Murderers*], not devoid of talent, but saturated with fanaticism and very unpleasant.[37] With my cold getting worse each day I live at a slower pace, working and thinking more and more about this letter that I would like to succeed in writing, about the words that I would like to write to you, about those that I would like to say to you, if you, Jacques, were here, if you were here.

---

* From "Palais Royal" to "salami" is highlighted by a black ink vertical line in the left margin.
† From "Zaza" to "wounded" is highlighted in the margin.

October 4—Thursday

One day follows another and they are all alike. Have read a very clear and intelligent book by Benedetto Croce on Hegel.[38] I enjoyed a letter from Madeleine Blomart. My friend, seated on the terrace where mimosas are in bloom, you my friend, who are dreaming, immobile, about this little child to be born—wouldn't you be happy? "diminished internally" ... I contemplate that marriage and the stability that it brings must be a very hard trial if even you feel the intensity of your life weakening. And yet, I am not afraid; and I wrote to you, Jacques, my dear friend, from this office, and I was not afraid and I was not sad. The peace that is in me when I think about my life, accepted and definitive, is an active, living thing, and not inactivity for which one feels remorse. She says that it is very strange to be calm and relaxed [abandonnée] after so many torments. I myself know that my happiness does not deny the moments of despair that prepared it. Perhaps as Mademoiselle Mercier says, this experience was truly original; I tended it with so much care. But because of having put so many doubts, tears, and scruples in the first impulse, which for others is a joyful presence, I have acquired the right not to cry today, at the time when others start to be disappointed. This evening I read Légende [Legend] by Clemence Dane, imperfect book, of mediocre artistic worth; but I understand why you liked it, Madeleine; and for me too Madala is a very dear sister.[39] So that sums it up ... There was someone who loved "for the bits of herself that she didn't tell anyone," the one whom others loved only for her worth, her worth which was not her—and to you too Jacques, thanks.[40] I will say this thanks to you—she was after all only a great and simple young woman, she loved this simple man; among exquisite expressions, this one touched me: "She used to say, 'don't hurt me' with a sword by her side ..." I read some rather good short stories by Thomas Mann. I wrote to you, Jacques. I told you about the peacefulness of this office and of your house, that awaits us. And I was near to you. And I was not sad.

Friday, October 5

I worked so well that I almost forgot to have lunch. I finished Caird, which was starting to bore me, read two mediocre books by Nicod on induction and La géométrie du monde sensible [Geometry in the Sensible World] and started Basch's thesis on the aesthetics of Kant.[41] Stépha came by about 4 o'clock. In the fog starting to envelop Paris, we walked along the quays, then we went up to her little blue room where the framed portrait of her very pretty mother is smiling, near the picture skillfully painted by one of her friends and some reproductions of Cézanne, Renoir, and El Greco. Simple pleasure of tea and cookies. We discuss Rivière and Mauriac.[42] She says: "Yesterday, I wanted to pray; I was at St. Sulpice.* It feels good to be in the chapel of the Blessed Virgin. I used to go there, even when I no longer wanted to pray. I knelt down; I wanted to confess my sins; and I could not pray. I walked back and forth like this for an hour in front of the church . . ." and she walks with her habitual gesture of her hands linked behind her back. "Some men paid me some stupid compliments; I found these men and all those like them so dumb that I wanted to shout at them. I felt hurt. Oh, how hurt one can feel! . . . I went to Le Bon Marché. I bought a little missal and then I couldn't say the prayers. However in Lourdes, I did go to confession and communion. I would so much like to; I know that it's the only way that I can be happy . . . but I cannot . . . So I picked up *Aimée*, and I read desperately to keep myself from thinking any longer."[43] I know, dear Stépha, I know . . . the prayers at night, the unanswered prayers, the awful anxiety.[44] And that is why I no longer want, I no longer try, and I no longer like this stifling religion from which I have suffered too much. I will never go back to it—my heart and my reason equally distance me from it. I do not regret it.[45]

Yet, is it this religion that left me with such a taste for purity that the slightest allusion to things of the flesh fills me with distress, an inexpressible desolation? I have read, I have seen many, many things, but the things roll off me and because I do not consent to believe in their existence, I say that they are not.† "You attribute too much nobility to life," Merleau-Ponty tells me. Tonight she said to me, "You're an idealist. The world is not like that, nor are men . . ." I think back to what Madeleine Blomart was telling me in her room, to what Pontremoli told me, to Mauriac's books; and Stépha too tells me "These things exist."[46] So in the black, black rain as I came back home, I felt hurt, I was afraid, I was telling myself, "Maybe a young girl never can understand a man. Speak to me, Jacques, tell me if the soul of a pure young man is so different after all from that of the highly educated young girl. Tell me if he has struggles, troubles, disgust, and scorn, tears, and weakness, perhaps exactly where his intransigence refuses to see anything—and that maybe this intransigent purity is from pride and because one finds such causes for suffering unworthy, it is

---

* From "In the fog" to "St. Sulpice" is highlighted in the text.
† This paragraph is highlighted from "Yet" through "not."

inhumane to scorn this very suffering." And cruelly, I sensed this abyss that, despite everything, widens between us due to this simple fact: that you are a man and I a woman. Stépha told me: "yes, indeed dear, physical love is so important; . . . yes, indeed, especially for the man." She told me the story of this very intelligent man with whom she was so flattered to chat, and who one day started to court her despite his age of 50 and his wife; other stories. Idealist! My first reaction is to smile with pride saying, that's another world—but there is only one world. I force myself to speak of this instead of shrugging my shoulders. It seems to me that I would not have any excessive modesty—"and that is why I am a woman, to be held in the arms of a man," says Claudel; and this great silent gift of the body abandoning itself is the precious symbol of this trusting release of the soul to this other soul which chose it.[47] This seems beautiful to me. There was a time when I used to write that one word, one gesture of tenderness would have offended me to the depths of my self—now, no. Thus, at night only during this vacation, I was able to desire that Zaza embrace me as she leaned over my bed and that this banal sweetness make us even more sensitive to an affection that finally had nothing to reserve. Because there are words that one cannot say, because putting one's head on someone's shoulder to sleep, seriously, is a gesture of humility and faith more expressive than any sentence. It seems to me that I would not blush, and that it is even a rather great thing to prove through simple human gestures a love that one has established beyond the human. Claudel expressed the true grandeur of this while Jammes expressed its simplicity.[48]

I do not like that Mauriac shows us man dragging sin along in his flesh. I hate that article in the *Nouvelle revue française*: "Souffrance du chrétien [The Christian's suffering]."[49] And it is for the same exact reason that horrified, I threw away the last book by Jules Romains. The one who denounces what the other exalts resembles him in the excessive importance that they both give to the physical part of love, and to this hold that they suppose it has over men.[50]* And my entire self shrinks away from this. That two beings consent to a physical gesture, that they even take pleasure in it, so be it, and so why would they blush over this more than over eating and drinking? But if they feel governed by their desire, if their consent is not requested, it makes me sick and I feel like running away.†

---

* This paragraph is highlighted in the margin from "Claudel" through "Romains." Instead of writing out the word "physical," in the manuscript Beauvoir has used the Greek symbol for "phi" to represent the idea.

† From "And" through "away" is highlighted in the margin.

I have no contempt; I have no contempt for what I do of my own liking, but I want for it to be entirely of my own liking, a gift that my heart makes of my body, not because of a troubled appeal coming from the body itself. I would hate any solely carnal caress. And then why should I attend to something of which I am so totally unaware? Because perhaps others are not unaware of it? But it will be a long time before what I see will oblige me to modify this universe that I have created and in which I live. It is something so other!

Nevertheless, this hour at Stépha's was very good. She describes life well. She spoke of the Dôme, of the Rotonde, and of the Jockey, of her Slavic soul, of young people, of young girls, of the socialist ardors of her youth.[51] I like her a lot.

Saturday, October 6

I am finishing Basch's book on Kant and the one by Nicod on geometry. We have lunch "like true shop-girls" in Le petit Biard, bareheaded.[52] The sun in the small garden outside feels good while we are finishing our grapes; I try to explain how I believe in beings, and how it is enough for me to believe in them. We speak of Zaza who "wavers between her family and us," and that is exactly what I was writing to Jacques; there is a certain weakness in her that holds her back. An ardor for studying, for intellectual life, seizes me towards the end of the day, hot and poignant. Oh, thought gives me such silent and calm exaltation! We have some chocolate and brioches at Place du Théâtre Français while discussing literature. I take out some German books at Adrienne Monnier's after perusing the summer issue of Commerce in which there is a piece by Fargue and a rather pretty piece by Larbaud; moreover, I haven't finished it.[53] And in the evening I read Le tunnel [The Tunnel] by Kellermann, too much like a serialized novel.[54] I try to admire the passage on the catastrophe, but invincibly I think of Métropolis [Metropolis].[55] I prefer Mademoiselle Else by Schnitzler.[56]

How beautiful the gilded plane trees were in the descending fog of the evening!

Sunday, October 7

Such splendor this fall! At 9 o'clock I went down to the Luxembourg Gardens; and I saw the fountain emerging slowly out of the night's fog. I saw the russet colored chestnut trees, the clumps of salvia and heliotropes whose fragrance stopped me along the way; the pomegranate trees with red flowers and the paths strewn with dead leaves; the long, damp and sumptuous vaults over my head, pierced by a white sash of vapor on the side overlooking the terrace. And there I read *La mort à Venise* [*Death in Venice*] by Thomas Mann, which is a rather good book.[57] A small child was picking up papers and throwing them into the basket of the ragman, who, someone had tried to convince him, was the bogeyman. In passing by, a sailor and a young bearded man said, "You understand, a method is given to someone who doesn't yet know how to think for himself . . ." They made me think of serious and intelligent friends, which they probably were not. Everything was important . . . the tiniest drop of my life is important at the moment . . .

The sky was an extraordinary blue. I caught sight of J. Boigne with a young man. In the past she existed for me. Once inside the museum I looked at only Cézanne and some busts by Rodin and Bourdelle. Back home, I finished Lequier and Séailles's book on Renouvier.[58] Wrote to Pontremoli, to M.-P. from whom I found a pneumatic message upon coming downstairs; "my dear friend," I said in the bus bringing us to the concert.[59] Stépha dressed all in gray is exquisite. Wolff is conducting; mediocre program: Schumann's *First Symphony*, Mendelssohn's scherzo of *Songe*, Nin's *Spanish dances* sung by a good *cantatrice*, who also sings Mussorgsky, and finally Schmitt's *Salomé*— nothing good.[60] But it feels good, seated between Stépha and Poupette, to think about M.-P. whom I will see tomorrow, and about all the joys that the year will bring to my life.

Perfectly satisfied, yes on a certain plane . . . I understand the theory of "degrees of being;" this is the inferior degree that seems to be plenitude when one is there, just as Spinoza's second order of knowledge seems perfect: without this positive and irresistible something . . .

I have just read some articles on Kant. And then suddenly I am thinking of you . . . it is not a disruption or a fever like in the past. No, simply I am here, I have just worked, and I am thinking of you. Jacques, my brother—no, more than brother: Jacques, my life.

So, it is true. It is really true that five months ago (five months minus five days) you said to me, "So I won't see you anymore?" and the car fled up the street. I stayed there on the boulevard—I no longer knew what move to make. I didn't even think about crying. I was there and the car had turned onto another street. And you were in the car. So it is true that all year long, I will not go kneel on the low stool next to the desk where you will be sitting and reading things . . . I see you at this moment. I see you—and it is so difficult to grasp you again when you are not here.*

Jacques, my life. You are the only one, you see, who has ever known how to love me, who took me as a totality, without diminishing me in order to love me. You accept my intelligence, but you also accept the torment that it has been for me—and my destitute heart, and also all the other bits of me that the others don't see. I live enveloped in your tenderness that you have expressed to me better than if you had used words—and if I feel safe, serene, and splendidly indifferent to a thousand things, it is because I know the place that there is for me within you. "And your profound love which watches over my soul . . ."[61] You told me, "A person can be admirable even with a college degree . . . The woman who wanted to eat all the flowers . . . There are exemplary beings . . . When I think of you it is always involuntarily." You told me: "You are not only a woman . . ." One day you told me "thanks . . ."[62]

You also told me, "I especially don't feel like saying goodbye to you."†

And I know so well the value of each word in your mouth. Jacques, my life . . . you know my great torments and my small problems—my refuge, my support, my companion. We have laughed together so much that I laugh again every time I think of you, and we have stifled so many tears together that you must forgive me if I am crying at the same time . . . Sometimes you used to give me a look that seemed to say, "It's you, hello Simone, it really is you . . . I am always in a good mood when you are here." Oh, Jacques, you did say that one day. Jacques . . . has anyone ever loved you as I love you?

My brother, my companion, my refuge, my life . . .

Monday, October 8

A good long letter from Zaza welcomed me when I awoke. It was wholeheartedly her, and her love for me. Dear Zaza, I quickly sent her a very short note so that she would know simply that I was thinking of her as I waited for her to be here. I dispatched a brief note to Pontremoli.‡

As I wait for M.-P., I am reading *La vie de Racine* [Racine's life] by Mauriac; now there's a good book, a humane book in which Mauriac has put the best of himself—some female chair attendants are arguing, the trees are a bit redder than before and the sun welcoming.[63] With a slight limp in his

---

* This previous paragraph is highlighted with a black vertical line in the right margin.

† This sentence is highlighted in the margin of the manuscript.

‡ From "A good long letter" through "Pontremoli" is highlighted in the manuscript.

step, he arrives and we go take a seat on the terrace, like so often; I destroy the stone columns while I talk; people about two feet from us are locked in a ridiculous embrace; we are two friends, we are young, it is nice out and we are living through a very good hour together—because we are very close this morning: our friends Montherlant, Mauriac, and Barrès march by; we are not saying anything profound, but there is a pleasant harmony about the slightest of things.[64] We go back to the Latin Quarter. At Picard's we flip through the pages of some books, (I make a note of Ludwig's *Napoléon* [*Napoleon*]: Stépha told me it is very good) and some journals.[65] A young man who seems to be interested in us tries to take part in our conversation by speaking of Pierre Naville and *Libres propos*.[66] And with a kind gesture, with such smiling shyness and such an attractive look that excuses itself without coaxing, he holds out a copy of *Nord* [North] to me . . . [67] I invite him over with his sister, but we will see each other again before that; you know quite well what measured and pacifying joy your affectionate solicitude gives me, my dear good friend.

Lunch here. Mama is young, smiling and so sweet that I am moved.

At the Institut Catholique I read the articles by Nabert and Brunschvicg on Kant; and the *Leçons de métaphysiques* [*Lectures on Metaphysics*] by Kant in which it is interesting to already find the dogmatic part of the *Critique*.[68] The male librarian is nattering on with me—pitiful.

Towards the end of the day a bit of pink runs across the cold sky out the window on the left. The lamps are lit. One hears only the noise of rustling pages; one thinks of a young man very much like Mauriac who while working quietly would listen to a reasonable distress rising within him. There is no world outside of this somber, religious, and soothing room. As I lean over this black table, it is good to enjoy this almost monastic silence made of work and resigned satisfaction while I simultaneously feel hovering over me a love such that these walls perhaps never sheltered.* A young man I mistakenly think I know asks a thousand questions in my imagination, which gets lost trying to trace a perhaps empty smile. I escape this ingratiating heat, this refuge without oblivion, where things are no longer the same as in the past.

The sadness of the evening grips my heart.

The young Monina Poliakoff is in the living room speaking to Poupette about their workshop. She is pretty and her words touch on things that I

---

* In the margin of the manuscript, the words from "would listen" through "satisfaction" are highlighted with vertical lines.

loved. I am reading *L'homme au cheval gris* [*The Man with the Gray Horse*] by Storm—insignificant.[69] Then *L'évolution de la mécanique* [*The Evolution of Mechanics*] by Duhem.[70] But if I think about you again, that's the end of my work.

Tuesday, October 9

I leave on the bus with Poupette who is going to her workshop. Rain, wet bag, water running off my stockings, drab morning—nothing is as sad as coming into this big room lit as when we used to wake up early in the morning to go to the first mass. Books on Kant (Souriau, Valensin, Basch) of no interest.[71] But the sky clears. At noon, we meet Poupette in the "Bar Napoléon," and the air is pleasantly warm then. We speak of Zaza who wants to leave for Vienna and in the hall of the library we chat for some time: Stépha and Poupette are pleasures in my life . . . The green lamps are lit at the end of the day; this lassitude, this well-known heaviness in my head and in my eyelids starts to come over me—beloved fatigue when the dying day movingly accepts its destiny. I find myself back in the obscure sweetness of fall nights, on the avenue de l'Opéra streaming with cars and people who, after their day of captivity, fly off towards their night of freedom—the long forgotten smell of the metro: I read *Quintus Fixlein* [*Life of Quintus Fixlein*] by Jean Paul which bores me and which I don't understand at all.[72] Near Buttes Chaumont an accordion plays out of tune; I walk through familiar streets. Clavel welcomes me.[73] Germaine Monod is smiling and kind, she tells me of her resignation to her sorrow and to her sister; she would not have the strength to rebel . . . at least she has some finesse and when the Forrain-Jacquemont-Drucher herd falls into the midst of our discussion a secret jubilation unites us.[74] They speak . . . they speak with importance and hostility, embittered from being old maids, women without grace or love; I care so little about all of that! Monique Drucher is more touching in her idiocy. "If I don't get married, you understand," with that sweet little voice. Finally they leave, not without hope of returning. Oh, big red face certainly not sculpted by thought and that judges my charming sister as too young to deal with Clavel, do you believe that you have to be old and ugly like you to seduce souls? I wait for G. Monod: a half-hour later she arrives and we leave together comforting each other about our boredom as we talk about it. Trip back alone in the metro—ugly faces, gnarled and deteriorated bodies, sadness.[75]

Madeleine, during the moment that I spent there in that study where I met you, how often I have thought of you, my friend. Just yesterday you were saying, "There is in women a great demand for modernity . . ."[76] A year ago you were still here. Why wasn't it you I was going to see yesterday evening, in the brilliance of your smile? Well . . . I am told that you are happy—not enough for you, not with such intensity as could have been granted to you, not without remorse, but more peaceful, you whom I saw suffer so much in this office, where yesterday I thought of you so tenderly. (Charming story of ladies coming to tea and speaking of children, nannies, noodles . . . Madeleine starts to cry, "I don't want to be like that.")

G. Monod spoke to me of someone else too . . . I tried to speak a bit about you [*toi*] with detachment, but how could I? She told me, "I saw him in rue de l'Argonne seated at a table, arms crossed, talking to them up close." I see you—oh, so well!—the fragrance of all of this youth from the depths of these years has risen in me. Fervent Jacques who discovered Garric, the Équipes and the world, Jacques . . . [77]

Wednesday, October 10

I am ardently studying Kant. The day ends at Stépha's home: tea, chocolate, and pastries . . . She is seated on the bed with Poupette. They are smoking. Stépha is looking at Poupette's wood engravings and telling her stories about Gagnepan.[78] She makes this funny gesture with her hand at her throat that signifies choking. She is at home, free and joyous. We make some plans for later—a very perfect hour between us, three serious girls. And who cares about dinner, the heat of the stove, the problem of the Bouchys and the Richons?[79] Stépha was so funny as she imitated the high society life of the salons and her future relations with Zon . . . [80] "Oh, what a witty remark! Oh, how wonderful you look!" . . . and after all Jean Richon is rather kind, a very good-looking boy who speaks of music with some intelligence and at least keeps quiet about what he doesn't understand.

Thursday, October 11

The very good work continues. Towards evening I caught sight of Galois who was working at the same table as me. I started to dream again of that ever so attractive life of others. This young man inspired by Barrès, disillusioned and charming, who divides the world into "noble and ignoble" things, pale face behind horn-rimmed glasses, modern young man ... and I sensed that at present I can with the same avidity examine the secret of this almost unknown soul. I know that for my soul, there is only one soul—yes, lack of "seriousness," I daresay in the sense that Rivière gives to the expression in speaking of Fournier, but a "grace" ... [81] (I imagined this subject for a novel: a young girl, some profound and inexplicable magic in her; a glow of admiration and affection surrounds her; every promise of success. The most serious, the strongest, the best young man of all gets close to her; and his seriousness, his strength and his worth impose upon her. She lets him get closer—she will be his. She is his, and life continues. And it becomes noticeable that something in her lively brilliance has dulled; she is no longer herself. The written work lacks the subtle breath that perhaps could have been genius. Her life lacks conviction; and he knows it himself and is surprised to find the young girl, who mysteriously attracted everything and everyone to her, almost banal. And she knows, she knows that she was mistaken. And everyone understands too and knows when they see this young man who used to be hers, to whom she belonged despite herself, the poet whose dream she carried, from whom she distanced herself by a strange mistake because she did not understand him, because she did not understand this uncontrollable love she had for him and believed it to be dead and absurd—while he remained attached to her as the only climate in which she could have blossomed).[82]

The meanderings of my imagination, all for someone unknown or almost ...

I am reading some works on relativity that fascinate me. Then we climb, with Stépha, towards Montmartre. The I Bus takes us from Bourse to Pigalle by brightly lit streets with sumptuously sparkling candy stores; crowds, taxis, in a car a little girl is half asleep stretched out on the knees of a woman whose face cannot be seen. Stépha talks about Nietzsche, whom she is studying at the moment, and of the God of the Christians, and why on earth would we love him?[83] She says how much she suffers from her solitude before the heavens, from her powerlessness to desire even this religion that she thought she could artificially reconstruct: false hope that I know well— and at place Dancourt I tell her how much happier I am since I managed to sever my ties to Christianity; and that we must will our happiness ourselves and make it; create our values.

On boulevard de Clichy; this atmosphere is odious; the girls are of a vulgarity that would make one cry; the café orchestras are setting up for the evening; people are determined to have fun tonight. She says, "I would like to go into one of these places and shout at these people how stupid they are and all that there is in the world that they disregard." And also, "Young girls believe they have to have love to be happy . . ."—I did not answer. I know that this frivolous pleasure of living is completely sustained by a serious and profound thing; and how when I hold this thing in my hands, there is no longer any need for any pleasure. For the moment, let's be happy with these simple pleasures, pastries eaten in the street, people encountered who make us laugh, the bus into which I jump while she stays on the sidewalk, our trip back . . . She has dinner here, she reads the cards for Poupette and Mama. See you tomorrow, smile of my life. I find Poupette in tears because I was a bit curt since she was annoying me. She has this almost unhealthy need for my approval. I would not want and I do not want life to be bad for her.

Friday, October 12

Joy at awakening; cheerful departure for this hospitable place where good books impatiently await me. Einstein, Bergson, Becquerel; I recognize the abstract exaltation that Poincaré's books gave me on a beautiful summer day of my year of philosophy.[84] Math and science are decidedly dear to me, and every time I rediscover these abandoned subjects with a joyful remorse; pride of the human mind. Of such bodies that will return to ashes are born books of immortal and timeless formulas—the difference between philosophical and scientific "brains." To think as a metaphysician or as a scientist, what a difference in the sentimental ambiance surrounding all of thought! And this scientific way of thinking is more comforting, more perfectly joyous for the mind.* The discussions by Bergson do not seem to me to have seized the essential in Einstein but are interesting. Meanwhile I am rereading this admirable book that is *Lord Jim*—to demonstrate, even to show the importance, the reality of a human being, to describe the innermost recesses of his being through gestures that one sees, words that one hears, to create a man—immense.[85] There would be thousands of other things to say about it.

I buy a hat at Le Bon Marché with Mama. But you, Jacques, loomed up at the end of the day, so vividly; I saw your intelligence, I no longer know what you were saying but I know that I could not stand anything else. In the metro I begin *Jeanne d'Arc* [*Joan of Arc*] by Delteil in which I manage to like some parts since this talent is so great although I find it unpleasant, and it offends almost everything in me.[86] The room is almost empty when I arrive,

---

* The text is highlighted in the margin of the manuscript from "Einstein" through "the mind."

and here in her beige ensemble is that dear face with the rosy smile full of spirit. I recognize this curtain where advertisements speak, this noise of the gong that replaces the three strikes.[87] The play opens onto a green and red décor: *À quoi penses-tu?* [What are you thinking about?] by Steve Passeur; two rather funny acts, little Brigitte in pink, with a black suit and blouse of a little girl, bad-tempered, is exquisite. Dullin is too deep for a role that he distorts by lending to it what its author of few designs is powerless to render. Some small things are amusing: the idea, for example, of playing heads or tails with one hundred thousand francs in order to become true friends. Stépha treats me to some very good Neapolitan ice cream.

Upon leaving we see a gathering: a policeman is fighting with a too well-groomed young man who might be 18; younger rather, whose hat has fallen in the gutter; at first, I don't understand, "Take a look at that p . . .," sniggers the crowd. A man picks up the hat and holds it out to him; the policeman cries out, "I saw him" . . . the other guy is pale, "I was with a friend, with Maurice . . ." Something indescribably awful envelops me; it seems to me that I am going to be ill on this sidewalk. I drag Stépha away, as I choke back tears, the sound of this voice, this light, these made-up faces, these vices; I am as overwhelmed as if I had never known of the existence of these things—to escape and to yell . . . [88] She speaks—calmly she explains that all men are thus and sometimes women: even from the Sorbonne—"disgusting" as she says.[89] "You always say 'even,' as though it were something extraordinary," she says to me. She is right; literature is full of such things; men and women think about them, and even the good ones, to defend themselves. Baseness. And always I say to myself, "We are not like that," and none of these stories that she tells me with such remarks—however subtle—reaches me.[90]

I contemplate *Colombe Béchard* who threw himself into the dark pond.[91] I reflect that lots of indulgence is required for unknown things, I think about how I am accused of idealizing life, but nobody knows my very beautiful treasure. I have read *Nord*, at moments one is reminded of M.-P. and that's amusing.[92]

Saturday, October 13

I have come to the end of relativity. I believe that I have understood it well. I feel that my brain is flexible, refreshed, and happy. Big welcoming room, where we encounter studious lives that we love, a spiritual community in which it is good to take part—and thanks to this blond presence by my side, even the most austere work is a gay diversion. How charming she was

Thursday when upset by her reading, she paced up and down the room with her hands behind her back, her coat thrown across her shoulders, and her cheeks on fire. Charming when in a biting tone she put the young German man, who is too eager to get to know her, in his place, "I'm an American girl" ... and she is so trapped when he starts to speak English to her. Despite her efforts, he shook her hand in leaving—she was furious. She shares her thoughts with me almost out loud about the person across from us who looks like a gendarme and who "is surely seeking a proof of his nobility" in his book on coats of arms to which he is talking all alone, and she stifles her laughter in her book. "It's delightful," she says rubbing her hands together, her head thrown back and her eyes oddly crinkled. Her joy today was as lighthearted as the waves of her hair on her rosy face. "I feel like kissing someone"—she carries me away with her gaiety; I, who am so used to leading, I find it precious to follow someone who has a will for life at least equal to my own. She is so seductive. Her brief "good night" and that "thanks" always said when she leaves me; the words that she says have wings. She knows numerous people whom she evokes in a few words; she should write; besides, she wrote in the past and will write again a bit later when she feels mature enough; she will have a lot of talent. There are some very beautiful stories in her life: the one about her father's friend who has loved her since she was nine, who found her again at sixteen and spoke at length with her about philosophy, about everything, who has shown her a never-failing interest and affection ever since. And many others ... This morning while we were having lunch, a shabby-looking man with a distracted air came into the bar. She spoke to me of this penniless Russian utopian, of the poverty of the Russian people, of the wonderful hospitality in Paris for them. There was one who was a dishwasher in a restaurant; he used to be a count and did a poor job of washing dishes, the woman boss fired him. He sat down at the piano and played his sadness: "Would you like to make me happy?" a voice said—she was blushing and emotional, "You can pay me back in two months—it doesn't matter, or in ten years"—he refused, and she left the money on the keyboard. That's her in a nutshell, her shyness and her audacity.

And this too, that Ukrainian shoemaker, to whom she brought money and provisions during the great period of impoverishment in her country, and who drank; one day she buys a half-empty bottle from him for twice its value so that he won't drink any more. The next day when he comes to pay her back and there is nobody home but her, and she is sick in bed, as she lays in bed, the penniless and ugly man right next to the bed—he says, "I so like to come to your house because I love you," and then since she blushes, "Oh, don't be offended—I don't love you as a man; I love you as a wretched animal whose tear you have wiped away."[93] French people would not know how to feel such words. It is truly a very great tenderness that unites me to her now. During the entire day while I work she recites to me sublime passages from Nietzsche.

Josée spent ten minutes at the Bibliothèque Nationale to see me—I was glad to see her again. I invited her for the afternoon snack on Wednesday.[94]

Mama and Papa went out tonight. Poupette chatted with me a bit. She spoke of Montherlant, of the academy where she works, and the unbelievable milieu with which she rubs shoulders. I am alone now; and you, Jacques, never leave me.

A little while ago, I was rereading some pages that I wrote in a notebook eighteen months ago when I was opposing my atrocious disgust for life to that power of love that I nevertheless felt within me; and I was suffering from letting that power of love be stifled by my disgust—but now, despite everything, the feeling of wanting to live all my life with love triumphs. I don't regret a thing. I do not regret anything.

Another memory from five months ago—it is almost with stupor that I remember my escapades and especially that evening with Magdeleine when I strayed into a revolting dive. I grasp the horror of all of this abstractly, without understanding it; without being stopped by this sinking feeling in my heart . . . and it is probably because I combine a bizarre powerlessness to imagine the real with a very great power to react (precisely because of the solidity of my ideal constructions). "He played with burning coals as if they had been pebbles."[95] But now I understand that it is also because I was stifling underneath a sorrow whose face I did not recognize; not melancholy, nor tears, nor complacency; but this madness for diversion, this liking for passionate and vulgar presences, this feverish indifference, it was another unexpected form of sorrow.*

Sunday, October 14

The rosy birth of the sun through the windowpanes still fogged-up from the night awakens me every morning; from deep oblivion, I spring forth to the fresh and robust joy of feeling my body alive, then after this short

---

* From "a bizarre powerlessness to imagine what's real" through "form of sorrow" is highlighted in the margin of the manuscript.

greeting to the light, for some time I fall back into a semi-drowsiness in which I feel myself half-heartedly gather together forces of happiness and a more intense liking for life.[96] I do some good morning work in this office: I have reread Meyerson (abstract deduction, of no great interest)—and Duhem (mechanics), and this afternoon, Kant's anthropology.[97] For half an hour I walked in the Luxembourg Gardens where flowers have excessively glossy colors, and leaves a shiny and wet brilliance without finesse. Then in the deserted and foreign Sorbonne I looked for the first schedule of upcoming classes, but it's not there. At the end of the day I read. *Mère Marie* [*Mother Mary*] by Heinrich Mann is boring and stupid, *Jeanne d'Arc* [*Joan of Arc*] by Delteil, admirably vibrant and absorbing, and *Le paradis à l'ombre des épées* [Paradise in the shadow of swords], in which I recognize and like the will for toughness that nourished me. I also recognize a success in toughness, a simplification masked by declamations that I hate; I recognize love and repugnance.[98] He is the one who lent me this book, standing in his room in front of the table. And when I gave it back to him, I know how moved I was to understand that for him I was not the little girl to be guided, but rather the little girl with sound judgment whose opinion is sought. The past is very near to me and drives back into nothingness all that I manage to be happy about by refusing to make comparisons. I know that—through no fault of my own—my gaiety is really not fervor; and that I use all of my strength to receive everything given to me and to turn it into the light by which I live, but I know that almost nothing is given, that nothing is given in comparison with all that I would turn into a dazzling sight. And although the others might believe me to be more joyful and more attentive to the world than in the past, I know that I am only a life in suspension.

Silly phrase by Montherlant: "I would be ashamed for her and for me if she were no longer free and loved me." Nothing is more free than love, free and necessary. It is not this cowardice of the heart that does not know how to go on alone—my heart would know how to go on alone if it were alone; it is not love that I love, but rather it is Jacques, and I could have "entered alongside him into these great regions where the head is held high with the support of reason." I will not deny him these tears.

Today it has been five months since you left Paris. I have looked at photos of Constantine. This region seems beautiful, but *there* is not where you are. You are here as someone absent.

Very kind note from M.-P. who will come for the afternoon snack on Thursday.

45

We just went to wish Aunt Lily a good name day with chrysanthemums that smelled like the cemetery. I would have burst into tears at the drop of a hat. Stépha, dear, I understand better what I owe you: having been able to stand these two weeks. Oh, to think that on family celebration nights I cannot say, tomorrow I will go see Jacques. Oh! you are really not here, my refuge, my brother, so beloved.

Monday, October 15

She had in the corners of her smile the splendor of a happy day that I have not lived. The Louvre where a marvelous Dürer is exhibited. *Siegfried*.[99] The sweetness of the gardens on the Champs-Elysées. Laforgue's poems.[100] Through the profound joy of her gaze, she knew how to make me see these things as if I had savored them myself. Nevertheless, it is misting out; we are cold. I went to get her at her place and we waited for the bus in the rain. We hastily drink some hot chocolate; I start to study Hume—she leaves me around three o'clock, and as night falls I have all the time in the world to hunger for you, Jacques, and to cry.[101] However, at the Institut Catholique, some borrowed books give me a childlike pleasure: Brunschvicg, Poincaré, and Eddington.[102] I go to Belleville, I meet everyone: Rachel, Bernadette, etc. They are gay and full of an energy that I momentarily share; we organize the action committee, some lectures, etc. I go home with Mademoiselle Forrain, Mademoiselle Jacquemont, and Mademoiselle Drucher, and in the window-pane of the metro I see myself as young, almost elegant, and lively next to these graceless old maids—and I think of you, and I really like myself, and I tell myself that "we will do good things." I was dancing as I walked back home, "You must be in good health not to be humiliated by what you saw and withstood tonight," I told myself. I believe that I have acquired a very good health. I am full of ardor at work and full of ardor for what is not work. All of this goes together well. If I do not pass the *agrégation*, at least I will have had a wonderful year; it is all the more precious because it is unexpected.[103]

Dear Jacques, I believe that you would like me a lot at the moment if you saw me.

Tuesday, October 16

I would like to cry for joy, for love and for I don't know what pure and unforgettable exhilaration. Oh, dazzling summits of my life where my heart

46

leaps in the wild dance of my body! Oh, serenity in such a whirlwind of happiness, my life for which I lack words. Paris, my life, Stépha, Zaza, my life . . . When I reread these lines, will I still be able to find such immense justification for my existence that is this day that I am passionately kissing at this very moment on its enchanted face. Some banal things nevertheless . . . I study Hume for two hours while I grow impatient since I don't see Stépha coming. She finally arrives in a winter coat, and right away our laughter: for "the gendarme" who is still muttering in the search for proof of his nobility, for "Raspoutine"—for her "boyfriend" as, to tease her, I call the young German guy who incessantly invites her for coffee, and whom she amusingly rebuffs, "Your books are more interesting than you." She leans back and laughs, her nose wrinkled and rubbing her hands together; she is wearing her blue dress with the white collar, and she is exquisite. She goes to lunch with her friend Fernand whom she introduces to me when I myself come back from a lunch of sandwiches and a pastry, and the marvelous October sun that was shining on the gardens of the Palais Royal.[104] To be in high spirits . . . how well I understand the meaning of these words tonight! I was already in high spirits.[105] Of Fernand I see only a round face beneath some curly hair and a kind smile. We work. M.-P. comes at about three o'clock, I introduce him to Stépha, and we walk back and forth as we chat in the vestibule while the German guy makes faces at me. We speak of *Nord*, of Gandillac who is bored by the program for the *agrégation*, of Kant, and I am simply happy that he is here with his serious smile.[106] I feel like throwing my arms around his neck . . . Zaza comes to get us: Zaza, Stépha, M.-P . . . rare seconds in time. This real meeting of those I so love is my treasured possession. Zaza in red is captivating. We walk through Paris up to the Galeries Lafayette where we eat ice cream and pastry. Oh, to be sitting like this, with a passion for delicious food, an average young girl smiling in the mirror in a gray felt hat that happens to suit her well. And then such great happiness began for me; walking between Zaza and Stépha, who is brimming over with that gaiety for which she holds the marvelous secret; the teasing and affectionate phrases flow between us, "The other day Simone was overcome by a good mood . . .," she says: It is so nice! She calls me an optimist, yes indeed, and even more—a puzzle—and more again. Zaza is a bit dumbfounded by the silly things that we utter while we update her on Paris and our occupations. We talk about Berlin where she is going to go, of books, and Aire-sur-l'Adour, of G. de Neuville etc. I sense a bit of reserve in Zaza.[107] I mean that she is not exactly on the same plane: she did not like *Le bar de l'amour* [The love bar] by Soupault; she is a bit like her family and withdraws

47

when Stépha says that "the more intelligent the people, the more international they are."[108] Above all, I believe, she has a desire to see me alone a bit. Tomorrow I hope. For one or two moments Stépha weighs a bit heavily on me too, and I would like to speak to Zaza. But not really, the three of us get along very well together.

At place de la Concorde Zaza leaves us and for a moment watching her leave, Stépha and I feel the same pull of tenderness towards her, and the same joy for Paris rises within us—these cars passing by, this falling night, our youth—to the dismay of passers-by, we do a crazy little dance; we dance away singing and eating chestnuts, arm in arm and so moved by our mutual affection that we have tears in our eyes; how I love you, Stépha. She told me another story about herself, and the more she talked, so sweet and so strong, feminine and virile, gay and serious, free and serene, as she was walking, rosy and blond, so young-looking, so mature in mind and soul, my arm squeezed hers more tightly and my tenderness was choking me. I told her that I would tell her a story too, and she is worthy of it. And one day we will go walking in Paris, one night in the nocturnal Paris that we cherish, and Stépha, I will tell you about myself. I mean about Jacques. "If love knocks at your door, don't let it slip away," she told me, and from her these words were not banal.

I know a lot of stories that I like from her, but this one touched me: it is the story of her companion Fernand. He has been her friend since high school. He is the one who made her read Nietzsche, Goethe, who taught her to love art; who guided her in her studies, he who knew her and advised her and consoled her.[109] When her cousin, to whom she was almost engaged to be married, abandoned her, it was in Fernand's workshop that she went to cry—he was the one who supported her.[110] And she is his conscience. He has been in Paris for four years—he goes to Montparnasse, has fun, and she preaches to him strictly, one would have to see her harsh look when she would tell him, "You, who have read Goethe and who can recognize a beautiful thing, you spend your nights in base jokes." He got involved with a woman, a very talented painter, but without morals; she made him break it off. Then she left Paris. Fernand went after the woman and hid it from her; she guessed it all—and one night while they were dining together in a restaurant, she said to him: Fernand, I forgive everything in friendship, but not lies; you saw that woman tonight; you lied to me. Red and apologetic, the other confessed—and she got up, went out without looking at him while he followed her, got on the train and kept him from getting on with her. The next day at eight o'clock there was a large bouquet of flowers with this card,

"Not for your enjoyment, but so that you forgive me" and he left the woman in question. I like this story. I like the fact that she has enough influence on a man to make his mother jealous of her; for so many nights, sick, she watches over him; so that he will do everything for her and hide nothing from her. Finally, after a sort of artistic retreat, he proposed to her that they unite their lives saying; maybe I love you. I like this maybe. She said no, and still between them there was this profound affection. And when she recounted this, with all of her soul, she was as beautiful as purity, as beautiful as intelligence and love. And silently I gave her a bit of my true self that I had previously decided not to reveal; I made her enter my true life; she is someone with whom not only to be happy, but also with whom to remember and cry. Stépha, you are my friend.

Stépha, Zaza, Maurice, Paris . . . and Poupette when I get home (her godfather and his wife are having dinner—we are told about the engagement of Jacques Wartelle—irony!).[111] All of this is in me like a stream of happiness. I would like to give everything to you, Jacques, all of that. I mean peace, joy, this blossoming of the entire being that can passionately give itself to everything without losing anything. And you, Jacques, on the horizon of all joys, and you, the salt of my joy.

Wednesday, October 17

A day of fatigue because my night was short. It is raining, I am a bit tired and I skip lunch.[112] I read Hume without pleasure or boredom while Stépha, in her growing excitement about Nietzsche, repeatedly kicks the gendarme. I go home at 3:30. Zaza comes; we chat about M. Blomart, about Paris, about everything. She is amused by my gaiety and my childishness (G. de Neuville is still an innocent girl), about this power, that I have and she does not, to lose myself in my pleasure.[113] Josée comes by, exquisite with her hair very short, and the funny face of a little boy who easily catches cold. We have tea. We speak of the coming year, of studies that are being organized, of Gandillac: a stupid desire for scholarly success comes over me just like when my dear friends from the school Cours Desir used to promise each other to drink champagne if I flunked. I like them a lot, they get along well together, and I enjoy them. Poupette comes by and shows her paintings—all of them good! I lend Josée some books and I keep her company in the rain. She is sad, without life, without desires. She is surprised that I find pleasure in being near her—she is surprised by the illumination that I feel on my entire being, by my good mood, by this shiver of happiness that spreads in waves

of tenderness and laughter. Take Josée, take—I have so much to give . . .
Take so that you can more gaily go back up to your eighth-floor room where
you have such a beautiful view and where you are doing Greek, alone, while
waiting for the current of love which will run from life to you to be switched
back on. Take, Marie-Louise who wrote me such a pitiful letter, moving in
its frankness. Dear girl friends who have loved us so purely for such a long
time, we no longer love them . . . but by poking about in the ashes of the
past, we rekindle the brief flame of a tenderness. I was wrong to promise
more than I desired to give, but I will go to see you; I feel like being good,
and I want everyone to be happy. On the way from Josée's to Marie-Louise's
because of a letter of excuses and promises, on the boulevard St. Michel
all of this rushed over me: my beloved girl friends—my great care for my
studies—the struggle, the delights of life, my beloved, cherished, and ardent
life. And you, Jacques, to whom I am going to write. I would so much like
for you to write to me so that I do not forget you, so that I don't forget the
flavor of your life—but even if sometimes its flavor slips away and even if
these past five months are already blurring your image, what does it matter?
I know that at the first word, or a sign from your hand on an envelope . . . ah!
you will be completely there, and suddenly I will rediscover myself, who, as
I walk in this garden of lighthearted and delicious joys, always look beyond
the fruit that I pick if you do not appear.

Thursday, October 18

It would be better to do nothing but work—yes. I laughed because of the
baron-Nutcracker and the German man who wanted to prostrate himself
before Stépha to make her have coffee with him. I wrote to you, Jacques—
my sadness vanished. She was sad too, but with very slight sorrows that
barely mark her soul and that she likes. She is taken with first one guy
and then another as long as they are impossible, but she is charming for
saying so with so much detachment. The rooms of the Louvre where I
cried so much enchant us. There is an admirable painting by Dürer that we
contemplate at length: Saint Jerome in red, with a pinkish brown face in a
green hat, with his finger leaning on a skeleton head—despair in his mouth
and doubt in his eyes. Profound and very human meaning, and perfection
of the drawing.[114] Afterwards I see the paintings by Gréco, da Vinci, and
Botticelli that I always go to greet as I walk across the Louvre. A very
beautiful Poussin: L'enterrement de Phocion [The Burial of Phocion]—clear
sky on a landscape with shades of a storm; some other paintings by him are

nice. But my soul is heavy in my hands as the rain strikes the Carrousel. Hume bores me. Zaza comes to get me at four o'clock and drags me along the quays where leaves are flying in the golden sweetness of October—this is good—as is her coming to talk with M.-P., who finds her charming, and with M.-P.'s very kind sister.[115] Poupette shows her paintings; to entertain them I show them *La famille cornichon* [The pickle family] that he compares to *Ubu Roi* [*King Ubu*].[116] I love them all a lot. But something childish, too simple and easygoing in them makes me impatient, and their tenderness stifles me a bit. I love you all very much; but it almost embarrasses me to care about you all so much, almost as a remedy—no; rather by leaving you first place because first place is empty—while you are all perfect in your own place and I love you—but in first place you don't fit very well.

It is not worth the trouble of looking for you, Jacques; indeed you come back on your own. Behind the nice affectionate look in M.-P.' s eyes, I saw a deeper and more secret look smiling at me—the smile from the day when I lent you, Jacques, the second "Fournier-Rivière" telling you that it was so I could have the first. And you told me that then you would not give it back to me . . . that was in Aunt Geneviève's room where with Uncle Pierre you were repairing some electrical problem. To console myself I read a likeable but slightly awkward book, *Battling le terrible* by Vialatte.[117]

Suddenly I understand that it really is true; that you will not be here for a year—that I very much need you, and that I don't care about the Sorbonne—and my exams—and Paris—and all of them—and that for a single word that you alone know how to say I would leave tomorrow without any hint of regret.

If you didn't exist I would feel cramped by all tenderness—if you did not exist, I would be alone in the midst of those who love me and against whom I would have to defend myself; because my fatigue would find no other repose than to be like everyone else. For me the only repose is a couch with cushions where one stretches out at the end of the afternoon while thinking that you are coming back. My repose, my life, my more beloved self, I would like to feel your hand squeezing my hand, and to keep it from placing itself like this over these eyes that would watch you as my tears disappeared. In front of you alone I feel like a little girl—I recognize that you alone have certain rights with me—the right to tell me, "Look at me Simone, calm down."

And from having written my name as if you were saying it, here I am overwhelmed.

These people annoy me; they are too well-behaved—not disdainful enough, too good—they don't savor enough what is useless and delicious in intelligence. How was I given the grace to meet you, so exactly in harmony with me . . . I become smaller and annoyed near them for whom life does not have as much importance. I wish to hate them, I wish to be near you, to be near you, and feel that you understand. I don't want to stay without you for 10 months; I am no longer me, I don't want to—please.*

And despite everything maybe I do not regret the head resting on the leather armchair as on the day I understood that I loved you—or having cried these tears—my love had to be put to this test that you almost chose. A happiness as total as the one that you promised me merits this waiting, and this recognition of our desire from a distance that makes confessions to oneself easier. In a year you will be here—in one year—or we will be dead.

Friday, October 19

And Stépha is gay today, "What must I do, dear?" Since I know nothing, it is difficult to answer. "Be selfish . . ." We are crossing the square, "him before you, you two before everyone, if you love him." "I can have everything, Simone . . ." "You don't mean that, be good, Stépha, it's decent enough as it is." She is charming. I am working very well. Zaza only stops by, looks a bit at Baudelaire and leaves us.[118] Stépha and I go up to the eighth floor of the avenue de l'Observatoire where Josée shows us Paris stretching into the night pierced with lights; a small room with a blue couch where we take a seat: Josée on the table, we on the couch. We chat—about Kant, Flaubert, and ourselves.[119] Stépha fills the room with gaiety, and Josée, with her restrained charm and her finesse—they smoke, they encourage each other, and we make plans, and I am happy to have gotten them together, to be the living ray that penetrates this solitude; happy that they exist and that I am. Stépha accompanies me to Surcouf where the family with the Mornac household expects me for dinner. She is so perfectly exquisite that in passing in front of the dear house, I tell her a bit about my waiting; she understands with a joy that goes straight to my heart: "It is so beautiful, Simone, it is so rare." Yes, it is beautiful. Oh, dear boulevard, and even in this restaurant where next to us an amusing scene of a false couple is being played out, miracle of these lights through the misted-up windowpane, and of the passing tramways.[120] We go home and with the pretext of going to sleep, I go to chat with a happy Poupette in full-bloom who tells me about her exaltation in Montmartre yesterday and her simple and reliable soul.

---

* This last paragraph is highlighted in pencil.

"It's beautiful, it's rare," and yet I do not say: I'm lucky. Happiness seems like something I deserve; I deserve life. I love it so much. I can only be desire satisfied and incessantly more voracious; I am not made for resignation.

"You are the one who will make the best marriage," Stépha told me. Does my face show that I must have a profound and tranquil certainty that everything in my life will be perfect, as it is already. Oh! Perfection of myself, my support—my hand is placed on your so strong and so weak soul—and I am walking, so weak and so strong, thanks to you, Jacques, thanks to us . . .

Saturday, October 20

I am still busy with Hume. We barely have a discussion. She leaves before me escorted by the German man. But within, I am conscious of our meeting yesterday, of our true life as female students that I am finally realizing—of our meeting promised for Monday—it's so wonderful! We agree to go to Montparnasse tomorrow. My eyes are a bit heavy-lidded as I exit, leaving behind the green lamp and the attendant's chant: "Gentlemen—we will— soon—be closing," and I find the cool and free Paris night with a whiff of unexpected but nevertheless granted adventure. To find in these streets a soul who is only a smiling welcome with an unexplored depth where gathered echoes might resonate. Dream of *Le grand Meaulnes* [*The Wanderer*].[121] In Montparnasse walking near you, Jacques, who think that you are far from me—what miraculous moments I experience after leaving the great room of wisdom.[122] The bus, like a consoling presence, takes me along the edge of the Seine to Marie-Louise's place. Sadness of her soul cramped in a room of white tulle stretched over a blue background, her soul, tacky like her room but humble, loving, and touching.[123] And in myself I feel more than in the past a bit of simple goodness, a possibility of truly understanding her, of putting myself in her place—so alone, so stripped of strength and grace. I like her a bit. "The good that one could have done" . . .

And I went home, and here I am—and I am telling all of this to you, Jacques, and you understand very well. I thought of you a lot today—for a change. I think that after November 1, I will have news from you, won't I?

Sunday, October 21

I worked all day on Brunschvicg. Brief walk of no interest this morning. In the evening I was supposed to go out with Stépha: I waited for her in vain at her place. A vague note of excuse . . . headache, blues (more likely someone,

I suppose . . .). I go alone up to Montparnasse. The Jockey and the Jungle are smiling at me—but the night is so pure and needs really nothing but myself.[124] I went home to work. I worked very well, snuggled up with his smile.[125]

Monday, October 22

Excuses, fatigue, "darling" . . . It seems that when she left on Saturday, I was laughing as I watched her "like an old grandmother who sees her grand-daughter leaving to have fun . . .," and it is a bit like that. All the same she lacks too much of that profound gravity that I like. I have the serious look of a woman "scholar" said the young German man; that's what I want. I study Hume, and in the evening Newman consoles me: *La grammaire de l'assentiment* [*Grammar of Assent*] is a good book.[126] Bareheaded in the beat-ing rain that "I force myself to prefer to all else," as Gide says.[127]

But I prefer more than anything this soul that came to touch me while the afternoon had almost died under the green lamps; I vainly tried to tell its sweetness, its goodness, and the unexpected secret of its humility to this soul.

I went to Stépha's where Poupette was waiting for me; happy walk on the boulevards St. Michel and Montparnasse; some chocolates sweetened our lives. At Picard's, glimpsed books and journals; some engravings farther on: Laurencin, Matisse, Foujita, Botticelli—paintings—people who pass by, who live—earth so beloved, earth so old and so young, delicious earth.[128]

A note from Pontremoli invites me over on Thursday. Brief desire that he might be capable of welcoming this affection and this trust that I fear are not addressed to him—calm and tender memories of our friendship . . . bizarre—I would go to you, Pontremoli, with such naked simplicity, if only you wanted to understand this language of truth. Will you want to?

And again: you, Jacques—and I don't feel like working oh, no! . ., but rather like putting my head on your hands that would be placed on the table while thinking only: you are here, you are here . . . [129]

Tuesday, October 23

And once again it's the time when I make my way towards the house with the sweetness of my expected destiny taking shape—and yet not existing. Every night, the shadow of happiness hovers over me—and I come back, confident: I do know however that there is nothing of you here, Jacques.

So why is this? I have developed the habit of shutting the door of the study on the minor incidents of the day and talking to you while I do my night's work, very close to you, very close. I am walking in contemplation towards the thought of you I daresay—or rather towards the birth of the new year that the end of each day brings closer.[130] I don't know. I am here; you have my letter now; and maybe you are thinking of me right now—and I am here; I am waiting. I am waiting without impatience just as from afar you watch someone who hurries towards you, and you cry, "hurry, hurry," but he runs straight towards you, his eyes on you and gestures, "I'm coming." Soon we will look at the countryside together.

Stépha introduced me to "her" German man with whom I have lunch; idiotic and odious—and suddenly an unexpected and rising hatred because he could be the one who might kill you in ten years. We have coffee and pastries chez Pocardi—not entertaining. He can speak of Friesz, Matisse etc., he is the German man "from the intersection of boulevard Montparnasse and boulevard Montmartre."[131] He reads in my hand that I will marry twice, that I will not have any children, and that I am not faithful . . .

Merleau-Ponty is here; Stépha chats with him in the little square and flabbergasts him a bit—we go back in to work.[132] I'm reading pages from Newman that bring tears of pleasure to my eyes. Galois is working not far from us. It is warm and comfortable. Zaza passes by reading Baudelaire. It is humid.

I take Zaza out for a stroll; chez Conti we eat ice cream, we talk about me for a change and about that annoying accusation of optimism. I know what I am (In the displays on boulevard Saint-Germain, we see *Nord* and some pictures of Eskimos.) Zaza is going to leave for Berlin.

I am barely living—"He is a man from our hometown," says Lord Jim in an admirable expression of which Zaza reminded me. Oh! Man who is from our hometown—who will give me back *our* life.[133]*

Wednesday, October 24

Brunschvicg brings me unexpected pleasures. In *L'idéalisme contemporain* [Contemporary idealism], I am taking note of humane pages, truly beautiful ones; in *Étapes* [Stages] I find a concept of the mind, which in fact is very similar to my own.[134] I follow this rather unexpected evolution of my thoughts with a pleasure destined for me alone; I used to hate him so much!

---

* Beauvoir underlined "our" in the manuscript.

Yet today I feel that no combat is won or lost in a non-existent heaven—that my desires are defined as they come into contact with my life and that my life takes them as guides, through a reciprocity similar to the one by which nature and mind identify with and enrich one another. I copied passages from him—and also from Poincaré and Newman, who ends with the same beauty that marked his point of departure. And ten times in my extreme pleasure, I throw my head back onto the round headrest of the armchair and placing the book on the table I laugh at an idea just as babies laugh in their sleep. I'm such an intellectual! And why not?

Yesterday I read *L'âme cachée* [The hidden soul] by Lacretelle, an excessively dry book with no life and in which the talent is stifled by a seeming lack of freedom—I don't like it much.[135] Stépha accompanies me to Belleville; she chats about clothes with Rachel and gets bored in my study circle on Greek tragedies where I am not having much fun—but down at l'Opéra we have a delicious fresh lemonade at Napolitain—we admire some peignoirs and some dresses that would be "very nice to wear."

So now she wants to marry Fernand in order to live in Paris and serve tea in the middle of a salon filled with talented artists . . . she tells me this on avenue de l'Opéra, as well as a thousand other things. The bitter joy of earning one's own money and livelihood—the possibility that there are men on Mars . . . between the somber mass of the Louvre and the mildewed pink spots in the bushes, we contemplate the sky and have fun getting excited about the stars . . . The so beautiful Seine where, with hats off, our hair drinks the wind. In the street she wants to help out a sleeping man . . . chitchat. Clear, cold, and pure night. In all this, you, Jacques, were not forgotten.

Thursday, October 25

I go to get *Zaza* at her home in the hope of having a good discussion.* She takes me with her to do some errands—and for a moment it is not boring to be a young girl roaming through department stores. The world of retail display counters is almost deserted in the morning. I return to the Bibliothèque Nationale after having eaten some rolls. I have on a red dress that I like and my hair has looked nice since yesterday—I am smiling from head to toe . . . merely *my* foot in pretty shoes—merely *my* face in the mirror at Galeries Lafayette—or my hand thus on the table.† Flesh that will be corrupted . . .

---

* "Zaza" is underlined in black; the text is written in blue.
† The first two uses of "my" are underlined in the manuscript.

skin that will no longer be rosy with blood ... what does it matter—living flesh or skin rosy with blood ... And alone, the eternal sleep of the mind, that so ardently keeps watch, sometimes takes on the features of horror, as evening falls. She writes a letter to Josée that makes me laugh for quite a while, "we will have a meeting that is feminine par excellence ... there will be tea, delicacies, and five or six charming faces"—I am happy.

On the way to see Pontremoli, in the metro I read a rather uninteresting book by Jacobsen that I went to get with Stépha yesterday.[136]

Profound joy of rediscovering this room, the couch, the shelves filled with nice books, the tiny table between the tiny chairs, the tall stools in front of the desks loaded with papers, two pretty paintings, a rather beautiful bust of a woman between the complete works of Baudelaire. It is with a true liking that I held my hand out to him. Did he know it? Full of sadness, he is seeking a social position. He speaks to me of Baudelaire and of Proust whom he likes—of Balzac whom he likes now—of Jean Prévost's *Dix-huitième année* [Eighteenth year] which he appreciates and which I detest along with Prévost in general and all of his works in particular.[137] Of *La nymphe au coeur fidèle* [*The Constant Nymph*],[138] that he places well beneath *Daphne Adeane*, of *Lord Jim* that we mutually admire—then of Germany.[139] On this subject he comes back to his well-known pet subject: the universal, the particular, and the conceptual—but he believes that nations exist. He shows me reproductions of beautiful paintings seen in Germany.[140] He shows me pictures of an admirable Greek villa that his father built in Beaulieu.[141] And he speaks of himself, of his failures, which are very painful for him, of his uncertainty, of his will not to be on the side of the conquered. What else? He realizes that *L'état de grâce* [The state of grace] is bad, that he has no talent and I do not dare to protest. He justly tells me that I have never met with resistance and that's why I doubt the reality of things—that I cut through everything like a well-sharpened blade—and that if I scorn success, it is because I am successful. Maybe it's true. He tells me that I know nothing and that I like that—and in that way I reduce life to my size. That is less accurate. For my ignorance is willed. Oh, how Barrès has made his mark on me! He seeks the esteem of others, he likes what is foreign to him—others, for me, are "adversaries," and I construct a world that I like against *this* world that I do not like.* He shows me the journal, *Prometheus*, that he was writing at 16 and where already under the name of Didier he lamented being ugly

---

* The French equivalent of "this" is underlined in the manuscript but not in the French edition (CJ 504).

and dull. What can I tell him? I exaggerate my optimism, my scorn for what I have that he is seeking, my assurance, and he probably has a harsh image of me as an egotistical female intellectual when he leaves me with his lamentable "have fun," which seems heavy with hidden reproaches. He asked me, "What has become of your male friend from Algeria," and I didn't understand of whom he wanted to speak, as his completely external definition detached what is attached to me like the very traits of my face—he must have believed that I disliked having talked to him ... Meanwhile there was a moment when I was very near to you, when with your face between your hands, finally sincere, you said in simple words the double failure of this summer: your talent and your soul—and the anxiety about the emptiness within you. I was watching you, the words that I should have said stuck in my throat; I uttered who knows what inept phrase to disguise your lack of composure. Yet out of my pity rose a bit of tenderness, the desire to put my hand on your shoulder while saying "my friend ..." Naturally, he didn't grasp any of this—and I told him to drink some cocktails in Montparnasse—and that he was too serious, intellectual and submissive—not living a sufficiently unexpected life—that he must get to know simple people—and that I was less intellectual than him in one way. "Yes, but more so in three ways," he told me. What bothers me is to be so totally unaware of what I feel for him: sympathy, antipathy? Desire to let myself trust the bit of true affection that I would express to him—but he is impenetrable—and then ... And yet I thought of him in the bus that brought me back to the house. And I was annoyed enough by our discussion, which led nowhere, and by my toothache to go to Vieux Colombier to see *Les nuits de Chicago* [*Underworld*] while Mama and Poupette were at [illegible].[142] Quick and brutal film, reminiscent of *Variété*, and that I mildly appreciate.[143]

Friday, October 26

Life is so beautiful that I could cry. Poor Stépha who was asking for advice this morning after having received a letter that calls her back home ... so I am rereading Poincaré, his clear, intelligent, noble, and firm words—the photo shows a solid, resolute, and yet delicate face; I tell myself that he is dead, the one who admired with ardent courage this brief spark that is life, great rush of enthusiasm for this dead man whose firm words make me understand and savor the gift of my life, the grandeur of thought.[144]

Green lamps, bald heads—a gentleman is studying the origin of hieroglyphics—such a strong desire for you, Jacques, that I could cry. Zaza fortunately saves me; we go to Le Bon Marché. She speaks to me of Stépha, speaks unkindly, well no, let's not judge, let's not bring Zaza down to our level. First one exquisite life passes by, then another—how can their strangeness and their apparent uselessness matter? They are poetry—they understand and include our poetry—let's love them with an emotion of thanks . . . [145]

Charming and perfect get-together in the room of perfectly recovered Stépha, who, disguised as an old German woman, satirizes the people at the library, mockingly describes Berlin, and chats unendingly while she serves us tea and coffee in liquor glasses. Seated on the bed or chairs are Poupette, Stépha, Zaza, Josée, and myself, who, surrounded by cigarette smoke, all eat so many chocolates and plates of petit fours that we feel sick. I accompany Josée back to her place after which she accompanies me to the metro St. Michel as she tells me about Marcel Arland, whom she doesn't like much, about *The [Constant] Nymph* that she adores, and about Laforgue, whom she grasped very well and whose charm she delightfully reconstructs— she is gay, friendly, and charming.[146] I feel enveloped by tenderness—I am thinking of these girls, of Merleau-Ponty, of Pontremoli, again of Merleau-Ponty—with my head leaned against the metro window I am nothing but suspended happiness.

And all of this is perhaps only the pretext into which I throw the joy born from a word said by you, Jacques, a sentence written by you. Too madly happy—everything is too harmonized, too welcoming, easy and good. My life!

Meeting of the action committee in Belleville where Mademoiselle Monod is presiding. Good projects, drive and life. We accompany Rachel, Bernadette, and Simone back to Botzaris. I like them. It seems that in Neuilly I am thought of and liked. Thérèse and Anne would like for me to write to them. I love them! How I love people! How I love the love of these people, how I love things because of these people, because of myself. How I love myself!

I am here now and I am writing . . . it is good—I am here—I love *us* so much . . . *

Saturday, October 27

I am reading some Meyerson.[147] Neuville marriage where Geneviève and Zaza are charming. But how such ceremonies and social competitions are ridiculous—we are suffocating in this church. I imagine that one day maybe

---

* "The word "us" is underlined in the manuscript.

I too will laugh to see people congratulating me about a happiness that they do not know . . . I work again, but I'm fatigued—I go home. Marie-Louise and Zaza come, then Stépha. Zaza is charming in red. It is amusing to see "the young girl from the French world" across from "the Polish student," but Zaza is wrong to find it extraordinary that Stépha is what she is and to tell her so, even in an amusing way.

Tonight I am going to work hard on Cournot's *Leçons* [Lessons].[148] I would like to write to Pontremoli the affection that I feel for him at the moment.

I am beginning to find it very hard for you not to be here. It's not a letter that I desire but rather your presence, to have you facing me and to talk and talk. I am "pining" for you, as they say—Jacques . . .

Sunday, October 28

Winter rain in which I remember the feeling of early morning classes. The Sorbonne where I always go in vain to look for the class schedule is deserted, a bit sad. Day of work: *L'expérience humaine* [Human experience] captivates me.[149] I have the afternoon snack with Jeanne and the little Quintins who came to wish me a happy name day—but that isn't important.[150] What is important is to hear the wood fire singing, to see myself in my red dress, hair nicely done and almost pretty—to feel the joys from when I was 17 coming back when thus seated in this armchair and oblivious to all of life, I proudly challenged it, and that challenge guaranteed my happiness. Oh, this is enough . . . tonight I am reading *L'esprit des lois* [*The Spirit of the Laws*]; before it was something else—but for the moment it is the same pretty soul full of ignorance and expectation.[151] Indecisive face of this expectation and faith that a triumph will spring forth from it; now I can draw the traits of this triumph—but I am expecting it with no more fervor than on the day when I had not decided my destiny—my destiny today is you, Jacques.

Brunschvicg's theory of intelligence seems to me to have greater impact than the one that he gives it; reason cannot foresee itself or anything of the mind. You can desire only the object of desire, yet it is in making contact with its accomplishment that the soul, which is powerless to foresee itself outside of this struggle with that which is given, sees new paths opening in itself and invents new manners of traveling on them.[152]

This morning I sent a letter to Madeleine Blomart in which I spoke to her of my small pleasures and the vague dissatisfaction that her letter betrays. A note to Pontremoli to tell him simply that I was sad to see him so sad. There will always be something in this story for me to [illegible word].[153]

Monday, October 29

I am reading Le Roy—and things of no great importance.[154] A bit of fatigue, like an opium; Merleau-Ponty is coming. We are having a brief discussion in the public gardens. I really feel like seeing him, but will I have a lot to say to him? He is dumbfounded by Stépha, and Stépha finds him too quiet . . . evidently. As for me I try to balance one with the other. Dentist, hairdresser. No longer being anything but a body in a chair for all of these adroit hands . . . in the evening I work on Brunschvicg again. I think of you, Jacques, as of a silhouette lost in the fog.

I had lunch with Bernadette in a home for women—innumerable young women who wait while they embroider and chat. Poor but young and elegant are these dear girls of Paris.

Tuesday, October 30

I start to plunge into Cournot and interesting studies of him, and I have lunch with Stépha who was complaining about no longer seeing me. Foncin and d'Aulnoy are still hanging around the library. Next to some ugly old maids are some good-looking teenaged girls. The librarians behind their polished pince-nez really have the School of Chartres look.[155] With *Zaza* who comes by in the evening we go to have coffee at chez Pocardi.*[156] Stépha composes a very funny ode of adieu—she knows everybody: a Russian guy gives her some concert tickets; a rosy German youth similar to Thomas Mann's hero in *La mort à Venise* [*Death in Venice*] is now her favorite and often asks all passers-by about her.[157] I leave them: dentist again. But in the metro the book on Greek religion that Pontremoli lent to me and that shines with all Hellade's beauty keeps me company.[158] And again the hairdresser who tells little stories that would have bored me so much long ago . . . And Brunschvicg again—and the vain effort to make you, Jacques, wake up this dead world.

Wednesday, October 31

Cournot interests me. *Zaza* came and I accompanied her on some errands while I ate roasted chestnuts.† I had to choose a book for G. de Neuville and I leafed through some new arrivals that might tempt me if I were, for

---

* "Zaza" is underlined in black. The notebook is written in blue ink.
† "Zaza" is underlined in the manuscript.

a year, confined to my soul from days gone past . . . Then we go upstairs to Josée's place with some plates full of cake. She informs me about the class schedule. Poupette looks good on this bed, and Zaza in red similar to the best painting of Charles Guérin—and Stépha, who is describing Berlin, looks more animated than ever—and a delightful Josée, discreet and fine.[159] On the trip back, Stépha is arm in arm with Poupette and me. She talks a lot about that awkward and serious German student who looks intelligent and reserved, who has passed the *agrégation*, and who appears to be interested in her; surely she is interested in him.[160] Is it with him that she will find this love that she expects, where she would invest more than a quarter of herself? He thinks that I am not womanly enough . . . and that at 20 years old one must not exist for books alone—of course—but . . .

It was blue outside today. At lunch Stépha spoke of Goethe for a change, and I said, Pascal or Goethe! Ah! we must stay like this, she answered me. Yes, life is so beautiful—and comprehending it every day even more so. Yes—from this purpose, I will no longer deviate. Severed from Christianity.

But why do I have to see the same students' faces again—the classes, the fervor of study—and being "Mademoiselle Bertrand de Beauvoir" whom people observe out of the corner of their eyes and judge without benevolence . . . yesterday Mademoiselle Schuler came to tell me hello and to speak to me of Françoise Cazamian who is giving up on the *agrégation*; of G. Lévy who is studying for it, etc. I hate these things . . . professors, exams, serious conversations, etc. It already makes me uneasy. But why can't I remember your exact face, Jacques? Now you are fading away . . . it's time to write to me, you know? Oh, the fact that you are silent never hurts me—I know too well who you are . . . but I would like a perceptible sign from you—in order not to be alone. It's obvious—it is a whole year of living without you—and I am worth nothing, I can do nothing without you—I am nothing-but expectation-and sometimes boredom.

Summary of My Life

First part: 1925–1928
(Written in October 1928)

I date my birth back to the beginning of the 1925–1926 school year, or three years ago. And because, in an identical appearance, I discover deep within me the blossoming of another life, of an accomplishment following what was an apprenticeship, I want to outline a rapid summary of this first cycle, the one with the difficult beginning.

In 1925 I am spending my last vacation as a child. I have just passed the second half of the baccalaureate, that is philosophy and math, with only one week in between the two, and cum laude. I am a schoolgirl who has worked with all of her forces and who has fun all the same. Education at the Cours Desir from 1913–1914.

Wisdom—applied studies, reading of serious books that did not talk about life—rigid ideas, ignorance of myself—from about 1922 the ardent piety of my childhood has been completely dead—after a slightly painful crisis, my emancipation is consummated. Happiness is held in the blue of the sky.

Thus many things end: the routine of classes and insignificant friend-ships with girls—my great passion for Zaza during the year of philosophy was resolved—the last ties to religion are cut. Empty hands at the entrance to life. And this unknown malaise, at the end of July, as I leaned against the armoire of the antechamber, announced a new need. October is coming.

For my BA in literature, Neuilly is proposed—novelty. I make the acquain-tance of Mademoiselle Mercier, of Garric, and of librairies; relentless work. Zaza—indifferent. Slowly as a result of my success, the consciousness of a possible intellectual worth rises within me; overcome with admiration, I watch Garric as he opens a new world for me . . .

I start to read Péguy; a lecture reveals the *Équipes* to me; with passion I promise myself to this work, to a complete employment of myself. Conversa-tions in the garden of Neuilly with Geneviève Manceron and some others—unknown names come to me.

Brisk and miraculous discovery of myself. Fervor, study, exaltation, passion. Unheard of strangeness and intensity of this awakening.

January 1926 marks my eighteenth birthday.

I study Ronsard, Balzac, etc. In March I pass my certificate in French literature magna cum laude. At the Institut Catholique I study general math on sinister amphitheater benches where I carry the weight of my heart and my intended life. I begin to keep a journal that I lose in Sainte-Geneviève. I start over.

* * *

Meeting with Jacques, one night when he notices my existence—I told this story elsewhere (see Notebook 2).[161] Life *at top speed.*[162]

Discovery of Rivière and Fournier (see the notebook of readings from Notebook 1), of thought, of art, and of love to which I did not yet give his name . . . I read five books every day, the world of modern literature opens up. I try to pave my way in the midst of contradictory feelings of admiration. Reconciling Garric and Jacques is difficult. Exaltation of Garric's Tuesday classes, ah! dark wood table! Exaltation of the evenings when Jacques comes, ah! the car in front of the door! Acute suffering, loneliness beyond human strength, and I am once again a shy child in front of paradises whose possibilities I have only described.

I pass the exams in Latin Studies and in General Math in June of 1926. Mademoiselle Mercier advises me to do philosophy. I leave on vacation.

1926 Vacation

Cauterets, Meyrignac is dead, abyss of suffering.

I discover Poupette's sweetness in the moonlight—the past, Zaza among others, is dead. I start to write *Denise*, I read philosophy.

Return to School in fall 1926

Unique day (see all of this in Notebook 2). I discover Zaza again, and Jacques becomes my friend in an unimaginable friendship. Suffocating, I drag my love through the philosophy in which I am drowning. Painting, reading (see the notebook); I am lost in my tenderness, lost in a life whose awful uselessness suddenly appears to me. "Nothing is"—tears, disgust, work, such a heavy and disquiet love!

I start the *Équipes*: Belleville, acquaintance of Madeleine Blomart. At the Sorbonne, acquaintance of Barbier and *L'esprit*. An intellectual ardor returns, conflict with my love; conflict Barbier-Jacques, faith and despair. Sentimental chill, I try to interest myself in other things: lectures by Garric and Deffontaines—long letters to Madeleine during Easter vacation.

Sunday walks in Paris with Zaza.

I discover Miquel at the Sorbonne and we have discussions. Alain is revealed to me, philosophy becomes alive. I construct a private life for myself. In March, I pass the exam in History of Philosophy.

In Neuilly, I play the role of confidant to Poupette.

I begin to entertain myself—I discover les Ursulines, the Atelier, Charlie Chaplin (see notebook 3).

Friendship with G. Lévy—Baruzi's class—Acquaintance of Pontremoli.

The end of the year distances me from Jacques. I pass the exams in Greek and General Philosophy. Discover Lautmann, Merleau-Ponty—two weeks of exquisite friendship.

G. Lévy taught me to express in sentences the metaphysical hurt underlying my feelings of despair at the return to school and the suffering from my useless conversations with Jacques.

Merleau-Ponty teaches me to hope again. Intense intellectual reaction.

1927 Vacation

Unrelenting work. I start my book. I live my thought. Discussions through letters. Zaza and Madeleine B. confide in me (see these letters). The memory of Jacques reappears—suffering. Two weeks at Gagnepan; no more indulgence for barbarians—conversations with X. du Moulin.

Return to school, completely hardened—two months without seeing Jacques.

Friendship with Pontremoli and Mauguë, then quarrel, or at least, sudden chill with Lautmann and G. Lévy.

My book is progressing, my intellectual position is taking shape (homework for Baruzi).

I give classes in Neuilly—interesting. I continue to discuss metaphysics a lot with Mademoiselle Mercier.

Josée Le Core has rapidly become my friend since vacation—tea in her room. I see M.-P. a lot. I go to Sainte-Anne's.[163] I fill the gaps in my knowledge of philosophy. I start to know what I am and want.

Équipes without fervor.

I see Jacques again, I learn that "it is he and not another" and forever. Abolition of all sentimental worries. Peaceful and safe friendship.

I start to listen to music—movies and theater—Stravinsky—outings at night with Poupette who is closer and closer to me.

In March, I pass the exams in Psychology and Ethics.

I am less occupied with myself—diary not kept regularly.

Inner drought, lesser intellectual work from March to June.

I end up exhausting the charm of the Sorbonne camaraderies—classes at l'École Normale—very strong feelings of intellectual fraternity.

I manage to focus my thought; influence of Ramón Fernandez; I become aware of my metaphysical intuitions (conversations with Mademoiselle Mercier, notes) little by little I conquer a joy and a force, I create my own values.

After modern literature that I know in depth, foreign literatures appeal to me. Rapid knowledge of amiable intellects.

Even greater closeness with Jacques—his departure.

Two months of exhilaration, that were incidentally lucid, "bar life." Vacation ends this last experience. Marriage of Madeleine Blomart—goodbye to my students.

1928 Vacation

In a happy torpor. Few letters exchanged. Passionate resurrection of Meryrignac and of my childhood memories—I start work on my *diplôme* [graduate thesis].[164]

Letter from Jacques.

At Gagnepan, exquisite closeness to Zaza. I make the acquaintance of Stépha Avdicovitch.

From the outset, very clear impression that the first cycle of my life is over, and that after three years of apprenticeship my true story is beginning.

Thursday, November 1

Rain on the boulevard St. Michel and in the courtyard of the Sorbonne where I am wandering in vain ... A good fire at the house; I spend the beginning of my day sunken into an armchair watching the flames live while I read Montesquieu, Cournot, and Blondel.[165] At four o'clock Thérèse Mathieu and Annie Vauthé kindly come; they talk to me about their studies, about Neuilly, already so far in the past ... about *Le grand Meaulnes*, about Rivière, and about Copeau and his troupe which travels from village to village.[166] I am happy to see them. When they leave me I go back up to Stépha's place. She looks delectable in her armchair before a table, as her friend Fernand, who seems to care about her a lot, gazes fondly at her. He speaks to me of Husserl, of German philosophy, of painting.[167] We are gay and lively, and for over an hour very happy.

On the way back cousin Charles takes us to dinner at the Simbad: the boredom of these family get-togethers when Papa exasperates me and I feel sorry for Mama. But I quite like this kind, but ill-mannered cousin who is cordial and frank, and who calls us "the Dolls" [*les Poupettes*] and is amused to see that I am elegant, animated, and funny. I like that he notices this blossoming that I feel within me and that he tells me so—and especially that he brings us to this dance party in the rue de Lappe where we pay five cents a dance in a dodgy street watched over by policemen ... here, like elsewhere ...

Friday, November 2

Finished Cournot—looked at Bergson again. Stépha is happy because her mother is giving her permission to stay in Paris where she is going to earn money in journalism. We are being bored stiff at the home of G. de Neuville who has gotten us together to make jokes about Lélette . . . young girls waiting to be married, in a rich and boring social gathering, who, without depth or gaiety, "are each trying to outdo each other's ridiculous moods."[168] "Brr . . I'm suffocating," says Stépha with her funny gesture. Fortunately we had a delightful cup of coffee at Chez Pocardi with "Bibichon," the small blond and rosy man from Germany, who is always laughing and who told us in his jargon that we are much funnier outside of the library than inside, so lively and so gay. Oh! My dear Stépha, when I linked my strong arm with yours while running in the rain on Place de la Bourse so that we could rush into the metro where you were going to make me laugh again by imitating all the ridiculous people; how I felt this youth, this gaiety, and this life that are so much ours and that make even stranger this meeting of high society girls where it hurt me to see Zaza. In the evening, despite cousin Charles, I was weary, weary from having thought of you, Jacques, too often and in vain.

Saturday, November 3

Dentist, hairdresser, Bibliothèque Nationale where I am working on Bergson. Stépha is telling me her stories: about the guy with an *agrégation* degree, who approaches her on the rue des Petits-Champs and then accompanies her back when she is alone, but who is too serious; and about the married doctor of law against whom she struggles in such an interesting way since they both love each other with a love that they must hide and as adversaries, each trying to get the upper hand. At 6 o'clock I go to see Marie-Louise, touched that she likes me so and by her silly blue room of a pious little girl, sentimental and alone.

Aunt Germaine came this afternoon.[169] Just her name sketching a tangible trace in the air sufficed to awaken this overexcited, sorrowful, and oppressed soul that I often had when you, Jacques, were here so insufficiently—mine and not mine. Your reality scares me; your mother makes me afraid of caring about you in an almost palpable way, and with everything that she is going to tell me tomorrow. Something that was asleep (and I knew it) is being revived in my *thought* of you! *Belief* in the reality of you; this belief that grabs me by the throat, that throws me into turmoil, that *possesses* me, I, who can only lend myself to any other reality. I *must* (it is the first time in a long time that I must do something) go see her. Even if I feel my courage fail me while ringing at your door—and all afternoon I drag around a desolate soul, full of boredom and anxiety from this boredom . . . I must.*

---

* The words italicized in this paragraph are underlined in the text of the manuscript.

And to defend myself I try to come back to the one who waits for me in the solitude of my heart, who is not such a face, such a house, such a family; who is only one or two sentences said or written for me. Oh! This presence poorly masks a more real absence. For the first time tonight I *see* your empty room, Jacques, where the books are bored; and all of Paris, which is only your place abandoned.[170] I feel that tomorrow I will suffer if I go to boulevard Montparnasse, and that I will go. *Sukkot amari aliquid* [Something bitter arises].[171]

Sunday, November 4

And still the same heart that does not want to believe in its happiness. Now I have woken up to a splendid autumn day, cool and sunny, full of little carts loaded with pungent flowers. Now after I had interrogated the notices posted at the Sorbonne (which finally answered me) with the disgust at the classes and schoolmates about to reappear almost completely unchanged, and after I had leafed through some journals at the bookstore, Librairie Picard, and then with a pounding heart followed the boulevard St. Michel as though you, Jacques, would be waiting for me at its end, I met the warm and tender face of my dear Aunt Germaine in her room behind the door at which I rang. Then on boulevard Montparnasse while we were going to Notre-Dame-des-Champs, I felt enveloped in her safe and warm affection. And she spoke to me of you, Jacques.

For yesterday evening's sadness, forgive me, my dear; forgive me.

I went to Studio 28 where they were showing a not very funny Buster Keaton movie, a good film on the machine with accompaniment by rhumharmonium and *La puissance des ténèbres* [The Power of Darkness], nothing sensational—but so what?[172] It's a place to lean my cheek on my hand and speak to him, the one who isn't here. Oh! the elevated subway and the streets of Montmartre where I walked in this clear beginning of the afternoon, and the bedlam that was stretching and awakening throughout my daydream . . . I spent an hour at Josée's speaking of Max Jacob, Marcel Schwob, and the Sorbonne, and trying to explain painting to her.[173] I just read *Rabevel* by L. Fabre that I hardly like and a mediocre Conrad, *Gaspar Ruiz*.[174] But all of that was nothing. What was, was this hour in the church of Montmartre where it was good to hear you, Jacques, in the silence.[175] What is, is you and what I would like to say to you so dear—never too dear.

Your mother knows how to talk about you, Jacques—I saw you again as you are, pouring forth the perfection of your tenderness and your inner distinction onto the ones who approach you, "He has never hurt my feelings at all," she said to me. And also she told me that you are alone there, and that you never go out but instead you reflect, remember, and wait. You wrote to her telling her to speak to you of "the only person here who interests you." You want my news, my Jacques? Haven't I sent it to you? But thanks, for your mother and for me, for having asked her to look at me and to tell you . . . You also wrote, "I almost came back to Paris for four days—there are some things that I so desire to see again. But I would not have the heart to leave again."*

And maybe I am among these things. Tonight, with intensity, I imagine that you are able to love me enough to desire to come back for me—enough to think of me with this heartbreak that is often in me when I think of you. And I am overwhelmed.

My darling, my darling . . . if you noticed and if your mother told you what to say, you would notice only one thing, she would say only one thing: that I am yours forever—"winter as in spring, in sorrow as in joy, *usque ad mortem et plus ultra* [until death and beyond]."

Maybe you will come home on July 15—I would like for you to write to me before then, not so that I know anything else about you; this is enough; but so that I can answer you—but ah, to tell you in turn, darling dear, all that is in my heart only for you. Such a little girl, Jacques, this big person hides from the others in order to give only to you—such docility, such consenting weakness, and such an absolute tenderness. I myself have also repeated these words, "My God, if you are, make me love you one day as I love this man."[176]

It is with a love better than myself, a love in which there is room only for what is best in me—and in comparison with which I find myself to be contemptible, unimportant, and frivolous. Because to other things I lend myself; but by this reality supremely installed in the center of my soul, I am taken. Flavor of humility; it is only in the presence of he who knows how to make such a love spring forth in me that I succeeded in knowing your taste—this great desire to cry on my knees, and to prefer myself no longer . . .

But when for a moment I keep this image before me: of you coming up against a resistance similar to the one that I meet when I think of you, this image of you testing a reality stronger than you—the reality of love, the only one that allows life to be equal to death, as true and as tragic—what an

---

* The last paragraph is highlighted in black ink in the handwritten diary manuscript.

almost painful impulse toward you, what confidence more powerful than joy, and what worth suddenly attributed to myself through the one you are.

"I especially don't feel like saying good-bye to you."*[177]

Monday, November 5

Went to the Sorbonne for a class that didn't take place—but on such a clear morning when you, Jacques, were living very close to me. Moment of distress before these pince-nez, these unkempt heads of hair and these airs of importance that I am going to see every day of the year. Will they exist while you fade away?† I shake Gandillac's hand with a real pleasure at seeing him again; but it is a pleasure full of worry. Torrid and almost empty library where I read *Le progrès de la conscience* [The progress of consciousness] while I remembered the scent of other mornings when I so passionately waited to see you, Jacques . . . [178]

Afternoon at Sainte-Geneviève, have read some Bergson, then afternoon snack. Pontremoli thanks me for my note. Conversation on Gide and Mauriac, which drags a bit. Fortunately Stépha arrives more charming than ever in a very simple blue dress; she speaks, sings her Ukrainian songs with an exquisite mobility in her very young and very sensitive face; then reads the cards so drolly for Pontremoli—she declares that he is a bit boring . . . oh, yes! Aunt Germaine comes; Stépha stays for dinner and reads her cards. They like each other—I have so much love in me that I would like to cry; cheeks on fire, head feverish I embrace Stépha who is too touching with her grace and simplicity "with the entirely unexpected surprise" of having met her. Apparently I am more animated and lively than ever, she tells me. I feel within me this very unusual exhilaration that makes me sing, jump on one foot and speak very quickly, which causes me to be more exhausted than happy when they are about to leave. Desirous of a sound sleep.

Work: 5 1/2 hours.

Tuesday, November 6

It's beginning! Too many people, things, ideas, intensive training, overheated atmosphere—and tonight I wonder if it's really me? At the Institut Catholique this morning, I am reading Hamelin—how nice it is outside.

---

* This last sentence "I especially don't feel like saying good-bye to you" is highlighted in black ink—the text is in blue. The same sentence is also found in the 1926–27 notebook.

† "Will they exist while you fade away?" is highlighted in pencil.

Xavier du Moulin is working not far from me—some quick exchanges that make me happy on Newman, St. Augustin and the "Left-wing Catholicism" as Daniel Rops says.[179] Then Sorbonne—Rivaud's classes where these people are too serious, tense, implacable—we are suffocating—I don't say hello to anyone: oh! Lévy-Strauss, Boivin, Ducassé, Hippolyte, Schmit, Lecas, Gamochaud . . . pet peeves of my year . . . without counting the others![180] I hurry to the Bibliothèque Nationale to console myself with Hamelin and Spinoza, and to try to believe that I am still in this charming month that has just ended.[181] On the bus I start to read *Le vent du monde* [The world's wind] by Spitz—very likeable.[182] Gandillac approaches me; we speak of the exam, of the Greek skeptics. He is friendly and attentive; he gives me some tips. He tells me, "There are so many people who have confidence in your lucky star—everywhere people tell me that you always succeed." It seems that Merleau-Ponty told him, "What Mademoiselle de Beauvoir wants, she gets."

And this amuses me, and I am happy—but do I have to be Mademoiselle de Beauvoir?

Afternoon snack at Zaza's home; a large gathering where only *Elisabeth Boulenger*, dazzling in her black attire was a pleasure to see.* We take a taxi back with Josée and Stépha. Stépha too tells me, "Your life will be so good, Simone, you will always have what you want." I feel so finely tailor-made, yes, for every success! And for one year, succeeding will have to be fun for me.

Tonight I am thinking in particular about Gandillac, leaning on the table, speaking of Giraudoux, and advising me with a real sympathy in which I did not detect any condescendence—a soul that I would like to love, about whom I *care* perhaps more than others whom I like much better—I know that he is complex, so rich, so alone, so unyielding—I watch closely for a softening, a minute of weakness, a narrow door that would give me access to him and from that the least hint of a sign moves me. There is some strange hostility in me at the same time. I expect a lot—we'll see . . .

Oh! What if I didn't know that he exists, the one who, with a single word will cast all these vain things into nothingness! That is what I would be if you hadn't come, Jacques—but you did come and tomorrow I know "Mademoiselle de Beauvoir" will no longer exist—but only me who loves you and the life I am living. You alone—so different, so rare. Jacques, my Jacques, oh! So loved—you without whom I would not be. Simply: Jacques.

Work: 9 hours and one hour of class.

---

* "Elisabeth Boulenger" is underlined in black ink or pencil in the manuscript.

Wednesday, November 7

Life is good, dear friends, despite everything, at twenty years of age.

Getting up is a pain when one has slept poorly; but Zaza's ringing at the door is joyous although expected. "We walk," as she says, in the streets of the sixth arrondissement and in the Luxembourg Gardens where we sit down. I really like the phrase by Baudelaire that she cites for me about painters without genius who always finish a corner of the painting before all of the rest whereas for the painter with genius everything comes at once.

Robin's class. Always the same faces. Gandillac is increasingly cordial. He tells me that he spoke of me yesterday with some people who know me, and he marveled at my universal knowledge. I reach the Bibliothèque Nationale repeating to myself his words and authoritarian smile that I like a lot, and eating rolls as I walk along the Seine. Everything is lighthearted, full of pleasure and force—my life is tidy, clear, and always followed by every success.

I study Spinoza; Stépha and Bibichon say hello to me. As Gandillac leaves at three o'clock, he tells me, "You will write a doctoral dissertation on Spinoza." "I will not write a dissertation." "Why? That is all there is in life: to write a dissertation." "Do you believe that's all there is?" Then while giving a slight bow to say goodbye, he aptly retorted, "Getting married and writing a dissertation, that's all there is in life." Very well. Then dentist. At the Nord-Sud exit, I see a very friendly Pontremoli who tells me that the cards lied, but that he spent a charming day at my place. I go up to Mademoiselle Jacquemart's home; her apartment looks like her: let's escape. There I run into Magdeleine who has just arrived. But I don't care about all that.

What do you have to say about it, Jacques? Must I get married? since everybody tells me so. As for me, you know, whenever you want, but there's always this secret thrill because the others are unaware that for me this word means: Jacques, and not a thing that people place next to a dissertation in their lives. Rather the very essence of self. They do not know you, silent Jacques, too timid Jacques whose every word I would hear, ah! with so much joy.

Work: seven and one-half hours and one hour of class.

Thursday, November 8

It is a very beautiful day beneath its banal appearance. I meet Stépha at her place at eight thirty and together we go up to the École Normale where I am starting to get used to the graceless faces of these *agrégation* candidates.

Sorbonne. Lunch at the house with Magdeleine. At two o'clock Bréhier's class on the stoics—then Bibliothèque Victor Cousin, then Brunschvicg's class at the École Normale. Yes, but . . . Gandillac is so friendly in the rainy courtyard between the two classes by Bréhier and Brunschvicg, and especially before and during Brunschvicg's class where I finally meet Merleau-Ponty again and with an almost unexpected joy, and as for the return trip, between the two of them in the gloomy rain, nothing could render its sweetness. "You have a delightful naturalness," G. said to me, and also, "It is one reason to admire you that I add to those that your friends have already given me." It's idiotic but coming from him and proving so much affection from Merleau-Ponty, it brings me an infinite joy—how I love them! Merleau-Ponty sees me to my door—so close to my heart.

Beauty of these strong friendships, of this unity in work, of this solicitude that surrounds us. Grandeur. And what an unexpected thing it is that a sentiment other than these might exist—a sentiment that did not arise from any of these other sentiments and that I would not even suspect—in a separate corner of my life, outside of my life (if my life is this present).

I read the last Bedel: *Molinoff, Indre et Loire* [*Molinoff or The Count in the Kitchen*]—rather amusing.[183]

Work. Six and a half hours—three hours of class.

Friday, November 9—Zaza's departure*

Adieu to Zaza. This morning at her place, then we run some errands and I meet Stépha at the Bibliothèque Nationale. Merleau-Ponty glimpsed, disappears. Work.

Bibichon accompanies me back; he is kind . . . In the afternoon I was with Zaza having Prévost chocolate. I said a real good-bye to her that hurt me a bit . . . but so what! I have said an even more painful goodbye . . . that must be repeated every day.

In a little while we are going to the theater. Oh! Why, Jacques, are you getting further away from me? . . . from my sight, but not from my heart.

Work: Five and a half hours. oh!

Exquisite evening. We are at the orchestra in the midst of elegant but rarely pretty women, both of us *in high spirits*.† Pitoëff is admirable, his wife, as always, charming but less simply moving than he, the man who is always

---

* "Zaza's departure" is written in brown ink. The notebook is written in blue.
† Beauvoir wrote "in high spirits" in English herself.

ashamed. Dialogue between the prince and Fédia in the second act perfectly admirable. We leave as we discuss *Cadavre vivant* [*The Living Corpse*]—to get some chocolate we go into an empty blue tavern where three men, one of whom is a Negro, watch us in astonishment.[184] Stépha tells me about her adventures in Berlin—and how pleasant the night is.

Saturday, November 10

Bibliothèque Nationale all day long next to Stépha. Glimpsed Merleau-Ponty and Gandillac, who, seated in front of me, gives me loads of information and chats a lot with me. Both go off together leaving me to contemplate Cicero.[185] Evening of work.

Work: ten hours

Sunday, November 11

All day long at home; I've read Hannequin, Delbos, Höffding—late afternoon snack in front of the wood fire—without joy or sadness.[186] I go to visit Stépha who is not there. The air is gentle as a caress, light and free as an appeal. As I walk along the streets, my heart is suddenly swollen with desires—with a desire to live.

But someone has taken my life from me. I am waiting for you, Jacques, to give it back to me. I go back up to work. Fortunately, at night I stay alone with Poupette and we chat next to the fire; she evokes evenings from the past, evenings when we expected something . . . when we waited for your possible ringing of the doorbell, your hat removed, your "hello Poupette, how are you?" that I can recite by heart. The evenings don't expect anything anymore.[187]

Work: Nine and a half hours.

Monday, November 12

Hairdresser—two hours of Laporte's class where I catch sight of Josée—then work at the Bibliothèque Nationale, as always Merleau-Ponty and Gandillac. Stépha accompanies me to the Institut Catholique. We walk there on a beautiful night, and I listen to her reeling off stories that are just as fresh and new as ever. Marvelous evening of work, although it was on the skeptics. I no longer know where you are, Jacques. I can't find you anymore.

Work: Nine hours—Two hours of class.

Tuesday, November 13

Dentist—Rivaud's class. Bibliothèque Nationale: Epicurius, Lucretius.[188] Stépha isn't here. Five minutes of chatting with Merleau-Ponty. Night is falling dark and oppressive; a gentleman next to me is reading a book on happiness. Why? Do I still know the face of this word? I feel cloistered in these books, and arid, without thought and without desire. Infinite gratefulness to Gandillac to whom I lent a notebook and gave some book titles, and whose friendly esteem supports me in a way of which even he is unaware. Exalted by the *agrégation!*—he tells me, "There are not a lot of women like you in the world," phrase that I have desired from him for 18 months and that he tosses at me as if it were without value to me—a bit of the great esteem and the strong affection that I have for him returns. I said very quickly, "but all of my existence is not there." He gave me an intelligent and radiant look. So, let this gift of not being like other women be useful for something; let it be useful to that someone who knows how to see that I am not only a woman, this is useful, this he knows. Six months behind me, eight months ahead, I am in the depths of your absence, Jacques. Abstract certainty that you exist, but no passage from you to me. Shall I write to you again? No. I would hold it against myself afterwards like an insistence, a constraint with regard to you—I am not so weak.

But if you were not, would I then have lived in this way? Would I have a tidy and simple soul, unaware of torment and desire, and of the truest reality of this drama that we are living and that at present I only brush against—without believing in it even enough to scorn myself or be dissatisfied.

Gandillac can do a lot for me—much more than Merleau-Ponty in whom I find a too easygoing soul, in him there is a judgment of me that intimidates me. At present I desire to become part of him [*entrer en lui*] and to have him take me with him, I desire his friendship. He is capable of something other than his life. However, never beside him do I feel this total movement where the soul no longer keeps anything of itself— this tenderness, this abdication that J. Daniélou for example made me experience [*connaître*] only after an hour. Shall we speak of you tonight, Jacques? No, I must work—in spite of you, you must not be pulled out of the silence.

Have read *Le mauvais sort* [Bad fortune] by Beucler—book that I would have liked a lot if it had been a bit otherwise—and that barely touches me.[189]

Work: eight hours; one hour of class.

Wednesday, November 14

I am studying Sextus Empiricus. Robin's class. Bibliothèque Nationale. Evening in Belleville where I see Germaine Monod who tells me that Madeleine is happy. Good for her. On the way home I work some more. Glimpsed Gandillac at the Bibliothèque Nationale, but not Stépha.

Seven and a half hours of work, one hour of class. Wrote to Zaza.

Thursday, November 15

For the first time, great moral lassitude. Nevertheless the morning class at the École Normale is young and gay. Sarthe [sic] does a very good-natured *explication de texte*; he has a likeable face, and a hysterical old maid makes us laugh by pontificating in her sluggish voice. Afternoon with Bréhier and Brunschvicg during which Gandillac speaks—then Lautmann. Saw Mauguë and Pontremoli again . . . too many people—and this always creates such lassitude in me.[190] With Merleau-Ponty we go up to Stépha's place where Poupette is already. Tea, cakes, chatting. I stay alone with her in the veiled glimmer of the lamp; she tells me sad stories about her brother. As I leave her place I am distressed beyond words . . . under the pretense of going out we pace up and down the boulevard Raspail; and passing by the Vikings, I remember . . . oh! having been other, now foreign to myself!

Upon my return, I wrote you a letter that you will probably never receive, Jacques. I worked a little, had a discussion with Poupette who was happy and wanted to say so. But why?

Work: two hours, six hours of classes.

Friday, November 16

Relaxed day. I have lunch at the restaurant with Stépha. In the morning I see Gandillac and at night, Merleau-Ponty so simply kind. I do admirable work after dinner. Started to read *Climats* [*The Climates of Love*] by Maurois.[191]

Ten hours of work.

I received a card from Zaza.

Saturday, November 17

A sudden and passionate scorn for myself! Stépha gave me an exquisite picture of her, and I love it with all of my heart. Merleau-Ponty said a very kind hello to me. Gandillac is closer than ever (I even told him this morning how much he used to intimidate me). The book by Duhem on "the system of the world" is very interesting. A little while ago I saw Mademoiselle Mercier who is doing a doctoral dissertation on Leibniz.[192] What else?

No, it is not that it is too hot here and so nice outside . . . not that there are theaters, books, and bars . . . not that these studies are boring. "It is a better age and a more beautiful world that I seek."[193] I give your name, Jacques, to the girl who was what I am today, but without restraint . . . you approached her in a letter one day, in an afternoon of confidences. Ah, I believed then in beings, in values, and in an ethics that was poetry; I believed in life; and in myself. Ah! I was alive then—I suffered—I sought—and above all, I loved. Words resounded in me, as they awoke streams of passion. My eyes were not heavy from reading but washed by lucid tears. There was a domain in which the beautiful and the true possessed a face (that others judged as paradoxical) but that was sound for me. There were risks, victories, defeats, and rules—there were recompenses—"a poignant existence . . ."[194] There was above all a toughness and exigencies. Now . . . now it is with a more cowardly tenderness that I think of you; does my tenderness forget what allowed it? Now I too often confuse you with my happiness, and it doesn't do you justice. Ah! you are much more than that.

I despise myself—"the work-ing ma-chine . . ."—others could read these books, say these things, but as for me, there was a book that I had started and that I alone could write. There was a quest, a calling. There was a love that was not only a love.

At times in the past in this life that you had given me Jacques, I feared losing *my* life as it was supposed to be.* Is it the one that I have today—unreal series of shallow events? At least now I will know that every dignity is not here, but only in the life whose truth you hold. Success must be restored by reassuring my other self, which exists only near you—my faith in the importance of things must be restored—my ethics must be given back to me.[195]

I loved you in such an exalted way! "Ah, this was something entirely other than any marriage . . ."

It is not one of life's sweet pleasures, but a grandeur that I miss—to which I was closer in the times of the Stryx and the Jockey because at least this cry remained wide-open.[196]

Come on, in ten months it will be over. Calm down.

---

* The word "my" is underlined in the manuscript.

For you will be just like yourself, won't you? And not that man "obsessed with happiness?" Ah! Better the shameful life that some can lead, and from which with fierce disgust for the self they draw at least the love for an inaccessible perfection, than this wisdom of abstinence in which no passion boils. Such people forget to live; others have fun and believe that they are living. Give me, give me life and its beautiful harsh exigencies.

Rediscovered purity of this love. Indifference to all of your acts, Jacques, shedding of all desires and all fears. Between us is something greater and stronger than us. Whatever you have given and are giving of yourself, whatever you want, you are solely mine, since I alone am thus yours. You can't do anything about it, neither you nor I. Nothing can be done about it.

You did not believe, did you Simone, that he would respond so quickly to your call [appel], this lost face of the world, that he would so quickly raise his eyes, brimming with tears and passion, to you? Unforgettable, extraordinary night while our parents believed that we were sensibly at the Théâtre de l'Oeuvre. First simply the Dôme where Poupette, charming in a blue suit, with painted lips and a dazzling complexion, calls out to the soldier, laughs, amuses and delights me. Then the Jockey where I rediscover too many habits and where the alcohol starts to go to my head. Feigned dispute between me and Poupette, her smiles, and her funny way of sticking out her tongue. I don't know what idea made me want to go to the Stryx, sure of this tug at my heartstrings, of this upset once the first glass of Martini was served and my hello to Michel . . . then Riquet came in. I can't say more . . . the ink is going to be completely washed away . . .

Was it because we had both drunk a bit that our encounter was so profound and so sincere? Oh, suddenly remembered accents, this breath of life, this climate desperately requested from a faded memory! What simple and profound things did he say to me? On impossible happiness, women from whom he expects too much, books in which he seeks himself, the three classes of people: those who have the notion of good without attaining it, those who have no notion, or those who need no one. And so kindly, "I myself need everything . . . I need to need everything." Cerebral being, he also used to say, or sentimental: Jacques is cerebral and sentimental. About Jean Delrive—about weakness and strength.[197] "More than 30 people who would love me in my strength, I would want one who knew me in my weakness." And about Jacques again, about the way that he transforms his weakness into strength, about his gestures, and these precise and profound words on his pomposity which is really sincerity precisely because it does not appear to be. About the misunderstandings between man and woman. And with an affection for Jacques and a perfectly overwhelming understanding of him. How well he knew how to give me back my true Jacques, my only Jacques, weak and strong, who measures the vanity of all things, who is unaware of happiness, who speaks of serious and painful things between two cocktails. He told me, "Jacques adores Jean Delrive . . ." I would want him to say in the same exact tone, "Jacques adores Simone." He said this awful sentence to me, "Jacques will never be happy" . . . "But what if someone gave him everything?" "It would humiliate him." Yes, but not if everything were asked of him.

We made a date to meet on Wednesday night—it seemed to me that he had always been my beloved friend. Oh, how I cried coming back down the boulevard Raspail and biting ferociously into the bouquet of violets given to Poupette by a slightly drunk and unlikable sailor who had been introduced to us as one of Jacques's pals! I was devoured by regrets, fears, fatigue and love.[198] I was wrong to want to see him again on Wednesday—we will no longer attain this unique intimacy—I will be disappointed.

And I understand why it will always be "you and not another."[199] Why is it that Gandillac, Merleau-Ponty, and others whom I esteem and admire, who perhaps have a more rigorous mind and more intellectual *value* than you, can give me some joys, but only with effort, at least with a bias, whereas with you my soul is granted something which comes with long moans and thrashes the air with its arms in the extremes of its intensity.

Maybe I could have loved one of your friends, people similar to you, but never those lifeless people, whom I have resembled these days, who are strong because they are unaware of ordeals that would try their strength, and satisfied due to lack of desires and due to certainties that I would not be able to share, and which, in any case, should not satisfy them in this way but rather leave them open-mouthed like a cry of love.[200]

I wept all though my sleep—and I awoke sick and with tear-filled eyes and an aching head.

Work: seven hours.

Sunday, November 18

I stayed here to spend the day alone with you, Jacques. I read a bit: *Climats* by Maurois and *Siegfried* by Giraudoux in order not to burst with despair while *they* were here.[201] So here I am finally with this swollen face, oh! so similar to the girl in the prairies of Limousin two years ago who learned the extent to which we continue to see the light of the day despite a broken heart

79

...and since... since: twenty-eight months, with brief or long respites, my days have followed the rhythm of the return of such irrepressible and sense-less difficulties, a *physical* suffering: stinging eyes—a dry throat that cannot swallow even a sip of water, a head throbbing on both sides with pain, the chest only a heart ripped asunder—hands, hands, above all, that seek to grasp onto something, something that can be only you, Jacques... and that isn't here, that isn't here at all. We whirl about in the void, and all of it hope-lessly dark, in wild astonishment. I cannot endure that you are so far from me for another eight months, so far, and that I have no news of you.

The first wave has passed—I am more in control of my thought. I would like to untangle the intertwined threads forming the very complex web of this impossible-to-imagine love. Mania for intellectual justifications. Every contradiction will always shock me. I seem to have always come to you armed with a joy and a taste for life entirely acquired and willed by me, the only reality to which these intellectual justifications are attached; and I have found in you a doubt, a despair, and an expectation—all as real as I am since I love you (or did I love you because you knew how to impose their reality on me, it doesn't matter)—and to reconcile them I sometimes gave up one and sometimes the other. I tried to put them together into a synthesis: do not *accept a* life but *will my* life. That is what I call my joy. But this joyously willed *life* must indeed be the entire reality of my life, with its irremediable sufferings and miseries as well as its sweet pleasures. This form of my will inhales a content that does not come from it—presences—and therein lies the immense moral value of our love: this reality which you compel me to take into account, this reality that is you and that is communicated to things through your poetry—mysterious powers of the mind freed by the move-ment that engages it.

What need to put everything into a system?[202] I must always say "Jacques and me" and not confuse us with the rest of the world even if we consent to prefer some of the beings in it.

You, Jacques—Oh, a little while ago, such a desire to write you—to tell you that you do not realize that you are asking for too much, that I am not a strong woman, that I ask for your forgiveness, but that you must write to me because I am too unhappy. No, it's all right, it's of no importance: I said "whenever you want, Jacques," whenever you want.

But you know—you must not believe that you'll have finished with me so quickly. You must not believe that I will let you go before I have forced you to say: I am happy. You always want more than you have? But there will always be something to give to each of your desires. You will see, you will see who is the strongest if I arm myself against you—believe me, and maybe because of this very need that I have for you.

You focus on all of the paradises that you do not have. They are all open to me through your desire. You are the only being who could give me a feeling of insufficiency, that is to say, of reality that I might cherish, for if there were nothing left for me to expect from myself, how would I love myself?

Within me more solidity—within you more . . . intensity [*violence*]. Participate in this intensity and make it participate in my stability. He writes to Riquet: "I like you—I am going to write you a long letter," and the letter never comes. Why would I make demands?

Ah, Jacques, I am waiting for you, I am waiting for you . . . you will see.

"He had some hard knocks—he always got the upper hand."[203]

I would like to go down on my knees and cry from gratitude upon seeing that he really is the same one who, two years ago, wrote me the letter through which he became a part of me, not as I had expected, but in the beyond of myself and of him [*par l'au-delà de moi-même et de lui*], and about which Riquet was telling me yesterday.

The embarrassing question asked despite my reluctance: Does he love me, does he truly love me? doesn't count—"It concerns him."[204]

Stépha just left me—how charming was this chat by the fireside—with tea and cookies. She had a charming green dress, her beige hat and her coat with the fur in which her face was deliciously lost. She told me some short stories by Conrad with so much intensity that the book is surely not as beautiful as the animation in her words and gestures. She spoke to me of herself, of her fondness for struggle, for domination, and for the eternal feminine within her that she describes in such a curiously objective way like everything that touches her. Seated on the arm of the chair or standing and leaning on the fireplace and speaking with all of her body. Strange and precious Stépha who cannot understand me well but to whom I so love to listen. This appetite that she has for *all* of life: books, ideas, interesting guys, as she says.* I don't care as much about interesting things, or about having events and movement in my life, but only about listening within myself at length, to the echo of some very pure minutes. She cares about all that without knowing why she is driven by such a demon—maybe a vocation to be a writer who will one day soon gather together such adventures. Her feelings change in the moment; she abandons herself to each of them, and then moves on. She is strong at heart—more alive than I? I don't know. She

---

* The French equivalent of "all" is underlined in Simone de Beauvoir's manuscript.

takes in more things—but does she take them as far within herself? I will be so curious to see her face-to-face with Jacques.

Louise came too—she told me some nighttime stories from a very distant past.[205]

Desire to write to Jacques. I had said no, it would be better not to write. I would go further than perhaps he would want to go himself. I must wait for his letter that will not come.

There is something extraordinary in all of this, extraordinary. That I might conceive of my life so well without love, and even live it. That I feel no lack when I don't love except by comparison, and that I love thus, with a love that is a plenitude so incommensurable with the false plenitude of the other.

Oh, to tell him so, to tell you so, Jacques!

I would like to place my hand like this on the edge of the table and my head on my hand, and you, standing behind me, very near, you would listen to all that I would say—all, without saying anything.

Monday, November 19

On the contrary, everything is so perfect this evening. Quiet, tidy, and complete. This morning I slept a bit late and woefully. I had written you such a long letter that I probably will not send. In Laporte's class—so boring—I felt my heart being torn out of me and the need for a lively scream was on my lips in the midst of these satisfied students. I forced myself to go to the Bibliothèque Nationale. I made Merleau-Ponty and Stépha read Zaza's nice long letter received this morning in my bed. She says, "my dear Simone," and I was thinking of her, but in the meantime my heart discovered these words "my dear Jacques."[206] Finally I worked on Kant rather well. I came back with Merleau-Ponty—and tonight I have just worked with an exquisite pleasure.

By the fireside, I think that it is good to have learned how to lose myself in so many dear faces during the course of the day: of Josée and Gandillac during class—of Miquel met at noon with so much pleasure (he was well-dressed and comfortable, which makes me happy for him), of Stépha only glimpsed, of Zaza reunited through her letter—and above all of you, Maurice, on the plaza where the sky was blue around two o'clock, and at six o'clock on the banks of the very beautiful Seine, telling me what I had thought during my excessive solitude today: the artifice of this atmosphere, the disdain that is born from so much work, the bad pleasure that can be found in it and that this is more despicable than living it up. Maybe this simple half-hour managed to restore my serenity; once more you have helped me to get a grip on everything again, wise friend.

I would like to know why there is always this secret wound after each intense movement of new affinity. Is it for Jacques? Yes probably, but also for you, Riquet, over whom I cried so the other night, and again when I think of you, such a distressful stabbing pain. Already, I remember three years ago . . . this clash with an inaccessible reality suddenly imposed with as much force as your own—this irreparable failure against the real, showing the collapse of this ideal that wanted to take itself for the *entire* world. Nothing is attractive but this resistance and this sudden renewal of the world that is another soul—but neither is anything as serious or as alarming—beyond one's control.

Tonight is admirable. I seem to know in advance the happy peace that will be mine in a year perhaps. Thus I imagine such nights with an admirable intensity, completely enveloped in your existence, adventurous and passionate beneath their peaceful appearance, and yet so lucid and so free too. Tonight again I think tenderly of the book that I will write, we will read beautiful things and see some of them, and this plenitude will flawlessly keep all its doors open. Tonight it is thus . . . Stronger than anything, even your sadness is my very own joy; and it will prevail. You told me, Riquet, when I claimed to be intelligent and happy, that I would have to be a genius, but why not? Oh, this Saturday night is so good and the miracle of such midnights is there in its poignant poetry; I am not overwhelmed by it; it no longer upsets all of my life, it attached itself to my life and the junction was made. I am waiting for Wednesday when I will not drink and when I hope nevertheless to rediscover this shock, this happy surprise. It seems to me that a double spell is broken: the spell of the stifling library that is no longer going to keep me from living in your renewed presence, Jacques, and the exigencies that it entails—and the spell of the bars, of their sadness, of the nostalgia of unsatisfied souls; it seems to me that I can cherish and take with me without modeling on them a soul that I want to be harmonious and fulfilled by its own forces.

Oh, Jacques—so many things, so many things . . . and I will probably not write. But all of this is addressed only to you.

Tuesday, November 20

Institut Catholique then Sorbonne, then Bibliothèque Nationale where I catch sight as always of Gandillac and Merleau-Ponty. Hairdresser. Evening with Duhem and Plato's *La république* [*The Republic*], by the fireside and marvelously complete—nothing but a smile, nothing but a word ... the intersection of two souls a bit tipsy in a Montparnasse bar, some books unopened for a long while and some promises of paintings, hours of profound dreaming about your friend's face and about all that it includes of you, Jacques—about Poupette and about her pleasure that we used to renew together—delicious thrill at the mere memory of a smell.[207]

Wednesday, November 21

Tangerine peels that joyously leap off under the blue sweetness of the sky, the class neither fun nor boring at the Sorbonne, the slice of pâté melting on the very blue quays of the Seine. Gandillac is kind, his doubts are amorous— we catch a whiff of dead leaves laced with a calm sadness ... expectation of tonight.

Delicious taste of the world, delicious taste of the world.

Oh! heart armed with so much strength to bring joy—strength of having so much need and so much ardor to consent to it—strength of having such a need to love, and so little need to be loved. Unless ... unless this is about the only one through whom the pleasure of being sensitive to the world can come. Oh, just because of Saturday's tears watering the violets, this abstract world of ideas has been swept away. There are only a thousand memories of droll adventures at nearly one o'clock in the morning, of confused men, of fragrant nights, of cold cocktails in the soothing heat of bars.

Above all of a face for which I thirst as one thirsts for a glass of water in the month of August, of this look that says "the woman who wanted to eat all the flowers ... !" of this smile that commands while looking as though it is requesting (or the opposite? and the opposite): "Stay a bit longer or I will believe that you are a strong woman ..."

I could touch the form of certain of our silences, I can picture every curve of your hand in your hair, Jacques, or this habit that you have of watching yourself in the mirror as you speak. I imagine you in that part of your life that was truly mine, probably better than tonight when once again I will see myself in your life as if I had not already been there.

Marvelous night. A very delicious taste of the world ... At six o'clock I stop by Stépha's who decides to meet me at the Stryx. At ten thirty I enter the Stryx; there is a large crowd of strangers in front of the bar; one pretty American. Stépha in her green dress is drinking a Rose cocktail with her compatriot, Levinsky, who, as he is idle, uses his leisure time to study

Japanese in some odd books that he shows us. Enter Riquet and his friend, Mr. Carra who tells me that Saturday my sister was "tipsy, but in a delightful way." A Rose for me, some gin for them, and introductions. Stépha speaks every language with the Oriental Jew. I have a discussion with Riquet— unexpected pleasure, rediscovered life. We discuss Soupault whose *Le bar de l'amour* I lend to him, then Giraudoux, Bloch, Cocteau, Chadourne, Fournier, Gide, and Proust whom he does not like.[208] We discuss Lucian and the cock of Pythagoras.[209] Then we talk of life, women, Jacques, Jean Delrive, him, men . . . their weakness, his weakness.[210] "Oh! if only one by Herself would come one fine evening . . ."[211] He told me that Jacques would get married on an impulse, not without missing "love affairs"—that however, home might be enough for him. At times I feel something extraordinarily painful when through him I see a Jacques too similar to this Riquet whom I like a lot; I don't want intelligent and sensitive Jacques with his charming smile to resemble him too closely. We talk about the friendship between men, about his desire to some day reunite life's experience and science with all the enthusiasm of his youth. (Oh! how despite everything I feel more mature and stronger, having already attained that, and not at all by mere chance). He talks of the theater and cinema, and tells me that Jacques finds "that I must not misuse my intelligence, that I feel too intellectually"—but that is me, Jacques, . . . you must take me as I am.[212] Profound intimacy and cordiality . . . A "gin sherry-brandy" says Mr. Carra. We speak of Plato and Aristotle a bit loudly; some people—rich and chic Poles who are dining— quiet down to listen . . . "Michel, what do you think of Plato?" "I think that I have good customers." Stépha is getting drunk. A bit sad at first, she livens up and rants about bars. I put my feet on the table to prove my freedom. Now she is battling with Riquet and Mr. Carra about feminism, Turkish women, Japanese women, love life, and friendship between women. Riquet is badmouthing women; I protest even though I share his opinion, "she was always treading on men's territory . . ." (and despite myself, my expression was shocked, wounded by this liberty, a bit too great, by their words, and by this importance attached to sexual life. Frantic craving for purity. Ah! the love he describes, what a meager and undesirable thing . . . there is a passion so great, there are such real encounters, there is one soul facing another, and that is enough for greatness to be there—"Does that concern you?"[213] He himself would say, "take this into account . . ." I rather like his phrase too, but not with such women, I mean, not a desire for pleasure, a desire for greatness, but so what? Can I prejudge anything about you through your friend? Meanwhile I tell myself that it is perhaps insane to have wanted to fit you with happiness rather than the very salvation of my soul—a sort of distress—you distance yourself while appearing even closer, and yet, this portrait is indeed the one that *Riquet* was supposed to sketch of *you [toi]* if you are such as *I* see you). Another gin—not enough gin, Michel! Michel replies oddly . . . replies are comically exchanged back and forth. Mr. Carra speaks of gin from the heights of his forty years of experience, blasé but intelligent he explains his theories on life. Riquet is so young, so young in his disillusioned attitude (without romanticism).[214] "Let's leave, Stépha . . ." "Oh, I am so gay, so tipsy." Impossible to take her away—the minutes fly by so quickly. Yet, we are going out—marvel of this return trip . . . date for Saturday, Wednesday, and at her place also on Tuesday. We call out to vulgar passers-by, who start a quarrel with us. Stépha, out of her mind, sings and dances on the boulevard. Her compatriot tries to quiet her down, the two others double up with laughter . . . Stépha invites them all to her place: exchange of addresses. Some policemen eye us warily. Riquet and his male friend, noticeably delighted with their evening, are a bit dumbfounded however. Yes, perhaps I must have a very pure heart, and a powerlessness to see in all of this something other than a show offered for my pleasure, such a safe refuge in itself . . . But to focus on one of these moments: the one for example in front of the Rotonde, boulevard Raspail when Stépha stopped to sing that she is drunk, or when Riquet watches her with his questioning smile, and the other guy with his knowing look. Levinsky lectures her a bit on morality—priceless! He thanked her with emotion for such an interesting evening. She found Riquet so young and so intelligent. As for me, I am happy about everything; curious experience of other intelligent beings, and frame of mind to rediscover you and myself.[215] I am storing up memories.

Thursday, November 22

After such a night a certain headache makes Robin's lectures a bit painful to follow . . . In Bréhier's class Josée is very thin, tired, and sad—poor Josée. At noon I stopped by Stépha's place. A Stépha, delighted with her evening, shows me letters from her brother and speaks to me of interesting people. Brunschvicg's class. A woman-elephant is pontificating with an inert face that opens for awful imbecilic smiles. Lecture by Merleau-Ponty that is as like him as two peas in a pod, simple, serious, and charming. How I love him! He is so sure, upright, calm, and young in his gravity. Courteous and firm discussion with Brunschvicg. Both are witty and despite the heat it is cordial and almost lively. We go up to Stépha's place, she doesn't have the time to read his cards and the three of us come back down. Aunt Marguerite is dining here.

I myself came here; I am thinking of you, Jacques, and of me. One very anxious question: what am I for you? Or rather, what for you is the affection that you have for me? A desperate refuge because there is nothing else? Or a real thing worthy of being chosen for itself, not only preferred with a gratitude mixed with desolation. I don't know anymore, I don't know anymore. However, it appears to me . . . ah! Jacques, sometimes so truly close to you—ah! Jacques, tell me that it is I, really I who am close to the truest of yourself, that it is really *you* to whom I have written so many letters and silently listened so many times . . . Yes, of course, of course . . . why always suppose that he has a grudge or a distrust when he would be incapable of it.

My strength: feeling that I am above everything that I choose to love, uplifting the world with the sheer will of this love that I give him. Meeting no resistance, I feel all things with intense passion and as a gift of myself.[216] Sincerity of moments, but at the same time, I raise myself above my moments. I extract my own truth from the becoming of time. One thing alone is stronger than me, one thing alone is not subject to this moral and rational control—but that one, Jacques, that one . . . "What is more necessary than oneself, there is only one victory, which is to make it the strongest forever!"[217] I have that victory.

You do not know me yet—you don't know how I love you . . . that I managed to cry the tears of a wounded animal, walk like a madwoman through the wet nights, suffer without expectations.

I can't explain such melancholy tonight . . . yet while I was waiting for Stépha this afternoon, I liked myself in the mirror so much in this red coat and this gray hat that gives me a profound and sweet face.* My silhouette was relaxed, assured, and joyous . . . Melancholy . . . I was too proud. I put too many requirements into a human story. I wanted too much to believe that we have only souls . . . I ask for so much, too much, from you, Jacques. But not for me, for you.[218]

How alone I am before my love, how your love is, if it is, indeed yours and not mine. How silent you are, how far away you begin to be tonight . . . very far away, in a desert of silence . . .

---

* In the handwritten manuscript of *Diary*, the French equivalent of "I liked myself in the mirror so much in this red coat and this gray hat that gives me a profound and sweet face" is highlighted in pencil.

Friday, November 23

How many letters have I written or recited that he will never receive?

This rainy morning as I sit before my *diplôme* without adding a word, it is too strangely similar to mornings of two years ago when I would make progress in the midst of a dream.[219] Ah, never mind this nostalgia, never mind this powerlessness to study. I remembered the "better times, the brighter world," as painfully lacking but with truths that envelop me. The eyes of my life, the perceptible face of my universe. This alone matters, this alone matters: for me to live again. Time is nothing . . . Delicious, delicious taste of the world . . . so many pure moments intersect that we can only open our hands wide to reach for so much pleasure.

The Salon d'Automne smelling of humidity, oil paint, and solitude speaks to me of Jacques with every step.[220] I am dragging Magdeleine behind me as a pretext . . . beautiful and compelling paintings. Favory's mediocre lady with a flower—Kalli's boats tilting into the storm, white sails.[221] The mystery of this angler by Paulemile—Pissarro, minuscule on a pond with green depths under the green shadow of the silent trees.[222] By Mérinoff a strange green and faded pink carnival, formless and with unexpected tints—a small boat lost in a landscape ravaged by rain by someone named John Hura.[223] Le Ricolais, names to remember.[224] By a certain Vaudou a woman in pink nursing her child in the folds of a dress treated in Bosshard's manner; delicious skin tones.[225] By Lempicka a woman in pink with a blue scarf and boats in the distance—also a girl making her first communion; all of it in the genre of tole work but captivating and strong.[226] A lake between hills by Médici that moves me.[227] Whöffer. Babij, a woman in brown with chestnut blond hair, rather beautiful.[228] Some disgusting flowers and women by Marval, with tulle, whiteness, and toothpaste.[229] A likeable Souverbie.[230] Some landscapes signed by unknown authors that tap you on the shoulder.

The thought of Jacques haunts me—desire to know, to know and to tell . . . But let's see, but let's see, he does love me. But who can say how he wants to be loved . . .

An admirable Van Dongen, a long-legged woman in blue taffeta with a dog under her arm.[231] A rather good Dunoyer de Segonzac. The current retrospective: a Flandrin by chance bearable (*Matin de chasse* [Morning hunt]), a truly perfect Ottman.[232] A Van Dongen that I don't like much: a nude woman in a wide-open coat with yellow stockings, an ugly Renoir . . . a Renoir. Some whining and superficial Ch. Guérin, a good Fauconnet, that, moreover, I already knew—a good Othon Friesz, when one likes this painter.[233] A Desvallières, a Waroquier, admirable in its simplicity next to a still life by Cézanne that disappoints me because I expected too much from it, a Le Fauconnier, scholastic in its simplicity and poignant with its lighthouse lost in the brown rocks.[234] Curious A. Lhôte: woman running near a green bench; I don't like it much at all.[235] A Eugène Zak, very beautiful because of these two blond heads of the mother and child, because of her way of holding him on her shoulders, because of the tones of the fabrics and of the flesh.[236] A Carrière![237] Vallotton! Asselin, a man stretched out in the sand, rather good.[238] Maillol presents his female dancers, cover of a catalog, moreover, very pleasing to the eye. A mediocre Matisse: portrait of a woman in a complicated hat, some nice Gluckmann: nude women in a brown room, some flowers and a landscape by Y. Gilles whom I did not know but who has lots of talent.[239] But above all this black, green, and red Vlaminck, fruits and basket on a table, full of simplicity and mystery, unforgettable.

Lots of other things that must be seen again. Some fans, some pianos, some jewelry, some bars . . . some furniture, some marvelous interiors—oh! to live there . . . Oh! how wonderful that such delicious things are: this glassware by Lalique, this furniture with the simple lines, this ingenious lighting, these rugs—pleasure of the world.

And above all, the room of books, the red armchairs so comfortable beneath the appearance of being only elegant, the art journals on the long table, the wood engravings, the wonderful drawings, and some titles, some dear names, some phrases that one gathers in passing, "I sing on the summit where the heart is reason" (Suarès).[240] Moments when one could believe that the heart is going to burst. In front of these very beautiful things I rediscovered you in this profound point of our souls where we could not be mistaken.

Return in the rain, tramway; the boulevard St. Michel welcomes me. My heart sings. At the Sorbonne, I fortunately meet someone who will be able to take in all this joy: Miquel. We have the late afternoon snack in this new delicious bar, Alissa, place de la Sorbonne. Embraced by Paris and the world. The Fratellinis, Chevalier, Montparnasse, *Topaze*, *Siegfried*, the cinema passes by during our joyous discussion.[241] Your beautiful dark gaze, Miquel, your eagle eyes like on the day when I met you for the first time. After almost a year of forgetting—this rediscovered fraternity. Thank you, dear companion. We went to Adrienne Monnier's to skim through some books and pick up some theater tickets while he told me of his life in St. Germain-en-Laye, some works that he has undertaken and will show me, and together we make plans for going out. We go back up to the La Jeune Parque where I admire some *beautiful* paintings by an unknown artist: Le Scouezec—simple and strong landscapes of Brittany.[242] The gentleman, very friendly and with a likeable appearance, told us to go visit his workshop on Tuesday. We make a date while we look for the *Onze chapitres sur Platon* [Eleven chapters on Plato] by Alain—it costs eight cocktails: too expensive. I am joyful, joyful. Stépha, Miquel, Riquet are of primary importance at the moment. Tomorrow we will think about working, tomorrow—but nothing![243]

There is nothing in the world but friendship.

I picked up a super-mediocre book by César Santelli, where at least he notes two pretty expressions—by Duhamel, "Friendship, beautiful adventure more mysterious than love . . .," and by René Arcos whom I do not know: "There will be these delicate preludes / That are in the beginning new friendships."[244]

On my table I have some beautiful works by Plato taken out at Victor Cousin.[245]

This is good. But there is this desire to write to Jacques and this powerlessness to do it.

Saturday, November 24

Morning at the house. Interesting work: *Les atomes* [*Atoms*], by Perrin—*L'idéal du mathématicien* [The mathematician's ideal] by Boutroux.

Afternoon of work. Then I finish *Siegfried et le Limousin* by Giraudoux—that I so like! To render all of life's fantasies in this way . . . stopped by the library and then Stépha's where I find her and her friend Fernand. Discussed the Salon d'Automne and Cocteau whom she does not like—pleasant hour. Fernand is intelligent and sensitive, touching with his sudden bursts of nervousness, "We sell peanuts too . . ." Together we go to see some of the paintings by this painter that I saw yesterday with Miquel and that they find too dry.

In *Les nouvelles littéraires*, I find interviews: with Savin, which amuses me, and with Gandillac, which displeases me.[246] I think back to the phrase "the tattered flesh and its tragic suzerainty"—behind such harshness, maybe a suffering? but also public life, his career . . . I like only his words on *Les nourritures terrestres* [*Fruits of the Earth*]—try to speak to him of "Souffrances du chrétien"—of himself . . . I am happy that M.-P. did not accept.[247]

But all of this is not my life. Pretty lithographs by Poupette; a rather interesting oil painting. Jacques, I do not have anything of much worth to say tonight.[248]

Sunday, November 25

Finished the book on atoms—interesting. But how my thoughts wander, wander towards you, Jacques.

This mechanical jazz at the Ciné-Latin warmed my heart as always when I hear a saxophone. Douglas Fairbanks is delightful with his elastic hat, his umbrella, his pantomimes and his good dumb laugh, "Did you see that?" So natural while pretending to be an imbecile, and the crazy races, the daring jumps, the unexpected apparitions—and that wonder of the umbrella, upon his first entrance, *Le signe de Zorro* [*The Mark of Zorro*] very good.[249] The second film, science fiction, on Dr. Jeckyll and Dr. Hyde [*sic*], aside from one little idea is very, very bad. I like to think when I see these things that I will be able to speak of them.[250]

La nuit tombe [Night is falling] is an admirable book, decidedly admirable.[251]

Charming end of the day at the home of Stépha and Fernand (I talk as though they were married). We drink some Curacao in teacups and eat a strange mixture of honey, pistachios, and almonds, we talk a lot about painting: Van Dongen, Foujita, Soutine (Fernand shows me some very beautiful reproductions of his work) and much finer than all, Modigliani's portrait of him. He has good taste in painting; shows me the photo of one of his paintings that I like a lot; tells me about his start in painting. Extremely nice. Stépha seems to like him a lot, she will never love him, but will perhaps marry him. He is beside her as you, Jacques, were beside me without their being able to see you—and I enjoyed their intimacy as the reflection of the intimacy that plays itself out in my heart.

Wrote to Zaza.

Completely enveloped by you . . .

Monday, November 26

Bibliothèque de la Sorbonne in the morning. Institut Catholique in the afternoon. Night in the office with Aristotle and Plato. Approaching irritation, I think of you, Jacques. Questions form as threats of suffering. I ask for your forgiveness. I told you that I didn't want to know anything except from you. You believed me, I dare say. Despite myself, I imagine possibilities for suffering. Requirement of such perfection from you.

Write to me.

Tuesday, November 27

Bad night, or too good, it's the same. I saw you again, Jacques, and we had *so many* things to say . . . Rain in the morning. Sadness that pursues me to Rivaud's class, but I work well in the afternoon at the Institut Catholique in the midst of college graduates with lorgnettes. Saw Michel in the morning with Poupette, good discussion in the Luxembourg Gardens and on rue Delambre to see a painter that we had not yet seen.

Night at Stépha's. Disguised as a bartender, she was making mixtures of gin, sherry, and Curaçao. Fernand is joking with Poupette. Levinsky is very attentive to me. Stépha is tipsy and sings on the bed as she embraces Poupette; the gaiety rises in a delicious cordiality. I adore Stépha, Poupette is charming, Levinsky kind, and I love Fernand with all of my heart. He is trying to make me tipsy. Wait a bit . . .

We leave Poupette at place St. Sulpice; Fernand and I race each other to get to Montparnasse in the cool, harsh, and beautiful night. Songs and laughter from our hearts without any ulterior motives; nothing but this happy moment. At the Stryx, drinking menthes and inhaling the violets offered by Fernand, we greet Michel. Fernand is on a table, and Levinsky on a stool next to me. Stépha, disguised as a bartender, is crushing ice next to Michel. She is singing in Ukrainian and shouting, "I am drunk, come drink for *in vino veritas* [in wine is truth] and we must make life sweeter." She goes to the tables to take orders from customers, gives some drawings to the audience, calls out to some Germans and to people of all languages, gives her violets to two rather stunned young women, . . . arrival of Riquet's friend, of Riquet—reproaches. Their mood clashes with ours so we change our mood to theirs: we talk of theater, cinema, and literature (Laforgue, Rimbaud, Soupault). A woman gets kissed in the stairwell; Stépha tenses up. Riquet claims that he approves—tells me about a theory on the sentimental value of the cinema: oh! my God! . . . But why is there this need for women, this sentimental dupery, pretext for anything but a true feeling. To take the precise desires of his twenty years of age for an emptiness of the soul . . . and don't try to make me believe that to love means to pick up the feather that fell from this woman's coat. Desperate desire for purity and harsh lucidity.

Joyous return, we spoke of our future works—arm in arm I descend the boulevard Raspail with Fernand, dramatically taking our hats off to every metro entrance that we find—him on the left and me on the right.

Good sleep when I get home, without my being too oppressed by the inevitable "amari aliquid."[252] Oh! Jacques???

Wednesday, November 28

After Robin's insipid class on the skeptics I saw Gandillac whom I accompanied to place St. Michel. The way that he holds me in high esteem and makes me feel it with his very precious kind of ingenuousness almost makes me feel like crying. We talked about marriage: *La vie de Saint Alexis* [*The Life of St. Alexis*] and *Le grand Meaulnes* which is not a high point for him but which he likes—I say to him, "There are no rules . . ."[253] Spoke a bit about philosophy, of the necessity of being shaken up, of being transplanted. He told me, "You are right, but a boy must be very strong to withstand the transplants." A girl also has to be very strong! Oh! It is so fatiguing to want to understand and acknowledge everything, and yet to reserve the right to obtain more. I can acknowledge everything, but to be happy I must be seized by this profound feeling of membership [*adhésion*], this plenitude of the soul that needs no effort to be fulfilled . . . All of this hurts me, I have visions of Jacques that hurt me, and Riquet distresses me, he and all that he represents—this particular cowardice is not only in libraries . . . work is an opium; so is alcohol. Gandillac, alone, is for me like a certitude that would preserve me from all the rest, but one that I can no longer reach; I feel that he is the greatest strength near me for the moment. I desire to confess to him . . . a cowardly desire since he would respond in the name of rules that I do not recognize. (I would like to love him, despise myself, and tell him so—I do not love him, I do not despise myself— he is not absolution!) Jacques is not absolution. Jacques *allows* everything.*
But require of me instead, Jacques . . .

I am alone.

There is no camaraderie possible in my life—so heavily does every moment weigh on me, like a request for justification. Desire for morality, for value.

Desire to write—my book is taking form. I will cut many episodes. The first part will barely change. The second will be situated in the bars of Montparnasse: there, across from one another, both will suffer and she will seek oblivion. I will tell about the temptations from others' lives, the changes of position, the liking for risk—her solitude, and from him, a desperate pride; a madness for destruction. In both a purity and a haughtiness that will not even be mentioned. I will put more imagination into the style and the details—but just as much seriousness into the content.

It will be a *beautiful* book.†[254]

---

* The French equivalent of "allows" is underlined in the diary manuscript.
† The French equivalent of "beautiful" is underlined in the manuscript.

A bit of confidence is returning. But I would want to lean on someone . . . There is nobody. There is only me. Oh! my life has a tragic and delicious flavor . . .

After Belleville, brief appearance in the Jungle; very pretty but too chic—familiar faces and women—sometimes the mirage of a soul with whom one could be taken—glimpsed Riquet—sudden disgust. Beautiful night.

Thursday, November 29

Class at Normale. Return with Gandillac; we speak of marriage, of the Normalians' protest against his article, of Nizan and his wife who wrote to demand the right to love, of the ideal stoic. One day I would like to chat with Gandillac and to tell him . . . a lot of things. Would he understand?

Classes again this afternoon. Saw Josée, glimpsed M.-P. Regret having missed him between the class at Normale and the pedagogy lecture where I am reading pages by Rilke that break my heart. After some minutes in the rue Gay-Lussac I am bathed in light, first lost, then suddenly rediscovered.

I stop by Stépha's; she is with Fernand who is charming. Effort to place myself in their universe, so different from mine—but admirable. Discussed *Le grand Meaulnes*. He speaks of it with intelligence—but he hasn't felt it. He looks at me weirdly and asks me to explain my conception of the world to him. I explain. The more I explain the more I feel the need for a book where the poetry of images will perhaps make one feel what words cannot say. Levinsky comes in; I feel so at home, they are so much my friends already! We speak of Rilke, of the difference between poetry and art, of combat with the demon . . . They are a thousand miles from me—and yet very close.

Will I write to you tonight? I could perhaps, a long confiding letter. Something however, some doubt or some almost desperate taste for solitude, or some fear of saying too much about it now. I daresay I do know how to remain silent . . .

Friday, November 30

From morning to evening at the Bibliothèque Nationale. I worked well, had lunch with Stépha, stopped by at the hairdresser in the evening, caught sight of Gandillac. I think of Jacques, of Jacques . . .

Stopped by Stépha's where I am seeing Fernand and Levinsky.

Saturday, December 1

Worked again, and without even having lunch. Stopped by the home of Marie Louise who had nothing to say to me, nor I to her. In the evening, read the *N.R.F.* [*Nouvelle revue française*] without interest and some short stories by Stevenson. I finally started to write this letter that I shall not send . . . yes, perhaps I shall . . .

Sunday, December 2

Woke up late with my heart still overwhelmed from an entire night that I had given to him. Went to look for seats at the Avenue, and walked home because I didn't have a cent.*

I spent the afternoon at the house as in the past, with a book in front of a dancing flame. Then I described everything. There was no longer anything but the shadows dancing on the walls and the red glow on my dress. I told you more and more things . . . I would have wanted to write them to you and almost all of it stuck in my throat. This love, Jacques, this love—why is it so serious? Why can't I think of you without trembling and more, always the same powerlessness to dream anything ugly—and in the meantime this entire gift of myself that calls out to you, calling out to you in these sad postures that look just like you on the leather of the armchair where I laid my head. My refuge, my brother, my great friend, my life.

Evening at the theater. Stépha in a gray hat and a navy blue coat decorated with a blue leather flower and gray fur, is more touching than ever. She is sad, Fernand too. I took her hand in my hand, and I feel it throbbing while she turns her tear-stained face away.

The play by Gantillon *Départs* [Departures] is very bad—superficial, crude, and disjointed.[255] Marguerite Jamois annoys me a bit, Baty's staging is excellent, especially the boat. We walk down the chilly avenue des Champs-Elysées. I like their brave effort not to cry.

Monday, December 3

Laporte's deadly class![256] Josée asks me to accompany her. It's raining, I want to go work, so I need to be persuaded. She tells me, place Médécis, with

---

* This last sentence is highlighted in the margin of the manuscript.

something a bit odd in her voice as I prepare to take the bus, "Then I will tell you on Thursday what I wanted to tell you." Suddenly my heart skipped a beat, "No, right away, Josée . . ." She drags me into the damp and deserted Luxembourg Gardens. She is short and skinny beneath her hat shaped like an inverted flower and slightly worn like her too thin coat. She laughs, but averts her gaze slightly, "Don't tell anyone; it's too ridiculous . . ." Then suddenly, "So here it is, I would like to marry Merleau-Ponty." I sat down on the wire and looked at her, dumbfounded . . . I thought that she found him to be a bit cold and stilted? "It means I like him a lot; more than I have ever liked anybody." With such cautious audacity, such simple frankness that barely expects anything. I was so embarrassed to explain to her that someone else also loved M.-P.[257] "I somewhat suspected it," she simply responded. I now see that all the words that we had laughingly pronounced were quite serious. For an hour we walked on the rainy terrace. She spoke of him with simple and precise words that rendered a great straightforward love without grandiloquence. She spoke of love in general, of this new liking for the world that she had never believed that she would discover, of the impossibility of no longer experiencing this liking . . . of this evolution that she had felt begin within her. "I would tolerate anything . . ." she told me with an accent so sincere, such profound simplicity, such resignation to unhappiness that I like so much in her, so very much. She told me that she had always found him charming; and especially since the beginning of this school year. I was in such distress. "What am I going to do?" I murmured. "Act as if I hadn't told you anything . . ." "You too, Josée, you must be frank; he must know you with all there is within you for him, he really must know her, and must choose . . ." She shook her head, without protesting out loud. Saying, simply, on the doorstep where I could not leave her, "I know that we say that out of cowardice. I will do as I like . . ." "Ah, my dear Josée!" And it's my fault! Why did I call her on the phone to talk about Hamelin over a cup of tea?[258] And what about this profound and secret heart, that gave itself silently, faithfully? To unleash such consequences as these with only a few words—imprudent girl, imprudent girl, you believe that you can always control yourself and others. Life resists despite everything and there is no way out. I feel bad . . . [259]

And he knows nothing, nothing. What am I to do?

I found Stépha who listened to me with all of her intelligence—she told me that Poupette is more than Merleau-Ponty, more cheerful, imaginative, and poetic, and it's true—but so what, if she loves him. And she made me notice too how little he cares about Josée, because the other day when we were saying how sad, sick, and alone she was, he interrupted us without showing any interest. It's true. Poupette has more spark, more life, more youth. After having tried in vain to work at the Bibliothèque Nationale I went by her school to get her; through the window I watched her playing the piano and dancing, radiant, and so close to my heart. I went in and she ran towards me enthusiastically. She got dressed, so pink, pretty, and victorious. We walked, in the Latin Quarter, in Montparnasse. I told her everything, she felt sorry for Josée whom she so likes, but so what? She hopes to be loved, she hopes for happiness; how could one not understand this egotism? (which however wounds me a bit when I think of you, Josée, who with a smiling handshake gave up everything without a word).

Here I am, so distraught. I would like Zaza to be here, to tell her. I would like Jacques to be here to make me forget. I would like to tell everything to Merleau-Ponty and I would like to keep my mouth shut. I believe that if I were not supposed to see him tomorrow, I would write him a long letter. Tomorrow if I see him, I must tell him. I would like to write to Josée. I would like to have something that I could do. I would not like life to start having other intentions [*volontés*] than my own.

Don't take this as a tragedy? It's always easy not to take the sorrow of others as a tragedy.

I am no longer working. I will flunk—I don't care.[260] This is not a novel.

Tuesday, December 4

I work on Plato here in the morning. Class at eleven o'clock. I have lunch in Luxembourg Gardens where I work in the cold, partly because I have lots to do, and partly because every presence weighs heavily on me. In Brunschvicg's class I doze. Going out, I catch sight of Merleau-Ponty, Gandillac and Lautmann in the courtyard where it is raining. I grab Merleau-Ponty as he flies by (did I come for anything other than to see him?) We go down the boulevard St. Michel together, and then we go back up and take la rue Soufflot as far as the Panthéon. I look at him—I understand . . . I understand *so* well!* As it happens, after a few words on Gandillac he starts to talk of marriage. He has just come from a wedding. We discuss the appropriateness of these gatherings that so displease me whereas he finds them very enjoyable. He says, "When we are married, it will be fun to travel all around France to see nice people . . . and when we are old—but I must not speak to you of that" . . .

---

* The word "so" is underlined in the manuscript.

I get up a bit of courage (we are in front of the Tavern of the Panthéon). "Yes, I often think of your marriage. I wonder what your wife will be like."

"Ah, if only you could tell me, but you are not a fortune-teller. I even wonder how I will ever manage to choose a girl if I don't find one who particularly suits me between now and then."

"You will call me."

"Do you arrange marriages?"

"Oh, I don't do it professionally, but it does happen."

Short silence . . . then kindly he asks me for news of Jacques. I give him some hastily—does he sense the words that I would want to say? (We are in front of the Law School). "There is something embarrassing that I would like to tell you . . . it is so difficult . . . I know so little about what you might think, how you will take this . . . no, I will write it to you, it will be simpler"—silence—"Did you ever think about how important one can become in someone's life without suspecting it?"

"I have thought about it theoretically."

"Well, I will leave you with this subject of meditation until I write you the letter . . ."

"I am very surprised."

"There is nothing surprising about it."

Silence. "Let's talk about something else. How is your *diplôme* progressing?" Now we turn at the square. We go as far as the alma mater, École Normale—I am not inclined to talk, I watch him endlessly signing papers that the concierge hands to him from his glass cage, dressed with such an elegant sobriety in this tie, this hat, and this overcoat with a sensible extravagance very similar to his own, with this shining face, lit by intelligence, purity, and goodness, with this smile that offers all of his soul while simultaneously reserving it so well, with everything . . . We return to the Sorbonne side by side. He leaves me at the door of the science auditorium promising me that we will see each other again soon. The more I love him, the more I understand why people love him, and the more uncomfortable I feel. An hour at Victor Cousin Library.

Fortunately Stépha comes over at night and sings, and going down the stairs to Vieux-Colombier I give her a big hug.[261] The most visible tenderness that I have ever shown; I love her smile like the wind that passes through the poplar trees in the big meadow. I love her warm hand near mine as I love mysterious and supple cats whose sadness you hug in your arms. I love the stories that she has told me as I love Giraudoux's novels. The story of her cousin; and her cousin's friend who in a hospital bed asked her to forgive him for having separated her from him . . . I love this evening when a fairytale by Pushkin unfolds on camera through shots of animated puppets, when Max Linder is sometimes oddly amusing in his parody of the three musketeers, when a film on "nature and life" offers some dream images.[262]

Merleau-Ponty, must I write to you, Maurice, my very good friend, so dear, so dear, must I write to you almost in tears?

Wednesday, December 5

Sorbonne, Bibliothèque Nationale where Stépha, glimpsed, soon leaves me. Work and bewilderment, work and tenderness.

Delicious evening—we, Poupette, Stépha, and I, go to Belleville. The three of us look good on the metro platform where we are jumping about together, so young and lively, pleasant to watch. Chit-chat, songs and laughter, in the big, cold and empty place where on the stage accompanying herself on a bad piano, Stépha is singing, exquisite. Stépha . . . the others listen delighted; the boy scouts on the other side of the door are noisy and strike up their song with enthusiasm. We have tea with Germaine Monod—friendly and happy meeting. Then we walk into the wondrous Parisian night through les Buttes-Chaumont and into the streets striped with rain; unexpected encounter with lights, gleaming roadways like pieces of silk in which the lamplights of dreams are reflected—arm in arm we sing "Le coeur de Jeannette [Jeannette's heart]" and "C'est pour ça qu'on s'a quitté [That's why we left each other]" . . . [263] Stépha speaks of her childhood—the good cheer increases with the alcohol. Upon reaching the boulevards, we drink some delicious coffee—"plain or fancy, ladies?"—in a Brazilian place where there is delightful lighting, and like animals in a cage we watch people passing freely along the sidewalk. The flavor of every night is in our mouths—we walk along the boulevard to St. Denis watching painted women who wait on the café terraces, and it is as if on this night during this simple walk all possibilities [possibles] had been harvested.

Thursday, December 6

École Normale. Gandillac presents a very good analysis. I catch sight of Merleau-Ponty who makes a date with me for the next day. Sorbonne in the afternoon. Normale; I go from the Sorbonne to Normale between Gandillac, who is talking about medicine, philosophy, etc., as if it truly interested him, and Josée, who, embarrassed, says nothing. After having signed up for the pedagogy lectures, I hastily leave her to take a bus; she walks away, alone and huddled over, she walks away.[264] On the way back I find M. de Ravinel, C. Mallutée, and A. Vanetti—they tell me about their studies, art, literature, etc. I interest them a lot. They don't interest me much.

In the evening I read *La vie inquiète de Jean Hermelin* [The troubled life of Jean Hermelin].[265] Every page reminds me of Jacques. Oh, such appeal, oh, such desire! There are days when seven months is very long.

Friday, December 7

Bibliothèque Nationale, I see Stépha. At the Sorbonne where I go at three o'clock, hastily devouring two rolls in the bus, and on through the cold Luxembourg Gardens, I find charming Miquel, with whom I make a date for the next day. Then Merleau-Ponty arrives; meandering walk through Luxembourg Gardens where he speaks very well to me of *Aimée*, of Rivière, of Fournier, and of Gide. On a cold bench we peruse *Les nouvelles littéraires*: response from Nizan and from a law student, Bouscard, who seems very nice. I hear some of Barrès's phrases, almost painfully since they are the ones that we so love, Jacques. We stroll to chez Picard and go back up to Normale. I attend a pedagogical lecture by Roustand who talks about the duties of professors, and I myself think about the students in the boarding school classes, about the students in the classrooms where one yawns in front of the black desks while the students learn to suffer, admire, and love ... Bizarre conversation with the secretary who signs an attendance sheet for me. Charlotte comes to dinner in the evening; she hurts me, burdened by too many memories.[266] I go to see *Le gaucho* [*The Gaucho*], a mediocre film by Douglas Fairbanks.[267] I am only a desire for your presence, for my hand on your shoulder, for your life—for you, Jacques, oh! Jacques. I finally sent my letter ...

Saturday, December 8—

I worked seriously on Kant with no break from nine in the morning to six at night. I go by Stépha's, she is with Fernand, both are sad. I spend a boring hour at her place, I have dinner, I wait for Charlotte in front of the door of the cinema where we were not supposed to go, then I rush towards the rue de la Sorbonne where I meet Miquel who was waiting for me in the cold. Raymond Duncan speaks about the "disquiet of being" of things; I think back to an evening when you were here ... a lady is taking notes.[268] I myself take the floor and we argue in the midst of laughter from the audience. We walk back up to Montparnasse. The Stryx is crowded. Riquet, Carra, and his nephew play poker at the back table with Jean Delrive near whom Olga is seated, in a marvelous red and white dress and a light gray coat, with blond hair cut above her ears and admirably curled, and a delicate and well-groomed face that I find infinitely attractive. We are having a discussion with Miquel. Stépha and Levinsky arrive, and Stépha argues with some fat Swedes, and with a common woman who insults her. We talk about the "resistances" of real things that life offers—and everyone says that nothing is stronger than oneself and that one must live without remedy, that passion subsides or leads to folly or sleep. I do not take part in this discussion. I know that within me there is something uncontrollably stronger than myself, and that none of these people could understand, and that I am other than all of them. Miquel gives me some violets and leaves us, after paying for everything, which embarrasses us a bit. Riquet comes to greet us and laughingly calls us intellectual little girls—he speaks at length of *Volpone* with Levinsky while Stépha calls Carra Mephisto.[269] We talk about *Départs* [Departures] that everyone agrees is boring.[270] Riquet complains about the monotony of the world. But everything irrefutably gains such a strong flavor, and it's precisely because several times you believed that you experienced something this strong that you never experienced it. A love like mine, Jacques . . .

Return with Stépha in this very great sonorous silence of nights along the wrought iron railing of Luxembourg Gardens. Fortunately, papa has not come home yet. I lie down, I think . . . Jacques, thus was your life, Jean Delrive, Olga, Riquet . . . they scare me less. Already a habit, it was no longer such a captivating thing that nothing else could matter next to it. Meanwhile, I imagine you as one of them and not as mine; I am alone. I doze off, just opening my eyes to see Poupette come back from the dance, ravishing in a pink dress.

Sunday, December 9

I sleep late. A letter from Zaza awakens me. She is opening up to the world, and I am delighted about it. I walk through the cold of Luxembourg Gardens, where for the first time a white frost covers the lawn, to go to Josée's—she is charming. Charlotte comes to lunch; complex feeling of affection, of defiance, and of sadness. The three of us, Josée, whom we went to pick up, and Charlotte and myself, go as far as avenue Bosquet where we drop off Charlotte, then we take the 43 bus to go to Neuilly, and in an empty creamery we have our afternoon snack. We talk so much that we walk up to l'Étoile and there we take the 43 bus as far as Montparnasse. At the bar of the Rotonde, with a glass of port wine, we continue our discussion until the night chases us away; then we discuss some more . . . Oh, the intensity of such hours! The jazz music from the dance hall reaches as far as the glasses placed on the table near the window that the checkered curtains separate from the boulevard Raspail. We feel inexpressibly in harmony with one another, with the same swelling of courage that fails at these moments that are too heavy to bear. She speaks to me in her clear and reflective voice that slowly seeks the truest of words; I feel all the difference in her solitude, in her defiant sadness about what she calls "my triumphant imagination," in her dependence in regard to beings, in the gratuitousness of the gift that I give to them, in my strength that goes beyond them—but even if our feelings are different, almost opposite, their sincerity, their strength, stronger than us, make us transparent to each other. I tell her of myself, of Jacques, who is here, here seated at each of the tables and standing in front of the bar also . . . she tells me of Merleau-Ponty, and that a being may be in you so strongly that nothing else exists in the world . . . and that simply because he will receive what cannot be expressed it will seem that everything is expressed for everyone, that everything is useful, and that everything is saved.[271] And too that sometimes it is this desire for such simple tenderness: to take someone's head in your hands, without saying anything, anything at all . . . She analyzes herself with so much lucidity, sincerity, and emotion that she makes me sensitive to the flavor that each instant in the world has for her. Something is there, as strong as death. And always being able to want only the impossible with such certainty of never obtaining it, and such emptiness, such solitude . . . she will leave for Saigon—she will endure. She is like a bird caught in the snares of tenderness.[272] She does not even try to struggle, expecting the worst. She is exquisite. She also speaks to me of beings, of her ethical exigencies—and this admirable expression: "so prompt to accuse and thus more quickly ready to excuse," and, Jacques, isn't that what makes me sometimes doubt, because even then I have already accepted . . . I am on the verge of excuse with such great suffering. Our love is here, in front of our eyes, each minute has the value of an eternity.

On boulevard Montparnasse, because of this pink glimmer through the curtains I suddenly felt heartsick—he used to be mine, in these surroundings of ours, in some moments when only we were real.

We have dinner at Lutetia with Aunt Valentine, and such a constricted throat cannot swallow even a single mouthful. Music.

Return in the cold—
I read some touching and accurate phrases in *Opales* [Opals] by
Jouhandeau.[273]
And there are seven more months to go . . .

Monday, December 10—

Rather interesting class by Laporte. At the Bibliothèque Nationale I exchange
words with Gandillac who tells me that he does not believe himself to be
gifted for literature because he has no sense of the particular. This is certainly not something that will stop me . . . Merleau-Ponty is here and his
presence weighs heavily on me. I am writing a letter to him tonight; what
will he do with it? I went by "the house;" there was no sign of life there;
Aunt Germaine was probably gone. I stopped by Stépha's, she is making me
reread parts from *Le grand écart* [*The Great Divide*] that she is learning to
like.[274]

Tuesday, December 11

I finished that letter this morning after the Sorbonne, in a café across from the
post office. I tossed it in the mailbox with a desperate gesture—I feel relieved,
lighter—it is so good. All day facing Kant, I did nothing but dream of him,
of the possible future, of everything. How I love life—and these very intense
encounters that we cannot even imagine when we no longer feel them.

I finish *Opales*—I liked the beginning more than the end. But there again,
on friendship and the universe, there are, in some corners of the pages,
remarks profound, brief, and accurate enough to elicit a moan of pleasure.

Wednesday, December 12

Bibliothèque Nationale. Stépha comes by just so we can have lunch together.
I am reading some not very interesting Mac Orlan at night since my return
home and I am working by the fireside.[275]
Thinking of you Maurice, great friend whose pneumatic message, with no
allusion to my letter, asks me to see him Saturday night. I am relieved that I
wrote it, as I stare at the fire thinking of you, Maurice, and wondering how
so much tenderness can not be the only tenderness—and why you will never
know exactly how immense it is—as immense perhaps as in those who love

you, only they can suffer from your not welcoming everything about them. I myself have no need of a welcome; my victory is to be above and beyond all that you will ever think to have found within me ... You are standing here, I hold your hand and you smile at me with this delicate and respectful affection that you know how to put in a smile—and I say only: you are here, you are here ... Oh, delights of friendship! Sometimes I find you too ... or not enough ... this or that, but real feelings are stronger than any of these gestures of indifference or bad temper; and the latter are of no importance. But you, how important you are ... Tuesday I would like to take you to the Jockey and explain it to you; we would speak of Jacques, of me, of you perhaps.[276] Oh, sure and calm fraternal tenderness for my great friend! ...

Wrote a note to Pontremoli.

Thursday, December 13

I have tears in my eyes because life is too good. In the morning darkened by the fog, the École Normale was only the delicious memory of our last year's encounters, dear Maurice. Class was not boring; it might have been a bit recklessly so, since you sat near me to make rude remarks about Brunschvicg.

The Knam is a dream place for eating Russian sausage and chops across from Stépha who tells me about her business projects and the good-byes that her Romanian friend said to her yesterday—her Romanian friend who at the Bibliothèque Nationale sits across from me and watches me because I am something to Stépha. He says good-bye to her because he loves her a bit too much—smoke, young people playing cards near us, handshakes: life. I chat until two o'clock giving myself over to this too easily welcomed ambiance. In Bréhier's class I exchange a few words with Gandillac. Josée takes me for a walk in Luxembourg Gardens. She recites some pages from Claudel for me: Violaine and Jacques, Pensée and Orian, la France and St. Louis—the very pages that so many times I repeated to myself with tears in my eyes.[277] She is so simply a young girl, completely enthralled—an exquisite child who loves and who marvels at discovering her heart, but will someone respond to it?

Brunschvicg's class. I go to the Museum of Pedagogy [Musée pédagogique] to sign in and I see him, cordial and charming as usual.[278] We look at Fauconnet's cranium next to those of some other nice guys (Audibert, Le Tellier) until the director of Normale who is keeping watch decides to slip away. So we slip away too: Savin's nice funny-looking face, Simone Weil's bizarre face at the door. I accompany Merleau-Ponty to Normale, and then bus. Here I find Monina and Poupette who are making pretty drawings. A letter from Belleville (action committee's report), notice from the Sorbonne that my *diplôme* proposal has been accepted—nice letter from Miquel who sends with it a marvelously detailed "chart of resistances" that I am going to bring tonight. Because of this friendly note, because of these intelligent lines in this intelligent handwriting, immense joy that makes me dance all over the house as I empty boxes of candy and cookies.[279] I am happy, happy . . . life will be so good, ah! Jacques, you will see. During these past few days I have made wonderful plans; we will have nice get-togethers, very good friends whose whole-hearted affection we will share and maintain, things, people and ourselves. You will see, you will see. You must come home quickly.

Stryx—with Poupette we go to get Josée and all three of us are the first to arrive, then Miquel comes, then Stépha and Lévinsky. Poupette is in brilliant form and very amusing; jokes with Michel to whom Stépha gives some flowers in front of a big elephant of a German guy, with Mr. Carra. A small Chinese woman with deformed feet juggles with swords and collects money with a silent smile.

Riquet does not greet us. He is with Olga whom I find less elegant and less shapely than I had thought; face too harsh and without charm—and with Jean Delrive.[280] Stépha reads the cards for a delighted Miquel while Levinsky, like an old Spanish knight, adds some sententious and intelligent words from time to time.[281] We are certainly witty, and replies fly back and forth above our cocktails, but why is someone over there speaking about a corporal in Algeria from whom Olga has just received a card? Why did he write her a card? Why isn't he here, why has he never been here, why am I here? The Dôme resembles a boat sunken under the sea, glass figures laugh strangely on its windowpanes; it's too hot, too few people respond to our gaiety. Broken glass, a Sidecar spills over onto empty peanut shells, candied fruit passes from hand to hand and I savor two delicious Alexanders. The "club of unrespectable people" is causing a scandal; we stupefy an intelligent and unpleasant German man, whom Stépha knows, by astounding him with questions on "resistances." A young man smiles kindly at us over the letters that he is writing to us. Rather cheerful return home—but . . .

Friday, December 14

So, poor work, poor work, and sadness oh, so great! . . . Why them and not me? Jacques—where is the truth, with them or with me? I do not dare believe in you, I don't dare anymore—I don't feel well. Because of this same despair on the grand boulevards, this same confused feeling of solitude and doubt so feared in the past, I left the Bibliothèque Nationale, and I walked in the cold up to this stupid cinema where I cried with irritation. Dismal trip back, night without joy.

Saturday, December 15

Good work at the Bibliothèque Nationale. At night for a laugh I stop by M. du Fraisaix's.[282] Merleau-Ponty comes to get me to go to the Cinéma Latin; Mama is young, Papa lighthearted, and for some moments in the parlor we are animated and happy. Together we walk up as far as the rue Souf-flot. There I propose to take him to the Jockey; he doesn't feel like it but he comes to make me happy. I talk to him of Jacques. As always, I don't describe Jacques well, but I read him a letter, and I feel that he understands better. He tells me that he is not scandalized to see me there, but that he doesn't like it. Do I like it, myself? He does not understand this compromise that justifies wasting one's days in such places; he cites Barrès with wisdom . . . I recognize the words that I myself used to say to Jacques two years ago. Was I right? Or hadn't I met this absolute of despair and solitude of which he too is unaware? No, instead, I was right. To go there while keeping [*gardant*] oneself is not bad; but what an opium for those who get drawn in as one can hardly keep from doing! I really understand Riquet, for example, and others, but I myself have other things to do. How easily I am influenced! No, I do not regret the moments that I have spent there; but I must not attribute too much importance to them. I must not want this "frenzy" of which he was speaking; and I no longer have a reason to want it since I want "a beautiful life." One cannot keep oneself; it's an illusion: the best values are lost and the difficult joys are no longer attained when the mind allows itself to be absorbed by casual encounters. Some rare and grave joys, not this laughter that fades into a serious irritation.

I feel sorry for Jacques, sorry that he needed all of that. Yet I know that into these things he put a poetry coming from within that really counted; and that Merleau-Ponty is wrong for never knowing how to understand that. Besides, with you present, Jacques, I would not lose myself this way; everything would take on a depth and a truth . . .

We went out; on a beautiful, cold and starry night we traverse the boulevard Montparnasse, Raspail, Saint-Germain. We speak of love, of Josée, whose pitiful efforts to get closer to him he has noticed; I talk to him about it too, with great emotion, since I know that she is so definitively condemned. He is going to change science programs.[283] He also told me, "Your sister worries me less . . ." We speak of friendship too; he tells me that he doesn't think he can ever love. Besides, people always say that when they do not love. But now I understand his calm and his little need for affection: his tenderness for his mother is so complete that none other is required.[284] He speaks well of his friends, of Gandillac, of Galois, but when I tell him how a being can suddenly be so present for me to the point that tears fill my eyes and nothing else exists, he tells me, "That's excessive, too . . ." Near you, friend Maurice, if you were the one I had loved, I would have suffered at times precisely because of this word. I feel that he finds rather strange what I tell him about my way of loving people, that I stiffen internally at the idea of any affectionate word. This inner gift is so total and violent that in order not to experience it as a slavery putting me at the mercy of the one I love, I must link it to the certainty of having no need for the other to know about this gift. I could not be so passionately generous, grateful, and lost without this assurance that I am really voluntarily thus, and that it is not because of even the slightest appeal within me.

All in all it was a beautiful evening that put me back under your influence, dear conscience, and restored my taste for joys without dissipation, for discreet moments of sadness . . . for how much time? How perfect you are, Maurice, and how I would like for Jacques to love you and for you to love Jacques, above all. Will you understand how tied he is to profound exigencies beneath his affectation of freedom? Will he understand how very free you are beneath your measured exterior? You have this strength of understanding, truly understanding, others without identifying with them and losing yourself in them, of accepting without suffering or believing yourself to be obligated to choose what you accept. Also you are very, very good, Maurice, you know. "Dear smile," you would say, "that, also, is excessive . . ." But no, I think of you without "frenzy" as of one of the purer sides of myself, as of an element of my life without which I would no longer be me, as of someone who must not leave me (Isn't that right?) until the final departure, and who becomes dearer to me every day than I believed him to be the day before.

Sunday, December 16

I sleep late—I do not like the sad lassitude of these Sunday mornings. And I feel lost among all of these different selves that like different things and that I try to reconcile by looking at them all in the same way—even without being able to make Jacques understand the "beast" Simone-Merleau-Ponty, or Merleau-Ponty the beast Jacques-Simone or either of them Simone all alone. These are the three aspects of Simone that count.

The afternoon starts at Josée's seated on her table, and her thin cheerless face is outlined in shadowgraphs while her very charming laughter, although all of human distress runs through it, sometimes throws her slightly back, shaking her short boyish hair. Stépha told me about the night that they spent together when Josée spoke unendingly of Merleau-Ponty and, how, with a touching docility, she liked Fernand's painting as soon as she learned that Merleau-Ponty liked it. First, I tell her about Zaza and read her parts of Zaza's letter, and she understands her very well. You are among us, Zaza, you are within me, very dear Zaza. Then I speak to her of my night out yesterday, trying to discourage her without touching on it too much. She leans forward, sometimes thoughtfully, her voice when she says with so much sadness, "I used to love this boy, I really did," speaks to me about his sister whom she admires so.[285] I accompany her to the metro. "I am used to unhappiness," she tells me, "people are born like that." . . . Poor, poor little being, alone and lost in Paris, alone and lost in life. She loves nothing but beings who reject her, and is interested in nothing other than these sorrows of her heart . . .

At home Stépha comes to see me. We speak of Zaza, whom I teach her to know better, and of Montparnasse where together we no longer want to go. Why do these things that existed so strongly yesterday suddenly cease to live? But only that which always exists must be conserved . . .

My own Jacques, how much simpler everything would be if you were here . . . Now I am waiting for your letter and I am afraid (but I know well that your letters are better than the thought of them, and you even better than your letters).*

Evening at *Volpone* whose final acts are truly a perfect thing—good evening out—Poupée is charming in her green dress with a big silver flower. She dumped Jean to chat at length with Merleau-Ponty, and Mama is scolding her, but she is so simply happy that he is giving her something with his time and his friendship—and she hopes for so much. I myself hope for less since Saturday. The world is not created to obey my desires. And yet the world is so great, so very great . . .

Madame Lacoin spoke to Mama about Zaza . . . "I don't know Stépha, I know Mademoiselle Avdicovitch who was a governess to the children . . ."

---

* "My own Jacques" is written in English in Beauvoir's handwritten diary.

Bang! "You raise Simone as you like." Bang! "Fortunately Zaza loves me a lot ..." Yes, well that is shameful, dear Madame, to bank on that, and I myself detest you, and I am with Zaza against you even if Zaza is wrong to love you too much. You are much better than that, Zaza!

Saturday, December 17

"With a hotheadedness of the South" a certain imbecile called Herment holds forth in Laporte's class while I start to write to Zaza, then Bibliothèque Nationale where I work rather well. Stépha. Of all of my friendships, the one that I have for Stépha most resembles what people call love—this means that I demand no inner perfection from her, and that I have no need for her esteem or to be understood by her. And what's more I know that she passes up the best of me, but I like for her to be by my side. I like her gray hat, the little greeting of her hand, her smile. I like her cheerful and not sad. I sometimes feel like taking her hand to feel her living or like embracing her because I find her to be so exquisite, but all of this without any moral feeling, without torment, without remorse or worry—just as I love damp roses or violets against my mouth.

December 26—Wednesday

Morning at the Bibliothèque Nationale. I have lunch with Josée in blue, silent, and very sad. Poor Josée. Stépha is there and tells me little things and leaves early. I read some beautiful texts from Le banquet [Symposium or The Drinking Party], Phèdre [Phaedrus] and exchange a few words with Gandillac on "Le bien [The Supremacy of Good]" by Plato.[286] This library is becoming a dear habit.

Bus trip back with Josée. She forces herself to speak to me—but through the windowpane, dear friend, I saw your defenseless face while the bus continued down the street I was crossing. A letter invites us to Merleau-Ponty's tomorrow. I received one from him this morning that brought tears to my eyes with one simple line: "Tonight is Christmas, dear Simone. I am wishing you well." Did I ever love with so much novelty and surprise as during this year when every day is a tender marvel? Evening in Belleville: I read Tristan et Yseult [Tristan and Yseult], which moves them and is a truly admirable thing.[287] Return in the rain with pleasure in my heart, and pleasure is in my heart in the metro where my reflection smiles at itself and where Jacques speaks to me as if he were there; and pleasure is in my heart in the warm and deserted parlor where each inch of the rug is a distinct moment of our great friendship. I walk with my handkerchief on my mouth and through the wet veil over my eyes I see you again, ah! in your so simple, so certain truth—my Jacques to whom I belong since the beginning of time and forever. My Poupée [Dolly] is at the Richon's in her blue dress with her red lips scandalizing people and trying to forget her poor little heart.[288]

I am rereading, an exquisite thing, *Elpénor* [*Elpenor*], by Giraudoux.[289] Sleep well.

December 27—Thursday

Bibliothèque Nationale, some notes to Gandillac who disappears around eleven o'clock. I have the habitual sandwich at lunch with Stépha, and she talks about Fernand, the crazy woman whom she saw the night before, Poupette, and Merleau-Ponty, as she digs her nails of a cat, of a loving tigress, into my arm—same Stépha. At four o'clock I leave her to go meet Merleau-Ponty. I catch sight of his buddy, Galois, at the table behind me who is reading with a mean look.

Waiting for the bus—getting on the bus on rue Soufflot I am completely joyous because of having so often gotten on the bus with people I love, because of the pleasure of rediscovering the bakery celebrated in my memory where so many good memories live on, and for being at the Sorbonne not alone but united to hearts that like me and make these places moments in my true life. Lévi-Strauss is already there with some Jewish friends who leave when I arrive. Merleau-Ponty soon arrives. We discuss, mock, and examine Rodriguès's notebooks.[290] They throw in some memories from junior high and some of their professor's phrases. We imagine fanciful classes for our teaching internship. We invoke Proust, Aragon, Kipling concerning affective life, without forgetting Claudel, André Breton etc.[291] This is going to be fun. Lévi-Strauss feels at ease and no longer puts on airs as in the past when I so disliked him. We reminisce about the psychology group, already memories! And already it feels good to be a girl with the life and soul of a man, for them a man and yet a girl, in the rain on the rue Soufflot and the boulevard St. Michel. We make an appointment to go see the professor and the principal—and I accompany Ponty to Monnier's, then I leave him. He informs me that I will see Galois tonight. And indeed a novel about friendship is as beautiful as a novel about love, since such a great joy comes to me, for the one who was worthy of causing it. I go home. My dear Poupette is troubled, a bit irritated. We carefully put on dressy clothes. Our parents waylay us because "it is not suitable for young girls to go out alone," and then they go to the cinema. We take the metro Raspail-Passy that calls to mind so many childhood memories, and we reflect each other's pleasure at sitting across from a nice silhouette with a rose in her coat—a light rose on the beige coat with the shiny black fur collar, a darker rose on the light fur of the red coat. In climbing the stairs, we are quite filled with emotion.

First impression: a bit annoying. On one side the men: Wagner, Maurice, Galois, and also Madame Ponty, who is presiding—across from them, some faded dresses topped by faces lacking grace: Mesdemoiselles de Gandillac and Wagner. Monique Merleau-Ponty seems truly charming; Poupette is a clear and joyous note in the midst of them, but this gathering is not very gay . . . Poupette is hardly having fun. At the end of the evening the girls went into the room of Maurice who went to keep them company. Then Poupette joined the men (where I was, of course), and I liked her presence and that Gandillac said to us, "Mesdemoiselles de Beauvoir, is it on purpose that you matched your dresses to match the tricolor flag? What's more, it is very beautiful." Gandillac didn't arrive until 10 o'clock. Then it was very, very good. With Wagner, I spoke about Xavier du Moulin and about Jean Daniélou; with Galois about Laforgue, with everyone about everything. Oh! To feel that I am also a woman and more fully in bloom than any other woman present! To feel that I have graceful gestures and a lively girl's face; and yet to be in the midst of these men a man whom they treat with the same seriousness, the same straightforwardness and barely a precious nuance of deference, let's say rather of a charmed astonishment to find me so similar to them underneath my silk dress. Very fine hours in the parlor where we discuss Montherlant and Valéry.[292] Even finer is standing around the table where we are served a delicious cake whereas in the doorway we discuss Barrès, the opportunity for hasty meals and forced work etc. Gandillac tells me, "Mademoiselle de Beauvoir, you must be Nietzschean . . . since you like Spinoza and Barrès," but there is so much warmth in his voice![293] He is young and animated. He puts a wastepaper basket on his head and resembles the Père Ubu.[294] Then he imitates the Orthodox priest in Russian weddings. And when he cries out concerning a wedding luncheon, "Moreover the mood that I was in is nobody's business." He tells me that I will get first place on the *agrégation* exam. Oh! No.

I remember another moment: when standing at the door of the parlor between Merleau-Ponty and Galois we speak of the pleasure of speed and dance—very, very astute and nuanced remarks from Galois who makes quite an impression on my heart with this smile of an unexpected simplicity, this very Barresian reserve, this goodness, this . . . ah! everything. Pleasure to see them relaxed, less solemn than in the library, speaking of very simple things: of Galois's pullover sweater, of their school chums, of Colette whom they rather like. I feel that they are closer to me than I would have dared to believe possible, closer to Jacques and his friends, who are attached to very concrete problems. They are becoming human, and I love them infinitely, and I sense between them and me waves of fraternity that they also seem to feel. I would like to remember everything about this admirable evening—and especially the trip back; their jokes about the female students [*khâgneuses*] in the stairwell and about Simone Weil whom Galois almost killed in his youth.[295] The welcoming clear night and the concierge who did not want to open the door for us, and the evocation of the Bibliothèque Nationale Club . . . and Gandillac's essays on the movement of the earth from the left to the right bringing about the development of cities and rivers to the west, and his handkerchief passionately waved in the air from one metro platform to another, and his joy over being cheerful . . . And above all, ah! you Galois, you Daniel Galois standing across from me in the metro saying, "I don't like intellectual work," speaking to me of your love for music, and books that are waiting in your dresser . . . and when we are leaving each other at metro Raspail and I speak of *La danse devant l'arche* [The dance before the arch] and of this later time which, I dare say, will separate us, what reserved, grave, and transparent words you choose to respond![296]

So at night I could not sleep. Head as heavy as when I come back from the Jockey. I hear every hour chime and each repeats the same face for me. Oh, don't sleep yet . . . this night is not yet another: it is tonight, it is the present; the day will already be another day and all of this will have passed. Plans, murmured words of affection, dreams, almost without suffering.

December 28—Friday

I love you, Galois, I love you—all of you, fancy that, with tears that you will probably never know about, with your smile before my eyes, your smile already of a man, and yet so young and full of welcome. Not with that shyness that the encounter of Barbier or of Merleau-Ponty gave me, but with a full-fledged confidence, as if I were meeting a very old friend who had been made to order for my heart. I arrived at the Bibliothèque Nationale at nine o'clock despite my sleepless night. Gandillac greets me and already there is sadness in me to see only that, the day after such a beautiful day. Nobody comes through the glass door, neither that soft gray fur whose view alone is a furtive caress on my hand, an arm around my neck, a sweet smile against my heart—nor that expected silhouette for whom I prepared so many words all night long. One of Stépha's chums whom I take for a stranger sits down near me and takes me away to have lunch with him. He knows Miquel, but doesn't know how to talk to me about him; he is apparently very bright but of no interest. I glimpse Laporte and Baruzi . . . I glimpse Galois at his habitual place. My heart does not pound as usual, but right away I go shake his hand as if it had always been agreed that from this moment onward we would be friends forever. How very charming is just his hello! My darling Stépha has been here for half an hour and rebuffs her pal who took her place and sat next to me . . . She speaks to me with such tenderness that in front of everyone, I would like at every instant to embrace her tenderly and at length. She tells me about her night out yesterday. A Hungarian with a rather nice face at the table facing us, and with whom she was in Montparnasse, approaches us and says that I have a smile "full of intelligence and finesse." Stépha writes to Fernand and speaks of me. She says, "my Simone." She says "I must tell you what I think and write about you." I sense so much emotion in her glance loaded with tenderness, and in secret I feel the caress of her hand on mine. Lévinsky, Fernand, and de Chamonix think "of their Parisian friend." Oh, my life, my life against my mouth! Oh, sweetness of the world, I will kiss you on your sunny face. Snares of affection envelop me. I sense Galois and his offered sympathy behind me. Stépha is near me almost trembling with emotion like the girl near the man whom she loves. This Frenchman and this Hungarian find me charming, Fernand and Lévinsky don't forget me, and I love myself; I love myself for the unexpected blossoming of this year, for the smile that I know I have, that I caught sight of unexpectedly and with so much emotion on the windowpane of the metro, for my red dress, the ease of my gestures, and this always new gift of my defenseless heart. Of my defenseless heart that no longer risks anything, for Jacques exists in the depths of all the thoughts that live far from him, in the depths of all the tenderness that is not for him.

The day passes. Stépha would like for me to go out at five o'clock with her, but somebody is there behind her reading with his lip slightly protruding, which gives him a nasty look and provides the exquisite surprise of seeing him transform at his first glance into a welcome that asks for nothing. So with the hope of daring my desire, I say no to Stépha, but not without agreeing to spend the evening with her tomorrow. I read Boutroux and I wait for my chance. My chance came. I had kept close watch. At 5:45 I get up and I bring back my books while I observe someone who is not moving behind me. I dally so long getting a call number that suddenly he is next to me—some words on my work, on Vitrac's *Victor* that is playing tomorrow on the Champs-Elysées, on *La coquille et le clergyman* [*The Seashell and the Clergyman*], on the cinema.[297] He likes everything, he is precisely the one I would have loved. We arrive back at the metro where I get two tickets for first class, and since I bought them he accepts so simply. He thinks that Gandillac is too sure about his path and his success. He talks to me of Maurice and finds him delightful. I like them together, and tonight I like Galois a bit more, more because of all his novelty, more because he is the one I have been watching for so long, knowing that there is a source of joy for me there, the source has gushed forth. In the metro I let my station pass by. We haven't said anything yet. I know that tomorrow if we want we will no longer have any secrets from each other since he does not like false proprieties that keep one from speaking of oneself. And how dear you are, newcomer, so dear that these tears are sweet, sweet without the worry that a perfect encounter has always given me until now? Do I already sense that your friendship has been acquired? Do I know how to see you again tomorrow and often afterwards? And above all for this grace that you have in being you. Daniel Galois, whose name suits him so well that I believed I had already loved it as someone else's.

Went by Adrienne Monnier's where I catch sight of Jean Prévost. Went by Aunt Marie's who gives me news of Jacques.[298] He is in the South in a mindless job as staff secretary. We send him ties and sausages. He will come back in July. These words sink into me without resonating—into an indifference, dear Jacques, you, that has nothing to do with forgetfulness.

Daniel Galois, I will spend tonight with you. I am going to read Colette and George Moore about whom you spoke to me yesterday.[299] I expected a lot from you, and you gave me precisely that plus yourself—I want you for my friend. You are the one . . . the one I could have awaited and discovered suddenly with this great desire of receiving every joy from him—but it is good this way; I would have had less audacity to take you for myself if I had thought that my fate was at stake here. I sense "the multiplicity of compossibles" united with each step . . . but the real so full that it suffices, and the rest will remain nevertheless, right?[300] Isn't it you who will suspect nothing of what I have written here? Oh, my life, my life, o things, o men, men of my heart.

(Solitude at home on this night when everyone has left for Arras—peace, joy, love for the world, love for myself).

My darling Poupée, what are you doing tonight? How dismal Arras must be! You have your blue dress. You are pink, blond, pretty, light-hearted, and within, you are desolate with so much courage. You are thinking of your Mone. You know so well that this year your Mone is a silly big girl who soaks handkerchiefs while thinking of people whom she loves too much—and of these people there is only you and one other who are not a marvelous gift of the moment, but the very flesh and blood, and breath of my life.

December 29—Saturday

Galois had told me that he would be here and is not. I saw Gandillac and wished him a happy new year. He responded very kindly, and I like him a lot. Lunch with Stépha and her guardian, who is light-hearted and pleasant. I have little use for pleasant people. Stépha keeps me from working, annoys me—almost a rancor within me—I bluntly send her away. Upon leaving me she runs her hand so gently across my hair . . . I find the chair next to me really empty. Fortunately she is coming tonight. Tenderness like a man has for a woman, yes; some undefined sensuality is in my heart—but not my friend, my equal, and without the most honest and true part of myself for her. Galois I am thinking of you who are not here almost with the same urge to cry as when Jacques used to leave too soon after dinner.

Desire to return to a more reserved and secret life—not to let myself be even slightly harmed by my acts; to be alone and not given over to a universal tenderness. Desire to go back to the enclosed garden of Bérénice.[301]

Stépha did not come to dinner and I was almost happy about it—marvelous night of reading—the *Nouvelle revue française* where there is some Valéry, some Marcel Arland, some Fernandez and some very interesting critical notes, *Sous les yeux de l'esprit* [*Under the eyes of the spirit*] by Béhaine, *Les mémoires de ma vie morte* [*Memoirs of My Dead Life*] by G. Moore.[302] An exquisite letter from my Zaza keeps me company. She speaks so well to me of Merleau-Ponty. I went to bed late, all numb and drunk on books and friendship.

December 30—Sunday

Blue sky of a noon that could be a spring morning. I take the metro—and it so happens that I can no longer take the metro without thinking of Galois. I get in a first class car in his honor, and I read some short stories by Pushkin while watching pass by a golden Paris stretching out in the warmth of the season, full of the past and deliciously present. I walk through the streets of Passy with the same premonition of joy and the same emotional attention as on the first few days, dear Maurice, when I got to know you and when I would say, so it's here, here that he lives, and these streets, with their look of ancient provinces, speak only of peace, fraternity, and welcome ... [303] Lévy-Strauss is already standing under the clock; the white trench coat does not keep anyone waiting. And the three student teachers (one woman and two men) make a comic opera entrance into an antiquated parlor where an eager bearded man comes in, cordially shakes hands and holds forth interminably while distributing instructions. At the end I fall into a light sleep. Lévy-Strauss leaves us and I can say to Merleau-Ponty a bit of what swells in my heart, about so much love, so much astonished happiness, so much confidence, and so many expectations. He is so near to me, such a friend, so good, I thought I cared about him less since I had begun to care about another; on the contrary, he is even dearer to me.

Oh! Let's give each other our hands, my friends! With our arms linked to advance together and yet each of us alone on the still very new path of our life. Oh! Let us raise our heads in joy towards the singing trees, and what does the world matter to us? Isn't the world us? Oh, multiply each of our joys by the number of hearts that beat to the same rhythm as our own! Believe in us with the faith of all others, and walk so well supported by our common strengths that each of us cannot even know if he is supporting or supported. Oh, my friends, let's really look into each other's eyes—these eyes that send our reflection back to us, but mixed with those who are in turn merged in our eyes—united and yet each reflection distinct. Because we are young together, because one day we will die together, each of us crying over each of the others, because we will have the same life, and because we know nevertheless that life is only that.

I will see you again Thursday, Maurice. I will see the others too. After a hasty lunch, I went to Stépha's and to Josée's; not finding them did not disappoint me, my entire heart in all of its joy is enough for me; my heart and this sunny cold that caresses a bundles of roses and violets on the boulevard St. Michel, and the gaiety of people passing by in the animated calm of a day of summer vacation.

I went to Studio Diamant.[304] There I saw life in Deauville, that made me love you a bit more, my friends who will never go to Deauville. An idiotic Maurice Chevalier film and *Crise* [*Crisis*] where Brigitte Helm in a script resembling *Rue sans joie* [*The Joyless Street*] is an admirable actress.[305] If I were a poet I would like to write a poem about the purity, intelligence, and intensity in this woman's face. And I took the bus home down streets that radiated happiness under a pure and starry sky. I thought that I would like to write these things to you, Jacques. I thought that I love you, Jacques, that we will have a beautiful life—that I no longer fear anything about you and that you and I will both be happy. Nobody can hurt me except by his own suffering. Shout with happiness.

You are one of them Jacques, the one the most involved in my past, the closest one, but also, one of them, as simply and joyously as any other (one of them, but if you were here, my dear, would my bliss be of this opinion?)

Oh, I like these things enough for life to be enough—oh! I like these beings enough for it to be awful to die.*

Wrote a lot of letters with New Year greetings. Family letters, and also to Pontremoli, Riquet, Besnard, Miquel, and Mademoiselle Mercier.

December 31, Monday

At the beginning of the day I worked. Stopped by to see Stépha, who tells me that Hans Miller is in Paris. She wants to spend the evening with him, others, and me in Montparnasse. I say no. Stépha is so fickle. Yes, I love her as a man loves a woman, with moody and rancorous reactions; her disappointment about this "no" irritates me.

Montparnasse is so far away on this calm day that I spend alone, concentrating from noon to seven o'clock on the admirable novel by Meredith, *La carrière de Beauchamp* [*Beauchamp's Career*] that I had gone to get chez Monnier.[306] Nevil, Renée, and Cecilia keep me company in the warm parlor where I am seated sometimes on the ground in front of the slow-combustion stove, sometimes in the armchair . . . My friends are so heartwarming that I cannot stand to lose them even for an instant by losing myself in some noise and some faces of newcomers. I really don't care if people are "interesting" as she says; I will be able to find their thoughts by myself; only their manner of being, their underlying attitude, or their secret interests me. The only people who interest me are those whom I can love.

A pneumatic message from Pontremoli drops into my afternoon. How kind of him to have answered me so quickly, so very quickly. His note is nice. I think about him a little and with affection. And tonight . . .

---

* This last line about things and beings is highlighted in black in the right margin.

No, I will not take stock of anything. I know what I am demanding of the coming year, of the coming years. What good does it do to return to the past? I am calm; I do not wish for dissipation or adventures now that I have experienced what they are. Free to be at the Jungle tonight and knowing what sort of pleasure awaits me there, being there is no longer worth anything more than any other occupation. My desire to read in peace *Un jardin sur l'Oronte* [A garden overlooking the Orontes] makes it worth less.[307]

I love them—I love myself. It's enough. Nothing has any solemnity, it's useless, but everything is pure and real. My most authentic soul is vigilant on this last night—the soul that, three years ago in this same place, was thrilled about Garric and Péguy, and two years ago passionately desired Jacques's presence . . . my ardor is better managed and less full of illusion; but the same contained and sure ardor; love that is not desolate, less avid, and tested, but perhaps more wanted.

The old despair has died, really died. I do not regret it. Tonight I feel that I am making progress in comparison to all the other nights, and maybe this spiritual progress of which I have spoken so often is not a vain expression: I will no longer cede to the false illusion of giving to the instant the value of my entire life. Each instant has a flavor, and a truth as great as when I called it irreparable, but I know that I am above this instant, I feel strong.

My photo smiles at me from its frame, and I like it. I would like to keep my equilibrium, to be serene henceforth and forever, not to be misled by grand words, not to get sidetracked by poetry or sudden despair.

I just took a walk through the festive streets—peace within me, and joy. None of the charm of the nights or the enchantment of the boulevard Montparnasse is dead, but only if I want it, and it's so useless.

I think of you, Jacques—with so much calm and confidence in you and in me. If you were wrong, what difference does it make? I do not need *your* perfection to believe in the goodness of the world. And you may have been mistaken without being worth less than anyone else—dear torment—I ask for your forgiveness. I don't know how to think about you very well once you cease to be present to me. Here is my peace, my very beloved. Here is my faith in you that will not be disappointed. Here is my desire for a very elevated and very pure life, for us to merge into a single destiny. Here are my friends so that they can be yours, my strength to increase yours, my weaknesses so that you erase them, and my demands so that together we meet them. Here are my joys so that you take part in them, my gravity so that you do not separate me from it, my sadness so that you push it gently away. Here is my great and calm love. Don't ever let it be less great; don't ever let me be less proud of it.

The clock is about to strike midnight . . . happiness for you, dear Zaza, happiness and the love that you merit and the most complete blossoming of yourself. Beloved Poupette, for you, you know what my dream truly is. Maurice, for you . . . the same calm perfection . . . Gandillac, whatever you desire of which I am unaware. Galois, almost unknown and so dear, a blank check with all possible joys including the one that I could perhaps have given to you . . . Riquet, everything that you do not expect of life . . . Miquel, a little money so that you can really be yourself. Stépha, Pontremoli, Happy New Year. Happy New Year to all.

Jacques, for you, happiness; the clock is striking midnight—for you all desires and their accomplishment. The clock has struck midnight—I am here Jacques . . . Peace be with you, and the rapid end of your military service, and good things upon your return.

For me? The same thing as for Jacques. Here we are upon this midnight, so far from each other. Grant that at midnight of next year, very close to one another, love and happiness will be our guests.

Happy New Year, o very beloved—my companion, my brother. Happy New Year, my classmates, strength of my life. Happy New Year, dear friends, dear Poupette. But for you, Jacques-Charles, you, oh! with such sweet heartbreak—with such a wordless yearning.

1929

Tuesday, January 1

Nice quiet day. Work at home. And in the evening Stépha comes and tells me about her adventure with the Romanian and with the Hungarian . . . We read some old letters from Maurice, from Zaza, I speak of Jacques; she says, "No—he doesn't need to write. When it is like this, there is no need for anything . . . I have seen many loves, but this is better than all that I have seen." Poupette returns from Arras in full bloom; we eat chocolates and chat; at midnight she leaves us. Stépha stays very far into the night, the house is sleeping, our eyelids are heavy; a low lamp and our whispering are the only living oasis in this silent obscurity whose intimacy envelops us. A delightful note from Miquel.[308]

Wednesday, January 2

I finish preparing my talk on Plato. Pontremoli comes to spend the afternoon. We have a discussion—neither boredom nor pleasure. I am reading *Les liaisons dangereuses* [*Dangerous Liaisons*].[309] At night, Belleville where G. Monod is very kind. Mama comes back from Arras.

Thursday, January 3

It is the kind of beautiful day that draws its plenitude from normal conditions in my life. Presentation in Robin's class; he congratulates me; Gandillac also congratulates me, simply because I am a woman and intelligent.[310] Warm feelings offered by Hyppolyte and Ducassé etc., I feel more adopted by them. But it is cold and my eyes are tired—this keeps me from fully enjoying this lunch at Knam with Merleau-Ponty; I invite him. After Bréhier's class, I also invite Gandillac who accepts with a charming "that is so kind of you." For half an hour, first climbing up from the Sorbonne to Normale, then to room D where I sit on the table in front of the board that I covered that very morning with the lines "equal or unequal"—he speaks to me about his way of working and the competitive exam, and Plato, but all in such a lively and friendly way that in my heart I experience only a great exhilaration.[311]

Maheu does a very droll *explication de texte* in Brunschvicg's class, and Brunschvicg responds even more drolly.* There is only pleasure of the heart and mind on this day.

I go by Stépha's. I find Fernand there, and we go up to his little room. We speak of Lévinsky who is in love with me, of Stephan Zweig, Galsworthy, etc., then we go to Stépha's, help ourselves to the cookies on the plate, and have such a good talk for two hours with him seated on the chair and me on the bed, with such complete cordiality and such an applied sincerity that Stépha, upon her return at eight o'clock makes me jump hastily to my feet and come back to a world where the clocks mark the hours . . . I really like Fernand.

In the evening I read *Blèche*, and I start to translate Aristotle.[312]

Friday, January 4

Bibliothèque Nationale. I come here to see Galois. I could work at home. I see Galois! We just had lunch together, talking about Barrès, painting, music, etc. He is delightful. He is perfect. I am happy. He is my friend, he will come Saturday; I am happy, I am going to work well.

His passion for Victor Hugo, whom he read between the ages of eight and ten and who overwhelmed him; the taste for grandeur which he took away from it . . . his emotion in a train taking him from Saint-Germain to Paris when he learned of the death of Barrès by whom he knew only a

---

* "Maheu" is underlined in brown ink in the manuscript.

few titles. Stépha arrives late afternoon, and I come back with her and the Hungarian.

Good night out with Miquel at the Theater of Champs-Elysées where a puppet show is being performed.[313] I catch sight of Stépha and the Hungarian who is leaning over her very tenderly. I am embarrassed, and especially because Miquel sees it, but when I go over, without blushing or giving the least hint of a reticent smile as the big fellow moves away embarrassed, she welcomes me with a charming tenderness and joy. We finish the night at the Sélect, avenue des Champs-Elysées. Today is the first snow; shop windows full of toys sparkle all along the white sidewalks where a chilly gaiety is hovering. Very merry return trip in the subway with Stépha and her friend, whom I wholeheartedly dislike. Received a kind note from Henri Besnard.

Saturday, January 5

From nine to six o'clock at the Bibliothèque Nationale on Aristotle, with lunch as my only interruption, when I read *Le perroquet vert* [*The Green Parrot*]—then passed by the home of Marie-Louise who is very kind.[314] Very enjoyable evening at Poupette's school; dances, songs, and cordial gaiety. And Poupette is ravishing as a shepherdess, and as a young girl. There are very pretty young girls, some lively smiles, bodies in full bloom, and the delicate grace of my sister. These are all pleasant things—but poor Poupette! So much charm and intelligence so uselessly spent . . . She has had everything to conquer success, but from some bad grace of fate until now, she has been unable to find any joy in it for herself. People who see her think that she should reign in first place, but she doesn't care about first place. And will she ever attain what she does desire?

For myself during this day of studying, I marveled simply at this peace that was my host and that had its source in this fact alone: that you [*vous*] could have been here. Being seated and working while knowing that at the table behind me, invisible and sure, he is working—this is such a perfect feeling of security, such a delicious feeling of reassurance that it could be called plenitude and happiness. I do not desire so much to delve into you; I am not so curious about you; I desire rather that you give me this smile, so impossible when you are not smiling; that you reach out your hand like this with this slightly hesitant ease—that I see you, or at least that you are there, or even that I know that you could be there. It's nothing: it is everything. Repose of the body coming out of the bath, so relaxed that it is only learning how to know how tired it was before; this body full of energy, fresh and sensitive to every nuance in the air and that no longer fears any lassitude. Thus in this armchair is the smiling wisdom of my mind. Nothing in the world is changed by this encounter, no new relationship has been created, no question asked; but this entire fog of bitterness or boredom that might intervene between my soul and him has been dispersed. Until Saturday . . . I am not in a hurry. Since all was already too definitive for anything to be irreparable any longer. Match won before it was played.

Sunday, January 6

I've been working in the office, near the wood fire, besides a half-hour spent this morning in the Luxembourg museum—in front of some impressionist paintings since you [vous] like them. A book by Jean Guéhenno (since you [vous] hold him in esteem), and on Michelet (since you are interested in him).[315] Half an hour also tonight to go to Stépha's, but she isn't at home. And in a little while I am going to work on Hume.[316]

There is never any solitude anymore. My life is so perfect, so intellectually ardent and so sentimentally rich and strong that I could dream about nothing else . . . *

And yet . . .

We will do such good things, Jacques, you will see, desert of silence— Jacques, you will not be silent forever . . .

Monday, January 7

Interesting class by Laporte. At the Bibliothèque Nationale, the Hungarian offers to buy me some coffee. We spend almost an hour in the hall of the library. He tells me interesting things about Hungary and about Maurras, and culture and civilization. He opposes Stendhal to Barrès in a way that explains a lot of things to me: that an upper-class bourgeois like Barrès might despise refinements that he has transcended, yes; but for the bourgeois who remains beneath him, disdain would be a defeat—however . . . grandeur of the individual, scorn for the social. He answers with some sound things on the impossibility of ever grasping oneself outside of the relationship that we sustain with the non-self: Bergson and Kant.[317] We walk home together. He tells me some nice things about coquetry in regard to life—do indeed be

---

* This paragraph starting "There is never any solitude anymore" is highlighted in black ink in the right margin.

flirtatious with happiness, but definitely not with life. Game theory. I would very much like to play alone, but as soon as I love, it is no longer a game; dying is not a game. We go up to the Bibliothèque Ste. Geneviève where Stépha is supposed to come. She doesn't come.

Evening of work and reading. I am well-behaved. I have such well-behaved and dear friends.

Tuesday, January 8

Sorbonne, lunch at Knam where I am working on Kant. Visit to the principal of Janson.[318] Trip back with Lévy-Strauss who talks in a rather interesting way about surrealism in literature, painting, and cinema. Studied Kant at the Institut Catholique, then the evening at home, Hume.

Wednesday, January 9

Day spent on working on my *diplôme*, which is progressing once again. Joy in doing something. Recovered a bit with the Hungarian. Very nice card from Merleau-Ponty who wishes me a happy birthday. And I am going to work.

No emotion on turning 21 or remembering that I had been so afraid of it when I was 19 and 20.

This silence is becoming almost hostile, burdensome like a confidence that one would prefer to have never received, but with the possibility, at least, of no longer thinking about it.

Saturday, January 26

Three long beautiful weeks of intelligent, young, and rich life in a beautiful, cold, blue winter where thought is clear, tasks are simple, and friends smiling.

Good news from Zaza and from Madeleine Blomart. Stépha is making up her mind to marry Fernand; they are both very nice; we spent a good evening at Ursulines the other day where they were showing a very interesting abstract film, *Lonesome*, a mediocre American film, and *La jalousie du barbouillé* [The jealousy of le barbouillé] by Cavalcanti, not much of a success despite some strokes of inspiration.[319] Moreover, she is having a love affair with this famous Hungarian who often leaves the Bibliothèque Nationale with me in the evening, and walks me back up to Deux Magots or to the

Place Médicis where we have chocolate as we talk about Stendhal, literature, life, and Stépha, whom he loves with a love that I do not like, since he loves this appearance that she offers him without worrying about knowing her true soul and helping her to exist. He represents a world truly foreign to me, but that interests me since he is after all very intelligent.

Poupette is working. The other evening I went by to pick her up at her workshop and we came back together in the Parisian night.

I don't go out anymore: I am so sensible! It is because my existence is so full that the feeling of other possibilities leaves me indifferent. The Sorbonne, Normale, the Bibliothèque Nationale are now places populated by living thoughts, by books that each of us has read, by the singular visions and ideas of each of us. Hippolyte is nice, Ducassé, Mademoiselle Richard, with whom I have had lunch, is a hardworking type of female *agrégation* candidate. In Robin's class we laugh so heartily as we propose places for Plato's Cave. Gandillac, and our trips from the Sorbonne to the École Normale.

A good evening at home with Gandillac, Merleau-Ponty, Stépha, and Galois whom I have not seen since and of whom I think as a happiness desired too late—without sadness, dear smile. My friends, my friends, how much stronger I am to think that I exist for you.

Josée is sad. For her, I am Merleau-Ponty's friend as I am Stépha's friend for the Hungarian. So many extra joys are given to me that would be life itself for others ... One day I stayed at her place so late that the dinner hour passed unnoticed; then the director's birthday celebration blocked the doors, and I wanted to jump out the window to leave—poor sad Josée.

Above all, there was my teaching internship which is just drawing to a close, sad days in a bleak and sleepy light when the students were sinister boors, Rodriguès excruciatingly dull, and when my own words fell onto deaf ears; still others when Rodriguès was funny, Lévi-Strauss and Maurice just as childish as me on the stage, under the ironic and sympathetic gazes riveted on us.[320] Sometimes such beautiful sunlight on blond and brown hair, so much complicit gaiety and joyous chaos on the benches, so much friendly malice from the young and charming black-eyed Samuel, gracefully elegant and flippant. Some afternoons perfectly beautiful: the one when I spoke with so much love about ideas that I like and that became present to me as I spoke of them: ideas about joy, about the power that we have over emotional life and its reality. The afternoon when Maurice spoke, standing, with his back to the wall, so simple, so young and serious, and so much the young man that they all must have desired to be. One day he read a page from *Aimée*, and each inflection of his voice revealed his soul in its strong and gentle tenderness.[321] He was at that moment so much like himself and yet so new that all of this great affection gathered in my throat, and I saw him through grateful and infinitely sweet tears that welled up in my eyes.

It is a good thing to work together like this, to walk as we nibble chocolate truffles in the courtyard where the students are in an uproar, and to go back up the avenue Henri Martin or the rue de la Pompe as we prolong the discussions begun under the gaze of the students. Lévi-Strauss is nicer than I believed, with such tongue-in-cheek composure as he speaks about mad passions . . . and Mauguë is different than I believed, simple, sincere, always direct and deliciously ironic. Yesterday the three of us had the afternoon snack together at Coquelin. And first I like the way that both of them like each other and that Merleau-Ponty, through his own straightforwardness, almost as candid and serious as children alone know how to be, brings Mauguë to be straightforward too. He explained his system of "agonism:" to suppress all perception by dint of action, to create success by action alone since the world is only representation and we are masters of these representations. He is funny, charming by this conscious and yet not feigned offhandedness. "I believed that I was someone very strong, I still find that I am not bad, but not as good as I imagined . . . I am tired, I am too busy . . ." Charming Mauguë; not for speaking: we would have to live together, do things with him—such chosen brutality in such a refined guy . . . interesting. Sad to think that in two or three years he will be, he and so many others, outside of my very regrets.

Today too was delightful. It was very cold in the courtyard where Mauguë introduced us to M. Drouin, who is shy, scrupulous and nice. Then we went out; Merleau-Ponty and Lévy-Strauss were arguing about Spinoza; Mauguë was encouraging it with a disinterested respect. Then he left us, as did Lévy-Strauss. I had the afternoon snack with Merleau-Ponty in a tearoom that looked as though it had been made for us; and the entire past, dear Maurice, and the good work of this year, and our future resolve [*volonté*] was between us. We passed by some admirable flowers: orchids, roses, and carnations. We took the AX bus. Across from each other, we discussed nothing and everything . . . Together in sweet and monotonous life.

A simple and full life that does not forget—such that one could dream of nothing else.* And yet tonight I am waiting for nothing but you, Jacques. I expect everything from you Jacques. Contemplate this. That without

---

* The lines, "Together in sweet and monotonous life. A simple, full life that does not forget---- such that one could dream of nothing else," are highlighted in pencil in the right margin.

fatigue, without sadness, in a full burst of enthusiasm and adventures, rich in thoughts, in feelings, and truly without desire because these days are now so simple and free, that in this happy equilibrium and without even a sharper awakening of your image imposing itself upon me, nevertheless, I know that I expect everything from you. I could live like this, by my own strengths I would attain the extreme point of life, divided into my love for Spinoza, my tenderness for my friends, and the joy of being myself.[322]

I could live like this, and I know that you possess such a secret of life that just thinking of it overwhelms me like something too strong. Jacques, my Jacques, it is something altogether other than all of this that the least word from you will give back to me in its entirety six months from now. Jacques of mine. I am able not to think of you, but once I think about you as I do today . . . ah! I know well that I am only waiting for you.

I, who, without you, am now only one among many, I know that one truth of my life hidden from all and veiled to myself will be given back to me in an upheaval that will last forever. And if there is heartbreak, what does it matter to me? You are so near to me tonight, after this long month when I learned only from afar that you existed, like an appeal beyond the present, like an exigency beyond all of my pleasures, a truth beyond my games, and almost a distress, as in the accepted and happy banality, I feel so beneath the gravity that your existence gives the world for me.

Oh, I know well that my life, that nothing is real except you standing near this desk, so sure and so shy! Oh, how sudden and unexpected is a sorrow, a presence, a love. Nothing is stronger than me, than you. Nothing is better than me, than my love for you, the only thing as sacred and hard as my death.

I am no longer only a little girl who cries, who had forgotten that she loved you so and that you perhaps loved her. Write to me, or don't write to me, but come back. Or didn't it exist? Of course it did; this past exists with more strength than this very day that is ending.

Is it the precise memory of you or of a certain intensity in myself that crosses my mind while I thought I was settled into a temporary indifference until the grace of your return? But how could I separate one from the other? And how could I accept this exile far from you and me, without a cry of revolt, of suffering that bursts forth suddenly and goes beyond the sea to join you to me—oh! Life is so short, and one year so long. Could one forget you so quickly?

Oh, my so beloved! Like he who was accustomed to snow and cold and who lived as if he had never known any season other than winter; but a breath of spring forgotten one morning awakens the smell of hay and the moonlight in the night when crickets chirp, and when the peace of summer reigns. Oh! my beloved, could I have believed that I could know only winter? Could I have said after all, this too is a life? But you are there and nothing is but you. Time can no longer promise me anything desirable but its passage. Only to hear your voice, only to see you. Please, please, Jacques.

What does it matter to me if an other is this or that? I don't care what you will do, what I will do. And living or dying, how can it matter? I am asking for a year—less: a month for you to understand and to know that you are understood—and that's all. Ah! I don't care what you succeeded in doing . . . I love you well beyond your acts—well beyond everything, everything.

February 15, 1929—Friday

What a life, poor dear girl! . . . [323] Long days when I think of nothing but Plato or Kant in the terrible cold of this winter as I watch through the window of room G of the Bibliothèque Nationale for the brief flash of blue that reminds me that life could exist . . .

The other Thursday Gandillac gives me the pleasure of a slightly private conversation in the halls of Normale—then he escapes so quickly! . . .

Josée is dragging her despair around me. Sunday we spent the night at the Jockey, and I heard her suffering atrociously whereas my great friend Merleau-Ponty is so calm and passes so sensibly through my life from time to time. Poor Josée; yesterday we spent the afternoon together speaking nonstop about the one she loves as madly as one might love, and who is worth it; but will he ever give more than he gives me, which is so much already, Maurice, so dear, but . . . ah! Walk by Josée's door in the cold counting the chances of a condemnation of which I know and she is still unaware . . .

Yesterday after such an afternoon I went to see Stépha. Spent the evening together at d'Harcourt to kill this growing distress that is perhaps only boredom; Thursday our fun evening out at Jockey ended up at a Russian bar—she tells stories about the girls in Montparnasse, about her youth, she is charming . . . The Hungarian—Eveski—after some ridiculous scenes is finally leaving her alone.[324] He offers to buy me a cup of coffee every day. Often I refuse. Amusing dinner together last Monday with a sausage from his country.

Return of *Zaza* who helps me to make it through days of flu by telling me about her stay in Germany.*

---

* "Zaza" is underlined in black or brown ink in the manuscript.

Some books, a bit of cinema, a bit of chatting with Poupette. And the rest, lifeless, divided between the animal need for inactivity, sleep, and relaxation of all of the body, and the tension of the mind that is no longer even thinking. It's not sad; it's tiring.

A while ago I caught sight of Galois—same turmoil and suffering as if I loved him. At the same time, something painfully indifferent to everyone and everything. Powerlessness to suffer or to be happy . . . Perhaps spring-time is all I would need. But above all, ah! Jacques! I barely have the time to think of you, but I do nothing but wait for you. I need, really need you. And every time that I realize your existence, that I remember the past, I can no longer believe in this future of which I am sure and which would be too beautiful. You alone can do something for me. I am weary of doing without you.

Memory of dinner at Rodriguès's where Merleau-Ponty was so delightful and Levi-Strauss nice. All three of us taking a walk at midnight in the very beautiful night. Then Maurice and I so lighthearted, walking down to the last metro. Maurice so dear, my beautiful, serious and carefree youth. I love you well beyond the need that you have of my love! And tonight I urgently need the only one, the only one who looks at me and lets nothing of me escape, and asks everything of me, and gives everything to me. Poor me. How long five months are.

March 9

Fourteen minus ten is still obstinately four; one can shake up the numbers like the glass pieces in a kaleidoscope, but without obtaining the wonder of any change.

And how would you sense from so far away that here it is springtime and the cumbersome resurrection of dreams buried in the cold of winter.[325]

March 13

Of what shall I speak? The afternoon snack at Brunschvicg's? The delightful evening where we "did Montmartre," Maurice and his sister, Gandillac, Zaza and I? The blue days between Gandillac and Merleau-Ponty? The always friendly Bibliothèque Nationale, the marvelous evening of *Prince Igor* with *Zaza*?[326] And that charming evening when with *Zaza* we went to get Poupette in Montmartre? The intoxicating evening with Poupette and

Germaine Dubois at the Jungle when we didn't have any money?*[327] Or rather the gloomy nights when Poupette and I drag ourselves through the gray streets of Montmartre where the houses—seedy-looking or not!—light up, and in cafés where primitive music dizzies us? Crazy fatigue and disgust for certain evenings . . .

Or this crazy day at the Louvre, the day when the first breath of spring has passed and when for four hours I wandered from Assyria to Egypt and from Egypt to Greece, when the Venus de Milo gave me a pure joy that I had not had for quite some time.

But today is all there is. Oh, chase away those bad angels, my pink and blond Stépha in pink and blond lace, in her bed and a bit weary yesterday. Stépha, who in two weeks will be Fernand's wife . . . And you my dear Josée stretched out a while ago in your room, so charming on Saturday when we were together at the Avenue to see *Le malade imaginaire* [*The Imaginary Invalid*], frail and upright in that black dress with the pleated white collar that drolly frames your delicate face, with a bizarre prettiness.[328] And you, Zaza in blue satin, happy and loving Zaza, sent back to me transformed by Berlin, and you, beloved Madeleine, near whom I spent a long afternoon, you stretched out on the cushions near the coffee table brought back from Morocco, happy, settled down, and yet lively, clairvoyant in your perfect love, and beaming. I love you all; and you especially, my darling blond girl. Take pity on me tonight, don't leave me like this, all alone with this absence.

Is it the coming spring? Or these days of illness, haunted by a single face in the emptiness of the vainly falling night? I don't know what it is, for one week I have been hungry and thirsty, and the one who can give me something to eat and drink is not here.

I am too tired tonight . . . I can do no more. These reread pages of *Le grand Meaulnes*, these memories aroused with Madeleine, these paintings by Foujita at the contemporary art gallery made me descend further and further into the faraway lands, where every beauty is an overwhelming lack because the key is missing.[329] I'm tired; I can no longer lose myself away from this country, in a world without ambush but foreign. Yet I cannot go into my country alone. Every day was the eve of the one when I was going to see you again, Jacques. I know tonight that tomorrow I will not see you; and it seems to me that I am going to die if you do not say to me right away, "Hello, Simone."

---

* "Zaza" is underlined in black ink throughout this paragraph of the handwritten manuscript.

I cannot write to you. I would only be able to repeat, I beseech you, write to me, beloved, write to me.[330] Beloved about whom I no longer know anything if not his past gestures and words whose memory causes so many tears to flow that my eyes seem to dissolve in memory. Beloved about whom I know nothing anymore if not that you will come back and that I will be able to resign from everything, from everything . . . I so need you, my big boy, my big boy, bitter about my expectation like this landscape within me that I often study vainly during the night. Oh, Limousin nights desired with a thirst that is an anxiety. Oh! Jacques's smile evoked with a fever mounting from my throat to my nostrils, to my buzzing ears, to my forehead where you are a haunting apparition.

I would like to write to you, I would like a letter, or I would like to sleep. Oh! These last ten months have passed quickly on the whole, but I feel that each day will now drag by, weighing heavily, too heavily, even alone. Who are you, what do you think, what do you want? I no longer know anything but this obsessive fear of some past gesture, some incredibly sweet phrase that remains before my very eyes during hours of madness.

I miss you. I really miss you.

Thursday, March 14

Day at Normale and at the Sorbonne interrupted by a lunch on rue St. Jacques. I think of Madeleine, of the sweetness of her home, whereas we are industrious, lonely, and weary girls. Mademoiselle Richard is very kind, so sweet, resigned, and courageous with a touch of revolt that is not bitterness. She speaks to me of Nançay, Meaulnes's country, where she was a teacher, of the classroom that one sweeps out in the evening, of bicycle races in the deep and savage country . . . Maurice comes to get me at Brunschwicg's. We catch sight of Lévy-Strauss and Galois. We have the afternoon snack together in a bakery on boulevard Saint-Germain. Thank you, I so needed you [vous], oh so much! Thank you for your gentleness that keeps me somewhat company tonight . . . he tells me that I have changed, that I am less accessible, more brusque—you [vous] mustn't be mad at me for it; I no longer believe in finding truth somewhere in a meditation or a discussion; I wish only to be happy, I so wish this. I love you. It warms my heart to think of you. I am completely weak before you and sincere if only you are listening to me. Do you understand how tired I am these nights?

I have a novel, L'envoûté [The Moon and Sixpence] by Somerset Maugham.[331] I feel so much like sobbing, really sobbing, oh! Nothing but fatigue, without feeling anything irreparable. My God, Jacques, my God, Jacques ... aren't you going to come in, to chase away this sadness that cannot continue. Oh! You are so lost, so lost, and I so love you, my poor departed and desired brother.

Friday, March 15

Bibliothèque Nationale, great fatigue, I just miss falling asleep ten times. I have some coffee and lunch with Bandi. He tells me about Stépha; he reveals to me a disloyal Stépha whose slightly petty ruses of an amorous cat would hurt me if I wasn't already so indifferent to her; blond and easily tender, a bit thoughtless, and despite all of her wrongs, always charming, right? At the École Normale a young botanist seems to be straight from a poem by Jammes.[332] He is sweet, he loves his mother; he is teaching his girlfriend the names of the flowers as he walks in the country.

Dinner at Nadine Landowski's. Room where I would like to live; an interior of a rare and very simple perfection. The mother is beautiful, young in her black dress with the white pearl collar. Saw her father's works, somewhat classical, somewhat "of a successful artist," but interesting.[333]

Saturday, March 16

Bibliothèque Nationale. Lassitude. Spoke a bit with Bandi. I vaguely dream of vague things, I don't work. I wait for Zaza and I think of Jacques. I feel like crying; or walking aimlessly in the streets; desire for a new affection, an adventure, a discovery, anything that would be other while waiting for the return of the past.*

Monday, March 25

So? *Sunday, March 17*, a blue and empty Sunday; so blue and empty; with a dazzling morning at Luxembourg Gardens, my hesitant gait into Paris laughing in the spring, my sleepiness in the cinema where *Le chanteur de jazz* [*The Jazz Singer*], a sound film was playing, the trip back through the Tuileries, suddenly heart-rending because of the man who came to sit beside me similar to all the other men who have sat beside me on similar nights when the rustling of the newspaper that he is reading dies down

---

* This paragraph is highlighted with brown pencil or ink in the handwritten manuscript.

like a moan silenced by the desert—horrible sadness.[334] Some little boys are racing. The people of Paris are strolling slowly into the evening with their families. Empty heart and listless legs, feeling like crying on someone's shoulder . . . I climb up to Josée's. Wonderful solitude of this room opening onto the roofs and the so blue and gentle sky, the sky of an uncertain spring at this hour that neither lives nor sleeps; I wait while reading a *Vie de Goya* [Life of Goya] by Eugenio d'Ors.[335] A boring girl is there and we don't have a discussion. Night of reading at home.

Monday, March 18: Laporte's class; Hume's skepticism rather interesting; afternoon at the Sorbonne after a wonderful lunch on the terrace of the Luxembourg; Gandillac runs by under the balustrade; unknown life; young man is reading not far from me; another one is reading his newspaper; I eat my sandwiches as I read *Le crime des justes* [*The Crime of the Just*]—sun, renewal of life; the world is good; my life is dazzling.[336] Already on climbing back up towards Ste. Geneviève before Lalande's class, the road begins to smell of hot tar. I work at the Sorbonne until eight o'clock.[337]

Tuesday, March 19: École Normale on a cold morning. An hour to spare since class isn't held until 10 o'clock. Enough time to bite into the sweetness of life. A tramway leads me to Champs de Mars. It is good to be too hot, to be sitting down while reading *Hécate* by P. J. Jouve and eating some rolls.[338]

Laporte keeps me waiting half an hour in a red parlor on avenue Bosquet on the seventh floor where the light dazzles the eyes.[339] Waiting is enjoyable, then his office, and very kind: great qualities, etc., but essay, very unpleasant: style is obscure and falsely profound . . . for what is said philosophically. Savage attack on Brunschvicg, Blondel, Le Roy ("I'm not saying anything bad about anyone"). Spinoza: a monster. The philosophers of Antiquity: simpletons, and Hamelin! poor imbecile . . . house of cards. Hume, however . . . yes, but: the practical problem. Oh! The practical does not pose any problems! Philosophy? A pleasure . . . Other pleasures might be preferred to it (I should think so . . .).—A convention?—Ah, no, Mademoiselle, this time you are exaggerating . . . Idealism, spiritual activity, I myself do not understand them . . . I do know that skepticism is no longer in fashion. Of course, go look for a doctrine more optimistic than mine. Philosophical fads . . . (funny guy), but delighted . . . you will succeed at the *agrégation* . . . [340]

Almost five o'clock! I speed to Zaza's; we go to rue d'Athènes where *L'effort* is sponsoring a film festival.[341] We see *Autour de L'argent* [About *Money*] and *L'invitation au voyage* [Invitation to a voyage] by Germaine Dulac.[342] Stupid. Some young men of modest means who believe that it is a success, but not too much of one, argue about Pure and Sound Cinema. I say good-bye to *Zaza* who is leaving for Bayonne.*[343] I go home.† I feel ill because I so wish to hear crickets chirping in the night, cows kicking the stable door, and this green area that wants *me* and that calls to me with a human voice.‡

Wednesday, March 20: I go by Stépha's. We agree to have lunch together on chairs in the Luxembourg Gardens with bananas and rays of sunlight. The window is open all afternoon against my cheek at the calm and bright Sorbonne library. Lévy-Strauss is working next to me. I am working admirably well; I am not thinking about anything. Life is good . . . I go up to Stépha's to correct some articles, and since the night is too beautiful to stay home, since I have a light-colored coat and a red hat that go well together and suit me very well, I spend the evening at the Studio des Champs-Elysées.[344] *Une vie secrète* [A secret life] by Lenormand is being performed, of little interest, but not boring.[345] And almost an hour of waiting in the admirable night, near the Seine.

Thursday, March 21—École Normale and Sorbonne until exhaustion. *Maheu* beside me is drawing Eugenes and beginning a hymn to springtime for which he writes only the dedication: "To my grandmother."§[346] I really like him; he is a cool comedian, an "I don't give a darn" sort, young, amoral and, it seems to me, marvelously independent, probably because of his cold-heartedness; he never says "at home" but "at my wife's home," he amuses me. You were really nice, Maurice, to come get me at that class when I was so tired. We have tea; you face me and I like you so much. I go home very weary, I fall asleep on the couch; my head is on fire. Long nap, until morning.

Friday, March 22: Day of fatigue at the Bibliothèque Nationale. I have coffee at Place de la Bourse with Bandi who is interesting; he tells me about his novels, talks about Cocteau whom he understands well. In the evening I work very well here.

Saturday, March 23: Bibliothèque Nationale. Lunch in the gardens of the Palais Royal. At six o'clock I exit into a cool, mild, and secret evening; I follow the passionately vibrant Boulevards where the displays and the cinemas grab my eager attention at every step. Pleasure of the boulevard Malesherbes, peace of such an hour, peace of my twenty-year-old body walking on its

---

* "Zaza" is underlined in pencil. The rest is in blue ink.

† In the handwritten manuscript the March 19 entry is highlighted in pencil from the name "Laporte" through the statement "I go home."

‡ The French word for "me" is underlined in the handwritten manuscript.

§ "Maheu" is underlined in brown ink in the manuscript.

healthy legs, peace of my silent heart. On the rue de Tocqueville Stépha comes to meet me, blond and white and pink in her fur collar and beige felt hat that suits her so well. She trots out her little stories, and I, mine. And on the rue de Clichy we buy a delicious pâté, our strolling dinner on the deserted streets of the Butte, deserted with the shining moon and the presence of the night. Beside the Moulin Rouge, some delicious still lemonade quenches our thirst; women and men are in the café. We watch for Poupette in front of her workshop, Poupette and Gégé. We walk down the streets together as we sing in unison. Gégé is singing "Pétronille, the poor girl . . ."[347] Dance steps, laughter—her delicious laughter—life, frivolity. Stépha hugs my arm to hers, Poupette and her friend sing; the Seine is smooth and deep, and the bluish black dots against the midnight blue sky make a more perfect classical etching tonight than ever seen until now.[348] How beautiful is the world, darling girls.

We drop Stépha off at her place—her foot hurt from having walked so much.* We go up to the Jockey. We talk about Jacques whom Gégé really wants to marry; I feel profoundly wounded in front of the brightly lit house where somebody, but not him, is going in. And jazz, women, and dance. Impure words, alcohol, bodies touching: how can I not be shocked, how can I accept here what I would not accept elsewhere, and joke with these men, sure of being pretty tonight? How can I like these things with this passion that comes from so far away and that holds me so firmly in its grasp? I dance and dance . . . I rediscover familiar faces; I rediscover that man whom I loved for one whole evening and who fondly reminds me of the evening "where we had so much fun together in that little corner." Yesterday. No, ten months ago already . . . then, here is what I come here to seek, "the little adventure of the day:" first, a young Swiss man from the Bibliothèque Nationale who dances with me and thanks me so much, surely a bit in love with me; and because it's here, this person of no interest becomes like a brother to me . . .

Then, a man who, smiling, asks me "if I am doing a study of manners." He is a doctor. He speaks to me of Poupette who has just left and who is my sister because of her dark blue eyes with the large pupils and her angelic look with her naively red lips. He keeps an eye on Gégé who is having a great time. He dances with me, interrogates me about them, about me, just a bit surprised

---

* From the beginning of the sentence starting, "We drop Stépha off at her place" through the end of the March 23 entry is highlighted in pencil in the manuscript.

to see us there, a bit ironic and without looking it, full of solicitude. At one o'clock he brings us back in a taxi. Gégé is tipsy and enumerates the dates that she has made ... He becomes aware of my slight embarrassment at coming back alone with him and observes me silently from the corner of his eye. Has he guessed that for two days, perhaps more, he will live ridiculously in my heart and I will feel on me his gaze that neither blames nor approves, and his solicitude, gratuitous since he will never see us again?

And what is it that I go seeking in these places of troubled charm if not the regret for the unknown man encountered and for having passed by without altering his unknown beauty? Only for you to be a nameless man who studied my nameless face with his curiosity and human cordiality. For me to remember the moment, the best of you, without knowing if you are above or beneath him, to be emotionally moved and happy to be a human being in the midst of humans.[349]

Sunday, March 24: Woke up to regrets and remorse, woke up to a weighty future, dear pain. Luxembourg Gardens in the sun. I go to get Stépha and find deliciously kind Fernand. It's an afternoon when I walk slowly through streets in a working-class neighborhood, where I enter into a popular cinema. *L'argent* [*Money*] doesn't interest me much although Brigitte Helm is beautiful, but this very young couple in front of me, they were teasing and embracing each other and smiling at one another, and without any vulgarity because she is slightly pretty, and he has a nice face ... but the life of all such men on their best Sunday behavior ... but life ... I feel like I have the soul of a sixteen-year old shopgirl at six o'clock at night.[350] I go to get Josée, and we take a walk in the evening. She speaks to me of Catholicism, of her joyless impotence to get rid of its precepts. She is as powerless to disobey as to believe and love ... "poorly weaned from Christianity." She says, yes, but what can she do about it? Be stronger. I hate this tyrannical religion. I hate ...

And today? Bibliothèque Nationale. I speak for two hours with Mademoiselle Schuller. She speaks to me of Françoise Cazamian who just got married. She doesn't know me, but I myself often think with great friendship of this young brunette with the serene and smiling face, sure of herself and of her happiness; with great friendship for this living success that seems to me to be sister to mine, for whom I feel incapable of ever feeling envy and about whom I care from afar. I daydream over my books; I go home early, now I am writing. I thought about some things today—how I feel now, and in comparison to myself last year, a woman. How "life" is more diverse for me than in the past—I daresay less pure, less passionately exclusive, but capable of everything, avid for every living thing. How well I understand attitudes, passions, desires, stalemates; how well I understand everything, everything that one could ever feel on earth! ... and how curious I feel, avid, avid to burn more ardently than any other, regardless of the flame.

My God! How many contradictory beings there are within me, or am I inventing them? The Jockey the other night, and the walks with Merleau-Ponty, is this the same girl? (I love you [*vous*] so much I could cry, do you know?). So much perversity is possible, the worst instincts, sensuality, coquetry, and vanity are lodged within me like curious little beasts that I would have fun parading before my eyes from time to time. And at other moments there is such a real disgust, and even the ignorance that such sentiments might exist.*

There is only one being who might give me back the authentic conscious-ness of myself, only one being who might define me and be the resistance for me to lean on, receiving my imprint, not this emptiness that lets me pass by without identifying traits that I seek almost with anxiety. I have hungered and thirsted for you, Jacques, these past few days, when I say words, there is no response, but sometimes suddenly a few words that you have really said emerge from the past with exactly your voice. Everything is swept away by these words that grow and grow until I can no longer see a thing.

Tuesday, March 26

Worked at home all day; philosophy of the sciences until five o'clock. I stop by Monnier's and read the most recent issues of *Commerce*: article by Gide on Montaigne, by Valéry on Vinci where I rediscover with pleasure some of the ideas that I tried to explain to Laporte the other day: on philosophy as an independent discipline, as rigorous and arbitrary as mathematics, subservi-ent to no object but to a logic and an inner aesthetic; thus today appears the work of a Spinoza. Then went by Stépha's. We walked about together.

In the evening I read *Moi, Juif* [My Jewish self] by René Schwob, of mediocre interest, and *Manhattan Transfer* by John dos Passos, which lacks subtlety and this hint of madness that is required to truly captivate me; and besides, the technique is too noticeable.†[351]

---

* This last paragraph is highlighted in the margin from "walks" to "might exist."

† This paragraph commenting on the works of René Schwob and Juan dos Passos is highlighted in pencil.

Wednesday, March 27

Bibliothèque Nationale, lunch in the gardens of the Palais-Royal, return home at four o'clock. Merleau-Ponty comes and we take a walk in Luxembourg Gardens where the green buds are starting to appear on the trees. The light is a bit strange and sad. We talk about our teaching internship, about Brunschvicg etc. Back at home we have the afternoon snack with Poupette.[352] He finds that she has a lot of talent. We are very lighthearted. We experience two hours so delightful that we forget the clock, and I no longer have time for dinner before going to Belleville. Discussion on Foch's burial, very animated, as intelligent as in any bourgeois parlor and younger and more vibrant. Stépha comes to get me; really very beautiful at the moment. We devour some chocolate, some cakes, and a plate of assorted cold roast meats at Félix's while correcting the articles in her Ukranian journal and chatting. Walked home on a beautiful night, spoke of her marriage. She is charming.

Thursday, March 28

Bibliothèque Nationale. Glorious weather. Very good work. We take Papa to the train station. We walk back with Mama very kind. Night of pleasures, sunk into the armchair in the office reading the *Extraits d'un journal* [Excerpts from a diary] by Charles Du Bos.[353] Intense exaltation: he speaks of Baruzi, G. Marcel, Fernandez ... the milieu of intelligent people who entice me, intellectual people. The purpose for writing, glorification of the mind ... I am again taken with the poignant desire to start living once again with all of my intelligence instead of using it to accumulate knowledge. Desire for books, paintings, music, and conversations ... How captivating is the diary form!

I have often thought that it would be very interesting to start keeping a diary to give a more real existence to my days, not to lose the precious encounters of ideas or sensations, but in everything I let myself be too guided by my pleasure alone. Above all and despite such moments when intellectual life exhilarates me, when I make plans for the future, etc., all of this really doesn't interest me much, and this face awakened in the depths of my heart has overwhelmed me with anxiety and expectation, chasing away what is only more or less a verbal game of the brain alone.

Friday, March 29

Desire renewed today in the peace of the Bibliothèque Nationale to write, to meet interesting people, to see things. Desire to conserve such riches in notes carefully taken every day and destined to be read, not to evoke the memory but to take its place. Desire to live more, to like my life, to be interested in me again. Many traits in these pages by Charles Du Bos reminded me of myself: this worthlessness of the periods when he is not thinking his life with each step, this death of sensation on days inflated with too many occupations, this impression of walking alongside a duration that doesn't affect you, and leaves you as inert as the tree branch not yet detached from the shore.[354]

I must resign myself to being an intellectual, but at the least I must know how to make use of this characteristic. I myself use writing to try to preserve the moments of perfect grace when the entire being is too overcome by life to not cry. Aside from such ardent and unpredictable waves of passion, nothing means anything to me, but even in savoring them, the idea of death embraces me. And that is the entire book that I had started to write. But I know nevertheless that writing is always a pale transcription of what was without it and, far beyond it. On the contrary one must ask of writing, as one feels so well that Charles Du Bos does, to put something into the instants that grace does not visit, to give to my face, to my occupations this distance without which I cannot like them. I think well only when I write—this year I let so much go by me without thinking anything, yet I feel as many ideas as before and at the moment if I had the time . . . *

Don't have regrets, I am not yet really old, it was understood that this year would be sacrificed. Four more months! But then, then . . . let me examine this truly neglected dear self of mine that I feel has so changed while I was not taking care of it, let me resume my attempts at a book—and start to elaborate on my work, my life, with care, with love.†

(Spiritual stimulants are a necessity for me: Proust's books, Rivière-Fournier correspondence, Gide's critique.) I will be alone, it is another thing altogether that Jacques will bring me, but this liking for a discipline, this "head for a career" as Georgette Lévy used to say, this delight that I

---

* The following lines are all highlighted in the margin of the text, "And that is the entire book that I had started to write. But I know in the meantime that writing is always a pale transcription of what was without it, far beyond it. On the contrary one must ask it, as one feels so well that Charles Du Bos does, to put something into such instances that grace does not visit."

† All of the paragraph starting "Don't have regrets" is highlighted.

feel when I take myself seriously, it will be (oh! without knowing it) rather *against* than *for.**

And then we will see . . .

Saturday, March 30

Morning of philosophy at home. In the afternoon I go to Luxembourg Gardens where Poupette meets me. We go to the Gare de l'Est to take the train to Nogent-sur-Marne. Walk on the riverbanks up to St. Maur, small boats, open-air dance halls where dances are beginning.

Sweetness of the night falling on the still leafless trees . . . At night we go, Mama, Poupette, and I to the Agriculteurs: *Une vie sans joie* [A life without joy] with C. Hessling, a great tramway race at the end.[355]

Fanchette is a stupid film.[356]

Sunday, March 31, Easter day

Warm and benevolent morning. I go to the musée Carnavalet to see the exhibition on eighteenth-century theater. There are some Watteaus including a very beautiful one, *La comédie italienne*, replica of the Louvre's *Gilles*. These are decidedly very reminiscent of *Grand Meaulnes*: two Fragonards, lively, less beautiful than the ones in the Louvre, paintings by Lancret, Pater—mediocre. Then I went to the Musée du jeu de Paume: canvasses by some foreign painters, I like almost nothing. Yet there is the Japanese painting and especially the admirable and monotone Foujita: *L'amitié*, a portrait of an old Russian peasant woman, a painting by Gluckmann that I don't like overall, but that keeps me spellbound with its brown background in relief. There are some Burne-Jones too perfectly dreamed to offer the least resistance, and thus the least reality.

But the most mediocre of these paintings does me good. I think back to what Charles Du Bos says in his journal about his powerlessness to feel and the awakening of sensations in him by paintings alone; thus I have a physical need for paintings. The themes of my inner life at the moment are no longer parts of phrases, but faces, colors, a piece of landscape: Watteau's *Gilles* in the uncertain evening light that brings to a close a very beautiful and empty day, immobile, doing nothing because there is nothing to do—nothing to do . . . on the contrary, Fragonard's portrait of a woman insolent with life, bold

---

* The French equivalents of "against" and "for" are underlined in the manuscript.

and impertinent in her big collar. Vinci's *Sainte Anne* [*The Virgin and Child with St. Anne*] and *La vierge* [Madonna]. Picasso's *La voyageuse* [The female traveler], about whom one knows nothing.

This afternoon I read *Thérèse Desqueyroux* for the second time; I liked Mauriac for having so liked this woman with a passion for life, happy about the lighter held out to her by a stranger and about the simple human crowd in which even a haphazard walk makes her feel carried away by life. At chez Picard, standing up, I read Julien Green's *Léviathan* [*The Dark Journey*], which gripped me by the throat: he seemed to me a *very* great novelist. This time the human drama does not envelop only a single destiny but engages several tragic figures, all monstrous and yet so close . . . again this hint of the terror-stricken crisis, the half delirious impulsiveness that serves too conveniently to explain gestures for which Mauriac would show, on the contrary, the irremediable necessity in the individual's heart; again this exaggeration of a passion, curiosity here, that absorbs the entire individual to such a point that he is only a carefully described appearance moved by a motive without complexity. But a gift for *narrative* that nobody possesses today: the end is poignant and admirable, and the character of Madame Grosgeorges is the most beautiful in the whole book. A work that would be worth a lengthy study.

Then I walked along the quays telling myself stories. I feel myself reviving on such a day when the worries about exams and the people who bind me to them are banished. I would like to know where I am in all this, it seems to me that I have infinitely lost, and the worst of it is that I cannot bring myself to suffer over it. First I developed a passion for psychological analysis; I wanted to sort out the tiniest nuances in my feelings. Then I developed a passion for my spiritual life: last year at this time, I was cultivating strange ecstasies. And now after such an ardent and devouring life, I am inert, carried along by the occupations and idle fancies of the moment. Nothing in me is committed to anything; I care for neither idea, nor affection because of this narrow, cruel, and exhilarating connection that attached me to so many things for so long. I am interested in everything with *moderation*. Oh! I am so reasonable that I am not even anxious about my non-existence.* I daresay the supposed temporariness of this state keeps me from suffering from it: at any rate this year was sacrificed. Inner life does not become fragmented, and

---

* From the beginning of this paragraph, "First I developed a passion for psychological analysis," through "about my non-existence" is highlighted in the text.

in suppressing what gives it its inexpressible intensity, it's crazy to believe that such strength will be transferred over to untouched domains.

Everything weakens simultaneously—Jacques brings me closer to everything from which he seems to be further separating me, for in me emptiness is not pain but rather indifference; thus every plentitude is an appeal. How I love myself when I love you, Jacques! How demanding I am of myself in order to be able to be demanding of you! How strongly the world and myself exist then, and how heartily does this existence request a meaning and rules! When I think of you as happiness and tranquility, it's nothing. When on nights of fatigue I murmur "darling Jacques" or "beloved," such words are directed to my lassitude and not to you. What is directed to you is this burning anxiety, this sudden importance of my heart, the echo of a silence that I solemnly relive. How scared I am of suffering again, yet how I desire it.

That was already three years ago now, and first I knew my sorrow; then my love and its strength, and now the place of such love in me and its role at the heart of my life, the only refuge against my egotism, my coldness, my distressing rapidity at squeezing the lemons dry. The only force stronger than me, that makes me know that I exist. I don't want a word of sweetness, or such a smile, no—but rather, Jacques, for you to say, for example . . . ah! whatever you want.*

I will go on living, I know that I will go on living and that time will be suspended in one great heartbeat.

Monday, April 1

In the morning I read at home, in the afternoon I go to hear Damia who is singing marvelously "J'ai le cafard [I have the blues]" and "La rue de la joie [Street of joy]" in a cinema on the rue de Sèvres.[357] I think of Miquel with great friendship, what has become of him? The movies playing are *Le vent* [*The Wind*], which is a rather good film with as its only hero the squall on the deserted prairie—and *Le rouge et le noir* [*The Red and the Black*], which admirably illustrates the crude deformation that the cinema imposes on a beautiful work.[358] Went by Stépha's. We agree to spend the evening together: Fernand is giving Poupette advice on her paintings, then, we go

---

* The entire paragraph starting, "That was already three years ago now," through "whatever you want," is highlighted in pencil.

to the Jockey where we are delightfully lighthearted. Return in the car of a poor trapped man (must tell Jacques).

Tuesday, April 2

Awakened by a note from Merleau-Ponty that upsets me by this simple reminder "of the times when I used to write a lot." I stay at the desk in the morning to write to him; and in the afternoon on the terrace in Luxembourg Gardens where we so often sit together, I read a bit and cover four long pages with my confidences. Outside it's a bit blue, a bit sad, rainy like inside of me. Profound release of tears, profound happiness of my intact tenderness, with such love I spoke to you! Soul searching, painful consciousness of an inner depletion due in part to my exam, in part to this terrible absence—humility—I am worth nothing alone—how little I like myself, how little I love myself! But at least for one day I have known this heartbreak of wanting to give more fully of myself, this emotion before a being so miraculously true to himself, this infinite desire for him to decipher in me my gratefulness for him and my great disgust for myself. We walked together, Maurice, on the quays of the Seine around six o'clock in the evening. I was going to the gare d'Orsay to get Papa. The trees are an ashen lace against the blushing sky: the water calm when suddenly the reflections of all the illuminated street lamps appear together, and you in me, my brother . . . and so much peace, and such a lively renewal . . .

Thank you, how can I ever thank you?

Wednesday, April 3

The Bibliothèque Nationale opens again. Spent the evening at the home of Zaza who has just come back from Bayonne. Dinner with the Mornacs and evening at the Cardinal where Poupette sketches.

Have read Gide's *L'école de femmes* [*The School for Wives*] at the Bibliothèque Nationale.[359]

Thursday, April 4

Bibliothèque Nationale, afternoon snack at M. de Ravinel's with A. Vanetti and M. Losson. I really like the latter, the others too, but they are so influenced by their Catholic, nationalistic etc. milieu. Their childish liking for action, their scorn for friendship (dear Maurice), their ignorance about

144

life baffles me. How often I think of you, Jacques who rescued me, Jacques . . . but they are very dear to me: so upright, serious, young. At the Bibliothèque Nationale, glimpsed Maheu, truly likeable: unpredictable!!

Spent the night rereading the story of this year here.

Friday, April 5

Bibliothèque Nationale. Zaza stops by to say hello; coffee and brief chat at chez Pocardi: Pierre de Vathaire who accompanies her is very funny. In the evening Bandi reads the beginning of his novel to me at the Café de Flore—not bad. Stopped by Stépha's.

And I am still here, as always, without liking or disliking it.

A card from Villandry, so affectionate, so good. Your solicitude, Maurice, your intelligence. How would I live without you, oh! the closest to my soul, so incomparably more helpful than any other, so sure, so forever new and yet the same and completely comforting, who gives me back the liking for my greatness. Thanks again.

Saturday, April 6

Bibliothèque Nationale. Glimpsed Maheu. Night of reading: Hawthorne, Strindberg, etc.

Sunday, April 7

Got up late—an hour at the Luxembourg Gardens. Afternoon of work and reading, alone in the peaceful office. Weary walk, a bit sad at the end of the day in Paris without a call. In the evening I read Thoreau which interests me and makes me dream of a free life, free and far from books in the heart of a carefree countryside.[360]

Monday, April 8

Vacation is over. And in the morning at the Institut Catholique as I studied Leibniz and Locke, I had the illusion that it would be easy to finally surrender the year's end to the discipline of the competitive exam. At two o'clock I meet Merleau-Ponty at the Sorbonne. We go all the way to the bright Luxembourg Gardens as we talk about Green, Mauriac, and Barrès. Pleasure to see him again and to be on this terrace again so simply. But after Lalande's class and the two words that Gandillac said to me about Davos, I recognize my refusal to bury my curiosity about a *different* moment. I accompany Mademoiselle Richard through the Luxembourg Gardens, then along the boulevard du Port Royal all the way to her home. I go upstairs. Tea; darkness, a sad face lined with wrinkles that disappear in the shadows; oppressed heart that does not try to recover, bowed under the tragedy of a lonely youth. She speaks to me of Barbier to whom she used to be very attached. Bizarre impression: two years older, I could also have written "my dear classmate" to him. He left for Sydney. This solitary figure is being humanized; the giant is becoming a man. But none of what she says in speaking of him, or, in short, of any other *agrégation* classmate, takes away any of this honest affection that I feel and that she, who was nevertheless his friend, will perhaps never feel.

Then she tells some rather tragic stories; lights go on in the cinema across from us, and cars pass. A young girl of 20 died from shooting herself with a bullet, a passionate and lonely young girl, prey to a woman and prey to a man, alone. Romanticism. Into the foggy sweetness of the night I carry shreds of this decadent romanticism; and I give in to this "unhealthy" and painful thing that invades me. Strange night. (And how can I say it all again in the calm and blue lucidity of noon?) In me is the dream of a woman as sorrowful, but more mysterious, more abandoned in any case than Josée or Mademoiselle Richard, of a woman who would be my friend and near whom it would be good to feel despair, cowardice, and madness descend surely upon oneself, in the nostalgia without a cure found in American bars or on some questionable street where we would walk. Not a man: this complicity with weakness, with whom shall I create a delightful reality of this complicity with weakness if not with Iris Storm or such another who exists and whom I will never meet . . . [361] I made up any old pretext to spend the night outside.*

Clichy, a pitiful singer, a place in the balcony for four francs in the midst of bareheaded couples locked in embrace—a deathly pale, atrocious girl at the end of the row, a sober-faced mother accompanied by two charming blond children, a young, pretty, blond woman with a pink and white pleated collar. One can glimpse below in a box, a lady and some very well dressed men. Songs stream past, crude, sentimental or funny—words, bravos, whistles travel between the stage and the audience. I look into myself with all the amazement of being there. What hidden affinities bind me so strongly,

---

* This whole passage from the sentence starting, "In me is the dream" through "outside," is highlighted in pencil.

so strongly to such a working-class life—not only working-class but an unsophisticated life, completely given to pleasure, and contrary to the mind. Rediscover within me—for she is there—the silly soul of the girl who would be plunged into a wordless excitement by the black hair surrounding the extremely pale face of the singer. Rediscover the cowardice of a lonely heart, soft, fed on nostalgia of the lowest class that would seek a calling to slavery in the smile of every man. Question myself about what each of these masks might conceal of self-importance, of foolishness, and perhaps in the most unexceptional mask, of an ardent liking for life. And I will never know . . . Between each of these beings and me, create a test that reveals them to me as I reveal myself to them. Ah! Music, tea, tango, *Fille du bédouin* [The bedouin's daughter][362] . . . and on the boulevard de Clichy and the boulevard Barbès why such love for brutal men with dangerous lives, for the spineless, but exceptionally handsome boy with the scornful cigarette, for the girl posted on the street corner, for the girl waiting in the questionable bar for the adventure which is for her only her daily bread? Why instead of horror or indifference, this sentiment that is not even curiosity, but rather desire . . .

Desire to be the girl who was saying near the metal gate of the metro, "48 hours . . . I don't give a damn, I've already done them—I've said it before, watch out, it's the tenth district roundup . . ." It's the brutal simplification of such lives, the crudeness of joys and misfortunes that attracts me, I think, with this required mask that doesn't fool anyone, whose artifice contrasts with the artless lives that it shelters. Within me is some perhaps monstrous desire, forever present and overwhelming, for noise, for struggle, for savagery, and especially for getting stuck in a rut. What more would it take today for me to also be a morphine addict, an alcoholic, and I don't know what else? Only an opportunity perhaps, a hunger a bit stronger for all that I will never know. Existences too well supported by their poverty.

What hours I have lived with the sole fear of blushing about them in the daylight! But not always—in the École Normale classroom, I wholeheartedly approved of that night at the Européen. I used to suffer simply by thinking: I am two-faced; I'm a hypocrite, I am loved for the noble appearance that I am not. The thought of Maurice ran through my heart. But does his friend exist any less because the side of her that he doesn't know also exists? I cannot reduce myself to him, I am not Gandillac and his wisdom; I want life, all of life.*

---

* In the manuscript, the text is highlighted from the equivalent of "I used to suffer" through "all of life."

What a book to be written here! But the heroine would be different from me in that she would not dream of making a book about it, and truly yesterday was not a memory that I was preparing for myself, rather I was caught up, and I was only a more complicated creature locked into the carnal sadness of the mere present.*

Strange trip back in the metro where a young anarchist was talking in the midst of a group, she was pretty with her big hat, her short-sleeved blouse, and her tie. The men had long hair and truly relaxed faces.

But it's impossible to draw a real bitterness out of all of it. Impossible for me to feel dissolved into a diversity, for I know such diversity understood and loved as a whole; and if I do not recount all of that, it will be because it would be too easy, not out of defiance. Yet, do you, Jacques, know of this madness within me, which would be a harmful punishment if in indulging in it I ever had the idea of calling it harmful and of mixing remorse with this passionate risk that I'm running: of going to the depths of the worst that I find within me to know if I would ever disgust myself.

Tuesday, April 9

I work here in the morning, very well—Rivaud's class at Normale. I come back with Gandillac and Merleau-Ponty up to the Luxembourg Gardens where I stop for lunch. I study Locke at the Sorbonne library. I go back home around seven o'clock. Night out with Poupette . . . at Bobino. Two marvelous numbers: the man who has fun all alone, juggles without balls (but juggles), does the trapeze without a trapeze (a real trapeze), and skates in place or even backs up running—movements in slow motion. Charming. His name is Lemenier; I must see him again. Then the clown who falls all the time, but with such a sweet smile and a tiny, but amazed voice: whimsical dream demanded by this show. A charming singer: Lily May. The main attraction, the big Mayol, provides nothing that even partially opens a door. And what does it matter if I don't tell you about it, Jacques. Even with Poupette, what does it matter?

Wednesday, April 10

Boredom—what is a four that has become a three? So many things could be savored if you tried them, Jacques. But I don't even know if you exist. How

* This last sentence is highlighted in the margin.

can I change this myth into a man, how can I expect a miracle? The closer I get the further away I am. The past is already no longer yesterday, and the future is entirely lost.

Now it's raining here, vacation is over, the same faces reappear, everything is terribly indifferent, and you, Jacques, seen through the tiny end of the telescope, far away . . . like the end of this class that goes on forever.*

Sorbonne—Gandillac's commentary, Robin's class when I sleep. Marie-Thérèse's wedding—flowers, music—does one have to go through this?[363] How beautiful *Zaza* is in blue . . . Scramble for lunch. Pleasant hours with Geneviève and Jacques de Neuville, Edgard du Moulin, superb in red, and Pierre de Vathaire. Champagne, dance, spinelessness, which keeps me chatting in the living room, while people like me pretend to have fun. M.-T. is great. The three young Vathaires are delightful little dolls and sing so well that I would like to hang on to their little voices, their little smiles, and this charm that will be lost tomorrow. Sadness because of Zaza—sadness for not feeling the mediocrity of this marriage more strongly—sadness for being exiled from my beautiful paradise of pride.[364]

And tonight I just read *Femmes* [Women] by Karin Michaëlis, a beautiful and moving book where women suffer and live simply, with a big heart that searches everywhere to find the one man—or who are silently faithful to one man, with a heart . . . [365]

A heart is so heavy if it's alive! Tonight it's not the best love, it's the desire to cry without words, without true suffering, and this staring at an invisible point. Write to you, Jacques—would I be able to do this? I would only be able to say one word, always the same, the only one that I hear when I *do not hear* you. When you are there, I know only you; I don't even know that I love you—if you move away, what would I know if not my love, this love that I will never tell you like this, that nobody will ever know like this, ever. Did anyone ever love a man like I love this man? Ah! It's something other, really something quite other than love. It is also love. When he is far from me, my feelings can be subtly complicated, disturbing, interesting—when he is there everything is terribly simple. When he is there, that is to say simply when his face lights up with a smile that gives or requests, when he tells me: you exist for me, even if it is his writing on a paper, and nothing, absolutely nothing in my life is elsewhere. This link that is between us, how strange, rigorous,

---

* The French equivalent of the text from "Boredom" through "forever" is not in my approved transcription of the manuscript; the translation of this portion is based solely on what appears in the French edition (CJ 608).

and inexorable it is, Jacques. How strongly we are linked to one another no matter what we do!

The past is so great that I cannot believe in it, but I do believe that it was *so great*, if it was! Ah! How well I understand that one might search through 40 years and even more for one minute that was lived beyond the earth—and for these last words about yourself that no other would have been able to reveal to you.

For three years now I have been yours, ever since that day when after a jaunt in the Bois de Boulogne I experienced emptiness as a heartache that can only be resolved in tears—April 1926—and since then we have lived, suffered, matured, and suffered one close to the other, and you far away from me at times. But what does it matter? And even if you have loved another woman, it is not as I love you. How frightened I am, how frightened I am of how you are going to hurt me when you speak to me, frightened as a woman is frightened of the pains of childbirth, horrible suffering, dear suffering, and I cannot free myself from this love any more than she can separate herself from this child which she bears. It is from this day however, that this child will be born, in the great light of the total truth, but I am frightened, I apologize.

And at the same time such an overwhelming joy.

Nobody will know, not even you, unless one day you love me as I love you, but never like this; and I wouldn't want that—oh! Definitely not that, not really.

I cannot wait three months—I beseech you, I cannot. When I hear his voice telling me, "I definitely don't want to," oh! such powerlessness against time, such powerlessness. Oh! Write to him and tell him, tell him, oh! I'm so distressed.

Thursday, April 11

École Normale. Once again we meet the good Robin! I take the bus with Maheu and Schwob, who is telling stories of Davos. Gandillac asks me to have lunch with him, but Stépha is waiting for me, we are correcting newspaper articles in the bar of the Sorbonne. Gandillac is very friendly on this clear afternoon; he speaks to me of German philosophy, of my *diplôme*, "if your friends want to read it," he tells me—my friends, how dear and necessary you are to me, and how secure is my place in your midst, but . . . It was good to chat with Hippolyte, Boivin, Schwob, Mademoiselle Richard, Gandillac . . . between the two classes. Relaxed from vacation, my classmates are all really good after all, so who doesn't have faults? And we are young together! How we laugh while the imbecile Ohanna reels off his analysis! Caught sight of Merleau-Ponty, who comes to get me at the end of class. I stop by chez Monnier where I catch sight of Fargue.

Night at home.

Friday, April 12

In the morning I work very well at home. At one o'clock I am at Stépha's and we work for half an hour while Fernand has lunch; he has a beautiful tie and brilliant black eyes. Exceedingly kind in general, he is very attentively affectionate with me, which I find delightful. Stépha makes me taste an exquisite rice cake while Fernand chats nicely with "the red hat" as he calls me. Plans for outings, for walks, gaiety, and his very friendly gesture of putting his hand on my shoulder like this . . .

I go to the Sorbonne with a warm heart and joyous; I work well on Leibniz. At Sainte-Geneviève I read Rousseau's life story. Desire for unrestricted reading, for literature, etc. I leave Sainte-Geneviève to go to the cinema. Anny Ondra is exquisite in a not very funny film, *Anny de Montparnasse* [Anny from Montparnasse].[366] How pleasant it is on the open platform of the bus on this cool night, with a clear head, a supple body, and a heart full of freedom. Freedom of Paris and of my life, joy of the other lives that intersect with mine, of the lights dancing from Montmartre to Montparnasse, of the deserted darkness on the banks of the Seine, and of myself in the heart of these promises. Wish to write to Jacques, to tell him about this simple and good night . . . *

Chatted with P., who comes back delighted with the Caveau de la Bolée, her hands full of drawings and songs.[367] At least our life is not banal, or imprisoned, or asleep—at least we feel, we enjoy pleasure, we suffer, and we love. We are still young and we will let nothing be lost, we will not leave the table without having tasted everything.

Saturday, April 13

This morning at the Louvre with *Zaza*.† First at the cast-making workshop, I see delightful busts by Raphaël, an *Amour* [Love] by Praxitèle, a *Psyche*, and a torso of a dancer of great beauty. We rush by the porcelains of the Far East

---

* From "Anny Ondra" through "simple and good night" is highlighted in the margin of the manuscript.
† "Zaza" is underlined in pencil in the manuscript.

wing, then we go to see the new halls of French painting: Renoir. Mixed pleasure. Two very different genres of painting, I like only the first without any effort: *La femme nue* [The nude woman], *Le moulin de la galette* [*Dance at Le Moulin de la Galette*], the meeting on a path where the flesh tones and the fabrics are a lively and joyous movement of spots of mauve and pink light. Exterior view of things (well-marked by the contrast between the landscape by Renoir and the one by Cézanne that is its counterpart; desire to stretch out on the grass and to pick these poppies; memories of summer walks in similar countrysides, the scent of this greenery, and the awakening of a physical intoxication. Yet this harbor by Cézanne is an appeal to the soul, a reflection become perceptible, the descent of the mind into the heart of a landscape that is no longer only itself but all of the universe where this mind lives), but a lively view. On the contrary, his big painting (from which it seems to me that many forms originate) interests me without seducing me. But this entire work is opposed to all of the painting that I like. Already I identify more with Manet. Certain portraits here are beautiful. A great charm emerges from their false precision: it seems that the traits are definite and constructed, but a contour, a tone escapes from this spiritual rigidity and mixes such elusive vanity of naked reality with the unity of thought. The great paintings, even *Olympia*, touch me less than this woman's face or this man's portrait. I find some Degas pleasing. Sisley resembles the *Grand Meaulnes*, Pissaro sometimes has a direct simplicity. Monet is inaccessible to me, I cannot like *Le déjeuner* [The lunch], the garden, the cathedrals or the train station, what I like (two paintings representing boats) is no longer by Monet, even though there is the great audacity and the great failure of *Nymphéas* [Water lilies], great as the overly abundant lyricism of Victor Hugo. Here there are only two Cézannes—as I face them there is no longer anything to seek, but only to silently love. Painter through whom one might live—there are so few!

At the Sorbonne, I work rather poorly. Growing desire to do nothing but wander through the literature of all times and of all countries. Afternoon snack at six o'clock at Evelynes with Merleau-Ponty; we are lighthearted and stupid in the rain, deliciously idiotic together. And now with Strindberg and Chekov. And every morning the impression that I will not get through the day, oh! without you still, still, day after day. Eleven months!

Sunday, April 14

I walk a bit in the morning. The air is touchingly sweet.

In the afternoon, to see Barbette, I bring Mama to the Moulin Rouge.[368] Nothing that suggests genius in this program; even Barbette doesn't touch me much, as anticipated. At night I cannot stay here calmly, I pass by Stépha's, but she isn't there. With Poupette we go up to Josée's, she just got back to Paris. Hélène Audurand is there too. We have dinner as we walk on boulevard Montparnasse, we have ice cream at the Dôme without saying anything that is in our hearts, then we go back up to her place. I leave her at ten o'clock and come back here, charmed by her delicate silhouette.

Monday, April 15

In the morning I work here—then in the afternoon, Sorbonne: Lalande's class and the library. At night we go to the Européen. Difference between life lived with Papa and Mama and life lived alone, adventurously. We are, seated on the foldaway seats in the orchestra, only spectators. And yet the other day I was acting in a drama that played itself out simultaneously in the room and on stage and that is life, life avid for distraction, for oblivion, and for song. However, tonight again I feel nostalgia for a hopelessly empty life, for a life dedicated to the body, and shrouded in the sleep of insipid pleasures. Oh! I excuse, I forgive everything—what wouldn't I have done myself. An irresistible comedian, Tricky, makes me laugh so hard that I cry. We have ice cream at Wepler—general good humor and tenderness for them.

Tuesday, April 16

In the morning at l'École Normale, hilarious commentary by Ohanna who gets into it with Hippolyte, chattering at the end of class with Ducassé, Maillet, etc. (Why am I always emotional when the voice of any classmate calls out, "Mademoiselle de Beauvoir?" Am I emotional about existing? About existing in the midst of other beings? About feeling their esteem and liking, and about having so easily established myself, in the midst of so many girls, as the only one who counts? I live so intensely, I live so very intensely! Oh! I will say all of that one day, won't I, won't I?)*

I have lunch at the bar of the Sorbonne while I prepare my analysis of Leibniz. At the Sorbonne library, I read Rousseau. How little it has changed in three years! The same students are there flirting with the same silly jokes,

---

* This entire paragraph is highlighted in pencil in the right margin of the manuscript.

the same fatigue settles over the room towards five o'clock . . . fortunately, Miquel suddenly appears.

He sent me two notes that I never received. I accompany him to Luxembourg Gardens and then to Châtelet as we speak of Damia, Triky, and of many others, as we speak of Baruzi, of his *diplôme*, and of him. After an hour of discussion, I feel light-hearted, happy, and simple. I go back up the boulevard St. Michel thinking a lot about you [*vous*], who were the pleasure of the evening. The deserted Luxembourg Gardens welcome me and slowly darken as I pore over Leibniz with whom I remain until midnight in the study at home. In the morning Gandillac spoke to me about cinema and Poupette's drawings and was charming.

Wednesday, April 17

Not a very successful analysis of Leibniz that Laporte admirably restates, then deadly class with Robin; fortunately, Gandillac is beside me and we chat a bit. He shows me the itinerary for his trip in Greece. I have lunch in the Luxembourg Gardens. It is so nice out that I would want to spend the day there—but reason takes the upper hand and I go off to study Rousseau at Sainte-Geneviève. From there I go to le Ciné Max-Lindor where I watch *Nouveaux messieurs* [New gentlemen].[369] Gaby Morlay is charming, and since the film is carefully done and witty, I have a very pleasant time. I think about lots of things . . .

I go home for dinner. I spend my evening with Goethe. *Goethe* by Ludwig is a really good book.[370] Volume one follows Goethe from ages 16 to 32; through his letters, his works, and his portraits, he is closer than the closest of classmates. This life is a long source of reflection for me. Why do I feel that it won't ever have any influence on me, I, who am so easily influenced? I don't love Goethe—no permission will ever come to me from a man whom I do not love, however great he may be. His works however made me tremble with admiration—but without speaking to that something that does not need to admire—he is splendidly foreign to me. Why? Overly carnal temperament, or maybe a more tragic carnality would be necessary; but I'm shocked by this place so tranquilly made for the life of the senses, without heartbreak and without worry. The worst debauchery, whether it's that of a Gide seeking nourishment for his spirit, a defense, or a provocation, touches me. Goethe's loves offend me: neither contrary enough to the penchant of his soul, nor sufficiently a part of his soul; in tune with it, yes—people always praise this Goethian harmony between body and soul, but in tune because they are strangers. Oh! Beauty of discords that arise from an overly deep friendship! How thrifty he is even if he believes that he is generous, how controlled . . . If he suffers, it is from coldness, not from an overflow of love. He has known emptiness from exhausting everything, but not this pure emptiness that is at the heart of everything. And then too, he really lacks this charm of fantasy, this irony, and for me, this necessary hint of madness. Pascal? No, but not Goethe, either! But why choose anything other than me?

Thursday, April 18*

And why always this distress at each encounter? Why so much hope and love that returns to my heart as tears. Will I never know how to say good-bye with a smile? The morning smelled delightfully like summer: the fragrance of leaves and sun penetrated all the way into the bus that drove me to l'École Normale. And already on the hard bench of Hall D, I am quivering at Gandillac's smile, at *Maheu*'s outstretched hand.† How I love you, men!

At eleven o'clock we go down into a garden that is beginning to come back to life. *Sarthe* [sic], *Nizan*, and *Maheu* toss pebbles into the fountain; Boivin, Hippolyte, and Borne come to smile at the goldfish and to toss them their metro tickets, cigarettes, "white gloves and spelling mistakes," Schwob and Gandillac appear at the window, authentic painting by Manet.‡ We endlessly discuss things as laughter abounds: slightly pedantic jokes on Robin and Sartre's ode, but we were just like schoolchildren released into a courtyard for recess in the summer; friends and enemies, but all bound by solidarity, classmates, united against exams and old age, singing of life and the joy of the body and mind. Morning that should have been enveloped with love and transported intact throughout time, yes, without forgetting even the fat Renaud, the most uninteresting of the group, was a friend, every face was a wide-open door.

I had lunch in a verdant Luxembourg Gardens while reading some letters by Goethe and a novel by Crevel. Then I sat through Bréhier's class between Gandillac and Josée. Josée, perfectly delicious beneath her straw hat, who goes down into the courtyard with me and is sweetly present to me although we say almost nothing. And the courtyard is festive, sown with likable faces from which blossoms the Molieresque head of Savin, holding forth with this

---

* There is a big "x" written in black or brown ink at the top of this page in the manuscript.
† "Maheu" is underlined in black or brown ink in the manuscript.
‡ "Sarthe," "Nizan," and "Maheu" are underlined in brown or black ink in the manuscript.

slightly protruding lip that gives him such a strange smile. I catch sight of Miquel who says a few words to me about his *diplôme*. I go up to Brunsch-wicg's to hear Savin's analysis and that of Mademoiselle Richard, I am barely paying attention to them, I am next to Maheu. (Oh! I am not, at any rate, going to start crying like an idiot . . .).

Do I have tenderness for him? No, nothing marvelously sweet embraces my heart when I look at him from within, as does happen for Galois or Merleau-Ponty. Do I have respect? No, I do not experience this solid resistance of esteem as I do for Gandillac. Do I simply have the impression of a fraternal solidarity as with Miquel? No, I do not like his friends; people have told me barely commendable things about him (his marriage for example for 800,000 francs and in fact, his wife does not look like a carefully chosen soul), this protruding jaw, this funny half-sardonic, half-easy-going smile does not invite affection.[371] Is it because of his singular newness, that today I would abandon Gandillac, Merleau-Ponty, Galois and Miquel together? Something else. He, too, is "a man from our hometown," there is a form of intelligence that I do not know how to resist; his Jean Cocteau-like drawings, his notes on the individualism of Sulla, Alcibiades, Barrès, and Stendhal made me change my mind.[372] To say that he brought me back to Jacques would be perhaps a lie; it was this very atmosphere that until now Jacques alone had been able to create around me. And if the following morning, in writing these lines, I am half-crying in the study opened in the spring, on other similar mornings, I used to hug the conversation of the night before to the same delighted heart. Encounter with René Maheu, or encounter with myself? Which one moved me so strongly!*

We discuss individualism, he is astonished to feel that I am so close, I who, he believed, was "catholic and social" before having heard me. How well he speaks of Cocteau, and of Barrès, whose "cult of the self" alone, he likes, and not the political bankruptcy! How well he speaks of all little things and how important they are for him! Conversation interspersed with promises of long discussions at the Bibliothèque Nationale. He tells me of a book that he will write. Sense of irony, oh! goddess without whom nobody will be able to find the path of my true self. I don't believe that he is sensitive, and this creates a gulf between him and Jacques, nor do I believe he is restless or sorrowful, but rather lively, intent upon his inner life, a detached and smiling analyst, joker but not a shirker, and masked, I think, happy to see people be

---

* On the verso page of the manuscript across from the beginning of this paragraph is written "May 26- Tenderness conquered by yesterday's silence."

taken in by his mask, and to speak ill of him. I would want to speak to him, to tell him my affinity, to make myself known to him as Jacques alone knows me. Why is he so friendly, he who keeps himself at such a distance from all? Why does he care about me?

And in a month perhaps he will no longer be anything to me.* This morning I am feeling completely out of kilter, as if something had truly happened to me.

This does not keep me from greatly enjoying the arrival of Merleau-Ponty and accompanying him joyously to the Ami des livres, and all the way to Passy on the AX bus. But it's so I can speak to him of Maheu the whole time. Six forty-five at Passy! the time when I am supposed to be at les Gobelins. A marvelous half-hour open-air taxi ride when I relive this entire day full of people, words, and impulses, when I relive each of Maheu's words, and when I wave in passing to the dear house with the lowered blinds. I told myself, "if Maheu wasn't married, wouldn't I be filled with great distress?" Yes—but why since in any case I . . . ? Security because the impossibility comes first from him? Brake placed on my so often vagabond imaginings? And I also thought: that at certain moments of exhaustion or even of disgust, a simply strong and tender man would have been able to arouse my body and my heart, and perhaps, on the plane of an ideal sincerity, conquer me (impressions of the Jockey, etc.) Whoever addresses my mind and overwhelms it so deliciously would not only know how to arouse me but also inspire the least of my desires for a more tender intimacy, for a protective gesture, since even Jacques . . . if it ever happens that I "rest" in him, then it will have been by a patient, slow, and arduous path. Here again, why?† How well I have dreamed in this taxi . . .

At Mademoiselle Richard's place, I find two good-natured young men (Lecoin, or something like that) with whom I had lunch once. Together, we go up to the Cité. I like Madmoiselle Richard a bit—affinity of complacency and weakness that does not affect my pride. Her friend, Jeanne Lecoin looks like a pure and strong archangel; all five of us spend the evening together in very banal conversations. But the Cité Universitaire is a kingdom of dreams in the great desert of the night; the sky is under the pure and immense moon; lights of every color watch over charming forms behind the windows; faces behind a curtain lean over books; shadows

---

* Next to this short sentence is written in black ink and vertically in the margin "On the contrary! May 26."

† From "And I also thought" through "Here again, why?" the text is highlighted in the left margin of the manuscript.

pass by in the park. Life, contained and ardent, surrounded and solitary. The restaurant is full of youth and noise. In a room of the central pavilion a few couples are dancing. Stupendous and almost dramatic poetry.

I return home by metro, exhausted. Delicious sleep.

Friday, April 19*

And this morning, here I am, as I don't remember having been for some time. Ill-at-ease, happy, and inundated with reminiscences of books by Barrès and phrases by Cocteau, or rather by the flavor the world had when I would open Barrès and Cocteau. Full of pride, a will to tell, and an intoxication of being. Full of songs and of tears. Oh! to return to myself, oh! as in the past wanting no other work but the perfection of my sentiments and my sensations, employing my thought only to clarify them, my paper only to solidify them, all my time to exhaust them. Oh! to live again! As much as Jacques, I would want to rediscover the girl who loved him so strongly—to drink at the Stryx, in the sole immensity of his heart.[373]

I receive an upsetting note from Josée. What? Because of having caught a brief glimpse of Merleau-Ponty yesterday at three o'clock? I barely noticed that he was there, and so much joy in her. Oh! Terrible and hard power of love, and that so many people deny you . . . Has someone like Goethe loved? To compare the passionate impulses that carry me towards one being or another with my one and only love is to respond. I am sure that most of the people who believed that they loved in this way did not know anything other than these desires, this distress, and these marvelous pleasures that many have given to me, that can die and come back to life with another, and the proof is that for Goethe, it was always slightly aside from his life—and even dying is not proof. But who has known a love like Josée's? And for me, it is still something other than a love—much more.[374]

Life! First day of life that summer awakens, old desires, old emotions, new ardors, and completely new joys. Ah! myself, my child, held close to my heart, for myself to become a god again in this afternoon of ecstasy . . .

It would have been madness to write the book of my despair so young. I need one or two more years of living to know the exact measure of my

---

* There is a big "x" in black or brown ink written before this entry, which begins this page of the manuscript and continues through the French equivalent of the sentence, "But who has known a love like Josée's?" in the same entry.

passion and my aversions.* For you, oh life, adored and heart-rending mistress. To tell of you in all of your tawny splendor.

Baudelaire, Mauriac, different types of music, paintings, and friendships intoxicate me. Seated before this table I possess the world. One could give a lifetime for a moment so rare. I falter before the beauty of a landscape that rises in my heart. O beauty, O poetry . . . and what does all suffering matter if there is such a pure cry to say it. You must come back, my Jacques. I am madly in need of you. I am rereading Mauriac's *La chair et le sang* [*Flesh and Blood*], and with each line I am gripped with a fear that you alone know how to chase away. I am afraid of me, I am afraid of me . . .

You must come back; this heart must no longer scatter itself in suffering over random encounters, and must no longer search among all the remnants of its goods—it must no longer suffer except for a single one. This day is empty without you—so beautiful and so useless—full of your presence, great as a calm appeal. In one such day of tears and joy, won't there be anything between you and me! How I remember all of you, Jacques, or all of the two of us. Oh! I ache all over. It is the first time in a year that such passion for life has awakened, not of physical life like during this vacation, of moving and golden life, of Paris with every particular scent in every street, with the particular melancholy of every hour, and you are not there, you who alone could share my very frantic thirst. I ache all over.†

But the end of the day was marvelous as bit by bit this distress relaxed—a few verses sent to the sad and delicate girlfriend who suffers, some verses by Mauriac, some verses by Claudel. The other girlfriend came, with whom I went down the verdant boulevard Saint-Germain, in a joy, in a peace, with, at my fingertips, the exquisite scent of the dear past reawakened by the papers from the desk. Slow walk in Paris, lulled by some verses of Paul Eluard, and in the Luxembourg Gardens, by a narrative of Gide; slow return here with a joyous heart. And delightful night with Magdeleine inexistent and Poupette a bit sad, that little by little invaded my happiness. All night long on the deck of the bus that led us to Pigalle. Dazzling presence of Jacques in the smoke-filled and picturesque room of the Lapin Agile, and on the very sweet Butte overlooking Paris drowned in dim light, the dazzling presence of myself.‡

---

* From the French equivalent of "It would have been madness" through "aversions," this paragraph is highlighted in the right margin of the manuscript.

† This last paragraph is highlighted in the right margin.

‡ From "Dazzling" through "myself" is highlighted in the margin of the manuscript.

Saturday, April 20

Worked on my *diplôme* and did Greek slowly all day long in my room, as I read a beginning for a short story that I like and will write as I think about my male friend, and as I devour the secret joy of being.* How I love you my child who even knows how to be rather pretty when you are so happy, how I love the books that I am in such a hurry, such a big hurry to see you write, and this reflective solitude, this security, this joy without reason, without words and so serious!

Sunday, April 21

Lazy girl who lingers in bed, numbed by the vague dreams of your body for so long in the morning . . . My beautiful, but too garishly green Luxembourg Gardens where Sunday morning I read *Les nouvelles littéraires*. Oh! afternoon with Barrès in such a poignant happiness to rediscover the ineffable music that gave me life. O Violante, O love for the King of Thulé, O Jacques . . . [375] Dinner at *Zaza*'s.† Evening in Salle Pleyel where Layton and Johnstone sing their songs with too many nuances and too much life for the public at large. Discreet appeal that can be barely heard above all these bare shoulders. Immense tenderness without sentimentality.‡

Monday, April 22

Perhaps one day I will regret this calm self so true to form after a quiet day of work at home, then an hour at the Sorbonne where I exchange friendly invitations with Gandillac.[376] Then a walk with Pontremoli in The Luxembourg Gardens, at the Utrillo exhibition where there are some beautiful paintings next to the images of Epinal, and then in the rue de Seine where he shows me some Siria works that I don't particularly like.[377] Quiet night with books, some friends' faces, with Poupette's paintings, Zaza's blue dress, Gandillac's handshake, *Maheu*'s slightly fiendish smile, the nearby smell of cocktails, the song of "Mystère en pleine lumière [Mystery in full light]" in my heart, and the waiting for Maurice whom I will see tomorrow. Quiet night when I write on an envelope a name arousing a phantom and when my brother becomes the same as me in an anxious happiness. Will I write to you?

---

* This paragraph is highlighted in the margin of the manuscript.
† "Zaza" is underlined in brown or black ink in the manuscript.
‡ This paragraph is highlighted in the right margin of the manuscript.

Tuesday, April 23

Nothing but the joy of lending *Les caves de Vatican* [*Lafcadio's Adventures*] to *Maheu* in the morning and to see him reading Gide while taking notes on Spinoza; a few words on J. Romains with Hippolyte.[378] Distinguished and disdainful Nizan is having a discussion with Bougle. Afternoon at the Bibliothèque Nationale where I quickly see Eveski.[379] Then I wander in the Tuileries where I read Giraudoux and Salacrou purchased for the occasion in small greenish yellow volumes. Outside it's green, it's a mild temperature, and it's sad. I get tired of waiting on the melancholy Place de la Concorde, I don't really enjoy seeing Merleau-Ponty and wandering on the boulevards with him: no wish for anything with him; Jacques would make me wish for everything (That's really not nice . . .). We have some chocolate and cookies across from a florist as we discuss Goethe, we wander around Montmartre and go look for Poupette at Hadler's. Streets of la Butte, so dear, and this view over Paris, masses of shadows dotted with light. What solitude, what distress, but very pure and free! Much talking about friendship, good evening, yes, indeed! I am thinking of another; I am thinking of Maheu, I am weary and nervous.

Wednesday, April 24

This morning at Laporte's, analysis by Schwob, next to fat Boivin. Neither sad nor happy I notice that "he" has ears so pink that one could easily mistake them for shining transparent petals, an odd neck with rather coarse blond hair, and a triangular forehead; I shake his hand. I carry away his handshake, *Cromedeyre-le-vieil*, lent by Hippolyte, and the excitement that this good-looking, scrupulous and intelligent boy without subtlety thought of me long enough to get this book, a few friendly words from Gandillac too, but the best seasoning for my rolls with ham is the new greenery of the Palais Royal and the novel blue of the sky.[380] Afterwards, strengthened by so much happiness, I tackle my *diplôme*; and unexpected today, he appears— tiny anxiety: will we speak today? will we be silent? But he brings me back Gide whom he doesn't like because Lafcadio's gesture leads to nothing, and I want to forget the boring dinner at Aunt Marguerite's with Magdeleine and Jeanne in order to think about you, Maheu, like afterwards during two hours from the Tuileries to the Luxembourg Gardens declining in beauty in the evening when with the slow and measured steps of a grown man, an unknown child moves off under the already somber arch of the trees. To you, René Maheu.

No anxiety when I face you, no timidity; a joy, a gaiety rather, a lightening of my entire self—physically you are youth, proud of its intact body, this rosy complexion so clear and pure, these eyes of a sixteen-year-old, this blond hair of a big boy, and this consciousness that you have of your strength. Do you remember how, by the fountain, the words that you said on the horror of ever seeing your body age moved me? And first in this very library we discussed Gide and Stendhal, I passed you my homework paper on individualism that you welcomed as if you had desired my friendship for such a long time. Yet you didn't know me, you believed that I was Thomist and social, and goodness knows what else. We had some coffee at Pocardi's: there you exposed your system to me, very close to mine but more developed, more certain, that integrates social life and the classes for the *agrégation* with the very individual. You spoke of the danger of social successes, for example, marriage, with what easy lack of constraint, and spoke of the Normalians: of Nizan whom he finds so distinguished, and it's true; of Sartre whose false eye I don't like, but whom he says is very interesting.*

Near the fountain we speak of death that he fears as much as I: to no longer see the grass, oh! the trees . . . He speaks to me of Rome and of his emotion on viewing the Forum, which from this skeptical boy infinitely touches me; how immediately we are in harmony! Not one word lost, no work to approach each other. When I speak to him of God, "but then the face of the universe would be changed" with a true gravity in his smile. He speaks so well to me of Uzerche! As for his marriage, he amuses me: it is a "social success" that most certainly has no place in his profound life. He said, "I hate camaraderie between a man and a woman," just as Jacques would have said.

Yesterday, Maheu, I imagined saying to you, "You are the type of boy that I prefer to all the world. Is that kind? Less perhaps than you think, if I am seeking someone else through you." Tonight I said, "No, not at all, it is really you [*vous*] and not an other."[381]

Do you know what you have done for me today? First, this delicious exhaustion of the mind that follows the too happy exchanges of words (I imagine that sensual gratitude must be something analagous but less irreparable), and then pride! Because from lassitude one reaches out to others: Boivin is a good sort after all, Schwob has a good face, Hippolyte is considerate, Mademoiselle Richard unhappy. But we will be without pity, without complacency, my dear equal, we will want to be scorned and we will like to

---

* A vertical dotted line is drawn from the middle of the top of the page to here with the comment penciled in above: "But he is blind in one eye, the dear little man--(August 6)."

scorn, and we will hold high the brief intoxication of our self-fulfillment. Big difference: he wants a social success, I, an inner success.*

Who will give this day back to me? Even from the dead waters of sleep I will not catch its reflection.

Thursday, April 25

What an astounding day! In the morning at the Bibliothèque Nationale I work on my *diplôme*, that is progressing well, and I say hello to Gandillac; I think about the day I had yesterday, and about Maheu. What emotion to see him before Bréhier's class; he hands me his article and talks to me about my homework paper in which he finds traces of Catholicism and romanticism: obviously. Hippolyte comes to me to talk about *Cromedeyre-le-vieil*. Maheu flees, then apologizes for having taken flight, "I don't care for Hippolyte." During all of Bréhier's class, I think of other things. Josée, who says nothing to me, is there, and I caught sight of Nadine Landowski. Brunschvicg's class when Gandillac has a very interesting discussion with Brunschvicg. We leave together. Hippolyte accompanies us to the house—gaiety—he is a Mortimer, but a nice boy.[382] Zaza is already there; afternoon snack: Poupette shows her drawings; Merleau-Ponty comes: gaiety, animation, cordiality. Gandillac stays for dinner and Papa really likes him. I suffer from feeling that people take such an interest in me at the Sorbonne—Georgette Lévy's malicious gossip saddens me despite myself.

We go (Gandillac, Zaza, and I) to Vieux Colombier; program neither bad, nor good; naturally Gandillac talks about marriage, then as we are going to Chez Lipp, I explain to him what is happening with this "unhappy passion," soon an exquisite tone of intimacy; having three people makes exchanges even easier when the three get along like this and send secrets flying back and forth. A great and delicious tenderness. He believes that I'm ambitious. I have too much pride, and above all, I like my pleasure too much.

Friday, April 26

I dreamt about Gandillac all night long.† He was crying on my shoulder in the Bibliothèque Nationale lobby, and then I on his in the big garden in front from which we saw Madame Lacoin who watched me from a car, scandalized

---

* The last two sentences are highlighted in the right margin of the manuscript.

† The French equivalent of "delicious" is written in ink and crossed out with pencil before the French equivalent of "dreamt" in the manuscript.

to see me hold hands with a young man. We were on a brand new bench and I was calling him, "my brother," then Poupette came by disguised as a dancer.* Alas, in the morning after such agitated dreams, telling secrets was no longer possible. I feel like crying, queasy stomach like after a night of cocktails. I feel like crying . . .

Fortunately *Maheu* sits down next to me, then invites me to lunch in a chic restaurant "La Fleur de Lys," where Baruzi is also having lunch; exposé of his individualism where he integrates love, admiration, and everything except for illness; we take a walk in Palais Royal; he communicates a desire for this Greek equilibrium, this harmonious serenity. He is happy, he is himself, and that is enough. Elegance of his system.† Short Gidian couplets, drawings, and formulas at the bottom of pages . . . I rediscover with more and more strength the passion for myself.

At six o'clock I leave the Bibliothèque Nationale uncertain and weary and I walk under the wet trees of the Luxembourg Gardens without getting anywhere; intolerable solitude and anguish. Once again I write (to Jacques and in this notebook) and writing saves me.

A joy, a pleasure of Maheu, and a tenderness for Gandillac. I carry them off into the streets that smell like rain and to the Studio des Ursulines where the program is good, *Rose d'ombre* [Shadow rose] and *Contrastes, Everest et amitié* [Contrasts, Everest, and friendship].[383]

I go home to sleep dreaming about strength and joy.

Saturday, April 27

If only Jacques were there after all, so that I could think so many things by his side and make new resolutions! Ah, break forever with Catholic deformations, with romantic restlessness, with the cult of sadness; detest them and trample them underfoot. Twenty-one years old, a free body, a rich thought, books, and the green grass . . . what then? With which moral exigencies and scruples shall I be burdened? But rather I shall take pleasure in the world and in my gaze upon the world, ah! Love myself. Ah, my beloved! Ah, myself! . . . I needed this exhilaration to become a God again![384]

What makes Maheu's position so strong is that he integrates everything, even the *agrégation*, without imprisoning his self [*son moi*] in a private garden. For my greatest joy . . .

---

* From the beginning of this entry to "dancer," is highlighted in the manuscript.

† All of this paragraph is highlighted through the French equivalent of "system" in pencil in the right margin of the manuscript.

It remains that the humility of someone like Gandillac and his sense of sin touch me in all that is dearest in me . . . And I know what horror I would have of certain degradations. But to do what one wants does not mean that one wants everything. "Give me inner beauty . . ." But this gets back to the evolution of an entire year: to want only joy. I have to beware of recreating these states of joy "blissfully in the rapture of emptiness"—or at least to make these states only elements of the synthesis. Finally constructive judgment alone permits the attainment of what did not exist before it. I must beware of regrets—beware of putting my entire destiny into every moment; every moment is on the line of a destiny that embraces years. Adieu, beautiful yesterday; adieu tragic yesterday when I so tortured myself. I will not permit even Jacques to make me unhappy. I must watch over myself unceasingly.

"I live! This alone is admirable . . ."

Sunday, April 28

It is admirably nice out. I take a walk in the morning, happy. In the afternoon I go out into the green and hot streets towards comedy on the Champs-Élysées. On Place de l'Alma people are inaugurating a statue by Bourdelle and women in Polish costumes are joyously parading; warmth and sweetness of the sun, of life, of the main solitary avenues . . .[385]

Jean de la Lune [Jean from the moon] is playing; grace of Achard's dialogues, perfection in the acting of Renoir, Tessier, Jouvet, and above all Michel Simon.[386] But Tessier is not the woman for this role, she is too noble, too really beautiful; and the play is not without monotony, philosophically a bit facile. I know that Jean de la Lune is intelligent; with Jouvet he attains a true grandeur; but decidedly the man-woman conflict does not manage to move me, however ingenious or noble the resolution may be. Perhaps I should reread the play.*

I like the Comédie des Champs-Elysées, the tunes from the phonograph and the bar during intermission . . . the photos exhibited in the halls where admirable faces are presented. Perhaps it is just such an aspect of his soul that Jean de la Lune wants to save . . . but I don't believe so. No, decidedly, I cannot vanquish this revolt that I always experience when I see love leaving two beings as strangers or turning them into adversaries.

I return home and go to Josée's, but I do not find her. I read *Dieu et Mammon* [*God and Mammon*] stretched out on her bed for an hour and a

---

* This sentence is crossed out with pencil in the manuscript.

165

half; Mauriac moves me in this strange book. What joy, however, not to be like him and to be freed from Catholic complications! . . . *

Very lighthearted evening; Poupette has me read her review, and together we sing the dear songs of Chevalier, and of Mistinguett.

Monday, April 29

Bibliothèque Nationale. At three o'clock class with Lalande at the Sorbonne. Return to the house at five o'clock, which is rare. Reading, and daydreams. With joy I rediscover *Le potomak* by Cocteau, the Eugenes and the Mortimers, and a thousand phrases that go straight to my heart.[387] Growing love for myself; serenity in my own garden; pleasure of being and of loving so many things.

I am reading *La mort du père* [Death of the father] by Martin du Gard.[388] I am reading *Don Quichotte* . . . I stroll within myself, charmed.

Tuesday, April 30

Class at École Normale in the morning. Two hours in the Luxembourg Gardens where a funny kind of a guy, a Sardinian, strikes up a conversation with me until I send him away. Afternoon at the library. I do some vague work. At the end of the day, I take out a book on Roman history, Salluste, and I dream about it again at the hairdresser's before going home.† Urbs, *the* city. Your name, our mother, must have been pronounced with such pounding of the heart. Strong, disdainful, and sublime Rome; was there ever a being greater than you. Marius, Sylla, and these legions hardened by great exploits, and the Senate, its pride, and its tenacious will. Rome, person loved as one who died; goddess who was born under the sign of immortality and who died; and thus mourned. I, so unsuited to historical exaltations, you suddenly seized me in a library and out of my childhood rose all the passion that I had ever conceived for you; and I was submerged in divine tenderness, and in regret as I was in front of the monstrance in the past. To go to Rome—but it seems to me that it would be too much for my heart not to break as a result.‡

---

* The word "however" is crossed out with pencil in the manuscript.

† This paragraph is highlighted at the beginning and end in pencil in the manuscript through the French equivalent of "home."

‡ There is an "x" penciled in the right margin of the manuscript between this paragraph and the next.

166

In the evening I felt too radiant to close myself up in books; Poupette and I, we go to meet her friend Germaine Dubois on Place St. Michel. While waiting for it to be ten o'clock we go listen to Layton and Jonstone records.

We hug the Parisian night to ourselves. Parisian night where the street lamps extinguish the stars. A deathly pale man passes by between two policemen; other men come out from a café surrounded by the police who push us out of the way; hint of vague fear, desire to have strong enough convictions to be ready to exchange punches while all around people shiver slightly. Parisian nights with the blue and still deserted Bateau Ivre where we gulp down our cocktails, then make music, disrupting the upstairs room not yet ready to receive customers; with the songs, boulevard Saint-Michel, boulevard Montparnasse, and the Dôme, and the Rotonde, and the Cigogne which surround us—and the Jockey where we end up. Music, dance, cocktails. The already familiar faces of women and men. Sharp-bladed poetry that cuts to the heart with a thud.*

I catch sight of Henri Besnard and go to say hello to him. Astonished at not being more distressed, I hear him speak to me of Jacques "who is changing, getting old, and will only come back on August 29."[389] His faith in Jacques is admirable. "In ten years he will do incredible things . . ." And once again Jacques becomes terribly present to me at the same time that I measure how much my life is now outside of this atmosphere that only belongs to him. We discuss *Jean de la Lune*—he tells me about Jean Delrive, friendship, and love.[390] He is intelligent and sensitive, too much so, at least, too given to what he feels. I understand the great advantage possessed by all of these young people whom I frequent and to whom a strong classical education gives the distance necessary for situating their individual adventures. Distance between Maheu and Riquet for example: considerable!

A dull pain, an exhausted desire, a paralysis of the heart, this is what I carry around vaguely; but all of it enveloped with confidence, certitude, and expectation.

Five more months, and this infinite silence while he writes to others. Am I nothing? Or am I too much? Oh! not nothing, I know indeed.

---

* The last three sentences of this paragraph are highlighted in pencil in the right margin of the manuscript.

Wednesday, May 1

But to know nothing of the other, will I consider that nothing? So splendidly rediscovered and unique! Oh! this ruse of my heart that would want to diminish you, Jacques, in order to suffer less. Is this suffering? Despite everything I feel that you are so near to me, and that it is towards me, not another that you advance; but this radiant tomorrow is so far . . . Oh! Henriette is at the moment playing "I'll love you always," and the name of Cocteau and the memory of his portrait glimpsed in Paris-Montparnasse strike my thought, what an amazing landscape of a moment that calls for you . . . The two hours of class this morning went over the heads of all those who were there; then I read *The Odyssey* at Ste. Geneviève to put all of humanity between me and my particular sorrow. Sublime pages, as fresh as if written yesterday, simple enough to explain what's most complicated. I returned here to read the May issue of *La nouvelle revue française* while waiting for Madeleine Blomart and her husband who has charmed me; I would like to see them again. But that's nothing . . .

There is me; there is you. There is me facing you and wanting to live even without you, but being able to live only through you. But then again, no. "Do you remember, dear girl, this spring of two years ago when you asked for a life of your own that would be outside of him as his is outside of you?" Yes. It was on the boulevards, I was looking at the posters, I didn't know anything yet. Now you have it, this life of your own; there is the Bibliothèque Nationale, the Sorbonne, École Normale, Monnier, there is Gandillac, Merleau-Ponty, Maheu, Miquel, and all your classmates; and Josée, and Stépha with Fernand, Poupette, and the cinemas, the theaters, Salle Pleyel, the cafés concerts. And the Lapin Agile, and the Européen, and Le Bateau Ivre and all of Montparnasse. And philosophy, the *agrégation*, plus my books and perhaps glory and success.

There is above all your very own garden: *Diane* by Gabies, a white church by Utrillo, the Gilles by Watteau, the Ste. Anne by Vinci . . . the Eugenes by Cocteau, and the songs by Chevalier and by Layton and Johnstone.[391] Sounds, phrases, books. And the grandeur of Rome that made you cry yesterday, Alcibiade and Athens, the sphinx in Egypt. There is your harmonious garden with secret recesses and vast horizons. And above all, there is in this garden, yourself, with your new desire to make of every sentiment, every suffering, and every gesture a trait of this irreplaceable drawing that is you! You said, "even Jacques will not make me unhappy . . ." It is true since today I did not cry over this great disappointment in me; or over his glimpsed writing; since the aged Homer appeased me; since I did not feel the desire to die. In this way I had to become a complete being, center of my universe, and not a satellite in yours. But now that this conquest is achieved, join this world to yours, and ah, be happy together! No, this is no longer the trembling in admiration; nor the anxiety of no longer being able to admire. I know that you love me; I know who you are. This is the desire for you to be near me and to see what is mine become truer as it passes through your eyes; to be exhilarated by what is yours. It is in facing a painting, a book, or an adventure, my gaze that turns towards you while gaily saying, "isn't that so Jacques?" and that encounters nothing. That's all; that is *all*. I love only you and me in the world; but indissolubly and without being able to seek refuge against the other in either of the two.

What an extraordinary being you are Jacques, extraordinary! Why not always dare confess to myself what I believe and confront, and distrust the judgment that my heart passes? You are an extraordinary being; the only one upon whom I have felt the sign of genius, incomparable with that of talent, success, or intelligence. The only one who leads me beyond peace, beyond joy, and into a region so full that there is no longer any emptiness. Your friend's faith in you really did me good! People live from knowing that you are alive; and generous, O man, and according to the beautiful Greek attribute: divine.*[392] If I am crying now, it is from serene admiration, from this boundless exhilaration of having been chosen for this destiny of loving you; it is about the strength that you juxtapose to my weaknesses, and it is, above all, about the weakness that I know is in your heart and in facing it, I know myself to be so strong. At the same time I have the vision of all that you can do for me and all that I can do for you; I don't know which of the two makes this waiting more bitter. What is winning out tonight is my veneration that makes me bow before you in body and soul, broken and in tears.

Thursday, May 2

École Normale. Daydreams and meditations while eating lunch on the rue St. Jacques. Class with Bréhier. Lecture by Borne at Brunschvicg's; intense pleasure of witty discussion; pleasure of having a new dress and of joking with these nice boys seated on the high windowledge and exchanging cheap jokes about Hippolyte, Borne, vital rhythm . . . Went to see *Zaza* rue

---

* Beauvoir wrote "O man" in Greek letters in the manuscript.

Oudinot; spoke about Gandillac whom she prefers to Merleau-Ponty too lacking in desire (made a date with the latter for Wednesday night).

Evening with Poupette, busy with going over old things.

Friday, May 3

Friendship, work. Friendship above all.

With Gandillac, I refrain from being ambitious: I care too much for myself; he asks me to explain to him how I reconcile this love for myself with marriage; I like him a lot. But my great happiness is *Maheu*; it's his manner of nudging me by the shoulder with a very masculine gesture, of laughing with this big young and malicious laugh while wagging his finger at me, of calling me "my poor friend!" when I speak of G. Lévy, of going into raptures over my ideas and his, of . . . I could go on forever. We chat for only an hour chez Pocardi, in the square, and in the street. But the hours that follow drift away as I prolong this discussion within me. And how dull this room is when he leaves . . . I no longer do anything but wait for tomorrow to give him back to me.*

So blunt? But sensitive. How Jacques would like him; how Jacques would please him! Oh, dear life, dear life!

Went to Marie-Louise's before going home.

Will you one day be a stranger to me, friend that I did not seek?

Saturday, [May] 4–Sunday, May 5

Here is the real event; won't I measure up to it? I have the dual refuge of an act of faith or an act of pride. Love him or love yourself with enough strength, my dear, to be able to be happy again. Do not forget, moreover, that you had already accepted (in the secret hope that it was useless, perhaps), accept today when it's sure.†

I knew that I was never indifferent to this Stryx and that something poignant was waiting for me there: how I hesitated before I entered, leaning towards the desire to go home to my unthreatening room without trying anything; then I shook off this cowardice, I sat down in front of a Rose cocktail; Riquet was talking with some friends. At the bar a woman: I knew right away that it was Magda. At this point a heart that hears the words that

---

* This whole paragraph from "But my great happiness is *Maheu*" to its end is highlighted in the margin of the manuscript. The name "Maheu" is underlined.

† From "my dear" to the end of this paragraph is highlighted in the manuscript.

I have immediately transcribed might experience itself as a sleepwalker, "Do you have news from Jacques-Charles? . . . He didn't ask for news of me? . . . That guy, he got the hell out of here a year ago and he doesn't even ask for news of me! . . . We didn't even last two years together, ah! I'm in luck, what a beast . . ." At the time no suffering; almost a relief. Because she is so pretty, so elegant in her fur coat, with her two long silken legs, so refined and such really that Jacques could have truly loved her. And then because she has a slightly unpleasant voice without tenderness and because in suffering (for her gaiety is false), she suffers because of Jacques, not truly for him: I am sure that she loves him much less than I love him. A final even more despicable feeling: he isn't asking for news of her; so he didn't love her for long.

And that's why, having heard this talk, I succeeded in staying calm and chatting rather serenely until one o'clock with Riquet and his friends. And then, bad taste in my mouth, eyes full of tears, atrocious night without sleep. I think of Colombe, of Colombe, who killed herself because the one whom she loved was no longer pure like her, and who threw herself into the pond; crazy desire to die also.[393] But what would this escape resolve? Oh, for the first time to feel weighing upon oneself an act that one cannot undo, words said that one cannot have not heard; for the first time, the irreparable. Is it a Catholic prejudice that makes me magnify an affair that so many young people seek and so many girls accept? But I myself loved us for not being like the others. It's atrocious, my God! So atrocious that I could scream. Jealousy? Oh, no! I remember too well Jacques dragging around a love that he no longer wanted; and I pity this woman for having been a burden to him, and for not having hated herself. Jealousy? And aren't I in you more than any other? But "What a pity, Iago, ah, Iago, what a pity!"

Desire to finish; to want nothing from the past since it was not as I believed; desire either to marry someone else, or to leave for Sydney alone in search of a complete break. Desire to burn all my bridges with the past. And certitude that there is no other place for me on earth; that I cannot start anything over; that this love despite everything will always be stronger than everything. Then desire to write to Jacques while shouting: help!

What a night! All my memories were grimacing with terrible irony—to think that I attributed his blues and his uncertainties to very subtle causes and to completely metaphysical anxieties . . . to think that I used to see him passing through this bar life as a free spectator who has fun without being taken in, to think that I judged others so harshly in comparing them to him . . . To think that I alone dreamed up this three-year friendship . . . to think that I care about it now because of its past, and that now this past is being demolished—everything is collapsing! Oh! So many days in his home—the one when he spoke with Maxime, for example, when I suffered from feeling that he was engaged in barbarian life in this way, above all the one when I saw him driving another woman in a car—surely her, and a child . . . such doubts, such tears, that today all swoop down on me.

Excuses . . . naturally excuses; I know that I would have been capable, perhaps, of much worse things; I know that a sensitive young man might be moved by a pretty face, I know . . . It is not about good or evil, what is it about?

Upon awakening I cry, upset again and defenseless—not only because of her; because of the mediocrity of these boys, even Riquet; likeable, rather intelligent, having an appetite for discussions and events, but spineless, without strength of mind, without profound passion in their hearts, but busy with facile loves, proposing hackneyed subjects for novels, using high-flown language to deny the poverty of their present: Merleau-Ponty, Maheu, Gandillac, Miquel, how dear you all are to me, my friends, and you too Galois . . . Sarment's cruel expression, "One is equal to the concessions one makes to oneself, never above," haunts me.[394] I know that Jacques told me that he had only one friend, Jean Delrive, but he spent his nights with the other boys—is he so different from them?

Run away from him: tell myself, "in regard to him, I constructed such and such an image of life; through him I was then led to modify it; he is a pretext. I have always been alone before him; alone I remain. I will marry him if he wants, I will still love him; alone by his side, alone with this love that will retain a reasonable place within me, and what does it matter if a greatness has been wrongly lent to him by me? I need to meet with greatness only in myself to believe in it." There is an easy way to run away from him; by returning to my life that is, without him, so victorious and fulfilled; but the true way is to run away in front of him, while accepting him as he is without expecting anything from him. Or maybe I must not block out the past; I must ask my friend Jacques for help against the hurt that he is causing me. The sentence by P. J. Jouve that he underlined, "I confide in this friend, but I embrace another." I thought, "So be it Jacques; I pity the other."[395] Jacques dear, when you spoke ill of women you used to tell me that I am not a woman; you wanted me to meet Magda; at the time you called me "your [military order] 'Attention!'" You did not permit yourself one word of those that you probably used for another woman; you tried to make me understand everything: it would have been so easy to set yourself up as a hero! I imagined this friendship as inhuman; I remember its ambiguity, its difficulty, and its constraint, but also its sincerity:

to the extent that it was human, this friendship was beautiful, Jacques. I have faith in you. I do have faith in you.

One day I sensed this in your life and I said: nothing that he might ever do will affect me; I believe in him beyond his weakness and some acts that I scorn. Yes, don't forget, Simone, your love for him is part of this resolution: whatever his life may be I understand him and will always be there; you consented to what you called "the worst"—put face to face with him, don't say then that everything was founded on an illusion; not at all, this was included in the tenderness that you used to give him. And when Marius said these words, you thought, "even if they are true," and when you received the letter from Jacques where he almost told you, you responded to him, "I understand everything." Not with the frivolity that girls are said to have before similar confidences—it weighs very heavily on my heart; but I am now crying with compassion, and the more I remember, the more I suffer as if it were simply from a misfortune that befell you.

But I am not thrown back into solitude. ("It's an episode that really cost us a lot," said Jacques while speaking of Magda.)

Besides, this ordeal allows me to better measure my strength; I now know that one must not ask life to model itself upon the ideal that one has posited a priori; that one must not make such and such configuration of events conditions of its success; but that one must joyously affront reality without demanding *anything* from it: and demand only of oneself to measure up to what is proposed. Then surely, life is great. There is a beautiful poem by Kipling in *Les silences du colonel Bramble* [*The Silence of Colonel Bramble*].[396] It is false to blind oneself voluntarily like Jean de la Lune, and false to believe that everything is lost when one no longer knows how to blind oneself; one must know how to transform even an apparent defeat into a much more magnificent victory.

I believe that I am in the midst of achieving a great victory while helping myself with some tears and a bit of ink. Without seeking refuge elsewhere, but in the very thing against which I am fighting; and always, still within me. Gide's precept: let today's beauty be not the beauty I dreamed of yesterday; a brand new beauty; in joy and pride, without the humiliating feeling that concessions are obligatory; this is not a concession.

I know that I have within me a source of profound joy that nothing and nobody will be able to weaken, not even you, Jacques; this love for myself and for my endurance, for what I have withstood and feel capable of withstanding again. This pride. When I didn't need it, I already liked to feel it so safe against my heart, and at present when I do need it, it is not letting me down—for this is my life; nobody can help me to be. I am not asking anything of anybody. If I love you, I understand everything; if I don't love you, what difference does it make to me if I no longer understand. But I do love you.

What weighs on me is only the expectation of the day when I will tell you all of this. And if my tenderness is a bit painful, my pride is joyful because life demands that it be this way, joyous because of all the threats, and sorrows and doubts that my pride controls. Thank you for giving me worry and not peace. What an admirable day this dramatically ended yesterday was!

First, conversation with Gandillac to whom I hand some excessively brief notes on love and individualism; he discusses with passion; he becomes animated and full of joy when I tell him that I so like his way of being interested in everything, so different from the placidity with which Merleau-Ponty decolorizes the world. He tells me, "You can trust me," in a way that captivates me; if I were ever weary of myself, I would lean on him.

This discussion gives me a lot of energy; I prolong it a thousand ways while *Maheu* is reading close to me; we have lunch together, we take a walk at Palais Royal, we exchange loads of jokes, and go out again for coffee.* My zest amuses him: so many stories, so many jokes, so much excitement! He is a demon of fantasy, a passionate eruption of gaiety and laughter, with Jacques beside me in the relaxation of such lighthearted hours, a pain that dissolves into laughter. Zaza comes to get me. We walk as we discuss her and me; she is also peaceful and happy; how I would like to take her to my dear Meyrignac! Went by the typist on boulevard Raspail; caught sight of Gégé and wandered about with her, then return and hesitation when it came to going out.[397] Decision to always run all risks. And the spell is cast . . .

Today I am only meditating over these things and writing them down in the Luxembourg Gardens; I feel tragically how my life is indeed, Jacques and me, and how what I love the most is nonexistent next to this, without possibilities. I also feel with exhilaration how beautiful such a dangerous life is. Oh, life so full of despair, of hope! Life made of real events, not of vague reveries; life that one must therefore not approach with the soul of a little girl, but with a maturity that keeps all of youth intact. Life where something happened; that I can confront—unique life . . .

Went to see Josée; she says that all that isn't important, "past is past," but for me there is no past—for four hours we chat stretched out on the couch in a calming lassitude.

Things are not going very well tonight, not very well . . .

---

* "Maheu" is highlighted in the manuscript.

Monday, May 6

Awakened by the news that grandfather is very ill. Slight sorrow—so am I insensitive? This expected death, natural despite everything, is lost in the persistent distress that made me write to Jacques last night. My forehead against the windowpane with this desire to cry. I go to see Jeanne and Magdeleine with whom I take a walk in Luxembourg Gardens; in the afternoon during Lalande's class I desire only to ask Gandillac one question that I will not ask him; despondency. With Magdeleine I go to have the afternoon snack at Lido only to become aware of the idleness of my soul. It's muggy, she is telling me her stupid stories, I don't care about anything; yet, this ice cream is cold, this greenery is indifferent, and on the avenue des Champs-Elysées life sways gently to and fro in a vague expectation without desire. Jacques is excessively close, or if not him, past days including him; a kind of slightly irritated peace.

Gare d'Orsay: Poupette and Papa leave, Aunt Marguerite; I drag Mama to the cinema again tonight so that I don't scream. In my bed I suffer for a long time from a contempt that I cannot subdue. "One is equal to the concessions that one makes to oneself, not above them."[398] Consolation in the unshakable certainty of my strength, I love myself, I have enough esteem for myself today to avoid despair over anything.

Tuesday, May 7—Day at Bagatelle Park

Perhaps the worst insult to you is the perfect indifference of this day in regard to you. Or perhaps the trees were too beautiful for me not to be assured that one day I would wake up loving the Jacques who had loved Magda? I didn't take one step towards him. What indifference to him as I got up this morning; I wasn't thinking about other things; but the phrases of his letter that most moved me in the past no longer touched me: faith in him, give him credit . . . Through the window at l'École Normale one can see the pink flowers of a chestnut tree blossoming: all of these determined faces would not hear my question; Maheu would smile with his big sly dog smile; what would Gandillac say? Great emotion of tenderness; I could ask him what I would not ask Merleau-Ponty, for I cannot speak of Jacques to someone whom I could have preferred to him. Gandillac is foreign enough to me; we will have lunch together tomorrow.

I meet Merleau-Ponty at l'École Normale and we have lunch together at Evelynes. This boy is extraordinary; such delicacy to have burned my letter about Josée: his emotion while speaking of her to me, his refusal to speak to me of Georgette Lévy; his discretion from one friend to another (he never said anything about me to Gandillac or about Gandillac to me), his independence, his strength, his conscience. He says that he has changed in two years; it's true. So many things he understands much better and how sensitive he is to all nuances. Such refusal to reveal himself which makes one sometimes suspect that he has much to reveal: meanwhile such wealth and the awe when he consents to open up a bit and, for example, to tell me of his concept of marriage (return of Ulysses recognized by Penelope). He assures me that it is unjust to reproach him for not being full of passion as Galois did before I said it: it remains that he does not know how to inspire others as do Maheu, Jacques, and Gandillac; but at any rate all morning long, he was joyous at the sole idea of our lunch together. He uses exquisite expressions and makes you feel with so much finesse how much he cares about you. His is a false simplicity; and he lives with a very great natural nobility whereas his indulgence for the "poor guys" would make one believe that he was closer to the majority: Jacques's opposite, perhaps (what a nasty thing to say . . .), he must not be very sad: he is without desire but not without need. What an admirable thing it will be to see him completely happy! And how full of scruples he is (not expressing his thought beyond his exact certainty as Gandillac does) and of wisdom. And how well he matures; and what an amazing man he will be in ten years; and how well he knows how to listen! His psychological finesse; if ever he wants to write novels, perhaps he will be able to have a lot of talent. How I admire him! How I love him! How unjust it is to believe only his most facile appearance; and with what openness of heart we talked! His reproaches are better for me than the praises of any other. O my friend.

I accompany him in the AX bus to Passy, after coffee on rue Soufflot. We spoke of Mauriac, Galois, Gandillac, and Zaza. With a few words he distanced from this world in which he places himself along with me, the "café aesthetes." I think back to Saturday evening: indeed, what a difference! No, true greatness does not compromise. Upon leaving him, I make my way towards the woods: just because Jacques did like the others, does it keep these boys I love from being different from others, or Homer from having written *The Odyssey*, or the world from being so green, so beautiful and swept with rain and sun? I follow the lakes while thinking of Merleau-Ponty, and also that it suffices to be near this terrestrial paradise bathed in light, cradled by the scent of cut grass that the mowers spread over the big lawns, animated with charming children, young women, and long silent cars . . .

The elegance of the Pré Catelan restaurant blossoms under the blue sky; this red beech tree ... the rows of red tulips, as the wind sweeps through, the tall grasses tremble, like love on a face. Then Bagatelle garden and the presence of joy during this two-hour walk. The flowerbeds of red tulips all leaning their heads to a single side; the beds of red and violet, the tulips of every color and the jonquils in the rose garden, the daisies sprinkling the lawns, and above all the dazzling sight of a pink and white tree; and all the human, generous, peaceful and mysterious trees, giants in the world where flowers are the only accessories, quivering with each breath and weathering the storms, the trees ... what chagrin could survive your presence? And as long as there are hedges of lilacs whose scent sways as a cheek brushes past the soft leaves, as long as all the grass on earth is not forever wilted, won't it still and despite everything be worth it to live? How the thought of my friends makes my heart pound, and how great is our youth! And what a perfectly harmonious thing it is to walk on these big solitary and living paths with the memory of pure, subtle, and profound words that we said; a network of winged words envelops my heart enough to soften all blows.

In the midst of my friends and the big trees, leaning on my elbows at the terrace from which people see the final lawns of the woods and the hills of Suresnes, I think about myself. I think that I must not rush my indecisive pain but rather let it mature and detach itself in an irreparable refusal or an unforeseen happiness. I think that I now know how to treat myself with more wisdom and how to find inexhaustible resources in myself even without calling for them. That after all Magda had been a very harmonious sight wandering in these paths: why refuse her passage in a soul similar to this park of numerous detours? I am indulgent and carefree; as though Jacques were not more within me than one of the trees in this garden. If it is less beautiful than one expected, it's probably a pity, but the garden remains. After all, the face of the world doesn't change; I still love him anyway for what the others don't have. But I form my ideal with the others who are of my opinion.* I am happy, not even because I am diverted from Jacques. He is no longer so important.†

Certainty that when he regains his importance I will know how to discover in what way Magda makes him even more attractive (yet ah! Yet ... if only she had kept quiet).

---

* From "After all" through "opinion" is highlighted in the margin of the manuscript.
† This sentence is highlighted in the left margin of the manuscript.

I stretch out in the grass, against the earth; I laugh with happiness; raindrops begin to play with my forehead and my cheeks: eyes closed, I offer myself to them. I walk back along tranquil little paths on the bank of the English stream. Near the lake, I sit down in the sun, with the hum of the cars and the smell of rain on the earth, I read Homer. It is beautiful on your earth, that you, unknown God or chance, have made. It is beautiful within my self that I know so well, in this dwelling place that I made for myself. I need nothing except to live.*

Wednesday, May 8

What I owe to Gandillac! Permission to follow the inclination so dear to my heart. Why must I always look for it elsewhere than in me?

After classes with Laporte and Robin I went with him to have lunch on the rue des Petits-Champs. Already in the bus, I started to tell him my story and to ask him the question that I was dying to ask; he looks surprised despite my misgivings and asks me if there truly isn't any jealousy in me? Women, says he, are always too harsh towards that which they should, nevertheless, be inclined to forgive. A man is not worth any less because of it . . . He likes Jacques's words that I quote to him; and everything that I tell him about us. He alludes to a similar weakness in himself: everything depends on the manner through which it has happened, he adds; but I am sure about the manner here. Oh, my Jacques, forgive me. I said forgive me in the Bibliothèque Nationale as soon as I was back inside; but it appears that "people could read on my face all the phases of my meditation since Kant was opened on the first page." This little card that G. passed to me stopped me in my tracks; I worked while clutching my books, while repressing the happy tears that came to my eyes. At five o'clock we went out together, and the sun was gilding the rainwashed earth; we were so fraternally joyous. I left him at the Louvre where I went to buy a hat, and here I am, happy, happy to know and to have accepted and that there is no longer any question . . .

Jacques, forgive me. I found by the most wonderful chance these admirable words in a book on induction, "to believe, here, is, in a word, to recognize." I recognize you. Oh, my false idealism, my harsh abstract judgments, my theoretical attitude, how I hate them! It is not about sending this letter; it's about coming back very quickly, dear you.

---

* This sentence is highlighted in the left margin of the manuscript.

Gandillac told me some things, banal perhaps, about which I had barely thought: that in love there is something intended for *this* irreplaceable being and something interchangeable suiting any woman: don't let the two be split: be a woman also, he told me; this splitting in two responded to a real need that I myself had to satisfy. Tenderness . . . what, after all, makes the idea of it almost painful to me? Yet, no, now it seems to me that tenderness will be able to be pure, precious, and a gift that is not a lack of restraint. His experience with Monique Merleau-Ponty is curious. He didn't name her but I recognized this nervous, stubborn, and strange girl; and sensual, he says, as one can see in looking at her. She loved him for the ideal that he represented while reproaching him for his harshness. For her he gave in, he became more smiling, more sensitive; and she, who had a noticeable need for this change, no longer recognized the one she had admired. And then he had to be theoretical and reasoning, when she simply needed tenderness. She was afraid of him, of his intellectual power, and of his Christian rigidity. Oh, how I understand this feeling of a non-believer facing a believer: this feeling of being the temptation, the enemy, of coming to survive a dialogue between God and this soul. For a woman it's overwhelming. And then he is always talking about making himself known: he didn't try to know her, to prefer her to himself; she felt alone facing him. I understand now Monique Merleau-Ponty's strange appearance, her fear of intellectuals, and her "one always gives, one never receives"—she was guilty of a lack of faith, he of a lack of selflessness; above all, I believe, there was such an irremediable difference of nature between them. But how strange is this sensuality and bodily abandon in a woman; such, he said, is imaginable only the night before the wedding, this exigency for compliments and sensitive caresses that unites you with an unseemly bond that is later impossible to break.* Or am I made of wood for never having been aroused by the desire for even one kiss. How strange to find in a man this revolt of his Christian asceticism against his carnal desire; and that she wasn't touched by such respect. And above all the designation of such questions as problematic: what must one and can one allow oneself? Isn't every caress only the unforeseen blossoming of a movement of the soul in lack of words? A harmony simultaneously commands it and justifies it. But how painful these calculations, these discussions must be! She suffered, so did he.†

---

* From "But how strange" through "break" is highlighted in the margin of the manuscript.
† This whole paragraph is highlighted in the right margin of the manuscript.

How I wish him a sensitive, but not sensual wife, who would submit with tenderness without asking for anything and who would understand this awkward heart.

He speaks often of Poupette with much liking. Why does she love Merleau-Ponty?[399] or perhaps Zaza who likes him a lot . . . ? He thanked me for my trust; I feel that it moved him. He is very close to my heart, and Merleau-Ponty, and Jacques. The world is beautiful.

There is so much sun in my room . . . so much admiration and love in my soul . . . the world is beautiful.

Thursday, May 9—Ascension

The courtyard of Normale is full of lilacs; Mademoiselle Richard is presenting a boring analysis, but Gandillac, who is watching me with so much friendship, is there; and *Maheu* is bored with a sly smile, alone on his bench, a little bowtie replacing his habitual tie and making him look even more like a kid.* Outside there is a festive fragrance; Gandillac is in a hurry and talks to me about Limousin; Schwob moans about Mademoiselle Richard; behind us Savin is singing with all his might. There are flowers on the little cacti. The world is so beautiful!

I drag G. to the Panthéon: we admire the Puvis de Chavannes; then go down the rue Soufflot together, cross through Luxembourg Gardens as we speak of Mauriac and wander down rue de Rennes without making up our minds to leave each other; I feel that his entirely new liking is very intense. I ask him if he doesn't think that the love of a Catholic for whom time is relative is not a bit cumbersome for a non-believing girl who saves herself only by making every moment an absolute? He shares my opinion. (I had outlined a novel about this—go back to it.)

In the afternoon, I go to see *Zaza*; on the Champs-Elysées, to calm my heart, I write to Poupette; I inhale the magnolias of Meyrignac and the chestnut trees of Paris at the same time: the long line of cars gliding by does not stifle the song of the nightingale; oh, earth! oh, delightful place! I chat with Zaza about Grandfather, about Gandillac and about love; I gossip with Germaine. Then I go to see Josée. We spend two hours stretched out on her bed gossiping about loads of things; she comes for dinner; she has a red dress that suits her well—she speaks to me of Merleau-Ponty, naturally; I of Jacques. How well she put it: "I would like to know him physically." We are

---

* "Maheu" is underlined in black ink in the manuscript.

alone in the living room; there is nothing in her but what's delicate, refined, and attentive. She tells me while I take her back home some delightful things about our friendship; about the way that people misrepresent you; about the mysterious affinities between beings.

I come back by the boulevard Montparnasse; Aunt Germaine is in her room with the light on; I think of Jacques. Once home, I read Proust, *Du côté de Guermantes* [*The Guermantes Way*]—I am more taken than at the first reading; these subtleties of high society are by their very uselessness a purely poetic construction; everything here is important and difficult.

Friday, May 10

The Bibliothèque Nationale no longer means work at all. In the morning it is Gandillac and in the afternoon *Maheu.** Gandillac is astonished that Jacques wanted me to meet Magda, "one must know how to behave during some breakups." I explain to him in the little square that I could not stand being separated from anything that touches Jacques; I read him some phrases from his letters that he seems to understand very well; he makes me feel how comprehensible it is that Jacques experiences difficulties in talking to me, in telling me . . . As I accompany him bareheaded to the avenue de l'Opéra, he tells me interesting things about himself: his intellectual attitude, his construction of feelings with his mind, his powerlessness to find a path, and the question of the pride aroused by such an attitude.

I have lunch at Palais Royal as I read Proust. Joy of seeing Maheu when I get home. He invites me to have coffee at four o'clock. As always I tell him my little stories; he presents to me his ideas on science and technique and in general on the possibility of an explanation of the singular as such. On a bench in the square we have a long discussion; I admire his ability to have his own theories on all things; perhaps because he doesn't know much philosophy. I like him enormously. (How weak a woman is in facing a man! They treat me as an equal, but when Maheu makes me pass in front of him by lightly nudging me on the shoulder, I learn how much this simple masculine assurance is able to affect me.) When he has gone, because tonight we are having dinner at Aunt Germaine's, an old anxiety, long forgotten, reappears: a shiver that runs down the length of my spine, contracts my throat, and soon takes over my entire body.† So I get up and walk the length of the quays in a very warm, almost hot

---

* "Maheu" is underlined in black ink in the manuscript.

† This paragraph is highlighted from "How weak" through "body" in the margin of the manuscript.

evening and in a pleasure embarrassed to recognize the emotional turmoil of the past. As I ring at this door that "he" will not come to open for me, I could almost faint. Uncle Pierre speaks of Titite; Aunt Germaine comes home and tells me of Jacques; he said, "You will say many things to Simone when you see her; I wasn't nice to her, but I am not nice to anyone; besides, it won't surprise her coming from me."[400] This seems like such a banal excuse that I draft a response in vain: "Many people are nice to me; what's more precious is someone to whom I feel like being nice."

I am but one among other people (?), I don't know; in the same evening, in the dining room and this gallery where he was my god, where I was so happy, another phrase hurts me: he said to his mother, "You will bring Claude back to me next year!"*[401] How sure I am that next year he will be mine! And what do I know? Isn't he free? I believe that my current peace comes from this certainty that perhaps responds to nothing in the other at all—I am frightened by the idea of all that I might suffer by this man. Have pity on me—know this well, when I'm face to face with you all of my defenses against you are worth nothing. Have pity on me.

Saturday, May 11

Morning spent dictating my *diplôme* in some student rooms on the boulevard Raspail. I eat Russian pastries for lunch on the rue Vavin. I cross through the Luxembourg Gardens, then with heart slightly pounding as always, I go to Gandillac's. Kindness of his sister and his mother, who worry about grandfather and Poupette. G's room looks like him; there is Renée Boismond, very ugly Mademoiselle Wagner, two unknowns, very elegant, nice, and likable Schwob, and Galois—shock in my heart that didn't dare hope for this. I understand the girls who go to ten parties to try to catch a glimpse in one of them of the boy they love. Merleau-Ponty arrives very late. The four of us leave together; I stay with Galois in the metro where as always I arrive at my station just when my shyness starts to fall away . . . Night of agitation invaded by him.

Sunday, May 12

So I don't know how to spend an evening alone with myself anymore? No wish to go out, or read, or translate Sextus Empiricus open beneath my eyes.

---

* This entire paragraph is highlighted in the right margin of the manuscript.

Hardly wish to remember. I slept until noon this morning, incapable of inventing any interest for the day. A dispatch announces that Grandfather is dead; I don't realize it right away; but while climbing the stairs at the Lacoins', I remember this nice smile, the outstretched hands, and the trembling gaze that sought us out to plant a big kiss on each cheek . . . beautiful death in the midst of his children and his trees; dead . . . not in Paris where it means nothing as there is no memory of Grandfather, but to imagine Meyrignac without him?* We go to the Bois with *Zaza* and return to her home for the afternoon snack. Germaine is charming, so naïve and childish, already with the grace of a girl, a romantic, yet sensible heart, a very sure taste despite the prejudices with which others burden her intelligence. I stay a long time; a bit from pleasure, a bit from spinelessness.[402]

Then walk down the wet avenues where the smell of damp leaves speaks of solitude; I think of Galois: this is the only man I could have completely loved (a girl with the illusion of still being free does not experience too much bitterness if faced with the ideal newcomer; she thinks of giving herself to him in this manner only thanks to her certitude of preferring the other, but also if she preferred him, she would accept this disruption. A young woman who looks even more secure must suffer much differently to think that now it's over for her). Galois told me, "there is nothing new." How could I respond to him that today my agitation was novel because of him?

Merleau-Ponty is my conscience, my brother, my friend, an overflowing tenderness and a smile of gratitude. Gandillac is an interest full of indulgence, intellectual joy, pride for having "moved up," emotion, and especially an infinite trust. Maheu is my great pleasure, my smile of youth, my laughing strength . . . oh! Galois is the always awakened and unassuaged desire, humility, the feeling of a richer, stronger, and more nuanced presence than my own, something that the slightest thing would transform into an immense love. Perhaps he will be nothing more in my life than these brief encounters, and these tomorrows with a tense heart; nothing more than these dreams around him, this malaise that doesn't quite turn into tears. And yet it's as though I were predestined for him; before I knew him he moved me. As soon as I saw him I was full of shyness and desire; I will never know him, but perhaps he will have been the great chance of my life that I will have lost . . . I used to imagine a whole novel: of him indifferent to me

---

* This paragraph is highlighted from "trembling gaze" through "without him" in the margin of the manuscript.

whom his friends so cordially surround, of me using his friends only to get to my love. I feel ridiculously hurt.

Not too hurt. A tricolor flag floats in the blue sky illuminated by an unseen light, it seems to burst forth from a mysterious flame; the Eiffel Tower lights up and goes out. A year ago Jacques left. Life is not only one word. Despite my torpor and the slightly spineless lethargy of this week, I am so sure of being, beyond all the events, myself! So sure of writing the books where I will lovingly set down the faces of all those I love!

I no longer have any desire for big risks or the desire to lose myself. Perhaps at the present time it would be advantageous to end this long story that has been mine for the past three years; and to start over with something completely other, and to rediscover a new being. But I can't manage to desire this; I barely sense enough passion and curiosity in me to resist such a storm (I mean, for example, that Jacques no longer loves me, for his death = my death, that's understood), I can no longer desire this.*

At heart, I am very happy; I love an infinite number of things: but I have an absolute need only for Jacques, and for me of whom I am sure.

Another idea for a novel pursues me: a girl (me) in a very noble and intelligent milieu that respects and admires her and that she herself admires and cherishes; a life of very exalted companionship; but in her life something; hidden struggle; triumph of something that seems contrary to everything that people know about her in other respects, either for her happiness, or for her unhappiness. (Either a believed-to-be-forgotten childhood love for a great adventurer who left, and who is no longer in her thoughts (or so she believes): but then he opens the door, and she sees that she is his. Or a passion, from which she tries to tear herself away, for an overly seductive brother who is oblivious to her love; or who, on the contrary, responds to it and keeps his sister from tearing herself away. Or she would get married and would know that this doesn't resolve anything, or he would get married and she would want to kill herself, powerless. Or an affair with a woman, in which she would be the strongest, moreover, not a prisoner, but an accomplice; and perhaps love would come to tame her and, despite herself, to save her.)

Perhaps nobody will ever love me. However, even then I will not have been a woman deprived of love: Merleau-Ponty would have loved me if I had wanted. Today Gandillac would love me if I wanted. I would love Galois if he wanted.

---

* This paragraph is highlighted in the right margin of the manuscript.

184

Poupette—how incapable she is of saving me from anything; when I speak to her about myself, does she understand? She is so simple: these complications of the heart escape her; I must not expect from her any insight about me, or advice. But I also never contemplate what she could not give; incapable of saving me from anything because she is me; but without her, because she is me, I am incapable of savoring anything. I care about her in an unimaginable fashion that I sense so well only in her absence.* I like that she is not dazzled by intellectuals and knows that her intelligence is more precious than any knowledge; that she is so visibly honest, upright, and pure with her daring words, so bold and strong, with a superficial weakness, so virginal with such solid good sense, so sensitive with a sense of the ridiculous, so ... so herself, my dear Poupette who, like me, knew every tree in Meyrignac, who denounces bad taste and silliness so quickly; so lively; so young, so rich, so pretty, so ... O my sister my darling Poupe who knows so well how to give to your Mone your ever present affection, without any displays of emotion, safe and sweet refuge, dear accomplice, dear myself.

I say that if Jacques died, I would kill myself; if you died, it seems to me that I would not even have to kill myself to die. Nothing resists analysis and every ruse of intelligence like such tenderness. Be happy, my so beloved, my sister. What admirable name is that of sister!

Monday, May 13

An exquisite note from Maurice Ponty welcomes me upon my awakening.[403] Friendliness from Gandillac at the Bibliothèque Nationale and the Sorbonne, *Maheu's* lecture.† Reading in the magnificent Luxembourg Gardens until dinner. (Caught sight of Maheu and *Sartre* as I was leaving. Did they see me? Vague hurt while I leave the garden. Why didn't I say something?)‡

I read *Ma vie* [*My Life*] by Isadora Duncan—strikingly bad taste.[404] Can one imagine a woman with an impassioned and also contemplative existence? One who would know how to live the most romantic incidents with the painstaking gaze of a Proust and with the miracle of an abstract analysis and an overflowing vitality? I do not desire a dazzling existence, but rather love, some good books, and some beautiful children, with some friends to

---

* This paragraph is highlighted from its beginning through the word "absence" in the margin of the manuscript.

† "Maheu" is underlined in darker ink than that used for writing the rest of the diary entry.

‡ This last comment in parentheses is in the same handwriting and ink as the body of the text but smaller, as though added as an afterthought.

whom I can dedicate my books and who will teach poetry and thinking to my children. Tomorrow's dream is one thing . . . I know. I am ready for almost anything. How I feel like writing! Come on, in two months and for all my life this will be possible. I will take my old novel along on vacation. Or no. I will start something completely new, without ulterior motives. At the beginning of the new school year I will see to writing the theory of my book, then my book.

Tuesday, May 14

Early morning departure. Travel. Through the country door full of life, of my life. Very dear faces, a very dear face. Splendid certainty of the future and the present. Emotion on arrival, feeling of profound ties that attach me to Papa and Aunt Hélène, even Robert for what they retain of this Beauvoir spirit that Grandfather also had and that I so much like to rediscover in the more delicately sensitive soul of Poupette; they evoke the gestures and the words of dear old Grandfather. This body. Insensitive wax—such a little thing that has been switched off, and so immense, even now when it has become almost vegetative: life. No emotion before this body that keeps nothing of this very loved smile. Meyrignac is less beautiful in the spring; green rye undulating in the wind, magnolias, purple beech trees, but the woods are not a profound shadow, the earth and the grass do not have this carnal odor that goes to your head, nor is the sun a scalding demand. There is all the difference between a very strong fondness and a true love. Walk with Poupette in the chestnut grove by the pond; she is so blond, and there are so many mauve hyacinths in the big field behind the stable, O life stronger than all death.

Chiming of the bells that the country folk ring with their crude affection for Grandfather and their strong arms, "So he let himself die, the poor guy!"—simple and direct words; their prayers near the bed.

There are too many of us and we talk too much for the objects to speak; I know that in this dining room the wallpaper, the bell, all the things have their own voice that could give Grandfather back to me and pierce my heart; for a moment in front of the bookshelves it seems that the smell of all the dear monotonous vacations is going to be condensed, and that I will then know that Grandfather is gone. But no, Meyrignac is not here; this is too short a break in unaccustomed circumstances that never involved Grandfather where not seeing him is unsurprising. I am not even captivated by the night through the dormer window. I feel surrounded by all possibilities; but

I would have to have such an entirely giving heart that from the first night on of a long stay, and in surrendering to this region, it would surrender to me in return. I know too well that Paris exists; this beautiful garden remains closed.

What impossible sleep elsewhere in this bed of our home, so much our home that it does not matter if another lives here.

Wednesday, May 15

Pleasure that this looks so much like Grandfather and that all the social horror with which Paris burdens death is banished here. He is leaving with flowers from his home, on a poor and touching hearse followed by country folk dressed in their Sunday best who are intently watching the funeral procession from behind the hedge of their field and who meet it with a great salute. The altar boys have umbrellas under their arms and surplices that are too short over their little pants. Besse, the headstrong, is carrying the cross, the fields are smiling with all of their flowers, the road is warm and calm, an exquisite naïveté in the air, a sadness that is so simply tender that it is no longer sad, and akin to Grandfather's good mood. And we, his grandchildren, are here so lively and so young as we walk in the calm spring of this warm countryside. All six of us gaily have lunch; we take a walk far from the adults; in the spot where I had so dreamed of the girl who I am, I stretch out on the ground. Magdeleine says silly things and I respond in kind; yet no impression of spinelessness—rather an agreement.

I read the life of Alcibiades, of Sylla, and of Marius in my bed. Sudden desire to stay here, with this pure, denuded, and confident soul that this region renews for me.

Thursday, May 16

Good-bye to Meyrignac, to the blue cedar, to the dwarf maples; but the ties between us are even stronger than a farewell. The car leads me to La Grillère in a long happy dream where Jacques is next to me, so strongly within me that nothing can happen to me, and that the world where he is not and the happiness of this walk that I live without him are part of a pleasure that brings me back to him and whisks me away in the same movement. The grounds of La Grillère, more moving in solitude than even the paths of Meyrignac; I cut off a branch from the pink chestnut tree, and I trample the smell of pine needles in the Rouler pathway with the

187

memory of a heart so heavy and yet so filled with joy. The region is beauti-ful all the way to Limoges. And it's fun to be a bit late, to accumulate pack-ages of provisions as I panic a bit until I meet Poupette, Papa, and Mama again in the train. Lunch that brings back my happy childhood when the family was everything and when its familiar jokes enchanted me and still amuse me today. I like our way of thinking, our disdain for others, our gaiety, and a quantity of subtle qualities that I cannot define but of which I detect the absence in Mama, for example.* To be once again for an hour this ten-year old child. . . . But the landscapes of the Sologne speak to me of higher joys; how I love these ponds, these copses, these thin grasses, and this deserted solitude! I would want a house here similar to that of Franck de Galais; how passionately one must be able to love these poor and untouched lands, monotonously wild with the unexpected pleasure of paths at nightfall.

Does all of this life propel me forward to do nothing with it? I think of the day when I will see you again with an immense peace that flies past the length of the embankment—I think of Gandillac's new friendship, of others, of myself stronger than all and who will always find in the most inclement hours a train similar to this one to take me away towards the conquest of a new relief. Dinner at Aunt Marguerite's; even in such boredom, it is enough to see Poupette's pose on the couch, smoking with her thighs crossed, with the very veiled glow of the lamp that gives Jeanne's sensible room the look of a place of ill repute that our remarks are hardly contradicting; how fun living will always be in spite of everything.

Friday, May 17

At Père-Lachaise Cemetery suddenly this incredible thing: above the graves so calm in the sun, the innumerable V's outlined by the planes with their powerful and peaceful flight; a flock of these tamed birds passes over our heads with a steady and moderate humming, at a set speed, and glides, har-monious—a song of life as I never live it and that overwhelms me. If all of those in graves are dead, these tamed birds are doing what these ancient dead never dreamed of doing: they are walking in the sky with a smiling and confident step, but also serious from all the beauty that they outline. To analyze such feeling is impossible: this incredible poem was simultaneously so conscious, and yet so stripped of literary artifice.

---

* From "I like" through "for example" is highlighted in the margin of the manuscript.

The rest of the day is the echo of this emotion. Lunch at my house where with pleasure I embrace the little Germaine Dubois who just lost her father and who is distressed, but with amazing pluck; in the street, my great girl friend from forever, at the Bibliothèque Nationale where I correct my boring *diplôme*. Gandillac accompanies me a bit on the way back and I talk to him about that place.

Difference in attitude once it is understood that a friendship is acquired; such ease. Presence and absence of Jacques in that spring of last year where his departure and my regret for it become indistinguishable.

Dinner here. Vague walk with the five of us, rather lighthearted; Robert treats us to ice cream at the Dôme.[405] We sprawl out on the beds in my room upon our return; but Poupette has such elegant poses that I can imagine her life without boredom for an hour as I match it with her gestures. What a pity that she cannot express, in the theater or in a life of adventure, such a great supply of feminine resources! Free show for us alone, the extent of which even her husband will probably not understand; perhaps it is better like this. I have an enormous love for us.

Saturday, May 18

Work at home on my *diplôme*; outing with Poupette to take it to the Sorbonne where I find Merleau-Ponty; we go up to l'École Normale. I wait for him on the green bench in the courtyard where water capriciously springs forth from the fountain, and where there are lilacs, a laburnum, some red thornbushes, and some Normalians in rope-soled sandals walking on the gravel with uncertain steps as they eat bread and chocolate; I exchange a few words on the *agrégation* with Boivin, a decent sort who quotes me some delightful words by *Maheu*. The subjects that he foresees for the competitive test are "Soul and Body—resemblances, differences, advantages, and disadvantages" and "Of all the authors on the program, say which you prefer and why . . ." I stop by chez Monnier to get *Les varais* by Chardonne.[406]

In my room open to the sun, perfect hour reading this very beautiful book; hour even more perfect after I read it, savoring the happy simplicity of these moments; Maheu's words are near me with him like a delicious diversion that is savored with one's hands behind one's head in order to sustain this slightly bowled-over smile; some words from *Les varais* are in my heart like the profound connection that keeps all the pleasures on the shores of my soul: "By giving her happiness one day, Frédéric had acquired a permanent power over her: he had closed the earth to her."[407] The happiness that you gave me . . .

Stupid prejudice which makes one refuse to assert, "I love him much more than he loves me," as if one were afraid to make oneself greater and to reproach the other—isn't this to say that you gave me more than I gave you, simply by living . . . Tonight so simply the same overflowing tenderness that so many times in the past made me bow my head; this could, as much as today, be an extremely old night, one of those nights when the Stryx did not yet exist, when I was revolted by Valéry Larbaud's words in *Enfantines* [*Childish Things*], whose grave beauty I have since learned, "nevertheless" [*quand même*].[408] Moreover, no, there is not any "nevertheless" because there is no event: there is a being, this thing as distinct from any ideal as from any fact, this unimaginable thing. Did I see you yesterday or a year ago? Will I see you tomorrow or in four months? Did you write to me or are you going to remain tirelessly silent? What does it matter? There is no time, there are no words, but I met you and you exist, and in that is everything.

I am well aware that I love Meyrignac with a love whose worth no one will even be able to sense; but are you aware that for one look from you, you know, like how you glanced at me the night when we were speaking of female friendship, I would give up ever remembering it? Are you aware, although I myself don't always know it, that I would bid adieu without one tear to this so loved Paris just so that you would say to me a single time, "hello, Simone?" However, it's true.

Interesting to reread what I used to write two years ago; then I used to write things that are only true now when I no longer feel like writing them because they are so habitual for me; this for example: "I have only myself."

The word "to mature" is right and beautiful; impression that through my two years of experience everything softened, merged, became richer, consistent and easily assimilated.* Jacques.

Sunday, May 19†

Gray weather. I work at home all morning; at noon I see some paintings in the Luxembourg Gardens again. Afternoon of quiet study; brief outing from

---

* This paragraph is highlighted in the left margin of the manuscript through the French equivalent of "assimilated."

† This whole entry is highlighted by pencil marks before and after it in the manuscript.

six to seven with Poupette in the Luxembourg Gardens and in a Russian pastry shop on the rue Vavin . . . I reread *Félicité* [*Bliss*], a charming book that makes more palpable this intense happiness that I have in being and in simply pronouncing the words: "azure," "fountain," "greenery," "violet," etc.[409] In the evening I write the plan for a novel that could be a hymn to all our delightful existence. Will I write it one day?

Monday, May 20

"As if someone had swallowed a bit of this brilliant sun." There is only one spring in the year and one youth in life, oh! Marvelous rarity of springs in my youth; what song of gratitude all of my body wishes to sing, while it can only rush fervently into streets, extinguishing the sun that burns it and intends to make all the other souls blossom as promised.

Zaza came this morning; I went down with her to the Luxembourg Gardens and up to the quays of the Seine as I told her a bit about this joy that I cannot contain. This room is too small to hold it all. I used as a pretense the art exhibit at the Tuileries that I visited with Poupette and G. Dubois. Very few good paintings; the Matisse is awful, and a Marval looks like a good Matisse; some Séverini, some Japanese paintings, some Boschard, others whose names I've forgotten detain us a bit: discussions, amusing critiques, and as the man I could have been would have probably dreamed in vain, my pleasure at being the companion of these two radiant girls.[410]

Oh, my happiness and the smell of paint!

At les Invalides, there was the fair, the smell of fries, mussels, and crepes, cones of cream and pink ice, swings that fly to the sky, the sun that melts nougats, and the sun! For the first time in the year, without a coat, I feel its rays penetrating everywhere through my crepe de chine dress and meeting the burning hearth of my heart. Sudden meeting with Charlot Troussel; amusing expedition to his place, in an apartment with new, modern, and intelligent papers and cluttered with jazz instruments, and old furniture covered with dust. We are playing beloved tunes on an out-of-tune piano, "Rien que votre main, madame . . . [Only your hand, m'am]" "Chiquita," and "Constantinople" on a phonograph that doesn't work. Gégé is dancing; port, and pastries: through the window we see the Seine and some trees; we say thousands of silly things—simply to get relief from this almost troublesome joy that has nobody to give itself to. Then we go back up the boulevard St. Michel—how fun is life's freedom, its unexpectedness, the adventure that it bestows upon us each day, and the delightful uniformity of its beautiful days.*

I go up to Josée's—she is coming to dinner for I can no longer leave her once I am near her; I read the letter that she tore into pieces and that I picked out of her wastepaper basket. We go downstairs with great tenderness to take a walk in the night so blue among the massive green shapes made by the chestnut trees of the little Luxembourg Gardens until the hour designated for her return and beyond. I like what we talked about: Gandillac, Galois, Merleau-Ponty, Renée Boismond; especially Josée herself who tells me so curiously that she is only interested in human consciousness and at the same time so disinterested in her own consciousness. She analyzes herself with finesse and above all a bizarre disinterest that is one of her greatest intellectual charms. I try to show her to herself, who knows herself too well to savor her presence as I see it and savor it, like a very rare and very discreet perfume that is never tiresome. I leave her only to walk for two hours in Paris, the length of the shimmering Seine, and near the fountains at Carrousel that I contemplate at length, seated under a fresh breeze scented with greenery.

It's because I was so sweetly overwhelmed by the interminable chatting under the luminous leaves that gave me such a keen consciousness of myself, and of her and other loved ones; the consciousness of our youth looking for itself, romances experienced so near to me, thoughts affirmed, hearts that lose each other or themselves to rediscover each other or themselves even richer, and paths followed in the night without knowing if they rise to the dazzling certainty of the self—all of this spiritual reality existed more than the trees themselves with such a noble welcome; the hum of Montparnasse was alive around her; and beyond Montparnasse all of the earth where somewhere there is Jacques, and just beyond this, the endless sky.[411] All of this sensed together, and I who sense all of this.

With the refrain of "Chiquita" so deliciously murmured by Layton and Johnstone; with the face of Iris Storm tilted in her green felt hat, and the slow-footed silhouette of the Grand Meaulnes. With all the dear ones of the past; with these shimmering waters near me and behind me an entire day of sun; and ahead me all of life. With myself and my joy that I will never stop expressing.

---

* This whole paragraph is highlighted.

Tuesday, May 21

I work at home, beside the memory of yesterday, the expectation of the night and the pleasure of being there calmly. Jacques's face haunts me; such power of one man over me! But my joy goes beyond him.

And tonight is dinner on a stool from Knam with Miquel who talks to me about his *diplôme*, about Baruzi, about the dispute between Brunschvicg and G. Marcel, about a novel of Jules Romains, about a satirical tract against Bergson, about Savin, Canguilhem, Alain and his *Libres propos*, and about himself.[412] Marvelous impression of freedom. I meet him at eight o'clock at night, in response to his unexpected call, on the barely somber boulevard St. Michel; pleasure to find him so cordial, lively, always and bizarrely close and far at the same time, far in the immense difference of our inner lives and all that we never said to one another; close in our common interests and the direct frankness of our relationship; something so unrefined in him, so plebeian; he is for me like none of the others; much less my friend; much more, in the largest sense of the word, "my classmate." We go to the Européen; very funny program: la Huppa, delightfully spirited in her multiple outfits, and Nolad; at intermission we watch the actresses so transformed in their street clothes in the somber little street where one little bar is lit up; I intensely ponder the lives of these women sought by men who occasionally offer a nice greeting or a pretty smile; some women are elegant: perhaps deceptive fraternity of these groups gathered around Damia's car; oh, to be one of these women. It's already good to be with Miquel in the street watching them. What powerful ties marriage and things always done together must form when such a tenderness arises from the simple fact of being seated next to each other and smiling at each other between songs, sensitive to the same absurdities, happy to exist for one another.[413] The "Darquez" are charming dancers—and Damia, a very beautiful singer.*

We go down to the St. Lazare train station and have coffee while we wait for his train; we discuss individualism and the dangers of the social climber's attitude; we speak of Wilde and Stendhal. I have so much esteem for this boy! for his intransigence, his power of solitude, the strength that I sense in him, his manner of moving straight ahead without worrying about others. And when our eyes smile at each other as we say goodbye, how I love to feel the charm of this mismatched and yet so solid friendship; mismatched by

---

* This entire paragraph is highlighted in the left margin of the manuscript.

a difference of intellectual power, sentimental refinement, origin, and education, but founded on a common taste for life, for independence and for sincerity.

What a beautiful night that still was, and when I think back to all this youth I will always have tears in my eyes! Night troubled by what all of these songs from the café-concert always arouse in me of fantasy, imagination, and chatting.

Wednesday, May 22

I awaken in a bizarre dream that did not leave me all day: a very mean man who resembles Laporte, whom I love insanely, and who for me softens until the day when he becomes cruel again with a cruelty that I control by accepting it; impression above all of the extraordinary security that an absolute love provides.*

I didn't sleep much, I don't eat well at lunch after leaving Robin's place, there is too much sunlight, and at the Bibliothèque Nationale I am riddled with a pain that I thought was dead and that at moments irreparably overwhelms me. With the book *Moravagine* by Cendrars I struggle against the vision of the Stryx, Riquet, Magda, and the words that they said.†[414] Fortunately along comes Gandillac who sits down (for the first time) next to me. We work side by side exchanging words on love, life, ourselves above all, and our past. Pleasure of finding a stickler for inner analysis who is intellectually interested in the least nuances in feeling; pleasure of this new face-to-face freedom, this absolute trust, and being sure of the sympathy of this man whose strengths outweigh his weaknesses. Incredibly great tenderness and esteem. I sense that he is so attentive to me, so ready to respond to any call, in order to avoid ever failing me. How can I put into words this sweetness in me, these tears that slide between his smiling face and my eyes, the impression of a physical contact like that of my hand on his shoulder or of him carrying me across a muddy path.

How I will have loved you, men, my brothers!

I go back through the already dusty Luxembourg Gardens, and I finish *Moravagine*. Tonight I am rereading *L'épithalame* [Wedding song].[415] Merleau-Ponty came by for an hour. At night on these days so free and open to all beings, when I feel so strong and independent, and very supported in a

---

* This entire paragraph is highlighted with pencil marks before and after it in the manuscript.

† From the beginning of this paragraph through "said" is highlighted in the right margin of the manuscript.

fine solitude, a fatigue sometimes very gently grabs hold of me—a desire, not overwhelming, but intense for a refuge, a sharing, a protected heart [*coeur clos*]—a desire for security, for what's definitive; not for a love, but for a marriage, for this infinitely solid and infinitely restful union, for this consensual resignation that is only a new strength. Without closing out anything, without losing any of the charm of adventurous detours, knowing the calm certainty of a safe haven. Woman's submission in the presence of man—only this is so banal: with two loving and strong arms. The sole repose, says Claudel, is to go where one can literally no longer leave. I believe that the only place that one can no longer leave is the prison of these two arms that hold you against the beating of another heart. For the first time, desire for this embrace that would be nothing like a caress but that would transfer into a bodily gesture the protecting and tender promise of the soul; like when Papa has tears in his eyes for Uncle Gaston and Grandfather. Leaving between my forehead and this shoulder only the roughness of the sheet.*

Monday, May 23

Robin's class—excitement because Maheu is perhaps there, behind me, and could lean over to say hello to me . . . but no, I have to make do with very kind Gandillac who walks me through the halls of Normale, with the beautiful fountain, with the good breeze in the courtyard, and with this insolent swelling of my joy while I joke with Hippolyte and Gandillac as G. Lévy in a pink dress angrily condemns me. The Luxembourg Gardens welcome me for two hours; the purple beech tree and the lawns while I read a satirical tract against Bergson.[416] Some young people pass by—a group of very young adolescent girls in summer dresses settles in with notebooks and laughter very close to me, in these beautiful English gardens where I am telling myself stories, sometimes reading, sometimes dreaming, with, as often this year, the fear that my peaceful happiness without name or cause will be wrenched away from me.

Maheu is there in the hallway, seated on the windowsill next to *Sartre*; he stands up with his great gesture of an apparent clumsiness and greets me with a hello that I cut short when I sense his sympathy-laden curiosity about my mourning clothes.† Must I admit to myself that I much desired to see

---

* These last two paragraphs are highlighted.

† Both "Maheu" and "Sartre" are underlined in the manuscript in a darker blackish ink than the rest of the manuscript.

him again? Now he is wearing a very light-colored summer suit with a beige and red tie. I sit down near Josée. He is somewhere behind me with Sartre.

Josée takes me in this intense heat to the Luxembourg Gardens where we buy ice cream from a little cart. We drink lemon-lime soda on green iron tables and chairs, almost without saying a word, vaguely lulled by the passing people and the heat that radiates from all things. We climb back up to her stifling room. I stretch out on the bed; I listen to my breath exuding my joy at existing—through the window a white terrace brings to mind Algeria which would be a less somber blue; the water from two faucets speaks of the countryside and chants the vague passage of time.* Josée put on a starched delicate linen nightgown, long with pink bouquets; stretched out on a chair, with a flower between her teeth, she is simply exquisite. On the table there is a large bouquet of pink and white hawthorns whose flowers we chew while exchanging rare words. I know that she is suffering, but I myself am too happy; too happy to see her like this, perfect and desirable like a very young woman whose husband would teach her to smile, happy with flowers, with the intense heat, and with believing ourselves transported into interstellar space, with our heads a bit fuzzy, to the song of the water that flows into our wide-awake dream.

We walk in the sun on boulevard St. Michel; at night I go home to read *Les rois aveugles* [*Blinded Kings*] by Kessel—remember today, think of tomorrow.[417]

Friday, May 24

Gandillac brings me his "Story of no interest." The title is accurate—literary platitude and essay from someone intelligent enough to substitute cerebral complications for a sentimental reality for which he does not possess the least rudiments. I don't know anybody whose sensitivity is so dull.† Yet I like him, we have a short discussion while I accompany him up to Palais Royal, about painting above all.

And then on the way back, what a delightful pleasure? Here comes *Maheu* who takes me for coffee "on the condition that I will pay since he has only one franc left in his pocket, having now lent too much money just as in the past he used to borrow too much." And we go to rue St. Marc to the bar Pocardi. As I walk I speak of Uzerche from where I would

---

* From "I stretch out" through "passage of time" is highlighted in the left margin of the manuscript.

† From the beginning of this entry through "dull" is highlighted in the manuscript.

have wanted to send him a postcard, and of Grandfather. "I thought," he said, "that you were in the country, and then I saw you dressed in mourning . . ." I am astonished that he thought of me. He also tells me that the other Monday he saw me at Luxembourg Gardens and wanted to invite me along with Sartre but that I was so buried in my meditations that he didn't dare, for even if he doesn't respect "the ruminations of Boivin," he would not dare to interrupt me when I am deep in thought. He said this with a sincere respect and without irony. Our disappointments are closely akin to one another over these last ten days when without admitting it to myself I was hurt to believe that he was so far away and that with Sartre he must be looking at me as a stranger; whereas he wanted to introduce Sartre to me and to give me a charming drawing from the latter that he had dedicated to me.*

How silly I am! Why believe in the slightly hostile indifference of people—even when they are full of solicitude and smiling welcome for me? But also what sweetness each time to see this phantom of defiance evaporate and to become aware that I am installed in the bosom of a friendship that I don't dare by far even hope to approach.

We speak of his lecture from the other day, of what he wants to write against Lalande, of our chances for the exam; he says some very funny things like always. What a pity to go home to work! During the trip back he tells me the stories that they are crafting about all the people at the Sorbonne, and about me; Merleau-Ponty has an unrequited love for me, but my father wants me to marry a country cousin . . . Such nice companionship, such a secure friendship, such a novel feeling of ease.

And if, after looking at Nizan's drawings of "Leibniz bathing with the monads," I remain lost in laughter and daydreams for nearly three hours instead of studying Kant, doesn't it mean that I am beginning to like you a bit too much, René Maheu? He tells me to accompany him to his student's home and takes a detour so that it takes longer.

"So what are you thinking about?" Zaza says to me when she comes to get me at five thirty—wonderful mischief [belle malice]. But it's good to end this hot day seated near Zaza in the Tuileries.

After dinner, I go to Germaine Dulac's lecture on the cinema to which Josée invited me; very beautiful parts of *Napoléon* are shown.[418] The night is divine.

---

* From "over these ten days" through "dedicated to me" is highlighted in the margin of the manuscript.

Saturday, May 25

"What I admire is that you never deprive yourself of anything," Josée told me. It's true; it's truer than ever, and by trusting in each of life's promises I so often receive such an immense recompense! And Galois who told me the other day that "life" is a word and novelty a myth! Will I ever weary of myself? Will I ever stop marveling at the wealth of every single day?

I gave Gandillac back his essay, without hiding my lack of enthusiasm; he was, moreover, very nice. But already, I don't care, since the other one is there who is going to ask me, "Are you coming to lunch?" And we go have lunch in the rue des Petits-Champs in the dining area of the bakery, seated next to one another just like the other day. He says to me, "Admit that if someone asked you the theory of complex numbers or that of derivatives . . ." and I respond, "I did general math." How his surprise amuses me! Is vanity this pleasure that I feel when, recounting these past four years to him, I hear him tell me, "It's incredible! I admire you, you know, I admire you; I never saw a woman like you—I will say so to Sartre." This touches me because it is not due to my exams, but rather to what I knew how to remain despite them. He speaks to me of the first time that he saw me, "I told my friends that I had seen a very nice young girl . . .," and tells me that he wants to introduce his wife to me, and speaks to me humorously and kindly of her. He tells me of his current life, of what he will do, of me, that I must get married, of what he would say to Papa if he saw him, "that we are friends." He finds me happier than when he began to know me: probably less work, the springtime, and perhaps him.

We enter "an historic place," which is to say the garden of Palais Royal. Speaking of what we will write later he says to me, "although for novels, one has to have genius"—thereupon I ask him his opinion of *Le grand Meaulnes*, and the depth of his admiration overwhelms me because I hadn't dared to expect it; doubly overwhelmed: like a homage to Jacques when he says with such true emotion, "It is incredible for a man to have written this; no, he's not a man—there are some enviable beings." I feel these words with such fervor, "If it is sometimes difficult to believe in you, it's because you are not a man either, it's because a thing does not cease to be because the reasons for it escape us and because if you attract attention like this, such charm must be recognized although the secret slips away"—since *Maheu* himself recognizes values stronger than any value that one dared to hope in speaking of one's self and one's friends, it is good that without being duped I can sense in you, Jacques, this "enviable" being who obligates one to extend the idea of man all the way to the heavens—these words, Jacques, I said them and say them again with such an ardent and wonderful peace!*[419]

And then for five long minutes I was overwhelmed to see the one who always speaks, silent; the one who is always gay, pensive; the one who always wants to be unemotional, moved. He was looking into himself with a hint of turmoil that he stifled with words although they betrayed a regret for which I loved him like I have never done before. "At heart I am much more intellectual than you; however, due to my origins, I recognize in myself the same sensibility, that I didn't want . . ." He makes a comparison to Barrès—he also speaks of English novels, *The Constant Nymph* where Lewis and Tess are admirable "Eugenes" as opposed to the "Mortimer" Florence, *The Mill on the Floss* whose Maggie Tulliver he loved for a year.[420] Passage on the supernatural in *Le grand Meaulnes*; he clarifies this for me too—I myself speak to him of the rarity of integrating a feeling into one's life like this. He remains pensive.

In the evening at six I meet Merleau-Ponty, and we have a discussion in the Luxembourg Gardens.

Sunday, May 26

What is this strange and banal feeling, this soft inner glow that makes the clarity of spring obscure and uncertain, this joy of having seen . . . this desire of seeing again . . . this marvelous exhaustion? What is this dialogue between me and a certain silence in the garden of Palais Royal that has continued indefinitely since yesterday? What is this desire to speak and to listen, this silent delight, and sometimes extremely brief and extremely rapid waves of tenderness, brief and rapid like one's very emotions, but coming out of this profound place in the heart which enjoys being thus scrutinized? This above all: that surrounding every idea, every event, and every fantasy arises a joyful desire to tell him, a desire that prolongs indefinitely and softly illuminates—what I will tell him. That every interest wishes to come through him—and that everything that comes through him is a source of interest.

But what then is love if now it's the same emotion that three years ago put the rare silhouette of Jacques in my heart? I recognize tomorrows that were tempered with certitude and appeased from not expecting anything else, tomorrows that were also the eves of another day, the vague melancholia in a happy soul, the anxious happiness, and the anxiety full of abandon.

---

* "Maheu" is underlined in black ink in the manuscript.

Between this and love, what is the difference, if my heart also skips a beat, and I stammer at Maheu's approach? If it's a similar distress once his voice has died and we are working side by side but already turned towards our departure? And if today I feel within me the possibility of suffering similar to those that made me wander the streets of Paris aimlessly to escape a hopeless boredom?

No, what links me to Jacques is something quite other than love—for this could also be called love—question of vocabulary perhaps. Oh! Certainly when he says, "I love my wife," his joy passes through me; but it is also certain, if he turned away from me in indifference, I could suffer, beyond perhaps even my consent.

I could suffer. I don't know how important this is . . . I know that there are some tears and that I write these lines to remember, I know that I would always want to see him. I know that at this moment, for him I would sacrifice every other presence.

How beautiful life is—how strong, safe, rich, and happy I feel! How good it is to work in my room, with the shutters closed, in the same atmosphere as on the night before an exam when I was 16, surrounded in this retreat by all the beings that I didn't suspect at age 16 and by my soul that did not yet have to expend itself with such restrained prodigality. (See what I wrote about him on April 18)

Moreover, instead of working I have just spent a long moment writing the story of these past days, and remembering, until happiness and tears prevent me from continuing. Merleau-Ponty yesterday, with his charming shyness, reproached me for the words "let's be happy" in the last letter that I wrote to him and reminded me that two years ago I asked him to put me on my guard against happiness. Dear, dear Maurice—how good it is to know that you are there, vigilant, loving, discreet, and attentive, my conscience. How to respond? I was right then; I am right today. It was important that this overly serious love would not annihilate me and would allow me the free reign of my thought. The content of my thought might have changed, but my freedom is intact; there is nothing to which I cannot give myself as if I were not already entirely captivated. You appeared pensive; you did not really understand when I said that it was difficult to establish a happy life, but I want such a lively happiness, every day new and boldly passionate; never sleeping is not so simple, nor is never being disappointed if one is always awake.

To give oneself, to keep oneself, wasn't that the admirable equilibrium that I proposed to myself and that I have attained today? I want to love like this forever, one man alone, and everybody. I want to love myself like this forever, in one man alone, in everybody, and in the sun that needs only me to intoxicate me. I want to write a book where I will express this love such that other men will be obligated to feel it with me.

Oh! I will have a wonderful destiny! I have already acted so much, learned so much, and burned so much during these past four years!*

If one day is beautiful, yet another is even more beautiful; I will not cry over yesterday if yesterday surpassed other days that I had lamented.

This is stupid—this is fun. Little Yvette, my goddaughter, a blond child charms this funny hollow in me.[421] And I had to flee in the heat to the Luxembourg Gardens, and for the presence of anyone, had to look for Marie-Louise with whom I walk on the quays up to the Jardin des Plantes. This evening I have just read the captivating *Tournant dangereux* [*Dangerous Corner*] by Vlaminck.[422] It's useless to count on a tomorrow that today knows nothing about. How much younger it makes me, this joy full of turmoil, this agitation full of tenderness, this emptiness outstretched towards plenitude ... an exact analysis is impossible that would reduce to precise desires or regrets the changing nuance of today. I will lend him *Le feutre vert* [*The Green Hat*] tomorrow. Iris Storm also dearly loved men, and yet never loved anyone but Napier.[423]

Monday, May 27

As in the times that preceded the baccalaureate exam! This haste is still rather calm in the closed room, where despite the shutters, all of summer is perceptible.

Classes at the Sorbonne: once again saw Mademoiselle Richard to whom I am quite indifferent and for whom I am not; Gandillac, and *Maheu* to whom I lend Iris Storm (with such childish joy a little while ago I recovered and glued the book that he was going to hold in his hands).† But I am pleased that Zaza comes to get me although he is in the courtyard alone and available; we take a seat in the Luxembourg Gardens; we speak of the novel that she would like to write, of the difficulties of a first work. I go home vaguely hoping on the boulevard St. Michel where with Zaza we crossed paths with him ... but no. And once again in my room, this hesitation between joy and sadness—joy of having met as he dangled the book in his

---

* From "I want to love" through "four years" is highlighted in the right margin.

† In Beauvoir's handwritten manuscript, "Maheu" is underlined in black ink; the writing is in blue.

fingers, uncertain about the place where he was going to read it, regretting that he couldn't invite me to have a snack, and bored to distraction. Joy that at this minute he is reading a book that I lent him . . . and sadness to be so powerless before him that I can't desire anything, not even his presence; I have nothing to say to him and nothing can happen between us other than by words. I myself don't know what is this desire whose unaccomplishment leaves me full of ennui. This silhouette on boulevard St. Michel . . . I would cry for it. I don't know what it is. It's nothing.

Tuesday, May 28

At the great risk of the *agrégation* . . . but what does it matter? For one more time I can review the complicated, minutely detailed, and lengthy texture of joys and pains of the mysteriously blossoming heart.

This morning Bouglé's class at Normale; Borne gives a lecture with his hands, around a table (we visited the center of social documentation) where we look like students of the former Cours Desir at the end of the year; the fountain spurts all the way to Gandillac and me when we sat down on a green bench in the courtyard to look at the Davos's periodical with the life-like portrait of Brunschvicg. Rivaud's class.

Arrival at the Bibliothèque Nationale, sad arrival, alone with Hume and a fatigue that coffee fights off. At three o'clock I am about to resign myself to no longer expecting anybody. Along comes Gandillac who talks to me about Aron's *diplôme* and when I leave with him at five thirty, I find Merleau-Ponty at the door and then chat with both of them until closing. Later, along comes Josée, and I go back with her. We take a seat at Deux Magots to drink some lemon-lime soda, then I accompany her home and come back through the Luxembourg Gardens where due to this stormy weather it's cooler. She shows me a beautiful passage by Valéry on love, an admirable passage that I would like to find again.*

Before her, along comes the one whom I no longer dared to expect—he is in gray today because he has just come back from a marriage. We go towards Palais Royal, he tells me, "Ever since I've known you I understand Berkeley who was a philosopher at 18 and Evariste Galois . . . I have less affection for you since I found out that you did general math: I admire you too much, it kills me." So I invited him with his wife to the afternoon snack. He clarifies, "What is charming about you is that you walk so quickly: one would say that

---

* This entire paragraph is highlighted in pencil in the manuscript.

you are going somewhere." He expounds on political economics theories, shows me some scraps of paper, vestiges of his trip in Italy; tells me that he is very pleased with *The Green Hat*. He jokes with me about my horrible writing and the scribbling that I put by way of a title on *The Green Hat*. Will I ever be able to tell this boy how much I love him? Ah! During vacation I will try.

"Affection for me . . . what's charming about me . . ." He has the same look of savoring me that Jacques sometimes had, but with more tenderness. I sense that I am, with him as with Jacques, the same light-hearted and witty self, and that it is for nearly the same reasons that they both love me, with the same charmed surprise. (These two words are stupid but they depict so well the difference between them and Merleau-Ponty, Zaza and the others who are more full of admiration than surprise, more attentive than charmed.) How I like to be loved in this way for reasons that even I don't know, for what is most unconscious, most truly my own in me: for all the little things . . . Oh! As we cross the street his hand nudges my shoulder to avoid a car . . . Oh, as he tells me good-bye his hand brushes the top of my chest: I would have stayed in this armchair for an hour to keep intact the sweetness of this gesture and of the smile that went with it. Do I write this because I don't believe it or to make myself believe that I don't believe it? Little risk in any case: a few months' peace. Never could he have been Napier for me—rather big risk that every evening might be the eve of an unknown surprise for my heart. What a love life I could count on, if only I did not love Jacques beyond love.

Now I understand loves full of esteem and tenderness that maintain almost a hostile pride and a refusal to be spoken, he might be the man in whose presence one would torture oneself to keep him unaware of being more than a good classmate. Nothing similar with Merleau-Ponty or Gandillac, supposing that one could love them in this way; nor with Galois, nor with Jacques.

I understand how in love the outcome of the affair depends upon the man; if he conquers the woman slowly, or if he doesn't conquer her, it is his fault: clumsiness or appetite for the most difficult of games. The basic rule is to avoid arriving at the perfect harmony of souls *before* having conquered the heart that one attacks: to leave it as a promise, the spoils to conquer, once one has followed love's royal path.* If I were a man I would bring the

---

* In Simone de Beauvoir's handwritten manuscript, the French equivalent of "before" is highlighted.

woman to the threshold of friendship, just to the point of interest and trust that alone permits something to be established; I would bring her there simply by speaking of myself without detour and of the world as I see it: then I would tell her about herself; then still unknown and full of promise, I would do her the homage of loving her with everything that she could suppose was wonderful in me; and when she would later become aware that all of it wasn't there, she would still believe in it because of the intoxication she felt in believing in it.

Men are not aware enough of how ready a woman is to be taken—how it only takes a sudden attack, a surprise, and the certainty of not being rejected (or at least the appearance of that certainty). Perhaps it is the sole authority of some familiar gestures that made a much greater impression on me with a single blow than the submissive thoughtfulness of Merleau-Ponty. What is more beautiful, friendship or love? This pounding heart or this restful smile? Being the one watched and waited for or the one taken for granted? Nothing here but what is lofty and honest; but the joy and the fever, and the pride to burn more ardently than another.

Maheu or Merleau-Ponty. Truly between these two feelings I cannot choose. And as every hesitation proves that the two parties are insufficient . . . Every analysis brings me back to an endless marvel at what depends on no circumstance and cannot be captured with any word.

Wednesday, May 29

This morning I feel no excitement when I see *Maheu*: he is seated on the windowsill; I on the table; then along come Gandillac, Boivin, Ducassé, Hippolyte, and Savin . . . gaiety and relaxation.* His face closes up, and with an admirable scorn he watches all of this—that is not his. Fun in Laporte and Robin's classes between him and Gandillac. Fun to be so calmly happy near him and to burst out laughing several times at the risk of seeing heads turn, in front of the facial expression of the crazy guy who asks if I am Mademoiselle de Beauvoir. "I thought you were a good student," he tells me. O my heart is overflowing, in the hallway where we are so light-hearted, and the relaxed classroom like in the old Cours Desir at the end of the year. Goodbye without sadness or desire; enough for today. Enough to go work at the Bibliothèque Nationale where I meet Gandillac, whom I accompany to Palais Royal, and to go home to work in peace.

---

* In Simone de Beauvoir's handwritten manuscript, *"Maheu"* is underlined.

Thursday, May 30

Robin's class. He isn't there. Mademoiselle Renaud is pontificating; Mademoiselle Richard is kinder than I would like; we wander in the garden's sunlight, watching tennis being played. Burnouf is climbing a rope. A sensational life is devouring me—this sun, this black dress that suits me so well, the consciousness of my body—two splendid hours on the terrace of the Luxembourg Gardens: the calm ornamental lake, where water flows into uniform metallic ripples, the pure and brilliant sky, passers-by, and the green and red trees; and myself.

I feel good between Josée and Gandillac; it doesn't matter that Maheu is not in this class. The steps of the stairwell extend into the sunlight that roasts my neck while students walk up and down it as if to intensify my feelings about my personal life; Josée says exquisite things. "What do you prefer about yourself?" she asks me. "Someone else . . ." "For me, you see," she tells me with her look of savoring a rare liqueur, "it's the exit door." For myself, I choose the entrance door. When interviewed, Gandillac declares, "my rare silences." How kindly she said with the look of a mischievous child who is exaggerating a very slight chagrin: "Oh, I am so unhappy!—why? Well, always the same thing," laughing with her eyes as if to reproach herself. We talk about K. Mansfield's *Bliss*, of *L'épithalame* that she finds too devoid of poetry.

Savin is giving a lecture on optimism; unintentionally funny; priceless reply from Brunschvicg; immense tenderness for his intelligent eyes, his fine, unexpected, witty, and so very exact speech that one could scream in delight to see him make such an astute comment; quivers of laughter that shake the entire class; for two hours pleasure of the rarest quality and keen consciousness of this pleasure.

At the hairdresser I have the leisure to repeat to myself eyes closed and numb with happiness: such a rich and perpetually renewed life; life of presences, peopled with words never heard, faces never seen, and words that can always be heard, and faces that could always be seen . . . Big plans: next year to move into *a place of my own*, in Grandmother's apartment; to receive visitors, write, earn money, and go out. What more beautiful undertaking is there than this destiny that I am fulfilling? Such certainty of no longer knowing emptiness! (Or does this certainty come only from my new love?)

I expound on my plans at home—they are very well received. My future life is taking shape. To think that I could have doubted you, my life; asked for something other than you, dear self . . .

Friday, May 31—Crossroads of Faces

What an incredible day! And in writing this what an overwhelming desire to cry—what an overwhelming happiness!

Nine o'clock. As I write a title on a report, I catch sight of a beige suit, a neck with thick blond hair like beards of wheat: contraction of my fearful heart (why always afraid and wanting to escape?). I take my seat: his things are set at the place next to it—two minutes later he is there. He starts to tell me about eugenic cosmology: the world is divided into Eugenes—Marrhanes—Mortimers—and Grand Dukes. The latter, associated with the earthy women [*femmes humeuses*] are the most awful enemies of the Eugenes. There is also a distinction between the Bardannes from the sensitive world and those from the intelligible world (R. Château) and a type of chameleon genus.

The Eugene was twelve years old the year of the Catalanic Fields . . . his parents sent him to harvest snails . . . his love affairs with the soul of the world and the enigmatic Rada Siva. They are going to write a book to tell about all of this.

Maheu! his deadpan look and his big smile while he reveals all this to me.* He also talks to me about *The Green Hat*. Then we start to work; I think only: here is a man that I like immensely and he is here; he is in the minute and the square meter that I am now living; he is here and knows that I am near him . . . I caught sight of the bespectacled face of Daniel Galois—emotion. I feel that my heart is divided, but the present is the stronger, and without regret I think: Galois is at the table behind me and sees me laughing with Maheu, whom he doesn't like; and I will have nothing from Galois today; but Maheu is near me.

Then along comes Gandillac, who sits down across from me; my pleasure is intense and this encounter so amusing! When I pass a funny passage from my book (by Charles Blondel: *Introduction à la psychologie sociale* [Introduction to Social Psychology]) to Maheu, Gandillac comes to put his head between us.[424] With a serious look, he asks me what I think of Brochard's affirmation: that Aristotle's God experiences pleasure. And Maheu, disdainful and cold, "I hope so for him." This depicts them. At another moment, when we are speaking of "the dignity of man," G. says to me, "and of woman also," and I reply, "Women don't have any dignity." My neighbor laughs and approves, the person opposite me is astonished with this slightly naïve interest that makes him

---

* In Simone de Beauvoir's handwritten notebook, "Maheu" is underlined.

very dear; between the two of them I evade the issue, feeling between M. and myself this wordless harmony, an intoxication that only Jacques had made me experience, but desiring not to frighten G. with this changed expression that I know I have. Indeed, for an hour I manage to maintain on our three faces of *agrégation* candidates a happy blossoming that is the profusion of the one that I carry within myself; exquisite morning.

Here is *Eveski* (Bandi) who bothers me twice to ask me to read his thesis on melodrama, and if one can put the word "gigolo" in the preface to a thesis.* I tell that to G. who doubles up with laughter. Here comes *Galois* to shake my hand upon leaving; G. leaves too; but he, dear accomplice, stays beside me.† He tells me that he knows Stépha and does not like her because she made eyes at him.

We go to lunch, on the rue des Petits Champs as usual, then take a seat at Palais-Royal, then have coffee chez Pocardi on the insolent pretext that when I haven't had coffee, I don't work, I get agitated and keep him from working. It is impossible to describe how deeply the words that he said to me during these two hours affected me. (My God! Is it possible to be happy to this degree without deserving to die?)

He says to me: "There are people who pounce on you at this library: it's unheard-of; the Hungarian comes twice to take you away, Gandillac, even Évariste . . . I am the first, moreover—you are so kind . . ." (We were seated side by side in front of the little black table, with our backs to the wall—his smile was adorned with a perceptible grace that is almost never seen in him, as if with an esteem that does not decline as it grows more tender, and he said, "you are so kind,"—such simple words that touched my heart because their tone responded so to everything desirous of goodness, of welcome, and yes, of kindness that I sense within me) . . . he said laughing, "you are the prey of a gang." He detests Galois, accepts Merleau-Ponty, as for Gandillac, he recognizes "that he becomes so kind when he speaks to me that he is much more likeable," and this too causes me great happiness, since I so desired to be the magic wand that reveals hidden resources to hasty passers-by, to be this tenderness so obstinate and so tranquil that it obliges all souls to yield to it what they sometimes do not know they possess themselves. Ah, let me love myself this evening, love myself through another and him in me. He talks to me of G. Lévy with so much partiality for me . . . then he tells me: "Besides, our relationship is strange

---

* In Simone de Beauvoir's handwritten diary entry, "Eveski" is underlined.
† In Simone de Beauvoir's handwritten diary entry, "Galois" is underlined.

... at least for me: I never had a friendship with a woman." I reply, "This is perhaps because I am not very womanly." Oh! such a look in response; such a look that I can compare only to the one that Jacques had one day ... and then he laughs as he tells me that to be as entirely welcoming as I am is astonishing: "It is what made our friendship possible," he says to me. I explain to him that I feel like, "a wide open door," and he says that this manner that I have of being open "is what is most surprising in me and so attractive." We speak of Iris Storm, of Violante, of women ... "I don't like easy women: it is not a question of morality, even Iris Storm does not endure contact with men without risk of punishment,"—and also "I cannot admire a woman, above all a woman that I have had ..." to which I retort, "that one does not *have* an Iris Storm." As he said watching me, "I so like it when a woman pleases me ..."—delicious consciousness when I am beside him of having no need to justify, of pleasing him, like Jacques, with what is the most myself, for which I am not responsible. I adore when from time to time he spontaneously responds to a word from me (which is always one of the truest of my heart), "Ah, you are charming!", as one would say thanks for a great pleasure, as one would take someone's hand in a moment of emotion, as one would smile in tenderness. I told him that I knew a Eugene very well, that I would introduce him to him next year, "Oh, yes! I will see you next year," he said with conviction. I add that he is "a soldier" with an ironic emphasis that much amuses him. We speak of the relationship between the earthy woman and Eugene and he gives me the responsibility of writing the chapter on earthy women in his book, "They are the ones who have a destiny. You have a destiny." Truly, to make allies of the Grand Dukes against the Eugenes is very profound: to love a Grand Duke would have been happiness and servitude for me; to love a Eugene is to struggle against him and create an admirable conflict; "The Eugene resists ..." he explains to me. "So I noticed!" I exclaimed. That's when he cried out, "Ah, you are charming!"

I really feel that I am not one of his dear classmates; but he sees that I am pretty today, and lively and animated and have a completely feminine grace; but without the coquetry that he detests. Neither a man, nor a female; an appearance of a total gift in which he senses a more secret reserve, an ease that is not at all facility; a lively and unequivocal affection—I feel that he likes me a lot.

And maybe there passes through him, something like regret for not having demanded more from life when there are woman such as me ... maybe; I say this because of a wave of melancholy when he declares that the Eugene is not happy, that insensitivity is an ideal that he doesn't attain. How well he understands the gift of life and what a marvel it is to be in the garden where water gently sprinkles us from one of the branches of the big fountain flourishing in the middle of the basins. We return to the Eugenes and to the books that we will write. Sweet pleasure of letting him buy me coffee as he bought it at lunch with such kind authority; sweet pleasure that it is already a habit to carry our cups out to the little coffee table, near the cashier who glares at us. We construct whimsical philosophical arguments: I say, "What a pity that God does not exist." "Yes, especially for him." We distinguish between three manners of swimming: like fish (Eugenes), in infinity (Marrhanes), in the sea (Mortimers). I make pertinent modifications to the eugenic cosmology. We say thousands of other things that seem to me to be entirely unforeseen, astute, and delicious. I am happy . . .

For an hour this happiness overflows; I am as though slightly intoxicated, shaken by the giggles while I read *L'auto* that I snitched from him. He tells me, "You are totally crazy," with a look of profound amusement, but astonished by such exuberance; he gives me a drawing and a hilarious article from *L'auto* as a present.

He says, "You are crystallizing the mystery."

Zaza comes to get me. "I am finally going to be able to work," he says to me mockingly, as he mocks my "ridiculous handwriting," but I well know that he is going to think about me at least as much as he will work. What a beautiful day! We walk along the quays. *Zaza* looks at me and listens to me, surprised by my exuberance.* We drink cold things at Evelynes while talking of the École Normale, Maheu, and the choice place that my position as a woman makes for me in the midst of these masculine rivalries.

I arrive at the Sorbonne, with my head empty from being so full, to meet *Miquel*.† We make our way to the Luxembourg Gardens; he lends me his *diplôme*; the lawn is green, green, and the fountain sunny; there are mauve irises and yellow irises, a red tree, and a cool shade. He tells me about the novels that he wants to write, and thus brings to life numerous adventures that he has witnessed. Together we speak passionately of the novelty of days, the riches lavished upon those who know how to come out of themselves to get them, of my hesitations of two years ago, of our trust and our faith in the world: if I support it, it will support me in return. People are playing tennis, and the evening is calm and grave. And I, a bit intoxicated from the day.

---

* In Beauvoir's handwritten diary entry, "Zaza" is underlined.
† In Beauvoir's handwritten diary entry, "Miquel" is underlined.

So I have to go out. How nice the night is! With great tenderness, we go, *Poupette* and I, along the caressing streets. I tell her about my day, we make plans for the future; we are filled with a strength, a certainty of success, and the passion for the present.* Banks of the Seine . . . calm waters where somber silver reflections sway; silent sky over our heads; white design of the bridge accentuated by the night; passage of silhouettes full of mystery in this landscape beyond life. The grand avenues are deserted, inhabited only by trees. The black veils in front of our eyes transform them into gods from German legends. Congested avenue, bars near l'Étoile, and at the end of the night our happy fatigue. What a joyous return, what happy sleep . . . †

Hands vainly gripped to keep such treasures; grasp that allows them to flee only drop by drop. My heart is bursting, split like an overly ripened fruit: what lands will be nourished by this golden pulp?

Do other beings know within themselves such a song of victory? Do they know themselves in this way beyond events, in a unique joy, and conspiring with all the pleasures of the world?

Living inside oneself; living inside a dear stranger—and uniting them in a single and endless affection.

Saturday, June 1

Is the day after a day when one was so happy a sad day? Not if yesterday is only deliciously prolonged in today; not if chair 283 is not empty, but rather where he was seated yesterday; not if I am not alone eating ice cream and brioches for lunch at chez Pocardi, but if I see Lama's silhouette once again.

Gandillac is here this morning; we speak little but amicably; I tell him about my plans for next year; I accompany him to Palais Royal while he talks away about the Russian mentality. In the afternoon, along comes *Josée*; we are going to walk around in the public gardens: inevitably I tell her about Maheu, about what he said to me.‡ She says, "It's true that all your doors are open; that's why people enter your life [*chez vous*] so frequently. I, in contrast, am always out and I take everything with me. What gave me the idea to enter your life one day? Or perhaps, it was you who had the idea of waiting. It's true that one could think, when the owner is gone, that he will come back any minute, but here's the rub, people don't usually

---

* In Beauvoir's handwritten diary entry, "Poupette" is underlined.

† From "I arrive at the Sorbonne" through "happy sleep" is highlighted in the margin of the manuscript.

‡ In Simone de Beauvoir's handwritten diary, "Josée" is underlined.

think this." We do Greek side by side all day long; or rather I watch myself dreaming with the desire to shout how passionate, fun, and interesting it is to exist.

Certain spiritual consciousnesses are more indiscreet than a physical gesture. We come back along the quays, on a marvelous evening; we leaf through some books at Monnier's bookstore. Then we go take a seat near the ornamental pond of the Luxembourg Gardens; smell of water, gravity in our hearts. She is afraid of this tomorrow from which I expect a superhuman destiny. She asks me why we like a book for making us think of a real landscape, and the real for reminding us of books. But it seems to me that this landscape is the memory of a future, of a dream lived elsewhere by purer beings, and not only the illustration of a written work that we would have liked.

We catch sight of *Nizan*, his wife, and his son—bizarre impression—refusal of marriage enslavement: great material freedom really makes the exigency of the heart's affiliations easier to feel.*

I leave her at her home, I walk on these paths carrying a marvelous feeling of weakness within me, without regret, without desire, a bit weary of this debauchery of sun and happiness, but with a dear lassitude that is nothing like a despondency.

In the evening, I settle in here with some work on my table, some books, next to the writing desk where more than three years of my life are sleeping.

I let myself trace my happiness, at the heart of my friendships and my solitude. Effort to hold onto words and smiles that are already dying out, but so what, this instant against my lips consoles me for all the delicious dreams that fall one by one behind me, lost.

And then suddenly all of that is nothing. Head prostrate on the table, a deadly desire for Jacques. The encounter of Jacques's smile with heartrending precision, a violence of love that throws me out of this room and out of my life against a past that is too dear for me to dare even to hope for a future. Tenderness . . . is really something else, something different than anything. Trust, sweetness, but what words can I say? Nothing but a name: Jacques.

With this abrupt silence in my soul, the passion of this sweetness that settles in me to tear me away from myself, with a stifling scream from not being understood, and a plenitude that takes away all meaning in the name of happiness.

---

* In Beauvoir's handwritten diary entry, "Nizan" is underlined and this paragraph is highlighted in the margin of the manuscript.

No, I cannot imagine seeing him again; it would be too much . . . Trembling with all the unhoped-for joys and the promised suffering . . .

In the midst of my free life, exalted and powerful, the passage of this terrible master, in the hands of whom I am such a little girl, who dismisses my life with the back of my hand and turns toward him alone my frightened face, my fulfilled face.[425] The passing of love. Same gravity, same stopping of my overwhelmed heart as at the passing of death, but with death nothing in me is complicit. Love has me entirely in its power as soon as it appears, silent; and it takes everything without asking for anything.

Half-past midnight . . . But sleep when the night behind me is so sweet, sweet as my bare arms and the gliding of crepe de chine on my shoulders, sweet as the contemplation of self.

A book by Rilke on Rodin, a tale by Giroudoux on the table, L'ordre [The order] by Arland that I just finished; emotional about the mediocre drama that he describes, certitude of having surpassed this and of being happy without being one of the awful herd.[426]

On this eve is there no other God to thank than myself? Grace of this world; grace of myself. Ah! How good are all things . . .

Sunday, June 2

Nothing but sleeping late, reading, and writing while trying to recapture these days. Nothing but being a bit weary and feeling a thirst welling up in oneself, counting the months in relation to Jacques, the days in relation to Maheu, nothing but shedding some tears and vaguely desiring vague things and singing beloved tunes with Poupette and Gégé. Then going to Josée's for an hour, weary and bland—and crossing through the Luxembourg Gardens where bizarre and blond young girls dressed in yellow are exchanging precise balls. Charm of the evening, but who am I running away from? Myself? Or a memory, or a desire. I flee all the way to the boulevards where I enter a cinema: Topaze, rather funny—and I think obstinately with my heart heavy and indecisive, of the light touch of a hand, of a smile, of a yielding of all of myself that he will never know.[427]

Monday, June 3

To tear myself away from this gray morning, from the fatigue of having slept so little, from the melancholy of having nothing to say to you, what power have you thus taken over me, René Maheu? Gandillac across from me, you by my side; you making drawings, G. trying to understand, me amusing you with a mathematical trick that not one of you can figure out, and trying to be interested or carefree, but half-heartedly, very half-heartedly. With the burden of you being so uselessly near to me; with the weight of the presence of G. so inconveniently between the two of us, although in himself he is very kind, with the long hours that separate us from a tête-a-tête that I know ahead of time I have to spoil. And you can easily see that I am "melancholic," but you take me to Palais Royal, chez Pocardi in the public gardens, you tell me of Italy, of your wedding trip, and of the sea with a great sweetness, as if I didn't always need to justify everything and as if you liked me a lot again when I do not know how to make you present for me . . . then a sensible joy warms me; laughing, you brought me L'auto, you make funny poems; you dedicate some "Eugenes" and the portrait of the average agrégation candidate to me. Now I am working well and I know that you are there, now the hours are very sweet, and the sweetest of all the hour when I accompany you to Palais Royal, when you offer me lemon-lime soda, when you speak to me of sports and cards, when I tell you stories of Jacques that you find fantastic, especially the one about the two deaf people . . . How nicely you reproached me for my impudence when I told you that I so loved to scandalize my parents, nicely promised that you would come with your wife, nicely said that we will go out with Sartre to whom you have spoken of me. I was light-hearted then, and so happy near you on this café terrace, so happy to accompany you all the way to your student's place, "This is so nice of you, I didn't dare request this from you." Oh! Your hand on my arm this morning to say hello to me; your familiar but respectful gestures, your affection of which I am so sure (you didn't used to come to the Bibliothèque Nationale so often before) and my affection that I don't quite know what to name. Am I saying too much? Or not enough? Like describing one's heart and the ever different taste of unique life?

Went home early. Evening with Poupette reading *Mon amie Nane* [My friend Nane] by Toulet, the NRF, Rilke's book on Rodin, and singing old love songs and Russian songs.[428] To live in you . . . Little girl, ah! Little girl . . . this calm is only the certitude of seeing him tomorrow and the caress of his pink gaze that envelops you again.

For moments in the morning, in the evening, a brutality of expectation, of desire for you who holds suspended from your tenderness all these joys that are not with you. Through your presence make me over into a soul capable of putting up with your distant presence, separated from me by even more than three months. That's a surprise . . . *

(I must have made his acquaintance *around February 15*, just at the moment when I did not write in this notebook, because it was a bit before handing in my term paper to Brunschvicg on February 21.† We had lunch together by chance at the Nationale. I had never said one word to him before; we spoke of Kant, Hume, freedom, and he professed individualism. So that already makes almost four months! I had noticed him before at an *explication de texte* in Brunschvicg's class on January 3, at two presentations in Robin's class, and at the Nationale where he was preparing them. He was in blue with an attractive scarf during the days that followed the New Year, and I felt like saying a word to him but I didn't. One day he brought his wife and that had a slightly disagreeable effect on me to see him climb the stairs, leaning over an unknown woman in gray, and later going up the rue Soufflot on her arm with Sartre and Nizan as escorts. That day when I saw him at the little restaurant, I went upstairs with the secret hope of meeting him: yet I knew nothing of him nor that he was having lunch there. a) On March 19 his appointment with Laporte is before mine; I hear him say, "Goodbye, Monsieur Maheu." Monsieur Maheu is a married and distant man for whom I will, alas, never be anything. One day I catch sight of him on Place St. Sulpice without even daring to say hello, but already it is as if there were something between us, and Mademoiselle Richard says, "But you meet Maheu all the time . . ." On Thursday, March 21, I say a few words to him and Brunschvicg's class brings us together. Since then, every Thursday we have been side by side and he has said friendly things to me while I admire his drawings. b) During Easter vacation he could be seen at the Bibliothèque Nationale; sometimes he would shake my hand; when I caught sight of him, my heart would pound with the desire to do him a favor, to find him a place or to tell him something intelligent. c) April 13 we take the bus together: series of fortunate random events. Then the long-awaited promise of April 18, then on April 23 and *April 24* the carrying out of this promise. And then the charming friendship of this month when we recognize each other, and then *May 24, Friday*, the certitude of confided affection.‡ And since . . . May 25, 28, and 31, and today June 3 without counting classes. Without

---

* The last line of this sentence and page is crumbling in the manuscript and not able to be read.
† In Beauvoir's handwritten diary, the French equivalent of "around February 15" is underlined.
‡ In Beauvoir's handwritten diary, the French equivalents of "April 24" and "May 24, Friday" are underlined.

counting the days when without seeing him at all I lived in him. Has it been only 10 days that my heart has managed to give itself in this way? And six weeks that it was offering itself?)

My friend.

Tuesday, June 4*

Indeed! He has his blue overcoat this morning when he climbs into the H bus where I am; near him in Bouglé's class, in the Center of Social Documentation is charming. There is Borne with whom I exchange some words and who is very nice, the fat Boivin, the chubby Schwob, Gandillac, Goblot, and Mademoiselle Roussel. Maheu makes drawings and takes imaginative notes that make us all laugh a lot. What beats everything is the absence of Bouglé and the letter to sick Hippolyte who cannot revise his curriculum for the tenth time. Maheu writes to him, "If you need for us to revise your curriculum, count on us," then superbly adds, "This is all that I can tell him; now if somebody wants to make an allusion to his wife . . ." G. also invents some funny things. Thereupon along comes G. Lévy who does not understand what we are doing there and who makes a speech while everyone is making fun of her. We hate her: isn't it simply because she approaches others as if it were given that they were enemies whereas I am immediately aware of them as brothers? Oh, sweetness of these final days of student life! And how charming Maheu is to me.

Afternoon at the Bibliothèque Nationale, he is across from me, pink and beige, clean and fresh. He gives drawings to me and to "Mademoiselle de Beauvoir's unknown friend," in this case to Josée; G. is a little further away. But the weather is a bit too gray; it's raining, and I am hungry and tired. After all it is enjoyable not to feel with too much intensity today, and to undergo as a habit the novel pleasure of each day. Josée speaks to me of Stépha who is going to get married and leave for Madrid. I cannot recall without emotion how much I loved her, and the sensual caress that was her smile, and her hand on my sleeve. We go, G., Josée, and I, to have ice cream chez Pocardi; the three of us come back chatting to the rue de Seine, then just the two of us all the way to Josée's. Coming back there was a flash of sun on the glistening Luxembourg Gardens, unexpected and beautiful like a teardrop held back at length.

---

* The first paragraph of this entry is highlighted in pencil and written above the date is "to recount" in pencil in the manuscript.

Then I climb up this stairway with the daily anxiety for the letter that I know is not here. I read an admirable Stendhal that has finally just been published, *Lucien Leuwen*. And Poupette came into my room to tell me good night.

Wednesday, June 5

There is barely a way out of this situation; I cannot desire to feel his presence less vividly. Let my true love take back his place and order will be re-established, but until then, I will have to drag this uncertain heart after every joy . . . I was very tired this morning; I dragged myself to the Bibliothèque Nationale at ten o'clock only to see him; weary and headachy, for two hours I find only Gandillac who is very kind, but no longer interests me. I skim through some reviews. It's raining. For lunch I go into a nice salon de thé on the rue de Richelieu; I read *Lucien Leuwen*; I feel like taking care of myself. It's raining and I am bored rereading my notes; the world is empty, and I am courageously waiting for six o'clock in goodness knows what hope . . .

And suddenly the blue overcoat . . . he has come to tell me that Saturday he will come with his wife for the afternoon snack at my place. It's raining, he saw Sartre and Nizan today, he is worried about the exam, and he laughs kindly at my fear of the rain. We take the H bus. Then, in the rain we look for a place to go. We end up at the café Danton, which is ridiculous, but no matter. We speak first of Kant, of the *agrégation*, and then of his book on individualism. He reproaches me for being too kind, for letting myself be monopolized by people and for wasting my time with it: either you are a psychologist or you are inexcusable, he tells me. I believe that I am inexcusable.

The truth is that next to Jacques these people are really only Mortimers; aside from J. everything seems to me to be on the same plane: Maheu makes me have faith again; it remains that even if I know how to distinguish worth, every human being can find in me, from the purely sentimental point of view, an offer of tenderness. In the past, no . . . We also discuss the point of knowing if one must publish or not: I explain to him how moments of awareness are sufficient for me to see an intoxicating written work in my life. I say, "I have marvelous moments," and he so tenderly, "I really hope so, mademoiselle, you deserve them . . . in contrast, I do not have any marvelous moments, I am a poor devil . . . but what I do is admirable." I tell him that I cannot tell him what I think of him because it would be too nice, "but I think it . . ." He teases Gandillac on the way back. I am defenseless; I like this man too much. I write these lines to outwit the sadness of this night when he disappeared as he ran off in the rain, but I must not hope to retain anything of him or of us here. It would be better to give in without resistance, without trying to justify myself, to explain myself, to invent questions and answers, without discounting the future, without snuggling up in what he told me. I must accept the marvelous gift of his friendship from day to day. When he tells me for example, "You must not judge me," I must, even beyond his irony, tell him things that would make him laugh, and accept the despondency that follows his too happy presence.

There, that's everything—that's everything.

Thursday, June 6

How surprising that tonight I can think only of seeing him tomorrow and saying to him "my friend" or anything at all. I search for passages in Fournier that I would like to read to him: how curious to feel today that I am on Fournier's side against him who is on Rivière's side, whereas I used to be opposed to Jacques who used to be close to Fournier. Make him like everything that I like and especially such admirable letters.

In the morning Bibliothèque Nationale. In the afternoon walk with the child Poupette and the Gandillacs at Bagatelle.[429] Beautiful roses, but rainy. Photos, afternoon snack, but light boredom. G. is no longer anything to me, he was exhausted in some reciprocal confidences ... error to believe that one will be rewarded for confiding in people. One finds a reward because one gives it to oneself, and soon one rediscovers oneself not any richer than before. There are only people who take you without asking your opinion.

Friday, June 7

In the morning nobody is at the Bibliothèque Nationale, and what's more, I don't work well. Then lunch, then I reread with fresh pleasure the delicious *Enfantines* by Larbaud. Thereupon Maheu arrives, and we go into the public garden to chat about "the Pontremolis," and about my future where there is no longer any room for him. I tell him a lot of kind things that I felt like telling him and I explain to him my way of using people, and that my sense of the particular demands that I recognize the interest of each being, one by one, even the most miserable. Those who are fixed in time are explored in a moment, those who are as gifted as the outpouring of life ask for a union of every minute, but all, if they are sincere, merit a spark of love. Incidentally,

I am not really feeling well: maybe it's physical. We find Gandillac settled in across from us, he annoys me. I work very poorly. Fortunately, Zaza comes to get me, and I accompany her to her place to ask her mother to let her have dinner at my place and to come with me to a meeting where Merleau-Ponty wants to take me.[430]

Emotional evening.

There, in the narrow salon of rue du Four, are *Garric* and *Ghéhenno* behind a table where Maxence is presiding. There is *Lacombe* to whom Merleau-Ponty introduces me, whose pale and delicate eyes I like. *Borne* and *Gandillac* are there. *Galois* is in an impeccable gray suit with ravishing cufflinks, with that smile that tugs at your heartstrings, that nuanced voice full of friendship and reserve, and always a book with him. Daniel Galois whose presence I feel all evening. There is my dear *Merleau-Ponty* whom I met with so much happiness after these ten days of absence, every time he is more perfect than I wanted to believe, and also the smile of Jean *Daniélou*. There are some other faces . . . Garric speaks and says some banalities that I do not like with the warm voice that I love. For the slightest thing I would cry because Jacques would fit in so well here, and outside of here, understanding and refusing as I do, alone, very alone in the midst of these dear companions. Jacques . . . I think of the day when Garric was speaking three years ago, when you were shaking hands in an inaccessible world where I felt so bad not to be able to follow you, and at the same time strangely, of a day last year when Garric was speaking and when I, exasperated by these great words at which we would have smiled together and more subtly emotional, was thinking of you. I am shaking hands today, I am firmly rooted in this inaccessible world; but what does it matter since you are not here so that we can judge it together? How willingly I would shed tears! How poignant is the past! Time is really an empty expression that dies in a heartbeat . . . Guéhenno is very likeable with his slow-speaking voice full of contained passion, which then explodes when these idiots exasperate him.[431] Session over, fight—hands shaken at the exit. Fraternity in the discussion of incidents, big young family . . . Garric drags Guéhenno, Daniélou, and others towards a bistro in an atmosphere that brings the Équipes of better days back to life. Galois leaves and Borne goes back to the École, and G. with his parents. Zaza, M.-Ponty and I go back up the boulevard Saint-Germain and the Champs-Elysées in the rain. Wonderful evening. How I like M. Ponty! This evening he is light-hearted, animated, and Zaza can match him. He is full of thoughtfulness and touching scruples. I would like to have his faith to understand its beauty and to give him the immense admiration that he merits.* What's more I like feeling that they are together and so kindly against me. Zaza says "the amoral lady," and they laugh deliciously when I ask "where?" M. Ponty says with so much tenderness, "You are a solitary consciousness [*conscience*]."[432] Zaza seems very moved by him. I would like to tell her how much I myself am too, with what wonder I meet him every time. I would especially like, Jacques, (oh! so much!) to tell you all that . . . †

Saturday, June 8

How breathtakingly [*vertigineusement*] individual is the color of each of our lives! *Maheu* and his wife came for the afternoon snack: she is charming, simple, a very well-brought-up young lady and a bit of a hick; he is kind to her like to a very dear sister, but love? She is "in love" with her husband, he is "taken with" his wife, but those delicious and cruel waves of electricity running through Aline in *Aimée*, for example, have they ever experienced them?[433] And "this approach more stern than death to the heart" . . . [434] As for me it is completely something else than always "this same banal play on words," and how can it be explained with words? But passing by Jacques's door and knowing that death's door is not more definitive, irreparable to anyone who goes through it . . .

This is for example Jacques and Magda, a liaison between lover and mistress that gives the illusion of a union of souls, especially if there is little feeling. I think of Madeleine Blomart, I think of myself . . . I don't want to be too hard on Maheu. Yet, I am shocked that he makes use of his individualism in his social relationships, that he creates a persona for himself instead of seeking a sentimental refinement, a true originality in what should be his truest life. And then again, what does it matter—there is only one man. How near you are tonight, tonight caught between our common past and my present, between Galois and Maheu, each of whom is a side of you. You, who are capable of laughing like my new very funny friend, and capable of being moved and serious like Merleau-Ponty. I passed by your house; no, to think that in three months your house will perhaps be alive, this desire was enough to be frightening. Then I will get to know myself, then I will know the key to my life, then there will be nothing else to do.

---

* This paragraph is highlighted in the right margin from about the mention of Zaza and M.-Ponty walking up the boulevards to "merits"

† All the names in italics in the diary entry for June 7 are underlined in Beauvoir's handwritten diary.

I was thinking this morning: that as always those who are absent are wrong, and that Maheu present is more than Galois thought, and that Galois present is more than the idea of Maheu. So what must Jacques be for this image from 13 months ago to be more than Maheu, Galois and all the others together? There are a lot of viewpoints on life, many ways to dodge suffering, but for me there is only one point of view, one destiny for which I must accept all suffering without being able to flee from it: "He shut me out of the earth."[435] All that is not him in this notebook is a game, or at least an occupation, all marked by the signs of the times. In him my life is eternal. There is salvation only through my self, but only with him. *Religious idea of life.* *

This morning I get up late. At the Bibliothèque Nationale I see Gandillac; he speaks to me quite nicely of Poupette: so much seriousness and simple spontaneity. He speaks to me of the powerlessness to attain a union of souls: dynamism, sensation that you are going to make it, then failure. I don't believe any of it. I dream for an hour about a million things, above all about Poupette—I care more for her each day, she is truly rare. I am a bit tired. I go back home early in anticipation of the Maheus. Such pleasure from the new intimacy developing between us through his wife, but sadness to feel that he has limits, and from telling oneself, "What? Is that all there is to his life?" One would want a man whom one loves to have near him a woman who opens infinite horizons; yet almost all these women close a door.

Jeanne and Riri come to dinner, we see them back, short walk with Poupette who is sad.[436] In me too, vague sadness. Gandillac sent a very kind letter to Poupette.

Sunday, June 9

Got up late. All day I thought of you alone, Jacques. Today sweet streets of Paris, how you speak to me of him . . . I go to "L'oeil de Paris," pretty red room with drawings by Paul Colin. An excellent fantasy, *Mirage de Hollywood,* and an admirable film by Epstein, *Finis terrae* are being shown, nothing but the savage sea, the hard earth and men, two men, nothing but their brief hatred, the solitude of the wounded man before this nature that overwhelms him without his comprehension, and the sweetness of their restored fraternity.[437] Jean-Marie's arm sliding as support under the injured arm of Ambroise, who is falling asleep near him, is a gesture of such grave beauty that it brought tears to my eyes.

---

* The French equivalent of the words, "Religious idea of life," is highlighted in the manuscript.

What does it matter to me if the love of Maheu, whose interesting term paper on history I have just read, is so banal and almost sickening like all the young married couples who don't understand a thing. What does it matter to me that it would be impossible to tell him the difference between him and me. I will say, "Your wife is charming." What does anything that is not you matter to me, Jacques? Here we are once again facing one another without the intervention of any joys that have not come to me through you, alone together as we haven't been for some time, o my friend. I have always known that you were here. Today, seeing you, I no longer see anything but you. The two of us and our world, with Rivière and Fournier, with the music of "Chiquita" and "Always" that I murmur as the only words of love that I know how to say, with your cigarette and our silences. With my desire for your face. What desire! What hunger! But nobody will ever understand. If you have loved another, what does it matter to me? Love is so little. I only desire it today as a new way of being a better friend to you, and to protect you from the love of another woman. Vague sadness that a being whom I esteem was content with so little, did not demand of life a woman who would only be "herself" and not an exemplar of the feminine type: smile, elegance, grace, tenderness. But you, I know that *just any* woman would never have been your share in this world and that perhaps I will be *this* woman alone with whom it will be possible for you to harvest our share of life.*

You alone, Jacques.

I wanted to say to Maheu: individualism for you is to carve out a figure of your name in society; for me it is to lean religiously towards this god who is named "me," a demanding god, with a solemn worship; and loving is not to annex to myself a certain number of amiable reactions, but to approach this divinity who alone can help me to feel that I myself am divine. The accession to a supernatural world, not the blossoming of my natural life—it is of a terrifying importance, not my happiness, my salvation—because my individualism is based on sentiment. It is only the theorizing of my passion for myself, and this passion is one and the same as my passion for an other. It is not about opposing a given and defining myself by this opposition, but about reflecting on what I am, completely turned toward myself and within this reflection giving birth to a world invisible to all others.

To make a success of my life will be to maintain, against the habitual world, the mysterious domain and to live there normally. The more *faith*

---

* In Beauvoir's handwritten diary, the French equivalents of "just any" and "this" before "woman" are underlined.

with which I live, the more beautiful this world will be, the more success-ful life will be. To live there with faith one can be unaware of the rest of the universe: in the first stage, one can also draw handfuls of all that is good from the given to transport it "home," to use everything, and to become familiar enough with it to manage to no longer see it or receive from it any brutal denials. Inner landscapes . . . But the foundation, even of this world, is Jacques. (I suspect Maheu of not having a very rich inner life).

Monday, June 10

Bibliothèque Nationale. I catch sight of Gandillac, then Maheu. We have lunch together. Seated near the fountain we have a long discussion: I explain my individualism to him as I wanted to explain it to him; he understands, he even admires that I possess a domain of my own. Then we discuss marriage: he tells me about his that he interprets exactly as I had; I oppose my conception to his; I astonish him by saying that my demands for purity are not limited to women. This seems to him to be Catholic shyness in a man: only, he adds, a man must not stop being free. How insensitive he is, but how dear to me! And how nicely he says when the moment arrives to return to the Bibliothèque Nationale, "It is truly a pity."

Zaza comes to get me. Together we go to the Sorbonne where I catch sight of Pontremoli, Maugüe, whom I introduce to her, and Merleau-Ponty with whom we stop by Monnier's.* She leaves us and M.-P. and I come back to the house while we chat. Evening with my diplôme, the Sorbonne class, and the pleasure of taking a test together. Rather dreary evening out with Josée who came to get me and who takes me to the Luxembourg Gardens and then to boulevard St. Michel.

Tuesday, June 11

I bring myself to the Sorbonne rather early. I catch sight of Galois who is taking his oral, Galois, for whom Zaza told me she had felt so much admiration. How close Zaza is to me at the moment. Yesterday as she drank some lemon-lime soda with me at the Tuileries, she told me that she is happy about this spiritual awakening that underlies her being moved to tears at an evening like the one on Friday. Her milieu oppresses her, but I don't think that she makes compromises, since she is as sensitive as I am to

---

* In Beauvoir's handwritten diary, "Zaza" and "Merleau-Ponty" are underlined.

the incomparable worth of a certain quality of the soul.* There she is this morning in the courtyard of the Sorbonne, and what does it matter that Geneviève de Neuville is accompanying her since the banks of the Seine are so blue. On boulevard Saint-Germain a hairdresser gives me a little-boy haircut. My heart is as light as my shaved neck! I meet Poupée at Evelynes where we have lunch on the terrace as people pass by. It is warm out, the ice cream is exquisite, the presence cherished. We walk around a bit and then I go up to take the exam for my *diplôme*. Brunschvicg was pleased with it but he riddles me with witty observations under the eyes of G. Lévy and Lautman who annoy me. I feel tenderness for this very gaze that is as intelligent as it is good.

Good day for a student: Merleau-Ponty at grips with Bréhier, so self-assured and polite at the same time; then in the courtyard Josée, Zaza, Gandillac, M.-Ponty and I have a discussion. We go to have the afternoon snack at Evelynes and to take a walk on the quays. Zaza shows an ease that delights everyone, G. is animated, M.-Ponty charming as always, and I, splendidly happy. Zaza leaves us and we come back to the Sorbonne. M.-Ponty laughs out loud while G. holds forth looking as though he is making fun of himself. A marvelous tenderness swells my heart, for example when he leaves us to take the AX bus. Josée and I accompany G. to his metro, and as always, he talks about his ideal wife. Alone with Josée, she reproaches me for sometimes being "social;" but it is only the blossoming of my *joie de vivre* that gives me this ease, and then too, I like these people, and then . . . Life is so beautiful, my goodness! But she is suffering excessively tonight while I accompany her back. She truly loves him, and he is really worth it! I'm sad not to be able to stay with her tonight. Live frantically all lives in addition to my own. Suffer these sufferings—taste these joys as my friends suffer and taste . . .

At night—Ballets Russes: *Pétrouchhka, La chatte, Apollon, Baba-Yaga*—but I am a bit distant from this show and absorbed with the music of laughter and words that I heard today.[438]

Wednesday, June 12

In the morning I do a critical analysis of Sextus Empiricus with Robin. I catch a glimpse of Galois who had high marks on his *diplôme*, and my heart is still marvelously sensitive to him. I attend Merleau-Ponty's oral exam.

---

* From the beginning of the June 11 entry to "soul" is highlighted in the right margin.

Together we go off walking toward the Bibliothèque Nationale. And there with a great and unexpected happiness I meet *my dear Lama*. We go have lunch together on the rue des Petits-Champs, as we speak of his *diplôme* and of what he calls "all my Pontremolis." It is hot—we take a seat in a café at Palais Royal where I am given a paper fan with which I have fun. We say silly things, both of us very animated. At a street corner, traveling singers bellow "J'irai revoir . . . la tour Eiffel [I will go to see the Eiffel Tower again]" to the sound of the accordion. He gives me *L'auto* as a present. I am happy to be here close to him. At five o'clock I accompany him to his lesson. How profoundly he is within me. Long discussion on Kant.

I go to the Sorbonne where I meet M.-Ponty. We are sitting, having a chat, on the courtyard bench when the rain chases us away, then we consult the list that gives us the results on our *diplômes*. I go back home to study Hume and Kant after stopping by the Sainte-Geneviève Library.

Exam atmosphere.

Thursday, June 13

Exquisite, adorable day. And first at the Bibliothèque Nationale where I read *Détective* and admire Maheu's notes on Kant. I pass him some books on Hume. We work until noon with a new frenzy that does not keep the Eugenes from walking across the white paper. We have a lunch of strawberry tarts on the rue des Petits-Champs. Then we walk around the Palais Royal garden ten times. How kindly he says to me, "Your hairstyle and your white collar really suit you well . . . you look like a little boy. With your funny husky voice, what's more your voice is very pretty, but it is husky. Both Sartre and I are really amused by it. The other day you were talking to Boivin . . ." He teases me about the "gonfalonnier de Padirac."[439] He also says to me with so much affection, "And you say that you are not feminine . . . you tell your Eugene that he is wrong not to take you for a woman, one could not be more wrong . . ." I drag him to the bizarre green Tuileries under a stormy sky. He teases me, pretending that I want to get him run over. We take a seat in front of a ridiculous lion killing a crocodile, and there we make conjectures about the *agrégation* exam. I joke about Hume's second philosophy and this document that he is going to seek. I feel that I am droll, a bit crazy, and he has fun seeing me. "You are a beaver [*castor*]," he says to me as we go back to the Bibliothèque Nationale, using as an argument my name (beaver = BEAUVOIR) and my constructive mind.[440]

We return home late. How quickly the time has passed, dear you. And how quickly it passes while I pretend to work by your side. We leave together to go to his wife's home; letters at the post office, the bus game (the V bus never gets taken unless it is the second time around). He shows me a charming Von Dongen in the rue du St. Père. He looks for *The Green Hat* for his wife, and a record for his sister-in-law at the Boite à Musique. These errands run together give birth to such intimacy. Compelling sweetness of remembering these hours . . .

And at his house it was absolutely delightful: his wife, Inès, in mauve with a ribbon in her hair, is truly straightforward and charming, and his sister-in-law Christine, kind.[441] They play some Layton and Johnston records, which make Jacques loom up alive before me, especially "So blue" and "Crying for the moon." Then along comes Poupette, we have the afternoon snack, and we offer ourselves an amusing session of thought transmission in which he does not content himself with walking, he runs. In his wife's room, some pictures of him, of her, very likeable, great friendship for her, and I believe that it's mutual. He keeps us late. Poupette and I return home radiant.

I find a deeply moving note from M.-Ponty thanking me for the affection that he has felt from me these past days and assuring me of his "inexplicable friendship." I spend the night responding to him in a letter that I will not send. What immense friendship, and always new, always more exalted, thanks to him alone, thanks to him . . .

Friday, June 14, Evening on the lake

Morning at the Bibliothèque Nationale. The weather is rainy, and I am sad because we are supposed to go boating on the lake tonight, and because I would like to see M.-P. and because it is going to rain. Fortunately Maheu takes me to have coffee at chez Pocardi and proves himself to be drolly vexed that I made fun of him the night before. I talk to him of his wife who is lucky not to have to worry about the *agrégation*, and for hours I read Boutroux's ridiculous book on Kant that he lends to me. He writes on a newspaper "to my dear Castor" in a writing that deeply moves me like an inflection in a very tender voice. He leaves early with a friend. I leave immediately afterwards.

The sky has cleared and I take a seat on the terrace in Luxembourg Gardens, one of Lalande's books on my lap. I do not read; there is a deliciously pink rose swinging to and fro in the midst of marvelously green leaves; little girls are getting splashed by the fountain and screaming; palm trees are glistening in the sun; my "heart is saturated with sunbeams."[442] Never, I believe, have I been so immensely happy; tonight I am going to see all my loves. In my purse I have a letter whose every word makes me cry with tenderness, and in a little while the one who wrote it will be before me. I am thinking of you, Maurice, for an hour, overcome with joy and sunlight, in a fervor comparable only to the one that a desired return will give me.

Then I go up to Josée's place. We dine hastily and go back down to Luxembourg Gardens where the light has softened. A tramway with wide-open windows takes us into a Paris beaming with peace. Together we say, "This is the most beautiful evening of the year. Let's savor it fervently, with an obedient exhilaration, with gratitude, without expectation. Here are the Trocadéro gardens, the trees on the contemplative avenue Henri Martin. Let's ponder our souls to savor such an absolute beauty; let's not ask for tomorrow. Tomorrow there will be desires that will not be able to be satisfied all at once, some regrets, some expectations, but this evening is the most beautiful of so many beautiful evenings, and our age is the most beautiful of all ages." L'allée du Bois led peacefully to pines whose trunks were blushing in the solitary sun; the smell of life itself was thick in the dying light and the lapping of the water; at the turn in the path dear smiles were going to appear: first Poupette with Gégé, then Gandillac, a bit stilted, then Zaza and Bernard whom I shower with candy, then the male friend so loved.[443] Soon the small boats are gliding on the water. Gandillac, Josée, and I set out on the sea of Sargasses; there are games with balls and races between the red and blue lanterns.[444] Then the most beautiful time of all when I am with Zaza and Maurice; I remain quiet, I have tears in my throat. Never, never in the world has there been a moment of such pure happiness: she is here; he is here with his white rayon shirt and knotted tie, so young, this young face dazzling with peaceful tenderness. He says to me, "You remind me of when you were four years old . . . come, come silly girl . . . but Simone . . ."—when he said Simone, I could have sobbed. How he loves me! How I love him! The incredible wealth of life, oh, life that answers all my dreams! How I love him like this, laughing, full of wit, carefree about joining whatever group hails us. I am also wonderfully close to feeling tenderness for Zaza; what gaiety and freedom! How well we get along, the three of us, like this.*

---

* This last part from "Zaza and Maurice" to the end of this paragraph is highlighted in the right margin.

Alas, boats have to be changed at the waterfall. I come back with Gandillac who aspires to be very sociable, etc. I manage to be friendly with a bit of effort. Josée and Zaza are with Maurice. We approach each other on the warm island where walking is a wonder.

Can't we shut ourselves away here, and stop time? (But tomorrow there will be still other joys).

Poupée gets into Bernard's boat next to me; we sing, our hearts overflowing; Zaza, found again, comes to join us; Maurice listens, beaming with all his heart. And in the woods our voices come together. Zaza is exquisite, blossoming as much as on the most joyous days in Gagnepan. Maurice is singing bass in a deep voice full of gusto; mad desire to hug them both. On the avenue des Champs-Elysées the flame of love only burns more ardently. Poupette feels a bit off and we go up to the Lacoin's: some port wine, Gandillac's attentiveness, and shyness. A taxi takes us back into this pure night that we leave only with regret: "Yes," says Josée, "life could be marvelous." She comes back to sleep here, caressing her dream. Very exhausted Poupette and I, who take part in her evident pain, sleep poorly together in the same bed.

Saturday, June 15

It doesn't matter; at the Bibliothèque Nationale I am brimming with gaiety. Maheu writes drolly on my notebook "Castor's philosophy or Parties in the Bois de Boulogne."

"You see, beavers travel in groups," he says to me, laughing. O dear Lama who "travels" all alone! I am absolutely unbearable; this ridiculous Boutroux excites my witty eloquence, and yesterday is prolonged in bursts of silent laughter. We have lunch in the rue de Richelieu where he draws up a bizarre list of animals that constitute the "metaphysical form of the pluralist universe." He is a bit worried about the *agrégation* exam; I am carefree and occupied with asking him riddles, telling stories, and making idiotic remarks. Then seated on the edge of the basin we discuss indefinitely what makes "the worth" of a being. As I pose the question from an excessively general viewpoint, he says: "That's the form of thinking that I detest," then, slapping me amicably on the shoulder, "It doesn't matter, it doesn't matter, Castor."

Back in the foyer, we discuss the Barrès case for another hour. Precisely then Zaza arrives and takes me away in the car to do some errands. She speaks to me of Merleau-Ponty with the greatest of admiration and animation, too

humble as always and envisioning marriage with disgust because she thinks she is not good enough for somebody good—but that's preposterous ... *
Josée was waiting for us at the Bibliothèque Nationale. All three of us have the afternoon snack together. Then I come back towards my Lama. He soon leaves, and I with him; slight malaise upon thinking that I will not see him here before the competitive exam; regret for yesterday evening's outing, sadness for what is ending, stormy weather.† I leave him at Palais Royal, and he kindly wishes me good luck. Bizarre distress! ... I would like to see Merleau-Ponty, and I go back to the Bibliothèque Nationale in case he comes by. The Tuileries welcome me, I am very strange, and I write him, weaker than my feelings tonight, overwhelmed by them. I write at length, and I wander around Paris cloudy-headed to send my pneumatic message.

I fall asleep with some idiotic newspapers.

Sunday, June 16

Picnic in Fontainebleau with Zaza and her family, Poupette (whom Gandillac does not leave alone all day), Merleau-Ponty (more exquisite than ever), G. de Neuville and some associates. Merleau-Ponty is close to me, but separated by these people who bother me: in the train he is having fun like a little boy. How I need his gaiety! In Fontainebleau we take a tram that takes us too far and gets us lost; he has a discussion with Zaza, he is casual, friendly, and charming. Then we get lost in the forest; the forest smells profoundly of earth, there are lilacs, all is good. Maurice looks like a horse, it's evident he is hungry; G. looks like a cricket, he is not complaining, but bores us. At the end, we meet again after running and crying out desperately—joyous lunch, games, walk, and return. In the train Poupette is very depressed, Maurice funnier than ever, and G. and I, slightly worried about tomorrow.

Monday, June 17

First day.[445]

Fun of rising early, of Paris so cool at six o'clock, of the Sorbonne courtyard with the worried groups: notebooks, thermoses, bananas, and sandwiches. We get settled in the library. Lama tells me, "Good luck, Castor," with so

---

* The French equivalent of the entire paragraph starting "Back in the foyer" though "but that's preposterous" is highlighted in the left margin of the handwritten diary.
† There is a pencil slash in the text between sentences as if to highlight.

much affection that I am still thinking about it when Lalande announces "Freedom and Contingency."

At two o'clock *Zaza* and *Merleau-Ponty* are there, and we wander in the streets half-heartedly.* Drinking lemonade at the Café de Flore comforts us. Then G. is of a mind to leave us, and Zaza, Maurice, and I have the most wonderful discussion in Luxembourg Gardens. We speak, above all, about our favorite topic of debate at the moment: "pity for mankind." Whereas Maheu reproaches me for too much benevolence, Merleau-Ponty accuses me of being acerbic and either impassioned or indifferent. I provide an explanation, which he cannot accept, but it doesn't matter. I no longer need for my ideas to be accepted. I like these people in their opposition; they speak to me with an exquisite subtlety that is rare in such a conversation with three people. Blushing, Zaza tells me, "I don't think that another boy as good as M.-Ponty exists," and also "I am happy because for the first time I didn't feel like a third wheel between you." I explain to her how, for a while, I dared less to confide in her since she was less understanding than today; she agreed about this change; our harmony is so great tonight that we cannot tear ourselves away from each other. She tells me that she doesn't think that either Poupette or Josée are suitable for Merleau-Ponty, her attitude on Sunday shows it.

I am sure that Zaza would be perfect for him. Who knows?

Tuesday, June 18

Hippolyte smokes like a chimney. Everyone is accumulating pages on "Intuition and reasoning in the deductive method."[446] I go out with a rather unhappy Maheu. I accompany him to his place. I feel wonderfully happy, this exam not having the importance that I had thought. I stop by Jeanne's, and from there a tramway takes me to the home of Madeleine Blomart (de Prandières).† O my good friend in your black and white dress, o familiar and imposing in your sovereign simplicity, o great pure forehead revealed by wavy hair, and every time such unexpectedly blue and profound eyes—o marvelous peace! She spoke to me of herself, of her present happiness, of her first boyfriend and the strange destiny that saved her from him; and with so much sincerity and straightforwardness, unskilled at masking your feelings no matter how surprising they might appear, how you dazzle in what you call this obscurity!

---

* In Beauvoir's handwritten diary, "Zaza" and "Merleau-Ponty" are underlined.
† From the beginning of the June 18 entry to here is highlighted with pencil marks before and after it.

Her husband came for the afternoon snack, amiable, straightforward, and very likeable. She spoke to me of Poupette; she would like to find her a husband. Maybe this would be very good. Poupette came, so delicate and precious with her Marie-Antoinette scarf, and her chignon so blond. One of Madeleine's simple and pleasant sisters was also there, sunken in the couch. What a delicious rum-flavored cake with this tea smelling like lemons, served on the very low Morrocan table. I was seated on leather cushions; I could not keep myself from mumbling, "How beautiful life is!" Oh, beautiful smile of my friend . . . Smile that dispenses joy, that gathers life; Poupette was entirely warmed by it as she left, and capable of confronting all of existence; and as for myself, I kept it within me as the perceptible sign of all the splendor revealed to me this year.

Wednesday, June 19*

We finish with "Ethics for the Stoics and Kant."[447] The caps pop off the bottles of lemon-lime soda. Maheu takes a walk in shirtsleeves, great relaxation of the last day. It's going very well.

Zaza and M.-Ponty come to get us. We chat in the courtyard under the envious gaze of G. Lévy. Then the AX bus drives us to Passy where some port wine comforts me. All four of us chat gaily, then Zaza leaves us, and it's a pleasure for me to speak of her. M.-Ponty, Gandillac and I walk in great harmony in the Bois de Boulogne; we remember the beginning of our friendship: I was much more of a little girl then, that's for sure. Then Merleau-Ponty leaves us. I go to see Mademoiselle Mercier who yesterday wrote me a rather pompous, but kind letter. We have a short discussion, but she no longer has anything to say, imprisoned in a dead-end life. A taxi takes me back home, exhausted and faint from the heat.

In the evening we go out to look for a bit of coolness on the boulevards. Poupette and Mama leave us; Papa is nice when he is gay like tonight. We explore the theaters of Montmartre and end up at the Théâtre de Dix Heures in a tiny and elegant room where Jean Bastia and especially Noël-Noël delight me. The songs are witty, the review funny and I exhaust the last legs of my fatigue. Another taxi in the fresh night leads us to Chez Lipp.

And then a big sleep.

---

* The whole June 19, 1929, entry is highlighted with pencil marks at the beginning and end of the entry in Beauvoir's handwritten diary.

Thursday, June 20

Until noon ... Pleasure of a day without homework, that would be light-hearted if the bizarre regime of these three days didn't make me feel a bit woozy. Poupette buys me ice cream at chez Pons. Dear treasure of wisdom ... she tells me that she is resigned to not being loved by M.-P. especially if his wife must be admirable. Besides what has been is worth it for itself and will give her good memories; and she feels her youth is open to all futures. It's true that she is dazzling, a poor match for my dear Maurice who is no match for her; she will be happiness for another. We walk in Luxembourg Gardens, touched to know that we already have a past, touched that it is so beautiful and that with our young strength we may promise to accept the challenge of the future. At the same time all becomes clear and with the greatest effort of disinterest that I have ever exerted, I manage to like Jacques's past in Jacques, without even knowing how to desire another face for him. Jacques, will you be able to recognize the arduous progress that my love has made? How this question weighs heavily on my nights ...

Then I go see Josée, with whom I chat at length. She is less sensible than Poupette and imprisoned in a path that appears desperate to me. Once home, I read part of *Dialogue avec A. Gide* [Dialogue with A. Gide] by du Bos, which interests me for the quotes from his writings and the conversations with a man whom I admire above all men. Such a true gift of self at the heart of this essential individualism, so much constraint and abandon, so much intelligence and sometimes madness—o dear image of myself, complex life, infinitely rich ... life is all of that, all of that! O wonder, and I too, I take on everything, with this heart of a woman in love devoted to a single love and capable of a thousand passions, with this head concerned with a single problem and knowing how to have fun with all intellectual games, and this body sensitive to the slightest ray of summer sunlight. Wallow in the world? Oh no! And even reproaching me for this is not to know me well; but with the reserve of Barrès, a more sincere passion, at least not as prudent, and generously dispensed to all these ardent things that constitute life day by day.

Friday, June 21

Ch. Favre comes to lunch; false animation, which makes me leave her soon.

Zaza is such a treasure. I find her in her living room where we speak of Gandillac and of M.-Ponty. Is it M.-Ponty's silent influence that softens her so and gives her the appreciation of his intelligence? She puts on a blue voile dress with black and white designs that makes her look taller and even more in blossom. A straw hat makes her face look astonishingly young. We go down the Champs-Elysées speaking of her. She tells me how she senses a new blossoming, an unexpected possibility of childishness, and after the sorrow that caused her to believe that her life was over, a beautiful expectation—she speaks softly, revealing nothing but what is just and sincere. She is marvelous, so alive in her reserve, so worthy of happiness, so astute, so profound. How close we feel . . . she questions me about myself with an infinite tact, asking me if J.'s silence doesn't hurt me and if I don't fear his return. I must answer her. Even to her, so tactful and accepting of my "way of loving" without being surprised, I cannot speak well of what is at the heart of my life; this excessive trust . . . these temptations of doubt, and my incredible certainty of the full worth of the being who is "all of my life." How can I say to any friend at the moment that I love them the most: but all of my life is a single word from that mouth, and you are no longer *anything* next to my destiny?

We arrive at Rumpelmayer's. I experience an acute pleasure in being a rather pretty girl in my veiled hat; alongside a dazzling girl eating ice cream and a piece of exquisite strawberry pie in an atmosphere of leisure. Yes, Elisabeth Boulenger is dazzling in her navy blue dress with white lace, in her very elegant horsehair hat. With a joyous heart, I accompany her along the Tuileries, the rue des St. Pères, where we admire some beautiful Foujitas, the rue de Rennes; we accompany each other indefinitely until taking a taxi to the Place d'Italie. I question her about herself: proud that she tells me what she tells nobody, joy of this beautiful show that is her triumphant body and her strong and clear soul.

Truly in the bus that was bringing me back I understood better than ever the sudden birth of love and its unjustified exigency. This birth is a life, and this soul would be nothing for me if it did not make such a splendid appearance poignant: nor would this rosy face be anything if these very beautiful eyes did not know how to welcome life so spontaneously. With all the distance that separates their inner lives, what charms me equally in Madeleine Blomart and E. Boulanger? It's this spontaneous self-affirmation, this taste for existence, this ardent independence, and the wealth of a very concrete experience. How easily I am exhilarated! How life goes to my head! Always the same refrain whose very monotony dazzles me: oh, marvelous life, o marvelous life . . .

At Agriculteurs I meet Gandillac and his sister—how dreary they are! G. talks to me endlessly about Poupette. I briefly see little Nathan who talks to me about my *agrégation* exam.[448] Surprise! M.-Ponty appears at eleven thirty; all of us go up together towards l'Étoile; I sense in him a joy of the same quality as my own, despite the boredom caused by his exam in physics, chemistry, and the natural sciences [*P.C.N.*], but the gonfalonnier, full of pettiness, puts a damper on everything. Fortunately, we ditch him, and walk down the Champ-Elysées together into a delightful evening. He tells me everything he resents about G; I remind him of the intelligent distinction that du Bos makes in *Dialogue avec Gide* between complicated and complex beings; G. is complicated, but hardly complex! M.-Ponty is complex. Jacques and I are also complex. He tells me in a charming way that he has had enough of people saying good things about him; it certainly won't keep me from thinking them. He tells me in a serious tone that deeply moves me that he finds my friend splendid, "she always speaks only of what she knows perfectly; also she speaks little, but every word carries all its weight." He also admires that in her difficult living circumstances she can be so true to herself. He tells me to invite her to go for a walk with us on Wednesday.*

How willingly I associate them in my heart. And how astonished I am to do it with such joy! Truly the day he loves Zaza more than me, and she, Maurice more than me, there will not be any jealousy in me, or this vague bitterness of being left out. Because it will be right and because they will know how to love each other despite how I love them, and then too because they also love me "in spite of," and because I am proud to break down their sensible behavior, and then too because their affection is clear-sighted and yet without reserve; and because I prefer neither of them—that above all! How willingly I would understand them together! As two present and involved beings, understanding them as a function of one another and not as a function of one's occasionally irritated self. But here they are united by what necessarily resists me, and this rare thing is produced that, because of their very high quality, they do not become deformed as they approach each other; instead they only become clearer. How very much I would like this!

I leave Maurice in an unending joy; I take the wrong way at Concorde and a taxi has to bring me back. Thus is the enchantment of my day prolonged.

---

* The part where M.P. admits to liking Zaza and wants her to be invited for the outing on Wednesday is highlighted in the right margin.

Mama tells me that Maheu stopped by, what a happy shock! I really care about him much more than I know . . .

Saturday, June 22

My whole morning was nothing but waiting. I am reading du Bos: I am so weary of this group, du Bos, Baruzi, Gabriel Marcel, Fernandez, who are nothing but Mortimers trying to pass themselves off as Marrhanes. A bit disappointed (my hair looks great, I am truly a beauty this morning), I go down to buy a heart-shaped creamy cheese: my friend Maheu is coming up to invite me to lunch. What a charming moment!

Slaves to a dear habit we go to the Fleur du Lys, then into the Palais Royal gardens. He tells me that my father made fun of him, "he took a playful tone . . .," that must have been really funny. He invites me to do some Leibniz with him and his dear friends [*petits camarades*], and tells me improbable stories about Sartre who wants to meet me, but Maheu does not want me to meet Sartre without him.[449] How kindly he speaks of our friendship; how nice he is when he says watching me, "Yesterday I worked on defending my dearest feelings." Sartre does not seem likeable to me. He is one of those people who interpret and do not concede: what an idea to have us spied on by Andrieux! Thus we will send Poupette to him on Tuesday to put him in his place, and he will deserve it. We speak of Sartre, Poupette, Maheu's wife, our friendship, books that we will write—he tells me, "You must get married. I will tell your Eugene that you must be treated as a woman and loved." (But maybe my Eugene will find this out by himself.)

I go off to read in Luxembourg repeating our conversation to myself. I stop by the home of Marie-Louise with whom I walk around for an hour. I return to the great joy of finding Poupette, who tells me of the hilarious conversation between Maheu and Papa. We go to the Coupole to eat a "banana royale" and we come back under a mauve-blue-gray sky from which all the trees in Luxembourg Gardens are standing out in precise masses of somber value.

Sunday, June 23

Entirely occupied by writing the story of these last two weeks. I also went by to see Josée. I find a letter from Stépha and Fernand who invite us over tomorrow. What great pleasure rises within me! It is like a very old memory that one would have wanted to bury in vain. I don't know what she is or what

I made her. I know after all what people tell me of her, and her forgetfulness, and my occasional indifference, the excitement of this evening when I am going to see her again, the excitement that makes the feather pen fall out of my hands in imagining her blond face. Her name is a certain almost sensual caress for me; I remember her tender gestures, her smile, her soft fur; I remember her catlike faces, the evenings in Montparnasse; Fernand's familiar and amiable gesture half-enveloping me with his arm. Stépha's room, Stryx, boulevard Raspail where we used to run so gaily, Bibliothèque Nationale where we were seated next to each other, cookies beneath the lamp, aimless chattering; Stépha, Fernand, dear past without grandeur but as soft and sweet as the sheets between which one slides after a weary day.

What a marvel these last two weeks have been! What a marvel this year has been! What a marvel my life is! One evening when I have written less, I will speak of it.

Monday, June 24

I spent yesterday evening writing to Zaza, thinking of Jacques and meditating with passion on the pages of my life. Today, at eight o'clock I meet *Stépha* who is waiting for me in the café downstairs.* We walk through Paris and go to lunch at Dominique's. Ice cream at the Dôme with Levinsky; cinema, afternoon snack, the purchase of books, dinner in the bright workshop hung with Ukranian rugs and full of skylight. Fernand is kind, but banality. Under this bohemian guise there are as many domestic preoccupations as among some of the bourgeois. Petty lives, very petty, where self-reflection is not essential.

The letters that Poupette brings me from Zaza, Mademoiselle Mercier, and Pontremoli, (the one from Zaza above all and incomparably), make me feel the distance between the pleasure of dining amid brightly lit greens and reds and the wordless happiness of a heartbeat.

Tuesday, June 25. Peace

Jacques—silently since this morning: Jacques. Oh, still three more months, it's enough to drive one to despair!

What a precious treasure, granted by what grace? And now I am as emotional about myself as I would be about someone else. It came on suddenly.

---

* In Beauvoir's handwritten diary, "Stépha" is underlined.

I read all morning and until three o'clock in the afternoon a book on Byron in which the endearing traits of Lady Byron captivated me. Then I met Gandillac at the Japanese art exhibition. Together we looked at two of Foujiita's big panels in which the poverty of his soul stands out too clearly. There is no beyond; expression is limited to itself without being a victory over an unforeseen real (thus certain expressions of terror). We spoke of this Japanese soul, very strange if one judges only by these works; a minuscule and diligent soul, not even sensual and always within the world. Nobody listened, but I said very astute things with an ease and a pleasure that astonish me; I would have liked to be beside someone who would have aided this unforeseen outpouring of thought.

And then while seated before a cup of tea and then along the length of the Champs-Elysées, as I listened to him analyze himself and tell me about his powerlessness to admire, to be committed, it came. I felt the solemn presence of a serious and reflective self [moi], close and yet as touching as that of a friend. I felt on the tip of my tongue marvelous words that I would like to say, marvelous words that nobody will hear but which resonate profoundly within me. And tonight is one of those nights from the past, detached from the earth and yet very real, a night when the soul is absolutely alone with itself without forgetting anything of the world; when I love myself with the same contemplative disinterest, the same pure happiness as the most beloved being.*

It is something completely different from the ecstatic radiance that flies off to the winged heights; something different from the ardent ecstasy of living that so often these last few days grabbed me by the throat. It's the calm beating of my heart against my chest, in a harmony that drowns out all idle noises. It is a silent and measured step, in a well-lit shade garden; an almost impersonal peace spreading over riches that are very particularly mine.

In the past, it was often like this. Must I regret such times, such times when every day I demanded a similar and silent fervor?

But this evening's peace is beautiful because I know myself to be capable of everything other than it also, and perhaps it appears to me to be less the end that it used to be for me, than a calm pinnacle whose grandeur dominates the entire landscape but from which one must also know how to descend. "The descent" goes poorly moreover; peace is a thing that one must carry with oneself and which must reside within you, not the tent that

---

*This sentence starting "And tonight" is highlighted in the right margin of the handwritten diary.

one unfolds to inhabit intermittently. If I am not content with ceding to this austere and very beautiful grace, if I question it, I will find in it a total, and almost awestruck approval of what I have made of myself until that day, but such approval itself is nourished by the inexhaustible spring whose calm murmur I hear within me. No, nothing is comparable to this feeling but love: and love is as demanding, and as full of acceptance, and as fulfilled as any other.*

Strange certitude that this wealth will be welcomed, that some words will be said and heard, that this life will be a fountainhead from which many others will draw. Certitude of a vocation—no longer as a calling to which one painfully responds: but advancing with full hands, and sensibly distributing a very rare good.†

This too is something other than happiness—something other than pride.

Oh! secret dialogue with myself, incomprehensible to all. Dialogue between the work and the artist, both being the same self. The most touching work of all since it becomes animated in response to the tenderness of this new Pygmalion who is sculpting a soul not out of marble, but out of life itself. When the statue speaks, what need is there for other men in the world, because who would bear her better witness than herself? Other statues do not speak.

Consciousness [*conscience*]—not vision: this understanding [*saisie*] is still too exterior, but like the Stoic's Zeus after the conflagration, I repose in myself and am entirely in myself. All that which is normally directed towards life: strength to deploy, love to give, and intelligence to exercise, turns back on itself and exerts itself to be understood [*se saisir*]—and in being better understood than in their direct use, they embrace all that to which they could be applied. (It would perhaps necessitate deploying Zeus and conserving in the meantime the grace of this very full concentration. I really believe that consciousness accompanies me at the very moments when I am the most generously lost, but then perhaps I do not yet know it well enough.)[450]

I like this year, I like this maturity that it brought me, this profound wisdom that I know to be within me, this infinite power to accept everything of the real without destroying my chosen domain, to understand everything without ceasing to prefer and to believe, I like no longer being surprised

---

* "No, nothing is comparable to this feeling but love: and love is as demanding, and as full of acceptance, and as fulfilled as any other" is highlighted in the right margin in darker ink than the original text.

† The paragraph starting "Strange certitude" is also highlighted in darker ink in the right margin.

and nevertheless filled with wonder.[451] I like that the novelty is not from my destiny but from myself. No, I no longer experience frightened hindsight in reaction to the apparent monotony of days; the admirable drama is deployed in the beyond. The immensity of my solitude, manifested in similar moments, is not pain; this moment belongs to nothing other than self, across souls and times. When I spoke "of carrying the world with me in this progress that ends in ecstasy," it was thus not a vain expression, but it happens in a slightly other way. Moreover it is so beautiful that in order to be faithful to a promise, one must modify it in its very accomplishment. Eighteen months ago I was thinking of a more direct and almost perceptible intuition of the world: what I grasp in this perfect state of joy in which I have been immersed for two hours is rather the imprint on me of this world, or rather, it is I as created and expressed by contact with the world. Thus everything is integrated, and better than if, in a single moment with materials taken from elsewhere, I were constructing a work that I would contemplate at the same time and that would vanish with this contemplation. This work *is*, independently of the joy that I have in feeling its spiritual emergence, and this certitude that tomorrow it will still be, although inscribed nowhere, gives such absolute worth to my joy.

No, it is not enough for me to have a destiny, to live ardently, or to understand—and if the ecstasy, although empty, of my 18 years is too slight for me at 21 (for at 18 it was full of the promises it contained), the simple accomplishment is also too little. Stendhal is really too little for me.*

I wanted to speak of others: of Maheu *first*—of Merleau-Ponty and Zaza—who are the only three judges whom I recognize for diverse reasons.† But judges of the manifestations through which I create myself, not of this supreme position of my self to which nobody has access. I also wanted to speak to you, Jacques, but the longer this colloquium with myself is prolonged, the more useless it is to invent a second person. How to differentiate us? Desire only in the presence of others to demand even more of myself, and this very consciousness that seems to exclude them. Disembodied joy, yet not depersonalization. It envelops the luminous face of Madeleine de Prandières; the inflection of Zaza's voice saying "the amoral lady," M. Ponty's gaze that penetrates to the depth of my soul, Maheu's smile as he touches me on the shoulder saying, "Ah, you are charming," and the distress of our last

---

* This paragraph starting "No, it is not enough" is highlighted with a vertical line in darker ink in the left margin.

† In Beauvoir's handwritten diary, the French equivalent of "first" is underlined.

handshake 13 months and 13 days ago. It envelops the pages sleeping in these desk drawers and also the book where my name will be printed, the chats that we will have together, beloved friends, and your rediscovered presence, Jacques.* Nothing but the purest of my spiritual life, nothing but that which carries in itself a word always present to me, and not even Poupette, not even Meyrignac!

Experience of such purity that it is impossible to imagine when one does not go through it.

Wednesday, June 26

Rather good day. At home in the morning I take a vague look at the authors on my oral. Afternoon, with Zaza and Merleau-Ponty; he is preparing for the exam in physics, chemistry, and the natural sciences [P.C.N.] and is ready to collapse; we spend an hour on the lake and the island where there is nobody. I am with myself: they are a bit foreign to me, but inwardly friends. We have the afternoon snack in Passy in that red pastry shop where I went with M.-P. one day of my internship when it was really cold. Then the AX bus drove us to the Sorbonne where Germaine took her baccalaureate exam.[452] Between Zaza and me a thousand memories return. Supreme sweetness of remembering that young girl in a white pleated skirt and a blue seersucker blouse, ponytail on her back, stepping fearfully into this place and dreaming of the glory she would harvest there: that's my dear friend . . . Here are Zaza and Merleau-Ponty on the edge of the ornamental pond of Luxembourg Gardens from which a bitter wind chases us. They each take their bus; I go up to Josée's home to find her awfully depressed with that deathly pale face she has when her fatigue is too overwhelming.

Some people have dinner here. Evening spent reading.

Thursday, June 27

Another vague day where I stay home meandering through a work, barely making any progress. It's cold. I was supposed to go boating with G.; he bores me, and a letter sent by pneumatic tube notifies him that I'm not going. Besides, my evening has very little need of anyone. Security, expectation, and calm happiness.

---

* From "And also the book" to "Jacques" is highlighted in darker ink in the right margin.

Friday, June 28

Finally two long hours spent with *Zaza*.* I went to get her around nine in the morning in rather nice weather. Naturally her mother welcomed me with her most sour face, but it doesn't matter to me. That lady who believes that she is elite because she is rich and has finally married off a daughter does not keep the avenue des Champs-Elysées or the avenue du Bois from being pleasant, or the paths that we followed afterwards. Zaza speaks to me of her delight over Wednesday—then of the absurd marriage into which her mother wants to force her through truly admirable arguments: "that women are loved and do not love; that Zaza would like to get married and has nothing against this young man, therefore . . . ; that Marie-Thérèse has after all married someone less intelligent." Is it possible that for people who call themselves men and women life is only this submission to conventional forms, without ever having the choice to decide where the entire being lives? Incredible! . . . And M.-P., and Zaza would like me to treat such people as "human beings!"† I deny them this name: it is not enough for me that each of them has two feet, two arms, and an illusion of a face for me to feel in my heart that he is wonderfully my brother. Never! Despite everything, their refusal to feel contempt seems to me to be more or less a lack of strength or of consciousness; and that is perhaps the greatest distance between them and me. Besides, from their point of view they are right since they are always souls.

What's more, Zaza is perfect. Her fervor for waiting, so contained and serene, yet so strong, touches me; this determination, in the past, weak, without revolt, and without brilliance has become firm and sure. She feels what life can bring her and that she must keep the door open. She told me moreover that had she not gotten close to superior beings, she might have been able to accept such a being as the one proposed for her; but that he would not have his rightful place between M.-P. and me, and that she doesn't want anyone to be dearer to her than the one she chooses. Correct also, that if no "unrest" immediately troubles the soul at the first encounter, as soon as one must truly love, no other strong feeling will ever be awakened. How much happiness I wish her!‡

I leave her to go to the Bibliothèque Nationale. How empty one seat is! And has it already been a year since I marveled at being seated at this

---

* In Beauvoir's handwritten diary, "Zaza" is underlined.
† From the beginning of the Friday, June 28 entry to "human beings!" is highlighted in the right margin.
‡ The paragraph starting "What's more, Zaza is perfect" is highlighted in the right margin.

number 271 and at having to present the *agrégation* the following year? I go home early, I work little. Above all, these days at the end of the afternoon and in the evening, I read. I reread Proust.

Saturday, June 29

How do those who live without love manage? As for me, I can thrive only on these intense impulses towards my sisters the souls. At this instant my peace has become radiant due to a note from Merleau-Ponty, and my heart focuses ahead on this evening when I am going to see *them* . . . my friends.

And the vague boredom of this heart is due to the absence of my dear Lama, o my smile, my pride, my pleasure, my exultation, dear René Maheu, and this uninterrupted silent song, sometimes deadly, sometimes drunk with life, is the expectation of you, Jacques. I say: two months, two months, and already I am getting so dizzy that I can no longer recognize myself.

The afternoon went by rather painfully; I went out into a humid evening; stopped by Mademoiselle Richard's knowing that I would not find her and with the vague remorse of moving forward and then immediately disappointing if some superiority in the other does not compel me to stay. I am reading *Caliban parle* [Caliban speaks] in which I hear, with emotion, the warm speech of Guéhenno, as I also reflect on the reasons for the pleasure that the dear half-stranger, Daniel Galois, took in this book, his delicate smile brings me such beautiful peace.[453]

And then it's "Art Seen by the Advertising Academy" at Poupette's school. She is exquisite in a white apron, jean-bart hat, and socks, with little pants hanging out.[454] It's Gandillac and his sister, the three Lacoins, Josée, a truly elegant and seductive Monique Merleau-Ponty, and Madeleine's beautiful smile near her husband's good-natured gaiety. It's the overheated room, Bruneau clapping his hands, charming and funny G.G. Dubois, blinking her eyes behind her horn-rimmed glasses and her very tiny waist cinched with a leather belt. It's Papa bustling about behind the poorly closed curtain, the jostling at a meager buffet, and some rather funny songs performed to beloved tunes. I accompany Josée back to her place. Beautiful night, fragrant and pure.

Sunday, June 30

Got up late. Work. Went by Josée's in the evening; charming. Naturally we speak of M.-P.—how she touches me when she says for example, "I wouldn't want him to have a wife unworthy of him; yet if he were to marry me . . ." I admire the totality of her disinterest, the depth of her humility before him, and that she is delicate and astute. But she lacks a certain . . . a taste for her inner life perhaps, a mastery, a directive. Bold and timid, so demanding and conquering so little. Not able to wish with you, my poor dear Josée . . .

Monday, July 1

Letter from G. to Poupette, rather untimely—everything I dislike about him is definitely there. Maheu's simple signature on a card addressed to the two of us by his wife makes me, on the contrary, dream of pleasure. I must tell him that Poupette spent an evening with Sartre on Tuesday that did not delight her because she does not find him very interesting.

How I like the rather original charm of our relationship, and what bizarre sympathy I feel for his wife who without him, nevertheless, would mean nothing to me! It's amusing.

I go out for an hour with Poupette. Then I work. A note from Zaza—her tenderness, my desire for her, for M.-Ponty. Madeleine. Poupette's dazzling youth. My youth and my peace. Always this indefinite happiness.

"Next year we will do this with Jacques," words that come back constantly between Poupette and me. I am not however imagining anything about what will be, and surely it will not be as simple as just including him in our charming life. Poupette is so other: a radiant young girl of whom he is unaware and who will delight him; I am *so* other: a woman so confident now, and so bold in my heart, so generous with this gift that I did not dare to give him eighteen months ago, of my thought and my life.* And him? We expect almost a stranger, with such a painful impatience to have him know us too. And for him to know what is offered and that everything is put to use. That in three months for sure, this unthinkable thing will have been accomplished: to say "hello Jacques." I am as afraid as three years ago in October after two months of vacation. But, ah! It will be marvelous! I am only afraid of the force of this joy that will carry me away, of our intensity of life that will completely overwhelm this unfortunate me over whom I so easily reign these days.

I found a charming expression in Toulet; he says that when he hears certain women's voices, it is as if "a hand hugged his heart." At times I felt so strongly this blue disorientation, this very sensual caress that are certain

---

* The French equivalent of "so" is underlined in Beauvoir's handwritten diary.

inflexions—of Madame Maheu for example—exquisite vacuity and something within one that melts.

Tuesday, July 2

In the morning, work here. Then around three o'clock I stop by Stépha's. Fernand and Poupette have painted rather pretty canvases, but vague sadness and boredom until the moment when Stépha is transformed thanks to a pretty dress. All four of us go for ice cream at place d'Orléans. Back here, work again, reading. Peace.

Wednesday, July 3

Very dear Zaza. How I looked forward to seeing you while studying Plato in this library so sadly empty. Your presence was already happiness, and nothing but telling stories, while the bus drove us to Luxembourg Gardens, about G., about Saturday's get-together, and about your interview so drolly led.[455] Having a lemon-lime soda in a sunny shade where students who are not studying and all our dear friends pass by joyously, as we speak meanwhile of beings more real than these pleasant appearances.

On boulevard St. Michel she thanked me for my letter; then I started to speak of you, Jacques. Don't accuse me of gossip; she was listening with my ears. The question posed: will he be in my life without all my life being in him, and him always incomprehensible, will I be the same me, simply with a husband—or will my friends be ours and will he be imperative to them as he is to me? Zaza believes that she will never know him and admits it. As for me, my friends whom I love so, pardon me, I care so little about this as long as it will be what he wants! Going out of L'Ami des Livres we went to take a seat in the public garden of St. Germain-des-Prés. Her foot hurt a bit, and then the tramway drove us to la Concorde. I followed her again on avenue des Champs-Elysées and in the metro to her place.[456] I will never forget those hours. Finally a portrait of him that conformed somewhat to him came out of my mouth; I saw him with growing excitement become an incredible presence within me once again, and I saw in Zaza's eyes the reflections of that very dear silhouette and that she was learning to cherish it. And what emotion in her when I read that letter, so direct that even three years later all the words catch in my throat. She believed him to be intelligent but insensitive, and that's why she was vaguely worried and bothered when we spoke of him, but she told me, "One cannot ever doubt the value of a being who wrote such a letter." She told me, "But to suspect what he is worth, you have only to hear the way you speak of him . . ." I told her everything. She listened with that admirable gravity which is hers, and accepted him entirely with faltering words, each weighted with such richness of soul because she was thinking them entirely; and I felt that for her so dear at this moment, Jacques was for a moment as perceptible to her as to me, both of our hearts intertwined together before this face, this face . . .

I walked back. Place de la Concorde I waited at length for the bus. Cars were happily shimmering by while the obelisk loomed calmly in the peaceful sky where the ashy evening clouds sprawled. An enveloping and meditative breath. And within me a supernatural rupture.

O Jacques. I know what profound flavor lives in the peace of my own presence and the marvelous hours that I have spent with myself; but the happiness that comes to me from you is other, as superior to me as I, myself, am to the rest of the world. Soul entirely required and filled with a divine gift.

No longer beaming from a heart profusely widespread, but with a mouth closed on the bouquet of exhilarating violets, a hand grasping a treasure, eyes focused on a single sketch, a life closed on one face. What comes from you, you. And nothing but this desire to flee from vain pleasures, to carry away within me these eyes, and these words, the rest of the world abolished. What is an entire life of the most beloved ones put together if compared to one hour of this life through which mine alone surpasses itself?

However a pleasure was waiting for me upon my return, the greatest pleasure: a charming note from *Maheu* inviting his dear Castor to spend the evening with him.* Indulgent life, charming life—how I also love these funny tufts of blond hair on his temples, this amiable gaze, these gestures full of the most affectionate camaraderie, and the tone with which he says "but my dear friend." We go to the Max Linder cinema where I see again Charlie Chaplin's *The Pilgrim*, with which he is not familiar and that he likes a lot, then a very American film but very well acted that is about an unfaithful husband.[457] It is the first time that I've gone out with Maheu, and I am savoring the pleasure. Rain comes: he puts his collar up in a funny way while we seek shelter under a canvas of sorts from which water is running everywhere. The V bus lets us get on the first time around: it is true that it's a V/AG bus and everyone knows that elderly people are kinder: how silly he is! He makes bad puns all evening and reproaches me for my relationships!

---

* In Beauvoir's handwritten diary, "Maheu" is underlined.

I adore the way he reproaches me for what he appears to want to praise me, exactly like Jacques—for example, "You are interested in everything, that's why I reproach you."

Oh, what a charming hour, dear Lama, at chez Lipp in the room upstairs where you are teaching me "Brazilian *écarté*," the card game invented by you to win at any cost, while discussing the customs of beavers [*castors*] and cassowaries [*casoars*] whose products are, I believe, gastronomes and deuteronomes. We do card tricks as stupid as ourselves, speak vaguely about our preparation for the *agrégation* that we are going to finish together, and we lay out 2F coins at each corner of the playing table with one in the middle. Dear crazy one, how we tease each other good-naturedly, and how nice it is to have met each other in the boring *agrégation* classes so that we could "frolic" together afterwards, and how long ago it was when I used to watch for the one whose improbable friendship was so desired, but not so delightful. He said kindly at the door, "So, my dear girl friend, goodbye, see you on Monday." Brief night completely wrapped up in him, to whom I would like to say if he didn't want to appear so cold, all the sensitive enthusiasm of my heart towards his apparent insensitivity. Dear Lama, I really will tell you one day. Dear, dear Lama.

Thursday, July 4

I go to Le Jardin des Plantes; a red beech tree, the pearly smile of fountains on green lawns, of unknown girls seated with some books—and myself with Boutroux.[458] I go look for Josée at noon, across the street, and we go to lunch together at Evelynes; walk the length of the quays in the wonderful heat, bus full of drafts, allées du Bois smelling like summer when the rain overtakes us, a heavy rain with the joyous sun filtering through and loading the earth with penetrating odors. At Bagatelle roses celebrate life under a stormy sky where gray darkens into a menacing blue; thunder and rain again from which the irises, and the clematis spring forth more sumptuous than before; certain roses are as beautiful as a soul.

Oh! Such muddy feet in the tram that brings us back, and for entering the room of *Pontremoli* who is going to tell me about his most recent failures!*
He tells me about books, which is good, and since I have not seen him for centuries we have enough to talk about without being bored. Besides, is getting bored possible with such a brimming soul? A very amusing man

---

* "Pontremoli" is underlined in Beauvoir's handwritten diary.

came to distract us by speaking of Basch, of Greece, of A. France, and Ch. Maurras. I went home late, just to learn that M.-P. had stopped by the house, and to go with Poupette and G.G. Dubois, while eating candy, to Stépha's place in Montrouge.

And how charming she is this evening, once again my blond and pink, blue-eyed darling, dear Madame Gérassi in her bizarrely cut pink and white sleeveless dress in crepe de Chine. Some people are walking on the roof; candy, cakes, and fruits are circulating. The record player is creaking out tunes to which "Hat" is dancing admirably while Poupette is singing some bawdy songs.[459] Everything is coming to life: costumes, a charming Russian woman disguised as a man dances some dances from her country; a neighbor lends his workshop; a singer sings in an admirable voice in Russian and dances and flirts with G.G. very drolly.[460] Fernand is lighthearted, his brother amusing—easy-going and joyous bohemian: some rather pretty Ukranians and a little Englishman, proper and funny. These people are of an astonishing and likeable childishness, without airs, but not vulgar; poor, but not miserable; almost all painters and without genius but with a spark of love in their lives. Stretched out on the couches we welcome fatigue; Stépha is right next to me, and we recall Gagnepan, our conversations under the lamp, and the promise of her future, which is already the present. With her straw hat she is once again the "mademoiselle" from over there. Joyous return; farandole and marching steps and songs in the streets of Montrouge; a taxi brings us back home and not sad from this evening that moralists would judge as saddening because we only had fun and much more with our bodies than with our minds.

Friday, July 5

This cannot last; such an ending to a year is too good. If I take stock of it again today, I see first *Maurice M.-P.* who comes to get me at ten o'clock and takes me to Luxembourg. We speak of the exam in physics, chemistry, and the natural sciences [*P.C.N.*], the *agrégation*, Guéhenno and culture, and the nature of intellectual joy: I explain to him the intensity for me of certain states of mind and their relationship to what is most direct and concrete in life. He seems to find that a bit strange, more ready to consider such joys of thought as fortuitous. At great ease, we also speak of Zaza, Galois, then his brother and his sister Monique, for whom he has a beautiful smile, then Wagner, music, and art in general. A nasty AX bus tears him away from me, alas! And a V bus drives me to the inevitable Bibliothèque Nationale.

I see Zaza crossing the grand reading room as so often before to come and get me; and at this end of the year everything is so emotional for being a possible "last time." We tell our little stories, then discuss *Manhattan Transfer* that she likes a lot, and we pace up and down the rue de Tocqueville until, coming out of her lesson under a charming beige fur hat, Stépha appears. This "married lady" buys us lemon-lime sodas in a big café at Villiers and our trio meets as if it had never been apart and as if we weren't going to have to be separated for a very long time as of tomorrow. I accompany Stépha in the metro up to Réamur, and once again, despite everything that I might not have liked in her, she is simply my darling Stépha. So many sessions at the Bibliothèque Nationale that would have been so gray, ends of the day that would have been so weary without her blue room, evenings that would have been sad alone. She is the one who used to call me "my Simone" with such a caressing tenderness; the one laughing during evenings in Montparnasse, the one who sang with such living grace, my Stépha. And it is probably not an "elevated" friendship, neither esteem, nor profound tenderness springing forth from admiration, nor the serenity of admirable moments of silence. But perhaps this completely "feminine" friendship is very particularly precious to me because it is so foreign to me. Nothing of what I have that is a bit great in me is shared with her; I cannot at all justify what I would call sentimentality in others. But when I remember her catlike ways, a certain delicate smile, an easy, but real goodness, a too extravagant but very discriminating tenderness, I simply feel like embracing her as I did when I left her, a bit emotional.

Above all, I see in the Bibliothèque Nationale a silent overwhelming hour where I spoke to you, Jacques, one on one. And while none of my friends compares to any other, nor present, imposes any absence, you when you appear throw them all back into a useless horizon, and I don't have need of anything. Everything that is other than this intense love is only waste from which you will save me; from which you are saving me. How intensely you were there! With words that you have said to me for each of which, I would give my life; with the promise (ah! impossible!) of your return; this idea alone brings me back down to earth—yourself Jacques, about whom I can no longer say anything since your name alone stops my heart.

Sunday, July 7

All day with a shattered Josée. Then Zaza and M.-Ponty of no great interest. A note from Lama asking me to work on Leibniz.

Monday, July 8

That's when everything started. Lama came to get me and the AE bus drove us to the Cité Universitaire. Shyness. Sartre politely welcomes me but intimidates me. I remember them so intensely: Lama in shirtsleeves half stretched out on the bed, Sartre seated across from me in front of the table, and all of that room, the big mess, the books, my surprise, the odor of tobacco . . . I explain Leibniz. In the afternoon, here they are, seated near the parc Montsouris in this café where so often in the morning we have had something, and then we will go, making our way together towards the dorm room. In the evening Sartre accompanies us along this boulevard Jourdan to the sinister wooden stalls of the fair. We play the lottery, and I win. Delicious return down the avenue of Maine next to Lama; I don't know what we said, but he was amiable, charming, so truly *my* Lama.

Tuesday, July 9

Arrival of the Grand-Duke without his wife (she weighs on me and annoys me with her false life): but he is a perfect object of contemplation, admirably handsome with his deep wrinkles, his sly and shrewd smile and this unparalleled elegance, made of who knows what.[461]

Oh! Unimaginable charm of such afternoons! Such witty jokes about Leibniz, Sartre's sketches of the Negro with the rational soul and the Lombards' wife's son, Nizan's drawings of this same monster, of Leibniz as a priest, and of the house that wants to escape out the window. And such "pleasant" words in their vocabulary, the handshake over my head, the name "dear *petit camarade*," the game with coins, the rituals, their jokes about my name, and the discussions about whether I am "Castor" or "Walkyrie," the virgin warrior, as Sartre would have it.

In the evening Sartre gives me an atrocious Japanese painting as a present that Lama helps me to bring back to my place. Lama reads, very poorly. The Grand-Duke reads, very well, and has fun. Sartre and I work.

Wednesday, July 10

All four of us again. I remember us drinking port wine near the AE bus stop without making up our minds to leave. I remember Lama curtly saying, "No, tonight I am going to the movies with Mademoiselle de Beauvoir," and the Grand-Duke replying, "Good, good," while Sartre says, "So be it." In the bus,

Lama tells me, "I want you to get along well with my *petits camarades*, but ..."—But you are Lama, right?—"Besides you will not be a *petit camarade*."—Of course. I am your Castor. Thus we emphasize what we are for each other; but he does not know how much he will always remain first for me.

In the afternoon we take a very big break, which means we go for drinks at chez Dupont, they have beer, I lemon-lime soda; they discuss the Eugenic cosmogony and the role of women; I argue with Sartre for a laugh while the Grand-Duke maintains a magnificent indifference. How much I also like their songs, how I like to be in their midst and take part in this marvelous existence that they create!

In the evening, Sartre, Lama and I go all the way to Denfert where I was taught to play Japanese billiards. Sartre gave me as a gift some absurd pieces of porcelain won for me last night, and a vile two-penny novel for my sister. It's late. A taxi brings Lama and me back; he is sad tonight, he would like to go out with his wife. I have a heavy heart upon leaving him, and I wander in Luxembourg Gardens eating pastries, astonished at the power of his smile over me, and exhausted. I barely make it back up to the house and meet him again. He tells me, "I am happy to go out with you, Castor."

Oh! night among nights ... Oh! the pleasure of coming together again as Lama-Castor on the Place St. Sulpice, of strolling along the boulevard, talking, without worrying about what we are going to see. He speaks to me of Sartre and Nizan, comparing himself to them, for he likes life in its simplicity, thoughtless amusement, and mixes his artistic ideas with such life; he values greenery, vacation, the great outdoors that the others don't know how to appreciate. His conception of women ... a mark of his respect. It's true that when in the morning he simply ran his hand over my head saying, "Beavers like this a lot," I was very moved. We see le Tour de France and a film by Buster Keaton that amuses us a lot. Before we had a drink in a little café right next door where he kept asking, "Are you bored?" I wouldn't want to lose any of him ...

We walked back, joking about the film. We had something at Deux Magots while talking about the workings of the divine analogy, his individualism, his in-laws, and his wife. He told me, "You have to get married ..."—there was an admirably pure, complete, trusting, and sweet tenderness between us. Oh, night among nights—oh! my Lama.

Thursday, July 11

Arrival of *Madame Nizan* whom I find absolutely unbearable—in fact because of her we don't work. We play Japanese billiards with her, and I win a superb red pitcher. I speak to her of her daughter with a look of empathy that, apparently, earns me hers, and also amuses *Sartre* and *Maheu* as proof that I am decidedly very feminine. The *Grand-Duke* drives us back. In the afternoon, he is not there, and we work with intensity. We first drank something close to the AE bus stop, and it seems that I angered Sartre quite a bit when for fun I compared him to Gandillac. What's more, I let loose this afternoon, and Maheu, collapsed on the bed, watches me in amazement saying from time to time, "How clever she is," for in fact I am getting the better of Sartre today; I am having great fun, but how well we are working too!

Stifling heat. But the drawn curtains create an obscure retreat. Maheu is on the chair next to me, Sartre has made it to his bed with his pipe in his mouth. We are studying the text—profound joy of such labor when time disappears, such very beautiful language, such captivating thoughts.[462] Sartre explains and explains, accusing me of making him reel off all of his knowledge at each difficulty—marvelous intellectual mentor—more and more, his thought appears extraordinarily strong to me. I admire him too with a great gratitude for so generously making an effort solely for our benefit.

We work until nine o'clock or almost. Then in great haste and without eating dinner I hurry to the Bois de Boulogne where "my gang" is waiting for me—what exhilaration I feel as I tumble down the avenue Henri-Martin while devouring brioches . . .

Evening on the lake with the *M.-Pontys* and the *Gandillacs*—how happy I am!* We drive poor Gandillac up the wall, but there is a charming moment with M.-Ponty and his sister in the small boat when he is so straightforwardly kind and she so tender with him. Great gaiety on the avenue du Bois where I execute my unfortunate hat. Gaiety in this café on the avenue Wagram where we devour something in such happy cordiality.

But all of this is no longer much of anything. My present happiness springs from a more informal atmosphere that dominates me.

Friday, July 12. Lama[463]

My heart beating with such joy! Have I ever so cherished, *L'éthique à Nicomaque* [*Nicomachean Ethics*]?[464] I hurry to the rue Vaneau.[465] Oh, this blue room, the velour armchair in front of the banal hotel table, the bed where he is stretched out in shirtsleeves telling me, "I am so happy to have

---

* The names "M.-Ponty" and "Gandillac" are underlined in Beauvoir's handwritten diary.

you here . . ." A portrait of his wife on the fireplace, some issues of *Détective*, and me, completely soothed, seated here, flooded with the sweetness of his presence and divinely explaining Aristotle to him while he reads notes by Hannequin and Sartre.[466] He shows me some very funny drawings by Nizan and Sartre of metaphysical animals and other things. He accompanies me on a beautiful sunny day to the bus that will take me, late, to Aunt Lili's while I read the admirable *Poussière* [*Dusty Answer*] by Rosamund Lehmann.[467] Life's pleasures . . .

In the afternoon, he warns me that he doesn't care about working; he shows me *Anabase* [*Anabasis*] by St. J. Perse and tells me stories about Buridan to keep me from going back to Aristotle.[468] In particular he shows me some deeply moving photos: three reproductions of Michelangelo, especially—the view of a man's profile with a magnificently generous gesture, a Sybil who brings to mind Vinci, and one who brings to mind men who would be gods, one who is sorrow and art and all things too poignant to ever be portrayed. Oh, visions evoked by such works! Oh, the fact that he shows them to me! Simply this banal room into which the summer heat filters just enough for it to be delicious to feel protected from it, simply this camaraderie nuanced with tenderness . . . I will be able to see it forever and ever. I will never forget even that the strap on my slip broke, that he went to get a pin and left me alone for a moment in the cabinet de toilette which had the most pleasant view in the world, that we went downstairs together and had a drink in a café on the boulevard Montparnasse where he spoke to me of his wife whom I do not want to see except through his eyes, and that I myself was madly in harmony with the splendor of this summer day in Paris. We came back bringing up vague and charming phrases, we tried to work a little bit, then he carted me off so that I could go have dinner at Zaza's.

Evening with Zaza in the garden of the Tuileries; she tells me about herself and about her odious mother. I am distressed for her, but my heart is full of an intoxication that I would like to tell her, of an astonishment filled with wonder, gratitude, admiration, and tenderness for these great young people who have adopted me in this way. Ah! Judith from *Dusty Answer*, how I recognize in you, this little girl with profound and calm passions, an insane confidence, a grave generosity, and so simply amoral . . . my sister Judith who is moved by blond hair, harmonious colors, and a park blooming with happiness, but who reserves her share of a more serious treasure—tragic and straightforward little girl, my sister Judith.

Saturday, July 13

Sartre explains *Le contrat social* [*The Social Contract*] always with this same intellectual devotion that already makes him very dear to me. I wandered at length before coming, prey to an excessively beautiful morning. In the tramway I met the Grand-Duke who speaks in his charming voice of English and Irish literature all the way to the café terrace where Lama and Sartre were seated . . . Delight of these arrivals, and sometimes one or the other already present . . . and sometimes one or the other whose approach we so tenderly seek, but always great and happy radiance.

That day, my Lama, we had lunch together at chez Chabin, and the parc Montsouris was coming in through the open window. We went to meet it in our turn all the way to the pond where there wasn't a soul yet. Do you remember the fountains with their great whirling of happy divinity, the pink tulips on the lawn, the sun and the things that you told me about the cruel little boy that you were? You told me about your childhood, the war, and adventures. How close I felt to you, and because of your very sensibility that also knows how to understand what is other than itself . . . Why did we have to go home? We hardly desired to work. The Grand-Duke's car took us into Paris by unexpected paths. I was in the back next to you, Lama, and I was singing, while we went to the government ministry office. You were also singing, "again concerning God, that He exists" and I was teasing Sartre while the Grand-Duke was saying, "it's a success" [*ça tourne*].[469]

And then the École Normale where you started to sing at the top of your lungs as you climbed the dirty stairways . . . In the now lifeless classroom D we wrote inscriptions praising the crazy Robin; we visited the disgusting dormitories, the suffocating study rooms; all those places where you lived. We stole Erland's paintings and climbed onto the roof to hang them there. What unparalleled moments, while they jumped with the agility of young males, I remained seated with a slight fear, a great confidence, a great tenderness and looked at the gardens of the École below me. Once again we jump into the car that brings us back to the Cité. How merry we are! Madame Nizan is there, we are barely working, we go to play Japanese billiards, and the Grand-Duke brings us all the way to rue Cassette where Lama accompanies back to my place. We listened to records too, very good records that overwhelm me.

Merleau-Ponty comes to dinner. He does not understand the charm of what I tell him, but on the pretext of studying Plato we have a very pleasant chat in the dining room until midnight strikes.

Sunday, July 14—the *petits camarades*

Did we work in the morning? No, rather slept until noon? I can still see our arrival at Sartre's with the promise of working until night. But there are a lot of people there: Zuorro and his girlfriend, Guille, Madame Nizan seated on the bed; the Grand-Duke on one chair, me on another, Lama with his back against the wall, Sartre also seated on the floor and striving hard in a charming way to act as host. The phonograph plays incessantly. There are some black gospel choirs, some records by Sophie Tucker whose voice I don't like and which Maheu compares to my wa-wa-wa that he mocks so well, and also Les Revellers who sing "Blue River" in such an admirable way, Jack Hylton who amuses me a lot, and especially Layton and Johnstone with the overwhelming "Ol' Man River," "So blue," "Crying for the moon," etc.[470] All of it speaks straight to my heart. All of it speaks of them, of another, of my life, of impossible lives . . . I would like to be alone to hear it better. Meanwhile the big reunion is a bit exhausting: we play with the cat; the Grand-Duke throws things out the window; Sartre is dressed up like an old man; and as for me, I feel oppressed by this entire reunion that distances me from them. But, on the other hand, what a party!

We go, Sartre, Maheu, and I, toward the parc Montsouris, which is already overflowing with crowds in expectation of the evening celebration. I can still see us seated on a bench, and they are teasing me . . . about soldiers and policemen . . . we cannot have dinner chez Chabin because it's too crowded; so through a complicated itinerary (oh, at the window, this man who *thinks*!) Sartre leads us to what will henceforth be known to us as *le dîner successif* [the successive dinner]. How kind they are to me during this dinner! . . . "Sartre is enchanted with you," Maheu tells me. "Besides, who is not enchanted with you? . . . The Grand-Duke is brimming with warm feelings . . . you have won over his wife."

"Yes, she is quite admirable," says Sartre. I tell them little stories about the opinion that I had of them, and they, on the way they came about accepting me. Lama is next to me, Sartre is across from me, and I am more moved than I want to appear.

Ah! What gaiety on the avenue d'Orléans, what profound and calm passion within me! We enter into a fair where Sartre thrills me by surprise and tests his strength; I shoot with an automatic rifle, and I listen with delight to "Dinah" . . . [471]

I feel attractive in this black dress that Lama likes, and bareheaded, and completely animated . . . they are singing; the coolness of the evening with the song that they are improvising, "Castilbeza, the man with the rifle / Used to sing this here / Does someone from here know the Sabine girl / Someone from here." Sartre sings "Old Man River" in his beautiful deep voice while on the boulevard Jourdan we make our way back to the Cité Universitaire. Stretched out on the lawn, we play at naming the firework displays: crackling, park ablaze, stars are falling on our heads, and we take them as omens. I would shout for joy; people are passing; the lawn is delightfully ours . . .

In Sartre's room the phonograph is locked up; with a noble gesture he stops a taxi saying that from now on he will take care of everything. Excitement to feel Lama's arm against my shoulder or sometimes to feel his hand slid under my arm in a protective and tender gesture. Giant steps on the boulevard Montparnassee . . . then the Falstaff welcomes us; around a barrel where I am served two cocktails, the evening develops a heartrending intimacy. Sartre praises me for avoiding, better than any other female *agrégation* student, the crude jokes and for taking them admirably well, "and for these two reasons, you are worthy of esteem." He does my psychological portrait and that of Lama, indicating that a very particular case permits only a friendship between us, since in general Lama sees women only as women or wives [*ne voit la femme que comme femme*], whereas my temperament should lead me further than friendship. Discussions on friendship and jealousy. I differentiate between the people who only cause pleasure and those for whom one suffers—at first, it doesn't interest him, then when I define precisely what such suffering is: the fear of an irreparable damage, he finds it very beautiful, if it's true. "But I told you that she was someone extraordinary," my dear Lama assures him.

We leave, going back up the rue Delambre and all the way back down to Stryx, where we stop in for only a second. Maheu took me by the arm, and both of them who saw great sadness in my eyes only a little while ago when I was thinking of Jacques, speak to me with a rare gentleness. Although I am a woman, Maheu wants to invite me to participate in his race and explains how the system works . . . We speak of dancing: Sartre will teach me. They see me back . . . rue Notre-Dame-des-Champs, they ask me absurd questions about the *agrégation* . . . chatting so gaily all the way to my door. Oh my friends, my friends.

O my Lama.

Monday, July 15

It's funny . . . why should I have been sad in thinking about not seeing him since by the greatest luck as I was about to take the AE bus I glimpsed that golden smile through the door. He speaks so kindly to me: they are afraid of having hurt me last night, but *Lama* is happy because Sartre recognized his priority in my friendship.* Accompanies me all the way to the Porte d'Orléans where we order something at chez Dupont. Speaks to me of jealousy, of his liking for special treatment in friendship. Finishes by going all the way to Sartre's place where he rediscovers the ring, pretext of his outing, and where we give a good explication of Plato. *Zaza* comes for lunch.† I take her for a walk in the parc Montsouris; Maheu sees us (oh! his beige suit, his raised hand) and walks us in the Cité Universitaire—he is very nice to Zaza whom we bring to Sartre's. Phonograph. She is out of place here—"Too severe a face," says Sartre and pointing at me: "Now look at that good face!" And then the Nizans come, I am fuming because I was supposed to go to the cinema with Sartre and they are interfering. It amuses Maheu, but taking pity he follows me out of the car of the Grand-Duke, who has driven us back, and leads me to the Deux Magots. It's there that he tells me, "I will kiss you when I leave: on your forehead and on your two eyes, but I shouldn't say so! Oh! . . . would you say something like that?"

I remember it so clearly. I accompanied him back to his place by the rue de Babylone. I was in terrible turmoil. He told me about his entering the École Normale, and consoled me about my exasperation of this evening, "Will you think of me?" he said to me with that sort of authoritarian coquetry so dear to me. And these words while squeezing my arm, "I like you a lot, Castor." I leave him to take the V bus, go to Luxembourg Gardens, without having dinner, meet the Nizans' car that takes us to the Ciné-Montparnasse, in discussion all the while with Sartre who is starting to interest me immensely. Went to the fair. Exquisite evening at Place Denfert-Rochereau. The Nizans take me back from the Cité in the car. Nizan explains his future works to me.

O my too dear Lama . . .

Tuesday, July 16—Lama

How that man can make me suffer! Oh! Friday it was too wonderful when he was there stretched out on his bed, smiling close to me welcomed by the big blue armchair on the pretext of explaining Greek.[472] Oh! Sunday evening with Sartre at the Falstaff, where we spent too much time explaining the friendship that was between us: our words perhaps led our friendship

---

* In Beauvoir's handwritten diary, "Lama" is underlined.
† In Beauvoir's handwritten diary, "Zaza" is underlined.

into this turmoil from which they claimed to differentiate it. Oh! last night so tender when he said to me, "I really like you, Castor" with his hot hand under my arm, and I, "I like you a lot, Lama."

Today I feel bad about that nasty departure at the Bibliothèque Nationale on the pretext that M.-P. came to get me, bad about this independence that I admire, about this cold atmosphere, magnificent for the strong, but heavy for the weak.

I feel bad about this weakness never before known to me, and about my penchant to give in to it. I so want his hand to caress my head again, his arm around my shoulder, or his hand briefly but repeatedly brushing against my cheek and my neck, so want this kiss that he promised me in such a way—oh! so slyly simple—that it was impossible to say no. And I am so frightened by what he could do with me if only he wanted it; and by my secret regret that he cannot want it. And yet, he is not the one whom I love. But for the first time, there is this pleasure that I would like to call odious, but that is delicious, to feel all excited just at the idea of leaning my head on his shoulder. I am going to suffer tonight. I am nervous, ready to cry at the drop of a hat, and feeling a terrible sense of dependence. Everything will be just as he wants. But I am not going to forget his high esteem that is so dear to me either.

I was at the Bibliothèque Nationale this morning to do some Plato; he was there, and it was a day from the past. Then lunch with Zaza and M.-P. who get along admirably well; some wonderful moments in the hall of the Bibliothèque Nationale when we said good things about each other, but they are attacking my friends, who are already more my friends than both of them, and I would prefer to be near Lama. He leaves, furious that M.-P. must come with us. I would cry at the drop of a hat, and I do cry.

At Normale we all meet again, collapsed in the grass not knowing what to do . . . I go home overwhelmed; fortunately Poupette gave me back a bit of peace.

And then with my too beloved Lama, what a night! What sweetness in his question, "Poor Castor, was I mean?" We walk the length of the quays and we stop at Pont de l'Alma. He tells me about his childhood, his coming to Paris. I listen to him, I am very weary, but it is delightful to be near him like this. We take a taxi that escapes into the very cool night all the way to the Stryx that he finds delightfully bizarre. He tells me, "You are a phenomenon," with so much tenderness. I feel like a poor Castor, but he tells me that I was wonderful tonight. Oh! On the rue Cassette how sweetly he assures me of that with his arm around my shoulder, his face so close to mine. How weak and absurd I am, how I love him!

Wednesday, July 17—Evening with Sartre

Worry. Sorbonne, ministry, École Normale with Zaza to find out if I passed; beginning of the afternoon at the Nizan's, then encounter with Sartre who announces my success.[473] Lama, who flunked, tells me goodbye with a profoundly affectionate smile. I have a drink with Sartre at the Balzar where I catch sight of Miquel. Sartre is delightful; he finds my joy to be perfectly "enjoyable." In a taxi, he takes me to the home of Maheu who is gone, and does whatever he wants with me, but I adore his way of being authoritarian, of adopting me, and of being so sternly indulgent.

I go to Zaza's, delighted with my success, and I meet Poupette and Merleau-Ponty there.

The *Grand-Duke* passes by to congratulate me; as always he is touching with his strangeness, his elegance, and his grace.*

I meet Sartre at the Koulak. What a night!

Walked all the way to the Tuileries, then from the Tuileries to the Falstaff where between two cocktails he tells me such profound things about myself. That I am not noble or moral, but generous, from many points of view a little girl. Intellectually less cultivated than instructed, and unpleasant when I speak of philosophy. But a very dear Castor. Overwhelming refinement and a "kindness" unexpected from this boy, so crude elsewhere, especially when he tells me that he knows that I am in love, that he has on that topic and on marriage some painful things to tell me. His advice as to my conduct with the three of them, the sweetness in his mouth of the words, "you are engaging." He tells me also that I am "a tragic girl," but that it's good because it means that I am not serious, the only hateful thing. Lama makes a woman feel attached to him just by softly caressing her neck, Sartre, by showing her heart to her—which one more surely enslaves her?† I don't know, but at present never seeing them again would be a death sentence.‡ O you alone dear ones with whom I can be myself, and who love me not for any nobleness, but for myself. "There is something tumultuous within you," he told me. How true it is!

---

* In Beauvoir's handwritten diary, the name "Grand-Duke" is underlined.

† In Beauvoir's handwritten diary, parentheses are penciled around the French equivalent of these words, "Lama attaches a woman to himself with nothing but softly caressing her neck, Sartre, by showing her heart to her--which one more surely enslaves her?"

‡ In Beauvoir's handwritten diary, the French equivalent of the words, "I don't know, but at present never seeing them again would be a death sentence," is highlighted in the left margin.

Thursday, July 18

How important these days are!

I do some Plato at *Sartre*'s in the morning.* Stopped by Lama's with my heart beating rapidly to see this room full of him, empty; in a note he told Sartre to "say that he wishes all the happiness in the world to Castor." O my Lama. Pleasure also that the Grand-Duke drove me to the Cité this morning while explaining to me the plan for his works and his philosophical position—a thousand fascinating things on Marxism taken as wisdom.

Worked alone, pleasant afternoon snack with Zaza, M.-P, and the de Prandières, but my heart is no longer with them. At eight thirty Miquel comes up to get me; I stay with him for a half-hour; he is rather exhausted, but still nice. Then I go up to Nizan's into the office covered with books, with a picture of Lenin, a poster of Cassandre and the sublime *Naissance de Venus* [*The Birth of Venus*] hung on the wall.[474] We translate Aristotle while drinking coffee. What good work, interspersed with chatting, and charmed by that voice, that oblique smile, that complicated gaze that is Nizan's alone.

Friday, July 19—[Beginning of the Oral Exam]

Good Greek explication, after the nervousness of the morning when seeing the *agrégation* students gathered before a paternal jury made me feel nauseated. *Merleau-Ponty* and *Zaza* kindly tried to help me shake it off, but in vain, until *Sartre* authoritatively took me to Luxembourg Gardens to do some Plato.† After lunch, instead of doing Plato we have a discussion. He takes me to the Balzar and gives me advice in a perfectly nice way: he is the only person for whom it is not a reproach to be called authoritarian. He himself presents an excellent explication, and the Grand-Duke drives us in his car through a terrible rain, thunder and lightning to have a drink on the Place du Châtelet. I write a letter to Lama in which I reveal myself perhaps too much. My God, how I miss him!

Gandillac comes to dinner; I am hot, I am nervous . . . my letter really touched him and we chat amicably all evening in the Tuileries and on the avenue du Bois. He tells me about his romance with Monique M.-Ponty.

---

* In Beauvoir's handwritten diary, "Sartre" is underlined.
† In Beauvoir's handwritten diary, "Merleau-Ponty," "Zaza," and "Sartre" are underlined.

Saturday, July 20

Work at Nizan's. Stopped by Zaza's who accompanies me along the rue Vavin, deeply moved by a conversation with M.-Ponty. They love each other; so be it. I am very happy, very.*[475]

The Nizans are playing funny and touching things on the phonograph. The couch is wide and pleasant, the Fargue editions marvelous, and the Grand-Duke, gray on red, admirable. We work little. The car takes us to the Sorbonne where I am told that I placed well, then to Montparnasse from where I walk alone with Sartre to work again. But we are, above all, having a very affectionate discussion. In the evening, work again. I steal from the bookshelves of Nizan who is brimming with liking for me.

Sunday, July 21

Today Nizan presented his lesson, which was excellent.[476] Aron was there during it—face intelligent and likeable. In the morning however I worked with Sartre.

When Aron, who went with us for a drink at the Balzar, leaves us, I go to Luxembourg Gardens with Sartre where we discuss good and evil for two hours. He interests me enormously, but destroys me [*mécrase*]; I am no longer sure of what I think or even of thinking.

Revelation of a richness of life incomparable with the one in the too exclusive garden in which I enclose myself, a strength of thought that demands the most serious work for me to attain it, and a maturity that I envy and promise myself to attain.†

In the evening I take a walk with Poupette, very exalted with such prospects of a fervent life. I demolish her Catholicism for her in a few words: ethics of cowardice that I abhor, sure safeguard, but one that I do not want. I feel within me something tumultuous that frightens me, an intensity that exhausts me. But I accept the great adventure of being me.

Monday, July 22

Extraordinary influence of Sartre—for the 13 days that I have known this boy, he has explored me, and now anticipates and knows me thoroughly.

---

* The paragraph, "Work at Nizan's . . . I am very happy, very," is highlighted in the right margin of Beauvoir's handwritten diary.

† In Beauvoir's handwritten diary, this paragraph is highlighted in right margin.

Intellectual need for his presence, and emotional turmoil in facing his affection. Doubts, upset, exaltation, I would like him to force me to be a real somebody, and I am afraid. I am a little girl, and frightened by the intensity of the renewal occurring within her. I will give myself over to this man with absolute confidence. Dominated by something too tender and sensitive when I think of Lama, and by something too strong when Sartre is there; what can be done with poor me?

He got through his lesson today, and after having listened to him, walk on the quays with him and Madame Nizan. He is blissfully happy; I like him a lot.

My Latin explication went well, and we are all taking a nice walk in the rues Monge and Mouffetard "where he was all fired up." At the École Normale we caught sight of Galois and Borne. Exquisite evening with Sartre whom I meet on the place Médicis and who apologizes for blunt things said yesterday. We walk in Luxembourg Gardens, and then a taxi takes us to the cinema. He is of an unimaginable kindness when he tells me, "You are a charming Castor," and places his hand so tenderly on my arm. He can tell me the most disagreeable things without upsetting me, for example, that astute remark that too much laughter is nervousness, and such nervousness in a pure little girl often comes from her sudden feeling of being a woman in the company of men. I appreciate more than I could convey that they treat me as a woman after all. We come back along the boulevard Sébastopol. I am peaceful and light-hearted near him.

Tuesday, July 23

Met Sartre in Luxembourg Gardens where we chat nicely for two hours. Excessively fatigued, I sleep for two hours at the Sorbonne. For a moment I see M.-Ponty, then Nizan takes me away with that indisputable air that I adore. We work a bit, then he reads me some articles on Brunschvicg, Epicurus, and French sociology, with his extraordinary charm. I am more relaxed with him today, I tell him that he is a little boy and so delightfully so with that sly smirk. I am overjoyed with the refined intelligence of these beings. Extraordinarily happy, I leave this Grand-Duke, who has been visited by all graces.

I tell all this to Sartre in the evening while I am eating peanuts and ice cream at the Closerie des Lilas. He tells me stories about himself, and in particular, about his engagement to a little girl whom he did not want to hurt. So touching coming from him who knew he had been duped and not unconsciously so . . . Sensitive Sartre; it surprises me, but why? my dear Sartre, while we are walking back through Luxembourg Gardens, delighted with one another and promising that we will see each other a lot next year.

Oh! All the blinds on the boulevard Montparnasse where I went by this morning are now lowered!

Wednesday, July 24

I take a walk around Luxembourg Gardens with very kind M.-Ponty. Oh! Such indescribable shock upon seeing the rosy smile of Lama at the Sorbonne; banality of the words exchanged that nevertheless inform me that he is upset. I go off to prepare an absurd lesson, anxious about this face to which I have revealed so much and that reveals nothing.

Bad lesson that my friends kindly call acceptable. But I would like to run back to Sartre, and M.-Ponty, his sister, and Poupette accompany us. Afternoon snack with M.-Ponty; I accompany him to Ducasse's place in the pouring rain with little to tell him. Fortunately a rediscovered Sartre takes me to the Balzar, tells me stories about his youth, and about him and Nizan to whose home we go for dinner.

There is Péron, the Grand-Duke (cold and magnificent), Madame Nizan excited and odious, Sartre a bit exhausted and me . . . poor me, at this dinner and in the streets where we wander cheerlessly. Poor me, *so* poor!

Lama got bored in Bagnoles, and his wife wasn't nice. Lama is not here. I wrote an absurd letter to Lama. Friday Lama is leaving for the entire vacation, and will I even get one word from him?

Sartre told me that his wife made a scene because of me. He belongs to that woman, and me, and me . . . Oh! René Maheu . . . as I walk at a distance from the others all evening I would like your arm around my shoulders like the other day and your excessively caressing voice. We will forget that all this is impossible: besides I know that you would be happier with me. For one night there would no longer be anyone but you and me on our horizon. Would you kiss me as you said? But then I would start to cry.

Thursday, July 25

I cannot know where all of it is going to lead me . . .

Oh! yes, very simply to the calm solitude of this vacation when I will get a hold of myself again—but let me cry. This morning let me cry all the rest of my tears during this too beautiful summer. When Maheu is going to leave, when Maheu must leave since after all he will not get a divorce to marry me as the Grand-Duke crazily imagines, and when I would not accept to do so. Jacques exists, but what tumult, what a tumultuous soul and tumultuous heart. And what crazy desire for this childish face, this unconsciously cruel grace.

Oh! my Lama, my Lama who knows only too well how too tenderly dear he is to me. I just saw him again, coming out of Sartre's Latin explication. He told me, "You wrote me some charming things about Sartre . . . what's more, you wrote me a charming letter . . . yes, indeed, I reread it twice . . . I understand that you were upset that you wrote it, as for me, however, it gave me great pleasure."

Oh! why upset, Lama, why upset that you would know what you mean to me; besides, you mean even more. As he said to Sartre, "Moreover, she *is* charming."

And Sartre, "You are physically very good-looking this morning—as always moreover."

He said, "Yes, I will probably write to you . . . I will get in touch in Uzerche." He said, "Goodbye Castor."

I am terribly happy to have made him happy, to be dear to him, to merit this smile that melts in my mouth like a piece of fruit. Terribly sad that this is such a long goodbye; and I do not even know which goodbye since next year will be so other.

Maybe it's for the best; maybe . . . and then two months will pass. Goodbye, oh! so dear Lama.

But what a delightful night, with such a delightful Sartre . . .

He comes to get me here, and my heart is too heavy to go to work at the Grand-Duke's. He takes me down long adventurous avenues, my arm hugged against his, as docile to his body as to his stories. Long avenues, cinemas, fairs, where we have as much fun as children . . . a fun fair, poignant walk towards Glacière, Corvisard, up to the Rotonde where I have a cocktail while he repeats, "You are a truly charming Castor." What kindness, what gaiety, what tenderness. Crazy moments, delightfully crazy and when I like him so intensely . . .

Friday, July 26

On the pretext of work, what a delightful day . . . I meet him at the Cité Universitaire and we vaguely study Boutroux together. I have on my sleeveless dress in crepe de Chine that suits me well . . . we take bus 8

262

together to go home for lunch. I hardly expect Merleau-Ponty to be there, and some family discussions exhaust me. But it is delightful to meet Sartre again in the Luxembourg Gardens, to try in vain to read Rousseau, as I am too caught up in the simple pleasure of being seated next to him, and then of listening to his theories on adventure, the work of art, and life. They are fascinating and I must reflect on them at leisure. Charming to go with him to boulevard Raspail, then alone to Le Bon Marché and into the public garden square to wait for him. Charming to get back into the taxi at the Cité and to go to *le dîner successif* while thinking of Maheu and of the delightful July 14 when he was here, and while listening to and telling stories about Mesdemoiselles Joint, Jollivet, and about Gandillac.[477]

We climb slowly back up to his room, and there we put off indefinitely the time to work . . . he on his bed, pipe in his mouth, examines my face in the flattering light; I look at him, I listen to him, as I trust in this worth that he affirms in speaking of himself with moving sincerity. How I like his calm fraternal arm against my arm; our laughter on the avenues, my hat stuck to one side, our plans, our happy confidence, and all to the way to the Select to become a more and more charming Castor, while he tells me that he doesn't know at what point our ever-growing liking for each other will end. Oh! Night among nights, oh! This trip back so full of emotion on the boulevard Raspail and the rue de Rennes, where we speak of the "great Sartre," oh! mad hope for our futures, our life, and insane sweetness of the present.

As I go to bed, I am truly intoxicated with him and with me.

Saturday, July 27

At the Cité again, in his room. We work, he on Boutroux, I on Rousseau, very little. Then we have lunch together at chez Chabin only to make our way slowly towards the Sorbonne. I take a seat in the courtyard so that he can see "my pretty face" from the library while he prepares French—but somebody comes along who changes everything: oh! you at last, Lama, for an instant, alone with each other. Your smile at the sight of my dress that you find pretty, your smile . . . and at the Balzar where you take me, these words: "In my day, it was lemon-lime soda."—"But it still is your day."—"That's what I wanted to hear you say." He tells me that he will come to Uzerche, even if he must go well out of his way, but only if he is without his wife, "I don't want to say anything bad about my wife, but if I come to Uzerche it's to see you." My Lama is sad, Bagnoles did not cheer him up, and that hurts me. When Sartre and Lama are together, why does Sartre pale in importance like this, if not because I am too intensely absorbed by the Lama. Oh! he alone, and so painful not to have him all to myself. We meet again with his wife at the Closerie des Lilas. Sartre is right: she is obnoxious, and it couldn't be sadder to think that his life is there, his help when he is sad, and his joy. Moreover, he gets rid of her, and we walk up towards École Normale. Great distress within me. I wait for him with Sartre in the garden. Then a taxi whisks the three of us away . . . My God, how I care for this man!

I am perfectly overwhelmed as I go up to my room. Fortunately, Sartre comes to get me in the evening; we go up to the Dôme where his encounter with a vague classmate amuses me for a moment; then, his arm against mine, we walk and take a seat in the little Luxembourg gardens, as we speak of Lama, of the beginning of our relationship, and of our interactions at the Sorbonne so amusing from afar. He sensibly brings me back so that I can work on Rousseau. Heart swollen with pleasure.

Sunday, July 28

Good explication of Leibniz, and glimpsed Merleau-Ponty who bids me adieu.

At two o'clock I go down with Poupette (that same morning Nizan, Sartre, and I had a drink with her at the Knam, chatting in a charming manner) and Sartre picks us up to go to the Dôme where they have a lively chat, then to La Boîte à Musique where he has us listen to some Sophie Tucker records. A wonderful moment, as I sit in the armchair near Poupette and watch the dear little man smoke his pipe to a tune on the phonograph reminiscent of the good old days. Went to Le Carillon with Poupette. Evening at home. I am reading *Er, l'Arménien* [Er, the Armenian], and I daydream about them, about the grace of this life into which they have led me.[478]

Monday, July 29

Lunch at the house in my honor.

Joy in the midst of these barbarians of telling myself: I am going to meet Sartre again and run to Luxembourg Gardens with my heart leaping. Joy of waiting for him with delightful abandon. Then, seated next to each other, joy of exchanging words with an exquisite ease. We are going to hear Nizan's explication, and then leave in the car with him, to Madeleine de Prandières's home. She is very kind, but I care so little about those beings now. Oh! My heart leaps for this evening alone. Trouble at first between the Grand-Duke and his wife who pounds on the piano, although Nizan is as always perfectly elegant, but when, at last, the doorbell rings I so feel that my dear Sartre is truly *mine*.

Gaiety of our walk in the rue de Saint-Benoît, the rue de Seine etc. Mock battles, cries, and games that enchant us. We tease each other kind-heartedly at chez Wepler, and on the Place du Châtelet. The Grand-Duke is admirable, and his wife, this evening, unbearable. Sartre sings, in this deep voice that moves me. He took my arm on the boulevard Saint-Michel and is hugging it very tightly. How comfortable we feel together. So comfortable that when the others leave us, we continue to walk, intertwined. We take a seat on a bench on the Place Saint-Sulpice. I am moved that his arm is around my shoulder while I tell him stories about Meyrignac . . . His gaze is full of amusement and tenderness . . . I could stay like this for ten hours. Tonight, he tells me in a very touching way, "You are a perfectly charming young girl." But I sleep poorly, agitated by such things.

Tuesday, July 30

I am agitated in the morning, when I go to get him at the Cité; some impatient words, "I don't like to be stifled," displease him as a call to order that in effect they were. We are playing on the boulevard Montsouris terrace, but I am not playing well. I would like to express my tenderness to him and I feel awkward . . . In the taxi, I am a bit unhappy, although he is being very good.

We have lunch at Chez André, chef de cuisine and there, telling him stories about Luxembourg Gardens, listening to him tell me about the École Normale, I again become charming Castor. But then, wandering around the Sorbonne exhausts me. We encounter the Nizans. With them and Politzer, whom I had already glimpsed, we have a drink at the Knam (for a change) and I feel, without knowing why, exhausted.[479] At the Balzar, I start to feel a bit livelier upon hearing Sartre maintain that it is not necessary to side with communism. Politzer is intelligent, lively, but how *serious* . . . which neither Sartre nor Lama is.

Waiting for the results; the great charm of being between Sartre and Nizan, joking with Boivin and Schwob, of having succeeded with only two points of difference from Sartre and of going with him to the home of "that lady" (Madame Morel), whom I like enormously as well as Guille. I sense that they like me, and I sense, above all, that Sartre is so at home here . . . I am brimming with tenderness for him. What's more I tell him so while, without having dinner, we are going to a cinema in the rue Monge and I am so happy to be with him—but all of it is too delightful, all of it is going to end, and I have despite everything this fear in my heart. In the rue Lacépède, on his arm, the bench on the bank of the Seine ... what pleasure ... He tells me about later, with the look of someone who will always be there. He speaks to me of my marriage, as almost a last resort, but he approves of it as such, for Castor is too honest to have a love life outside of it ... he says these things on the edge of a metaphysical garden where a white cat is circling.

Then his reflections in the street on the way we are holding each other— my response, "You are responsible for it"—his angry look—my sudden distress in the cinema: Who is this man? What is this conduct? and "Isn't he separating from me to judge me?" And my head in my hands, the little girl suffers, caught between her confident tenderness and her former prejudices. Oh! the gentleness of this voice, "What is wrong dear Castor?" Oh! his pleasure in seeing me take such pleasure in the film. A bit of peace returns, and I love him more than ever, while we are having an omelette at the Balzar, for being so good to a sad Castor.

He speaks to me of my future—sudden escape towards other possibilities than this former love in which, incidentally, I believe—after all, I will live. And in an unconstrained tenderness we travel the length of the boulevard Saint-Germain, from the quays, up to Invalides and then to my home. He tells me, "I found you infinitely pleasing tonight ... you are the most tender, the most faithful, the most profound, the most sincere, the most straightfor- ward little girl whom I know ..." Still agitated, but already accepting, I leave him with an abrupt "good bye" that amuses him.

Wednesday, July 31

Gandillac comes to congratulate me. He finds me at noon just barely up, he is dull and weary, my family odious. But I tell all of this to Sartre who waits for me downstairs at two o'clock and takes me to Deux Magots. Oh! wonderful afternoon ... the taxi to the Porte d'Orléans, the little tramway, Bourg- la-Reine where it is so funny to find ourselves, the little café where I wait reading Sherwood Anderson, and our trip back in the rain; and especially the train where I feel how much this total confidence that I have decided to have in him touches him, even in what will shock me, this train door through which we glimpse the Cité Universitaire and the parc Montsouris, and this train, where his arm appears to me as a delicious refuge. Then the station with the café Mahieu, and the song about Gandillac.[480] The dinner at cousin Paul's where I am so greedy for his beloved presence, the amusing apparition at Madame Morel's, the hour spent in the Tuileries Gardens near the basin with the little lights, and the quays where we play that he is Mademoiselle Richard. And the little café where I have a Mandarin and where I tell him, "Jean-Paul Sartre is J.-P. Sartre—that could get you far," but can I suppose that he would ever do anything that he would rebuke? It seems that tonight I am "a true miracle," and he assures me like every night, with a convincing inflection each time, that I have once again furthered his liking for me and that I have once again surprised him.

Tenderness never before experienced in the taxi that takes me back, where I listen silently to the inner turmoil at being hugged confidently to him.

Thursday, August 1. Sartre

Walk and lunch with *Gandillac* who is abject.* Encounter with the "Grand-Duke" to whom I am going to say goodbye. They chat with *Politzer* while Sartre prefers to see me, and pounds on the piano.†

A bit dismal with him at the Dôme, but Paris has on its most beautiful farewell attire, and the École Normale garden is radiant. He shows me some charming places, and we spend two hours laughing in the sun, without his movements frightening me any longer. Stopped by Madame Morel's.

Evening of unimaginable tenderness; at the cinema, in my heart, complete gift of myself, then in the street, delights of a sincerity that makes his tenderness grow even more.

Saturday, August 3. Meyrignac

From the first glance, what rediscovered peace, what profound joy! Painful lack of Sartre, more painful than I would have believed—boredom at being so far away from the *petits camarades*; and the memory of my expectations of last year is too fresh, but peaceful. Oh! The surest, the purest, the most beloved, how I rediscover you, Jacques, in these woods where you have never been—you and not another. Three years ago on these stones, life was you, Jacques, with such anxiety to see it refused; now it could also be Constantinople, free love, a thousand things . . . but with this magnificent and sweet approval, you alone, Jacques.

---

* "Gandillac" is underlined in Beauvoir's handwritten diary.
† "Politzer" is underlined in Beauvoir's handwritten diary.

Besides, we will see, this vacation is the eve of a definitive decision. I don't know *whom* I will meet, but I believe that it will truly be you, Jacques, in this dazzling perfection of which I am sure without ever trying to assure others of it.* O the most distant but most desired one is you, Jacques, to whom I offer this vacation.

And it was yesterday, Friday, August 2 that the metro brought me to him, my eyes cloudy with tears, when we spent three hours of tender intimacy and such amorous sweetness in his lost room. I accompanied him to the train station. And he told me such good things . . . that he loved these creatures who are not diaphanous and falsely devoted, but robust, gifted with biceps and good sense, hot-blooded and energetic, who protest sometimes laughingly but in fact sacrifice themselves without hesitation and with such grace that no effort is felt; that he loved little girls with deep and calm passions who give themselves entirely and never take themselves back, the generous souls. And then I said goodbye at his train . . . I took a taxi again that passed in front of the bench where we were seated together the other night. I did some errands, saw Madame Lama who was abject, and took the train thinking of Sartre with an expected persistence, and with an inner turmoil difficult to resolve.

Taking stock of what he is to me, of what they have all brought me will be the task of the days to come. But worried or agitated or whatever I am, I will not back away. I will believe in this man, I will believe that my tenderness for him is not an infidelity to either Lama or to you, Jacques, to whom I will say these things.

Meyrignac, my dear freedom . . . Easily a slave, this little girl, but with bonds so quickly broken. One day in the sun suffices, even though I am writing to Sartre. One hour suffices, especially in a deck chair, stretched out on the lawn in the murmur of grasshoppers and voices calling in the distance . . . and then, profound and calm passions, you are conquered. For, more than to any other, this little girl is faithful to the silent self that awakens during great solitude: who if not the self would know how to see that the great fir tree resembles an old man, and that in the clear sky the first star appears? Who would be wonderfully exhausted by the entire dear past and would thus rediscover the self's continuity? To hell with others! alone my dear dream, alone the sentences that I will slowly write, such perfect facility. Perhaps illusion. This love for self is one thing, my regret is another, and every morsel of my life is like this. To choose this morsel for the apparent

---

* The French equivalent of "whom" is underlined in Beauvoir's handwritten diary.

solemnity of the silence into which it flows is perhaps too simple. Always the same old idea of the *self* as purer if it strips away everything, even though it constructs itself with everything.*

Desire to keep the face of this dream faithfully in my heart, to gather these voices, to listen to this pure emotion through which all of my youth is remembered. Oh! "the green paradise of childish loves." How far away that was in Paris; yet, so necessary here. But desire to know the rest, less to say it perhaps than not to say stupid things by insisting on the essential. Desire to think about all of that, desire to work, to write.

Jacques—the only one to whom I can speak of heady magnolias, of this fragrance. Jacques. Everything put back in place from the first night on, in the awakening of the one who is neither catoboryx, nor *castor*, nor borboryx, nor *agrégation* candidate—but the same one who at 16 was ignorant of ethics and offered herself to life. Thanks to them, return to such freedom, thanks to them . . . etc. We will come back to this: it is advisable to seriously clarify all of this before the twentieth of August.

Sunday, August 4

I remember those very rare weeks. Oh! my Lama . . . What cowardice of heart in this haste to be absorbed by a close affection, pushing away the more devouring passion that would cause suffering. But now that both are an emptiness, the absence of Sartre is only a sense of uneasiness, whereas missing you, Maheu, alone overwhelms me with a despair in which I recognize, only attenuated, my chagrin at 18. In evoking you, tears come to my eyes. From you alone, I cannot wish to free myself.[481] I long for a letter from you.

Besides, why compare . . . affections that are each breathtakingly particular. What's curious is that the affection that appears to be the most intimate and close to a friendship between lovers is on the contrary much more peaceful and fraternal. Oh! There is no reason to suffer from all of this—all of this is beautiful, and Lama cannot be mad at me about my tenderness for Sartre, nor Sartre about my love for Lama. How these fields and these woods are peaceful in the sun. My harmonious heart . . . Jacques more clearly recognized every day.

---

* The French equivalent of the word "self" is underlined in Beauvoir's handwritten diary (CJ 744).

The idea of *nobleness*. How I protested two years ago when M.-Ponty applied it to me—at the same time I believed that one must move towards it. Lies. Jacques never proposed this to me, only consideration for the needs of other people, which is something else, and as for me alone, I would have never wanted this high-necked and ugly collar that I have discarded at present.

Monday, August 5

No matter how much I interposed vain letters, an entire world, between them and me, Sartre and my Lama alone remain my *petits camarades*. I am enveloped by them, with only a secret complicity between Jacques and me that gives me a greater solidity in their midst. Harmonious life, perfect rhythm of a time without emptiness or surprises. Tonight, for example, seated in the midst of buckwheat with the smell of the earth and the damp new greenery, with this clear blue sky that melts into the admirable landscape, with Claudel on my knees and such great peace, maybe for the first time in my life, everything had its proper weight. Have I ever known such moderation? Neither this frenzy of the countryside, nor the giddiness of solitude, nor the oblivion of the sun caused by a too passionate heart, nor the haste, nor the languor, but rather, all burnt by the summer, a divine wisdom that I did not seek.

Uzerche with Magdeleine today was neither an occupation, nor an ecstasy, but I was there without expectations, without memories, without the possibility of boredom and yet truly alive. One might call it a time, granted as a surplus to my life, that comes from nowhere, aims at nothing, and yet brings nothing uniquely its own. It is a feeling of unknown security. Maybe the certainty of seeing Sartre again right here plays a big part in this state of mind. I count on his coming; it is much more necessary to me than I think . . . *

Tuesday, August 6

Being seated in this pleasant corner separated from the world by the babbling of a brook, close to myself at 15 when I used to read Benson on these same cool stones with the same sense of abandon . . . and thinking of them.[482] Yes, I am the same as the blue dragonflies and the spots of light are the same; yes, the same, and yet so much richer!

---

* The passage, "It is a feeling of unknown security. . . . it is much more necessary to me than I think . . .," is highlighted in Beauvoir's handwritten diary.

Having *so* desired this return . . . and now being so afraid of it!

Wednesday, August 7

To the passionate cries of days such as the eighth of April, for example, what an answer you bring, dear Sartre. Yes, indeed, to you I can say what seems to me to be hypocrisy and baseness; you do not impose any false nobleness upon me, you understand. Ah! with all of my heart, such a big thank you! (And I even easily accept that you make fun of me).

Maheu! Why reread those days when we were together, why repeat to you that you are the most important; I can only suffer by you, only suffer. For it is absolutely incomparable . . . Evening in this room with the lamp intent on the night . . . I am thinking about the dear little man. "Calm and deep passion," he said, and within me I protested a bit, but this sweetness in my heart says that he is right. The others from this year, I gave and gave to them, and tried to take what they offered which was in vain—such a disappointing effort. Here I am fulfilled and dominated—with only the anxious fear of losing everything, of sliding off this very beautiful peak. Oh! Don't let me become bourgeois. Oh! Force me always to think, to be, my Leprechaun.[483] Whatever was too sensitive that embarrassed me the first few days has disappeared.* And I sense only this very strong, very creative, very beloved intellectual influence. I could always be freed from my heart: from the past, from promises, and from all emotional excitement, but if someone gives me access to a wider, higher life I am completely in his hands, capable of terrible sacrifices for him. Thus, although I cherish Lama so much more, perhaps I care about Sartre the most incomparably; all the more because I feel penetrated by his thought. What a charming letter I received from him this morning, but this charming Jean-Paul possesses me less than this man who is alone, and sure of his worth, and strong.

His weakness in love will always come from this, it seems to me: that he does not need . . . To love him is to receive from him, to be subjugated. So if, for an instant, one escapes him, one does not return to him because of the great need for devotion that makes a woman love, in a man especially that which she lacks, in order to justify this love. Sartre must start over and take again, and it is difficult for a woman to owe everything and to give nothing.

---

* After the sentence, "Whatever was too sensitive that embarrassed me the first few days has disappeared," there is an exclamation point added in pencil in the manuscript.

He said something false about love the other day: either one says, "I prefer you to speak to me" or "I prefer you to kiss me," never, "I like one as much as the other"—but you can prefer a kiss, and be brought around to preferring it nevertheless because of words, and no longer like it if these words disappoint you—love beyond esteem, but love for which esteem is necessary. Many men can move you emotionally, but to love this emotional turmoil, you must have deeply bowed your head and preferred it.

Thursday, August 8

Extraordinary hour—odor of straw burnt by the sun and of this carnal red earth, splendid Limousin, stretched out at the bottom of this field, and my heart completely full of the letter that I just received.

The same excitement as last year for a letter from Jacques, the same passionate desire that sadness would not reach this favorite of the gods, the same offering . . . Little girl, how many things you have learned these past months; and that you must say thanks to this man, and not to yourself, if today you are happy; because faced with these men marked with grace you are only tenderness offered and confidence; and because you could not, through any impossible going back on yourself, say no, but it's perhaps this very confidence that protects you. Perhaps revealing yourself like this, unarmed, compels them by its gentleness, to not want only to attack you, and compels them to protect you from yourself.

Your goodness, Lama, that would have rather protected me from myself; for if I was sometimes afraid, it was not of you, but of me, not of a request that you hadn't made, but of my excessive desire for a request—one night above all . . . And you know it, Lama, and there is no shame in it. I would always like to be only your sweetness like this, I would not like to be anyone's life, but rather this refuge, this "Attention!" or this sanctuary for the beings I love. There are two beings, two who overwhelm me with a similar turmoil, Lama and you, Jacques, you who left me, whom I reproach for nothing for you didn't know to what great dangers, to what great confusion in my heart you were abandoning me by your silence. Oh! I have really always felt that Sartre's audacities are less dangerous for my destiny than Lama's very tender and pure reserve.

Lama, I will write all of this to you when you are in London. And on that day I will commit myself to putting you first, before everyone except one man, before myself, my works, my happiness, and my honor. Miracle that at the same time, Jacques, you were given back to me in tears, with all the power of your weakness over me. Sartre was right when he told me that it's this type of man that I would love, and who will make me unhappy, and to whom I will give all without getting anything in return. Perhaps also when he said that I am the type of little girl who merits the best and with whom one is vile, but by the grace of those whom my heart has chosen, I feel, without defending myself, miraculously protected. But now, no longer true, what I wrote on the eighth of June, for example, is no longer true. You, Jacques, are no longer salvation, and the earth is not closed to me. You are preferred, but Maheu and even Sartre are at the same level of life as you, and I am asking you to justify yourself. And between the three of you and myself, I am alone with my destiny.

But also, the more my soul becomes "elegant and luminous," the more, detail by detail I approve of and love you, Jacques. Your presence continues to impose this approval, this love upon me with force—and now that I am finally conquered, there is a peace in the heart of the most awful dangers. Oh! I am so happy! Maggie Tulliver, my sister . . . [484]

I need Sartre; and I love Maheu. I love what Sartre brings me and what Maheu is. Reflection on myself and passionate selflessness. My Lama . . .

Friday, August 9

Letters to Sartre and to Lama. Arrival of Gandillac, I give him a tour of Uzerche while thinking only of Sartre. Afternoon walk with him, Jeanne, and Poupette in Gimel where there is dazzling sunshine. Celebration of body and soul. Gandillac is the last of the simpletons, but these hours are charming thanks to charming Poupette.

Saturday, August 10

Long walk with le Gandille on the banks of the Vézère where I think a lot about Lama.[485] Lunch in Meyrignac. In the afternoon we accompany la Gandille to Brive, much less pleasant that last year when I was there alone with Poupette. But I have so much joy within me . . .

Sunday, August 11

I read all day on the hill across from Meyrignac, buried in the big ferns. I write to Sartre as I do every day.

I am happy.

Monday, August 12

Magdeleine comes to Meyrignac with her family. We read side by side in a field all day long. She makes me sick. But I am still arrogantly happy.

Tuesday, August 13

I dedicate the incredible contentment of this evening to you, my prince of Lamas. Isn't it entirely yours? (Ah! to get it back, what anxieties, what passionate woes I would consent to endure again). The sweetness of a sky growing paler towards eight o'clock at night when the air takes on the most exquisite nuances; the trees are surrounded with peace; the cicadas begin to sing while the smell of earth and heather is rising.

I am glued to the earth with my face against only these fading clouds and this great stretch of blue made clearer by the rising moon; it outlines the ferns; one by one the stars light up. Voices pass over the fields with a quickly stifled uproar; the leaves of the ferns sway in a warm wind, a bumblebee passes from time to time, emphasizing the immobility of time with his brief buzzing. And I am this body with the smell of the earth and the grass, and this soul without regret or desire; fulfilled. Fulfilled by the purity of the hour, fulfilled by the purity of its memories, and by all of this weakness that endeavors to be a magnificent and perfectly sure strength.

Myself. Myself at sixteen ardently offering herself to life, my promises that are kept today. Myself: this eternally unchanging, calm, and profound countryside that so tenderly evokes a face. Your face, Lama. Perfectly mine, perfectly given and received, finally unthreatening. Now I finally dare, after the caution of those days when I feared how much I would suffer if I opened the doors to the recent past; now I finally dare to surrender and to think of you unreservedly—and now everything is given back to me: your smile, your grace, your tenderness and all the moments that I know; and now I am in the heart of your purer self that you know I have found; and you are irreparably mine without anything being able to harm this ideal union.

The last sunbeam of the day lit up that letter that I did not have the strength to reread; every word entered into me like a divine happiness—these tears were from a heart swollen only with too much joy; absence, presence no longer meant anything. Will you ever be able to be more present than in those moments when I was coming back down the field, when the crickets were chirping in the moonlight, and then along the avenue fragrant with pine needles—and even now at this very minute. Never have I been yours with such a definitive devotion and with the wonderful certainty that you are mine, never have time and distance been so vain. Never has my tenderness risen so high. There is only one being with as purified and as fragrant a soul whom I have cherished as much, as much, but not more, my prince of Lamas, my prince of Lamas who is no longer bitterness for me but now joy and satisfied renunciation.

Wednesday, August 14

Why this silence from Sartre, just after a letter in which I revealed so much, just when such a great nostalgia for Paris is rising in me, and when Paris is taking on his face? Oh, our evenings, his tenderness, my confidence, our gaiety—the hours pass slowly, one by one, all delightful, but so easily threatened with bitterness. How I loved you today, how I thirsted for your presence, with a great emptiness that is beginning to hurt.

Thursday, August 15

Same silence. Is he waiting until he has received another letter? An emptiness . . .

And then this note from Charlotte, with the treacherous sentence, "I will go to Aunt Germaine's." From afar I can think carefully about Jacques, make a choice, speak to him; yet nothing but his mother's name on the paper takes away all appetite for living. I am afraid, I am afraid of the harm that he can do me and afraid of imagining his face. I dreamt of him last night: I was suffering. In a month, will I have a visit from him? What haste to deal with this terrible danger! What fear!

Sunday, August 18

Happy Castor? Happy. A good letter Friday, and yesterday expectation and boredom, and beneath the weight of the stormy sky, all my weakness hits me again as a stomachache. But today there is a rain making the countryside more fragrant and tender, and an even better letter, a letter that is all of dear Jean-Paul's tenderness, his clear and benevolent tenderness, and that has an even more perfect grace than ordinarily.

I walked by chez Feugeat, by chez Fanchande, and up to Condat. I thought of Uncle Gaston and of those beautiful hungry mornings when I followed him as he hunted, of my past despairs and hopes, of the future, and of myself. Yes, a woman with a woman's destiny [*Oui, femme avec une destinée de femme*], and for which *my heart longed* forever.[486] How completely, passionately I accept all these risks that have scared me these last few days. How eager my soul is to suffer for all of the Toms in the world![487] What does it matter if only there are Toms in the world to love? O Jacques, o Lama, you were no longer bitter for me, and the threat of your grace was only benevolent for me. And what does it matter also if this witness to my life always remains attentive to me; my thought will know how to find him after all even in Constantinople, this dear Jean-Paul whom I have carried in my heart through damp fields in such a peaceful happiness. And at any rate there will always be the tall chestnut tree at the summit of a field, and for this dependent and too easily captured heart, that which is only for him, this gray and tender countryside in the rain, and a tender and tragic English novel waiting for the water to be silent. I am not afraid. I would be afraid only of uselessness and boredom, but already my life is full if I am for one of them a strength, for the other one a pleasure, and for yet another one a charm that helps him a bit to escape boredom; and if their lives are so important to me that one moment of them suffices to justify my own. And Sartre is going to come, Sartre who wrote me such a good letter, and I have so many things to say to him, and I so want his presence. And I am passionately happy.

Monday, August 19

Arrival at La Grillère.

Tuesday, August 20

Sartre's arrival. Immense joy. A bit of shyness that makes me artificial.

Wednesday, August 21 through September 1

Sartre's Stay

Every morning I wake up at seven o'clock and stay in bed for a long while, my heart beating with joy. I go down through the meadows, and I run all the way to Saint-Germain in the cool of the morning telling myself everything that I am going to say to him.[488] The first couple of times it was only up to the Boule d'Or and on the Place de Saint-Germain some curious faces were spying out the windows. He would be waiting on the bench, dressed in the beige sweater that I already knew from the Cité.

After the scene on Sunday, August 25 when Papa and Mama surprised us in the meadow, which will be one our funniest memories, I would sit down at the corner of the road to la Porcherie, and I would wait. Then we would go into some meadow: until Sunday, in the big meadow where he would not have lunch and when I would bring him cider, spice bread, etc. Then we would play at myths. Afterwards we were in a big field along the route to the train station. I would tell stories, all of my stories: the family cycle, the Sorbonne cycle, the Cours Desir cycle—etc. He liked them, and especially seeing my "ugly mug" while I recounted them.

In the afternoon, the first day we went to la Baga. Thursday was the delightful day at Uzerche with lunch at Chez Chavant after the walk in the dear old streets: he thinks they are made for lots of little boys to live in while reading in many little places that are theirs alone. Delight of this walk when together we feel so many pleasant things, then a pause in a big meadow that overlooks la Vézère, where we tell stories, where we are quiet together. There are small boats on the water and a fisherman who could be the Grand-Duke. He speaks to me of his friendship for little girls, and that he likes them better as friends than as mistresses. Now I accept without embarrassment the slight feeling of turmoil at being in his arms and feeling his power; my admiration for Jean-Paul and my faith in him are absolute, and my tenderness for my dear Leprechaun without reserve. He explains the theory of contingency to me while climbing up to Saint-Eulalie, an extremely beautiful philosophy that I understand with all of my heart. We have dinner at chez Ambroise; across from him, I don't even feel like speaking because I would have so many nice things to tell him. Trip back by train with the memory of Bourg-la-Reine and an immense tenderness. Long-lasting emotional turmoil when during the return trip we are silent in the dark, seated on the edge of the road, and me in his arms, given unreservedly to him, and I feel his excitement the entire length of my body.

Friday was la Porcherie, first the meadow by the railroad on the bank of the stream where I was such a blissfully happy Castor while he told me about his history with la Combes, and while I played freely with him, entirely given, entirely free and light-hearted.[489] Then there was a long interlude where the sun was beating down terribly hard—then an inn with green oilcloths and pink walls, with big mauve bouquets in porcelain vases.[490] I sense that his tenderness is slightly greater than mine on that day. My watch misinforms us and we go home terribly late; general disapproval.

Saturday, again, I believe, this dear inn.*

Sunday we go to the kilometer-marker 40 after the scene made by my parents. We find lemon-lime soda and beer that we drink in a shady spot while he tells the story of his passionate period.

Monday, in the little woods the "Playboy" appears to me for the first time: this face so tender and intelligent sings to me "Miss Hannah"; it's this expression on "my upside down mug" that he finds charming, and on my tender face that he finds wonderful with its half-smile, its flushed cheeks, and its half-closed eyes.[491] A little boy observes us and we laugh with him. Is it already that night his kiss, so light . . .

Tuesday is my two hours of fatigue and bad mood because I am tired and hot. It's his calm waiting at the bottom of the tree, dear Leprechaun, until the Castor reappears. And in the inn, it's his kisses, his shoulder, and his caresses for a tired little girl who returns with her heart overflowing with tenderness. "You are something very precious and very fragile, dear Castor," he said to me, "who must be handled all the more delicately because you give yourself more completely. I have a sort of admiration for you."

Wednesday is again the little woods, lemon-lime soda, chocolate, and his songs. He sings "My child, my sister" in a way that deeply moves me. My Playboy . . . and all of this tenderness is lighthearted and good, expressed as easily as felt, so sincerely and yet understood as part of the big game.

Thursday—we discover the meadow.

Friday, Saturday, it is there that we spend our last days. And it is there that these games of the "Playboy and the little girl" give way to a wonderful tenderness—"my beautiful tender mug" . . . "You are so delightful this way . . . charming, charming little girl."

There was a very fun evening with Magdeleine and Poupette, and what charming myths we concocted with my parents, the cousin, the sister, and the old aunt. Such stories I told him! And him . . . and such wonderful ideas: on doctors, history, art, contingency—admirable "song of contingency." Dear notebooks where so many strong thoughts are contained, wonderful serious face of my Jean-Paul while he is explaining things to me: on imagination, psychology, etc.[492]

How I love his advice, our plans, the applied and attentive way he speaks to me about myself. What perfect days with alternating narratives, ideas, and caresses!

---

* In Beauvoir's handwritten diary the next few lines are spotted with some form of liquid.

278

What delicious myths, showing on the horizon the beloved universe of our *petits camarades*: Lama, Grand-Duke, Madame Morel, Guille, and for fun, Aron and Politzer. And already behind us, what a great past, and what a great year to come!

Thus the days passed with a free heart and a body unembarrassed in the sun, and words that we said a short while before thinking them, only to think them all the more strongly.

And I loved my Leprechaun attentive to transforming everything into pleasure. And Jean-Paul, serious, strong, rich, and my Playboy whom I understood so well and of whom I asked nothing more than those moments that he really wanted to give me. And the Walkyrie, hidden in the depths of this tender little girl, poured out big waves of joy to him, and she knew that she was strong, as strong as he.

But last night, how tender this Playboy was! How this heart and body were touched! How these words still burn into me, "my dear love" and "I love you."

For these two faces: of the tender young woman in whom rests all the wisdom and intelligence in the world, of the innocent little girl; such love came to her in just a few days that he said she must not doubt. "You don't know what tenderness there is on your face, dear little girl." "You don't know how moving and tender your voice is like this," he said in the meadow. And from "this dear face of my little girl, my love has descended into her dear body."

"And I also love you with all of my heart and body," I told him. Awakening of this body, awakening of this woman who had not previously been spoken to as a woman. Emotional excitement to hear such words for the first time, for the first time to rest in a man's arms, docile, lost with tenderness and with the desire to give oneself entirely.

Oh! Whatever the future brings, these hours, hugged against his heart repeating, "I love you," and "how happy we are!" Ah, this unfamiliar voice that he had on the road as he arrived, this changed face when he left me, this assurance of his love, this fear of hurting me, and my burst of affection for him.[493]

Then his departure, and despite everything, running in the night, a sort of joy as if from a great liberation after these hours of too sweet surrender. And all morning the next day the joy of being alone, uniquely mine, free, and strong.

And then the uncertainty of the heart that tries finally to contemplate what it so crazily gave itself to for ten days, and that knows so surely how much it loves Sartre, how much it loves Lama, how much it could love Jacques, and each in a different way. But that doesn't know how to reconcile within itself all of these loves.

Monday, Tuesday, Wednesday, September 2, 3, and 4

Admirable days. I am completely understood, loved, and supported. And my soul of a Walkyrie is alone, joyous, and strong. And the awakening of my thought that wants to be and to be said; and the perfection of this happiness so full of promise, so full of certainty that I must go back four years to find anything like it. Here is the "life" for which I waited with so much contemplation on the same September evenings (and tonight the sheaves of freshly cut buckwheat were bloody bodies against the earth). Here is the great "world" as I had not hoped to know it. Here is my body free, my heart completely occupied, and my mind feeling alive, solid, ready at last to be put to use. Mixed up with all of that, Sartre is in my heart, in my body, and is above all (for many others could be in my heart and my body) the incomparable friend of my thought, which is extraordinarily happy to meet with him in such an extraordinary harmony (Oh, much more than with Lama or Jacques). This could be a total and incredible passion. It is still far from being that. It is incomparable to what I felt for Jacques in the past, incomparable to that madness, that obsession; but it is happiness, it is myself entirely given back to myself, and also an immense tenderness for him. It's pride for the two of us, the certainty of his overwhelming worth, the presence of his delicate, generous, and tender heart, and of his grace of mind. Never have I known such equilibrium, such happiness, this liking for myself and for the world that is given to me through him. It is exactly what I have always desired, and sought, and what is in such perfect harmony with myself.

And everything is simple. This already prepared year is going to be perfect. In a year there will be time to decide whatever will come after. I dream these days of travels, adventures, and of never stopping anywhere— of having a sensational life.

Nevertheless, tonight, alone on the porch with the lamp set on the iron table and the armchairs, it seemed possible that across from me that same presence was still expected: yours, Jacques.[494] That it was you, and not another that the bizarre reflection of the light on the pink impatiens required, you and not another, this sort of damp sweetness in my heart, with Almaïde d'Étremont who was passing by in the depths of the park. All I can do is wait.

I love each of them as if he were the only one. I will take from each all that he has for me; and I will give him all that I can give him. Who could reproach me for it?

I don't want to do a psychological analysis of my feelings for Sartre, and to compare them to the love that they indeed are not, at least, not yet. I must wait.

Everything is simple. Never have I so loved to read and think, never have I been so alive and happy or envisioned a future so rich. Oh! Jean-Paul, dear Jean-Paul, thank you.

Friday, Saturday, Sunday, September 6, 7, and 8

Lama's stay

One would think it was a two-day dream that I was still uncertain about.

A letter came that made me frightened, embarrassed, and quick-thinking: but it was only to meet him at night in a second-class train car, after the most tender of expectations, a Lama in a beige check jacket, unshaven, dirty, and tired, but already it was Lama to a tee on the Uzerche train station platform with his overcoat thrown around his shoulders, his hat on crooked, and his two suitcases (to be a true tourist). Indefinite wait for the omnibus, ascent up the dark street, arrival at Chez Reynier with the astonishment of getting a room here, unknown, a room overlooking the Vézère, and from where we are on the same level as all of Uzerche. Dear voice of Lama who sings as he freshens up near by, while it is delightful to wait. Dinner at Chez Chavant, where I eat his portion and mine, and walk through Uzerche at night. How calmly happy I am while he is looking at the sky upside down, stretched out on the stone balustrade on the Place de l'église. Ah, the charm of such a goodnight when he kisses my hand after an hour spent together in my room.

The next day, he strides off in all directions. Oh! Espartignac where "we went on purpose," the winding paths, the town council, and lemon-lime soda! He speaks of the Gallic people, "*omnis Gallia divina est,*" the Greeks, the Romans, and his life in Coutances.[495] He sings "So Blue." He is my Lama (more my Lama and dearer than ever; how you must measure up, Jean-Paul, for *you* to nevertheless . . . !!).

Lunch at Chez Chavant, meadow on la Vézère from where we send cards from the two of us. Then we go to drink some lemon-lime soda at Chez Chavant, in a ridiculous room with leather benches and green walls. It is delightful there. We exchange insolent remarks, and he is excessively witty, with such a comic lower lip, then he tells of loads of practical jokes from the École Normale. I will often remember him like this, in shirtsleeves stretched out on the bench. We go up to Ste. Eulalie and we take off at random. We follow le Bras d'Arsac where we play at racing boats with the Grand-Duke, we splash around in the water, and he climbs trees. I will never forget "the young erudite René Maheu" perched on a branch, with his gray flannel pants rolled up, his hair in his face, his feet the color of the sunset. Epic trip back, my aunt's shoes are soaked, my stockings in tatters, and I walk barefoot without recognizing my route while he throws pebbles into the water. However, we approach Chez Chavant without incident where they must take Maheu for a prince in disguise since they are so eager to please us. We speak of Sartre, my life, my marriage, and of everything with such exquisite sensitivity and tenderness. And what comes out of all of it at any rate is that we will always be Lama and Castor. Without noticing, I drink a bottle of Chablis Village 1923; so everything is swaying while he is stretched out on my bed telling me about the crazy year. He cannot make up his mind to leave, nor I to tell him to leave, and I watch him as if delirious, with this lanky appearance and such a funny face.

Atrocious night . . . [496]

But how tenderly I love both of those mornings, his voice, "Hello Castor," and his blue pajamas, the eau de cologne and the soap that he lends me, and his tender solicitude. Since I was sick upon going to la Pelouse, he took me tenderly by the arm, and with such gentleness towards noon he kissed my hair twice.[497] My Lama, so dear. Lunch made me feel better; he tells me about London for which he makes a map. We play Brazilian écarté, and we go down under the ramparts of Uzerche where, as on all the streets, bits and pieces of the houses hold onto the walls every which way. He recommends some books, talks of the cinema, history, poetry, and Shakespeare with an extraordinary gift for poetry: the one man in the world who knows how to breathe intense life into everything that he touches. Dinner, departure by car for the train station, he, across from me in the train, gives me some money that I am so pleased to receive from him, and there are promises to write. Goodbye. Goodbye with such a cold tenderness just like our relationship; marvelous grace of our feelings, marvelous grace of Lama. He couldn't be more like Lama these days—gay, witty, distant and close, ironic and tender, and already so familiar. And I understand exactly what he is, and what Sartre is. But of that I will speak later. Goodbye for a long month, prince of Lamas so quickly come and gone, but so happily within me.

Tuesday, September 10

Thus I understood what men who remind me of Grand Meaulnes are, and what a guy like Sartre is.[498] The former are beautiful to contemplate, and you are happy to serve them for the insatiable exigency in them, and for the very rare prize of their goodness and their tenderness at the heart of this life that is theirs alone. But to justify to yourself such joy in seeing them and the suffering that you are ready to endure for them, you are tempted to give them too much. "Don't ever judge me—have faith in me," they ask, and this touches you as an appeal to your generosity. But now that I know a man who can always be judged and who always provides justification, I no longer see in this request this sort of incantation that used to bind me. It is delightful to be partial towards such beings, but how could you not be conscious of such partiality when you see that there is somebody whom you could admire completely and impartially, and who compels your esteem?

I remember having distinguished at the Falstaff with Sartre, between people who are "others," as though surrounded by a halo of this strangeness and as such beyond reproach, and the people of my race who don't see me like that, whom I like less, but with whom I feel secure, understanding my harmony with them. It is still accurate, but something has changed: among these people of my race I have found one so great that my esteem has extended from him to my entire race, and I no longer feel defenseless before people from the other side. And as I sensed in Meyrignac, it's him alone and not another that I need. My admiration for the others is more or less bias and poetry; Sartre alone gives me the freedom of an absolutely integral sincerity, and of a straightfowardness that does not attempt to construct anything.

Now thanks to that I have understood my prince of Lamas. Well! No, I don't have much esteem for him, and I maintain the painful impression that he gave me when speaking of his wife, the world, and society—sensuality, ruthless ambition, a bit of vanity, childishness—and a lack of generosity. Ethically I haven't any esteem for him. Intellectually, he is not enough for me; he isn't interested in enough things, he does not understand quickly enough, and does not master all questions. In other words, everyday life could get boring near him; he does not sense loads of little things; he does not like stories, one cannot give unsparingly of oneself, and such clear and pure coldness of mind is a bit stifling for me. Upon seeing all of this, I thought of Sartre, of the way so similar to mine that things exist or do not exist for him—his relationships with women, the world, his culture,

283

his passion for ideas, all of it on the contrary I admire and esteem without reservation. I see him clearly. I rank him as extraordinarily worthy.

But . . . but Maheu is a poet and an artist, he has the extraordinary gift of bringing all that he has touched to life, with a depth that the object did not have before, as for example, when he speaks of history. He feels verses, and art, and beauty in such a direct and sure way which people like me, and even Sartre, will never manage to do, as for example, when he spoke to me of Shakespeare. He is young; he is witty although he denies it, and lively and unpredictable, in this again a poet. He plays as he lives; he loves the grass and the trees, and walking barefoot in a stream. He has an unequaled grace in his gestures; he is elegant, he is charming, he can be "taken" with a thought, an impression (when he spoke of England). He lives the adventure, he has an innate subtlety, and his tenderness resembles goodness. I love him as profoundly as in Paris, more familiarly, more calmly, as gaily, with as much offered devotion. Lama so loved, my prince of Lamas. That feeling has now entered into my life, and knows its place, asks for nothing more and risks nothing more either. It is the most delightful, the most sure, the most tender of friendships. And it is wonderful that precisely with this sensual man nothing physical intervenes between us and that our tenderness is so cold and pure—whereas with Sartre, who is not sensual, the harmony of our bodies has a meaning that renders our love even more wonderful.

So that's what is happening in this marvelous saga of the *petits camarades*, begun in the month of March. Here's what is happening in my friendship with Lama: curiosity filled with emotion, uneasy friendship, sure friendship, turmoil, uneasy passion, and now: passionate and sure, and calm friendship.

What is happening for me with Sartre is quite another question.

But these past few days have brought to a close this year that I so feared, and the most beautiful, richest, and most full of unexpected awakenings. For now it will be after the year of absence, the year of return. And my life with Sartre, and "after my studies," and all the unknown. A new year that I approach full of hope and joy. Only I want to come back to this a bit to see it better in its entirety and understand it.

Wednesday, September 11

Rain. The inn at kilometer-marker 40 where I find shelter. I thought of Sartre with that definitive love and devotion that I felt for Zaza in the past, for Jacques very often, and at one time for Lama. I thought of Jacques with a charming apprehension. Happy!

Thursday, September 12

I am going to see him again, however, I am going to see him again. Who knows what immense love for him is afoot? I loved him incomparably more than I will ever love any man again, even if there is one whom I love at the same time with my heart, my mind, and my body. I loved him as one cannot love twice, very few love even one in this way. And perhaps he will be nothing to me; perhaps I am going to recognize this great disruption that I imagine upon hearing him say to me, "Hello, Simone." And I don't know which of the two I desire.

Summary of this year—September 1928–September 1929

Jacques's absence.

The sadness had to be killed, and at first it's Stépha next to me at the Bibliothèque Nationale, having lunch with me on the squares and in les Biards, taking me to her blue room and enveloping me with well-being. That's one month during which I work enormously. It is still Stépha in November and December with all the rest of my life that starts up again, the gray Sorbonne, a bit Zaza, who then leaves for Germany, Josée in a sad residence for female students. There are charming discussions, afternoon snacks, outings to the theater after dinner, then to Montparnasse, the Ukranien compatriots, Fernand, the Stryx with Riquet, lunches at the Knam, a free, slightly bohemian, and very, very lighthearted life, while at the Sorbonne I believe that a friendship with Gandillac would be of interest and I see Merleau-Ponty from time to time. I learn how to meet strangers, about German literature, and already a bit more about men and all the divine possibilities that there are for men on earth—thanks to Stépha. Charming memories: evening at the Atelier, at the homes of the Pitoëff, Stépha, and Merleau-Ponty, *Départs* with Stépha and Fernand, and simply the streets of Paris where I have fits of good cheer. The Sorbonne is still an intimidating unknown, but the classes interest me, I have a lot of work, the students are curious beasts, my double life charming, Robin's classes pleasant, and the sky blue.

I write to Jacques twice—intense love in this tranquility, passion of expectation and certitude. I also go out with Miquel, whom I have rediscovered; the "club of unrespectable people," the Dôme, and Raymond Duncan. Everything is very pleasant. I read enormously, especially foreign authors. People are numerous and I inhale them intellectually and use them as decors for my outings and my occupations. My joy comes from myself, and all the rest are motifs with which I alone compose the songs that I like.

Then in January, *Galois, Merleau-Ponty*, and *Gandillac*.* Discovery of the first whom I start to like a lot, rediscovered tenderness for the second, desire for friendship with the third—impression of happy companionship, no more shyness: Mademoiselle de Beauvoir blossoms. There is a party at Merleau-Ponty's, meetings with Galois at the Bibliothèque Nationale, a party at my home and the period of the student teaching internship—that student teaching internship with Lévy-Strauss and Merleau-Ponty, the dinner at the Rodriguès's home, the afternoon snacks with Mauguë, my strength, and my assurance.

In February and March it is more of the same, with Zaza back from Germany, the party at Studio 28, my outings with Zaza (Borodine), the afternoon snack at Brunschvicg's. But all of this occurs while I am fatigued because to find something in these people, you always have to create it, because they are serious and stifling and distant from me, and I put on airs to avoid thinking of myself as alone. There are boring classes, less interesting work, the effort to be interested in Mademoiselle Richard, Hippolyte, etc, fatigue, the lack of pride that makes me accept helter-skelter all of these people, some very weary outings with Poupette, and the flu. And then the sad love affairs: Josée and Merleau-Ponty, Poupette and Merleau-Ponty, their confidences, sorry evenings with Josée at the Jockey, and a terrible despondency. Remembering Jacques as if he were a lost pride, and dying of thirst for him. Some cinema to put an end to this. However, there are some pleasant evenings with Stépha, G.G. Dubois, whom I discover, and Poupette. At the Bibliothèque Nationale, my distraction is the love affair with the Hungarian. He teaches me things. Spinelessness of these hours that I give up to him.

Great moment of depression at Easter. I offered everything to people who didn't give me anything; I lived their lives, but this wasn't mine, I gave myself, and I was not enriched by this gift, and I would like to live. Evenings at the Européen where I reach the depths of my disgust.

And then . . . from April 15 through June 15 *Maheu*.†

The lengthy desire—the painstaking approach—my hope confirmed every day. Sessions at the Bibliothèque Nationale next to him: work in the

---

* "Galois," "Merleau-Ponty," and "Gandillac" are underlined in Beauvoir's handwritten manuscript.
† "Maheu" is underlined in Beauvoir's handwritten diary.

morning, lunch together, discussion at the Palais Royal, gaiety into the evening when sometimes I accompany him to the home of his private student.[499] Friendship, then tenderness, and then some unknown beloved suffering. Pride that is reborn, life that lights up and all of this spring . . . Someone to whom there is nothing to offer; someone near whom I can be me, even more so than near myself, and whom I love. Perfect joy and numerous pleasures. I finish distancing myself from Catholicism, I start to show contempt again, and I learn the pleasure of being a woman. More and more the world opens up, and this saga among all sagas is exquisite because he searched for me without my knowledge, while I was searching for him without daring, even so, to say hello to him at the Sorbonne. Castor, his dear Castor . . . and he, extremely dear for me.

I think of Jacques with uneasiness, weary of his silence, I learn one thing about him that makes me suffer, I get over it, knowing that it will be justified, but he grows farther away. Meanwhile, in the background, great tenderness for Zaza, great heights of our friendship; great tenderness for Merleau-Ponty, and this approach of one towards the other. Then Madeleine de Prandières, whom I meet again, and always Josée's sadness. The lives of others. At times I still see Stépha with whom I do some journalism, and the Hungarian at the Deux Magots at night, and Fernand. Definitive renunciation of the romanticism of sadness and morality. Evenings on the lake with Gandillac and the gang—still some outings at the Stryx, but especially *L'auto*, *Détective*, the Eugenes and that great pout, so young and funny . . .

June–July: *The petits camarades* and *exams*.*

Immense. No longer only friendships, discovery of the world where I can live, of the thought that I like, of a thing for which I was always destined. Finally! Finally people stronger than me, and near whom I am myself. There again, exquisite saga. Lama's return and our evening outing, the two weeks when, together, we work or don't work, my first timidities in front of Sartre and Nizan who are only classmates of Maheu—my love for Maheu that is growing to the point of suffering, that extends into charming evenings, into calm and familiar hours—my esteem for Sartre that would want to become a friendship—a calm admiration for Nizan, and drinks, songs, Japanese billiards, outings, freedom, and the happiness of being a Castor. I am adopted.

Slight passionate fever at Lama's departure—meeting of Aron, Politzer, familiarity with Nizan, friendship with Sartre growing daily. Saw Stépha

---

* "Les petits camarades" and the French equivalent of "exams" are underlined in Beauvoir's handwritten diary.

again. End of the sagas of Josée, Zaza, and Merleau-Ponty—all of this is far from me.

Intellectual blossoming—joy, life. I think very little about Jacques, but understand him better. I dominate the world to which I became slowly acclimated this year. Furthermore, I pass my *diplôme* and the *agrégation*.

July–August–September. *Sartre.**

The world finishes opening. I learn that I have a woman's destiny [*destinée de femme*] and that it is the destiny that I like. I learn what it is to think, what a great man is, what the universe is. I free myself from all the old religious and moral prejudices and false instincts. I learn complete sincerity, the freedom of thinking, and of living one's thought with one's mind, one's heart, and one's body. Immense revelations—without distress, for everything was prepared. End of the past, opening towards a future different from these four years. And also there are exquisite nights in Paris, new people, charming inventions, cinema, cafés where we drink—and letters—and two weeks at La Grillère where I end up knowing him and loving him. And the promise of a strong love, and of a friendship forever.

Then the coming of Lama, some tender letters, and the expectation of later.

In summary

Diplôme and *agrégation*. French and foreign literatures. Theater, cinema, and night clubs.

Foreigners, students, and Montparnasse public. The life of others generously lived, waiting for Jacques and pleasant occupations in my own life.

Experience of my resources: joy despite everything. Contact with the world, maturity, and experience.

Discovery of the world as I must live in it, and discovery of my true friends.

Birth of the Castor who for so long hesitated between intellectual Mademoiselle de Beauvoir and passionate Mademoiselle de Beauvoir.

Tremendous year. Almost comparable to 1925–1926.

To do:[500]
From September 15 to October 1

100 francs from Lama. Borrow 100 francs from M. Blomart, and Papa.

---

* "Sartre" is underlined in Beauvoir's handwritten diary.

Take out the little Dubois, then Poupette when she returns, and the two of them together.

Go see Jacques.

Move completely in to Grandmother's place (table, bed, chairs, planks for the shelves and the writing-desk, wallpaper, a lamp).

Prepare my winter outfits with Poupette, at least in part.

Secure some private lessons in keeping with Sartre's advice.

Put my papers in order.

Read what Sartre and Lama have suggested to me.

Be a practical and effective Castor, and a joyous Castor.

From October 1 to November 1

Start to write, at least every morning. Hunt down the École Normale students who need private lessons. If possible catch one and give private lessons—Mercier, Parodi, Rodriguès, *petits camarades*.

Read what's on my list.

Returns: of Josée, of the Nizans, of Zaza, of Merleau-Ponty probably until October 10.

Return of *Sartre* hoped for the tenth—for sure by the twentieth—allow myself to be monopolized as much as possible!

Passing by of *Lama*—see him as much as possible.

Jacques and his constant gang, as much as possible.

Poupette to take out from time to time.

Money: borrow from M. Blomart, Zaza, and from Lama.

Be a working Castor and a Castor curious and happy about all the old and new people who turn up, and above all a Castor entirely devoted to the two *petits camarades* so rarely present.

November 1 to January 1

A) Lessons in the morning and from time to time another hour from 5:00 to 6:00; get 1057 francs between now and November 26, and 1162 francs and 50 centimes from November to January 1. Dress 200 francs, Grandmother 400 francs, Poupette 60 francs, wood 60 francs, and hairdresser 30 francs = 750F. 307 francs 50 centimes or 77 francs per week are left. Try to spend only 50 francs (cigarettes, communication, outing, entertaining at home)—thus put aside 100 francs on November 26.

In December: Grandmother 350 francs, wood, hairdresser, upkeep 150 francs equals 550 francs; reimburse Mama for 175 francs; 337 francs are left, or 66 francs per week; spend 45 francs per week in order to put aside 100 francs.

In January have 200 francs and 1000 francs free of debts.

Thus live with 45 francs per week during these two months.

B) Three or four hours reading at the Nationale—or writing at home.

C) Two hours twice a week with people.

D) Sartre almost every night and Saturdays and Sundays.*

Done:

From September 15 to October 1

Spent 100 francs from Lama, and 100 francs borrowed from Jacques.

Took out the little Dubois twice: Sunday, the 15th, brought her to Jacques's—and the 25th to the cinema, *La none.*

Poupette did not come home. Saw Jacques the 15th, 16th, *20th,* 22nd, 27th, and 29th, alone and with friends—Ayoub, Olga, and Miquel. Felt and savored this return in all ways.

Done.†

Not done (absence of Poupette)‡

Went to the Cours Desir—and wrote to Raoux through Zaza

Done.§

Have read Stendhal, Tallemant des Réaux, Mirabeau—etc.

Completely.¶

From October 1 to November 1**

Nothingness. Sartre's advice and reading a thousand things.††

Marcelle Marie; a little boy; the sixth grade class at Duruy.‡‡

A few foreigners and eighteenth-century literature.§§

Saw all of these people.¶¶

Monopolized from the 10th to the 23rd—happy.***

---

* In the handwritten diary, Beauvoir has written her plans on the verso page connected by dots to the parts on the recto page indicating what has been done or not done.

† This is written across from her plans to move in to her Grandmother's.

‡ This is written across from her plans to prepare her outfits with Poupette.

§ She did put her papers in order.

¶ She was completely a practical, effective, and yet joyous Castor.

** The following corresponds again to which of her plans she has accomplished and is written in the manuscript on the recto page facing the plans on the verso page.

†† This comment is facing "Start to write."

‡‡ This comment is facing the goal of giving private lessons.

§§ This comment is facing her plans to read.

¶¶ This comment is facing returns.

*** This comment is facing plans for Sartre's return.

Every day from November 3 to 23—happy.*
Jacques is avoiding me—letter from him that says nothing
Poupette's interview
1200F of debt!
Castor who didn't work, but who learned to dress well and to be pretty and a woman, who discovered her body in its joys and its tenderness, who was overwhelmed with happiness for her little husband, and by her dear Lama, and who learned to be of leisure, happy like never before perhaps . . .

November: gave 200 F to S. Reimbursed Poupette and M. de Prandières. Outfit purchased.†

SUMMARY OF MY LIFE (2)

The beginning of my life, I summarized last year in a notebook, but today I must clearly review this past.

Vacation 1926. Experience of solitude: affirmation of my individualism; ethics of opposition and will for life. Desire for a written work. Very painful love; vague consciousness of another possible, but too distant future; defiance of happiness. Yet wholeheartedly committed to waiting for this happiness. Bias of faith and trust.

Unhappy little girl, simple and worthy of esteem.

October. Passion, suffering, *atrocious* even evoked from afar, complete solitude. When I obtain a joy, it's because the God-myself is resuscitated: more and more definitive individualism. For Jacques a feeling that is a great compassion; that can do nothing for me although I live only in him. I love him, but different, foreign, bitter, it is not joy that he ever brings me. I do not admire him, and I always have to make an effort to esteem him. And revolt at the idea of limiting myself to him.

Elated little girl, less sincere because she wants to be in harmony with this passion that she cannot keep herself from judging. From the beginning deception, malaise, but an extraordinary poetry that still today I regret, and whose memory justifies everything. I am passionate, tormented, and too alone. But at moments still strong and lucid. For three years I was a slave to the poetry of this October.

---

* This comment is facing Lama's visit.
† Six pages are left blank in the manuscript after this comment.

November. Everything seems definitive; no more discussion. Tenderness and dream, two weeks of perfect and happy security (from afar). Atrocious boredom, suffering interrupted by brief extreme joys. Slave. Tragic little girl, but who doesn't think poorly when she rediscovers the strength to think.

December—January. A little more sentimental peace, few encounters and few things said, but prolonged in interminable dreams and in ruminations. I cling to this often fleeting love; even when I have it, it does not fill the void. I become agitated at night. Suffering. I do not dominate life; I am too young, and yet too old for my age. Sometimes revolt against this depressing love, against Jacques who doesn't know how to save me. But sweetness of certain moments. Extraordinary charm of Jacques and of his affection.

Little girl in distress. Such a need for simple tenderness and to be consoled.

February—March. The enchantment persists. Simplicity of our friendship, grave joy, from time to time I find that I am disgustingly sick and I try to escape from myself. Alternatives of pure and full serenity or revolt.

March 15. Abrupt and definitive revolt, on the boulevard des Italiens. Rejection of slavery, return to myself. Resurrection of my strength and unfolding of my life: Blomart, Mercier, Neuilly, Sorbonne, G. Lévy, Miquel, and the sun. And surges of love that go to my head but that no longer destroy me. Desire for a written work, need for nobody.

Love at times confident, at times uncertain. But this love is not worth as much. I experience my solitude and my strength; already I can no longer be absorbed in a dream (April 28). Sometimes *joy.**

End of April—May. Desires to believe and to act—I am obligated to recognize that I believe nothing and desire nothing. And yet many pleasures; a joyous strength that extends to a book or a new love; my life no longer appears to me to be already plotted out and around Jacques. How cold Jacques was already leaving me; and this horror of marriage remembered from my childhood, and the weight of life near J. is strongly felt, going back to the revolts of October and November. From this day on, I no longer love Jacques and I judge him—lucidity so great that I do not understand how I managed to get over it. And I have a great sentimental peace, having surpassed love. Intellectually, J. is an obstacle for me. Intellectual uncertainty, disquietudes of the mind. But strong, courageous, and lucid little girl who no longer deceives herself. I have esteem for her once again.

May—June. I no longer love Jacques, once or twice immense emotion upon seeing him again and remorse for no longer loving him. But my life

---

* The French equivalent of the word "joy" is underlined in Beauvoir's handwritten diary.

is outside of him. It is a vigorous renewal of myself, a program for life, a great outward dissipation that marks a desire to open myself to everything, a release, and inwardly the importance is granted to my intellectual life, not to my heart. Intellectual failures, from all parts, suffering for that to the point of despair. A bit ridiculous to be so tragic. But I wholeheartedly approve this will for life, for a written work, for an accomplishment. And I know how to make use of others while still preserving myself.

July. Sadness of solitude, of love that is distant. Will for thinking. Very painful metaphysical despair in this sun. Friendship with Merleau-Ponty, who brings me out of this despair and my solitude, and who causes my philosophical fervor to crystallize. Frenzy.

1927 Vacation. I've aged a lot since last year. No longer this beautiful dream alone, and nevertheless not yet known and dominated life. I struggle in my thought, with memories of the dream that remains dear. Resolutions of philosophy and strength. Loads of letters and ardor, but at heart I am very unhappy, very unhappy to love no longer. I write interminable pages. Intellectual and feverish little girl, studious too, which calms her, but she loses the simplicity of her thought and much of her worth. Intellectual elation and vague enthusiasm as bad for the heart as for the mind.

October–November–December 1927. Work and solitude. Strength, fatigue, intellectual elation, and vague mysticism. Inner tortures, but will for a grand life. Love was pushed aside for this grandeur. Love comes back at the end of December in an infinite pleasure.

January–February. Search for joy. In thought, in inner ecstasies, in adventure, in friendship, in this love come back to me, in everything. Search for an evasive truth. I struggle and drown. Little girl alone much too often, who sometimes stifles her heart and sometimes lets it burst. But watching all of this from afar, what a trial! And what a guarantee of all possible futures. Ardent life; and I knew that this intensity counted more than joy or sadness.

Superstition for inner life—this is still heart-rending for me.

March–April. Solitude, strength in solitude—too moody, and an emptiness in me that explains everything; need for someone who would understand everything and would help me. Nobody measures up to me. Never have I met my equal.

May. Lots of lighthearted and simple love. It is true that I rarely see Jacques and think of him little, but only with pleasure now, perhaps because I ask little of him. I become truly catoboryx and get lost in metaphysical intuitions. I am even tempted by Catholicism.

June, July, and 1928 vacation. I live in this love. I no longer think and am no longer worried. I love, I am sad and feel quite dizzy, or I am strong and work. I am even joyous. I calmly await the great happiness that will be his return. I prepare myself for a year of relaxation, which means a year of precise and thoughtless work.

And it is actually during the year 1928–1929 when I do not think and I do not love; I let myself live one day at a time in the most pleasant way possible.

Schedule for September 1929 through October 1930

And now I am impatient for the beginning of school and for this year in which I foresee so many things.

First, this love for Sartre which is unpredictable (it will die, or turn my life upside down, or calmly endure, a bit faded). That makes two nights at Versailles from six to ten o'clock, sometimes with Guille and Aron, and one long evening gathering in Paris on Saturday.[501] Stories, games, the entire past to tell him, the future to prepare, an intellectual direction. And for him, all that I will be able to give him.

Eight days in Paris at the beginning of October—eight days of marriage together at Easter in Guérande or in Alsace, and probably a month of my vacation in Versailles.

Second, Jacques. See him again, go out with him, and find out where we are, and in any case do not clarify anything before Easter, do not decide anything before next year. It's the great unknown.

Third, Lama, whom, alas! I will see little, the Grand-Duke, Zaza, Poupette, "that lady," Josée, maybe Stépha in January, and as many interesting people as possible.

Fourth, a book. Good or bad, but from three to four hours of work per day—to prepare with Sartre.

Fifth, readings—about three hours a day at the Bibliothèque Nationale or at home: history, literature, and a great philosopher.

Sixth, outings: concert at least once a week (I don't know music well enough), theater as good plays open, and with Poupette, and some random cinema according to my fatigue and people with whom to go out.

Seventh, two hours of lessons each day and 1500 francs per month to lead this life—set aside about 100 or 150 francs each month for my vacation.

Eighth, try to dress better for the pleasure of my *petits camarades*—learn the little tricks of maintaining a home, indispensable when one lives alone.

I see my days rather like this: 9:00–1:00 work, 2:00–5:00 reading, 5:30–7:30 lessons, dinner at Mama's, outing with Poupette or Zaza or Josée or alone, about twice a week.

Three other times: 9:00–1:00 work, 2:00–4:00 lessons, 4:00–6:00 classes or people or reading, 6:00–10:00 Sartre, 10:00–12:00 reading, or 6:00 to midnight Sartre (lunch at Mama's on these days).

Sunday, afternoon outing and in the evening reading—and then all of the unpredictable . . .

END OF SIXTH NOTEBOOK

NOTES

1. Beauvoir's *Diary of a Philosophy Student 1926–27*, published in 2006, (henceforth *Diary 1*) is the first volume of the annotated English translation of the French transcription that was established and approved for the English translation of Beauvoir's 1926–30 diary. In 2008, the published French version of that same manuscript from 1926–1930, *Cahiers de jeunesse*, (henceforth CJ) appeared. In this 2nd volume of the annotated English translation of Beauvoir's 1926–1930 diary, I thus include translations for and notes on the differences between the transcription that was established and approved for the translation of the first volume of the annotated English translation and the published French version of the 1926–1930 diary. My translations of Sylvie Le Bon de Beauvoir's additional notes are consistently preceded by her name and followed by the page number in CJ where they appear. All other notes and annotations are my own unless otherwise indicated.

2. Jacques Champigneulles is Beauvoir's slightly older cousin, who becomes her intellectual mentor during her adolescence and her first childhood sweetheart. Contrary to her autobiographical version of their childhood love affair in *Mémoires*, she still hoped to marry him until 1930 when he decided to marry another woman. See Klaw, "Simone de Beauvoir, Cousin Jacques du journal intime aux *Mémoires*, 84–91."

3. In her 1926–1930 diary, Beauvoir reserves the use of the informal word, often reserved for only the closest of friends, for "you" (*tu*) for her cousin Jacques. Except for Jacques Champigneulles and herself, Beauvoir uses the more formal pronoun "vous" to address others in her diary as "you." In the sixth and seventh notebooks, I have signaled in brackets the presence of (*tu*) or (*toi*) or (*te*) at the first occurrence of each section addressing Jacques or I have simply added the name, Jacques, to facilitate reading.

4. What I have transcribed as "au moment où ils éclorent," and translated as "at the moment when they blossomed," appears in the French edition as "au moment où ils naquirent," which could translate literally as "at the moment when they were born" (CJ 464).

5. Sylvie Le Bon de Beauvoir: During this same month, Simone de Beauvoir had returned to Gagnepan (CJ 464); Zaza is Elisabeth Lacoin, Beauvoir's first real school friend from the time Zaza was eleven until her death in 1929. Beauvoir calls her Elisabeth Mabille in *Mémoires*. For a better understanding of their friendship, see Lacoin, *Zaza*.

6. La Porte Étroite is a bookstore at 10, rue Bonaparte in Paris.

7. The Apollo is a music hall in Paris; Sylvie Le Bon de Beauvoir: Maurice de Chevalier was about to leave for Hollywood to star in the 1929 film, *The Love Parade* (CJ 465). Chevalier (1888–1972), the French actor and popular entertainer who started performing with the female star Mistinguett at the Folies Bergères in 1909, met with great success in France. By 1929 he was also a resident of Hollywood and starred in American films.

8. The "your soul" (*ton âme*) referred to in this passage is most likely Jacques, the only person Beauvoir referred to in the second person singular or "*tu*" in her 1926–1927 diary.

9. The Morris columns are the columns covered by publicity flyers showing the cultural events in the city of Paris. These columns are named after the printer Morris who, around 1820, came up with the idea of installing 100 columns to advertise musical and theatrical shows in a more orderly and attractive fashion throughout the city of Paris (Lesbros, 148).

10. Situated at 21, rue Royale, chez Weber, otherwise known as Brasserie Weber, served the public from 1899 through 1961. Before 1914, it was a popular meeting place for writers, artists, journalists, actors, and other well-known figures. (Rochegude. *Promenades dans toutes les rues de Paris*, 78); Located at 3, rue Royale, Maxim's was opened as a bistro by Maxime Gaillard in 1893. After some years, ownership of the bistro fell to Eugene Cornuché, who transformed it into a masterpiece of Art Nouveau. For many years, Maxim's remained a dining establishment for the Parisian elite. See *Maxim's de Paris* at http://www.maxims-de-paris.com/RECEPTION-RESTAURANT-US/paris.htm (accessed March 1, 2017).

11. Robert Louis Stevenson's *In the South Seas* is an account of experiences and observations in the Marquesas, Paumotus, and Gilbert Islands in the course of two cruises, on the yacht "Casco" (1888) and the schooner "Equato" (1889); Edgar Allen Poe's book of poems was translated as *Les poèmes d'Edgar Poe* by Mallarmé (1842–1898), a French poet sometimes considered as the master of symbolism in poetry and noted for his exploration of the themes of nothingness, the difficulty of being, and absence, and who became increasingly interested in depicting the effect produced by a thing as opposed to the thing itself. In her April 18, 1927, diary entry, Beauvoir speaks of Mallarmé's "L'après-midi d'un faune (The afternoon of a faun)," a poem composed of 101 alexandrines to retrace the thoughts of a faun envisioning memories, dreams, and reality (*Diary 1*, 227).

12. The Bibliothèque Nationale is the National Library in Paris at 58, rue Richelieu, which until 1999 still held the vast majority of books and manuscripts to be consulted in Paris. Throughout her diary, Beauvoir calls this library the B.N. (as do most students and academics in Paris). For clarity, I have spelled the name out in each instance; Sylvie le Bon de Beauvoir's note cites the book by Edward Caird as *The Critical Philosophy of Immanuel Kant*, Glasgow, 1889, and indicates that Charles Renouvier (1815–1903), promoted the return to Kantian criticism in France (CJ 466).

13. The words, "note 1," appear in the original French manuscript although they do not appear in the edition published as CJ. There is no apparent referent for "note 1" in Beauvoir's handwritten diary; Sylvie le Bon de Beauvoir: *Tristan* was a short story published in 1903 (CJ 466).

14. Octave Hamelin (1856–1907), was a French philosopher whose spiritualist doctrine relates to Renouvier's neocriticism and who wrote *Essai sur les éléments principaux de la représentation* (Essay on the principal elements of representation) (1907).

15. Jean Giraudoux's *Simon le pathéthique* is the story of a man named Simon who is looking for the right woman to marry. He falls in love with Anne and struggles with his love

for her when he learns that she is not the chaste and docile soul that he had imagined. He leaves her when he learns of her past lover, but finally returns to ask her to marry him. Anne refuses because she realizes that he doesn't like women as entire beings with emotions and passions of their own. As the story closes, Simon is still hoping to find "an animal who speaks" and "who sings" in the form of a woman. The text thus depicts the problems inherent in man's idea that a wife will be much like a pet that he can tame. Also of interest for Beauvoir's later writings on the myths concerning women are several elements such as Simon's comments that he was teaching Anne to be quiet and obey him, that a woman was more limited than a man, that she should listen to him about everything, love him, but never bother him, and should follow him everywhere (*Simon le pathéthique*, 150).

16. Mademoiselle Mercier (Mademoiselle Lambert in Simone de Beauvoir's *Mémoires*), who encouraged Beauvoir to return to her love of philosophy, is Jeanne Mercier (1896–1991), holder of the University *agrégation*, and a member of the Communauté Saint-François Xavier founded in 1913 by Madeleine Daniélou, a philosophy teacher at the Institut Sainte-Marie in Neuilly. See Léna, "Jeanne Mercier, lectrice de Maurice Blondel (Jeanne Mercier, reader of Maurice Blondel)." In 1926 Beauvoir was thus very familiar with the libraries and teachers at these schools and often returned for visits. (*Mémoires* 233–234, 272–273, 282–283; *Memoirs*, 168–169, 197, 204). See also *Diary 1* for numerous other references to Mercier.

17. Sylvie Le Bon de Beauvoir: Mauriac is the author of *L'enfant chargé de chaines* (1913) (CJ 467). The French edition, unlike Beauvoir's manuscript, does not include Mauriac's name in parenthesis. François Mauriac's *L'enfant chargé de chaînes* is the story of Jean-Paul who struggles with his faith in God before he finally consecrates himself to love to free himself from the chains of egoism and the refusal of love. His adolescent cousin Marthe is hopelessly in love with him, and only wishes "to devote herself, give herself away, and serve" (45); my translation. Several ideas that Beauvoir records in her diary are also in this novel such as the notion that people that love us more than we love them exasperate us (56) or that there is no merit in loving those who love you (63), or that one must ask forgiveness from all those whom one has made suffer (76) and finally that love is the path to freedom (78). Jean-Paul tells himself, "The day when my thought attached itself to Marthe with a tender and obstinate worry, that very day, I began to be freed from myself" (78). Beauvoir must be quoting from memory for the actual first quote literally translates as, "She has, like the other young girls . . ." instead of "She has, like all young girls . . ." (48). François Mauriac was a French novelist and essayist, renowned for his Catholicism. He created and discussed dark scenarios in which a lack of religious grace tortured its victims. The novels by Mauriac that Beauvoir most likely read between 1926 and 1930 include *Le baiser au lépreux* (*A Kiss for the Leper*), *La chair et le sang* (*Flesh and Blood*) *Génitrix* (*Genitrix*), *Le désert de l'amour* (*The Desert of Love*), and *Thérèse Desqueyroux*. Beauvoir also quoted Mauriac extensively in her 1926–1927 diary entries.

18. Henriette is Beauvoir's sister, Henriette-Hélène Bertrand de Beauvoir, more frequently called Poupette in Beauvoir's diary, and Hélène, years later.

19. Sylvie Le Bon de Beauvoir: *Dominique* (1863) is the novel of the artist and writer, Eugène Fromentin (CJ 467). His only novel, *Dominique*, tells the story of the adolescent boy, Dominique, who is in love with an older woman named Madeleine. Beauvoir speaks of this novel in her discussion of love on August 21, 1926 (*Diary 1*, 77).

20. Victor Delbos, *La philosophie pratique de Kant* (The practical philosophy of Kant) (Paris: Alcan, 1926).

21. Studio des Ursulines was the cinema where films were often shown for the first time in Paris during Beauvoir's youth.

22. Man Ray (1890–1976) was born in Philadelphia, Pennsylvania, and died in Paris, France. He was an American photographer, painter, and cinematographer, who participated in the first demonstrations of the dada movement in New York along with Marcel Duchamp and then collaborated with surrealists; Robert Desnos (1900–1945) was a French surrealist poet and pioneer of automatic writing before he eventually returned to more traditional poetic forms.

23. See Zaza's letter of September 28, 1928 (Lacoin, *Zaza*, 137–138).

24. "[T]he poignant feeling that a casual love is not possible, that I have too much to give—do you [*tu*] know this, you?" is a translation for "[L]e sentiment poignant qu'un passage n'est trop possible, que j'ai trop à donner—le sais-tu, toi?" but it is reasonable to assume that Beauvoir meant to write as I have translated and as CJ shows, "un passage n'est pas possible" (469).

25. What I transcribed as "tenant à tour de bras une botte de violettes et sautant par-dessus une corde" and translated as "holding onto a bunch of violets with all her might and jumping rope" appears in CJ as "tenant à bout de bras une botte de violettes et sautant par-dessus une corde," which would translate as "holding in her outstretched arms a bunch of violets and jumping rope" (CJ 469).

26. Sylvie Le Bon de Beauvoir: This is Aunt Marguerite de Beauvoir; Jeanne and Henri are cousins (CJ 469). In the manuscript, Beauvoir designates these relatives by their initials M., J. and nickname (Riri).

27. Josée Le Cor (known as Lisa Quermadec in *Mémoires*) was a shy student who felt an affinity with Beauvoir and who confided in her during their university studies. I initially transcribed her name as José from the manuscript and it thus appears in the first volume of *Diary* as José (spelled with one "e"). Henceforth in the subsequent volumes of *Diary*, I have reproduced this name, as has Sylvie Le Bon de Beauvoir in the French edition, with the standard spelling for the feminine version of this name.

28. What I transcribed as "l'avenue des Champs-Elysées" has been shortened to "les Champs-Elysées" in the French edition (CJ 469); What I transcribed as "tous pareils" and translate as "all of them the same," appears as "tout pareils," in the French edition, which would translate as "completely the same" (CJ 469).

29. Sylvie Le Bon de Beauvoir: *La robe prétexte* (1914) is a novel by Mauriac (CJ 470). François Mauriac's *La robe prétexte* is a coming of age story in which Jacques, the protagonist, falls in love with his slightly older cousin, Camille, and imagines that she has every charm. Once their love is discovered, he is sent away to Germany for three months to forget her. Upon his return, he sees that she is no longer a dreamy adolescent girl full of romantic dreams and poetry but has become a young lady concerned only with practical things. Of interest to studying Beauvoir's diary is the idea that adopting a single system means giving up millions of other systems (*La robe prétexte*, 202).

30. This description corresponds to Zaza's letter of September 30, 1928, in Lacoin, *Zaza*, 138–139. Rabindranath Tagore (Rabindranath Thakur) (1861–1941) was an Indian musician, painter, poet, and the author of more than one thousand poems and numerous novels, dramatic plays, and songs that greatly influenced modern literature in India. He won the Nobel Prize for Literature in 1913. This quotation is from section 79 of Tagore's English translation

of his own poetic work, *Gitanjali*, which André Gide later translated into French as *L'offrande lyrique*. See Tagore, *Gitanjali (Song Offerings)*, 78.

31. Jules Laforgue (1860–1887), French poet and contemporary of Gustave Kahn and Paul Bourget, published *Les complaintes (The Complaints)*, *Derniers vers (Last Verses)*, *L'imitation de Notre-Dame La Lune (The Imitation of Our Lady the Moon)*, and *Moralités légendaires (Moral Tales)*. He is noted for poetry combining audacity and fantasy. Beauvoir quotes several of his verses in 1926 (*Diary 1*, 127–128 and 161–162).

32. Sylvie Le Bon de Beauvoir: Stépha Avdicovitch was the Polish student who was hired during summer vacation as a governess to the Lacoin children and whom Beauvoir first met at Gagnepan (CJ 471). In Beauvoir's *Mémoires*, Stépha took care of the three smallest Mabille children during summer vacation. Beauvoir met her while visiting Zaza and her family in Laubardon. Stépha was very attractive, liberal, extroverted, outspoken, and pursued by many men. For all these reasons and more, although Zaza's mother quickly grew to hate her, Stépha continuously fascinated Beauvoir with her warmth, sensuality, and worldliness (*Mémoires*, 383–392; *Memoirs*, 278–288); What I have accurately translated as the sixth floor according to the American system, where the first floor is the ground floor, would literally translate as the fifth floor in the French system.

33. This is a quote from Ramuz also cited in 1926 (*Diary 1*, 81). Charles Ferdinand Ramuz (1878–1947) was a Swiss-born regionalist author whose works include *Aline, La beauté sur la terre (Beauty on Earth)*, and *Fête des vignerons* (Wine grower's feast). His writing is noted for its mixture of picturesque, tragedy, lyricism, sensuality, and mysticism. See also note 4 in Beauvoir's 1926 diary (*Diary 1*, 200). See Beauvoir's *Mémoires* to see how she reports somewhat differently this quote and Zaza's relationship with her mother (384; 398–399; *Memoirs*, 279, 300–303).

34. Note that what I have transcribed as "cher ami" and translated as "dear male friend," appears as "chère amie" in CJ, which would translate as "dear female friend," and change my interpretation of this sentence (CJ 471). Either interpretation is possible according to Zaza's letter of September 28, 1928, in which she describes her mother's refusal to allow her to go to outings planned by Simone or with people whose families her mother does not know including Merleau-Ponty (Lacoin, *Zaza*, 137–138). The "dear male friend" to whom Beauvoir might be referring would thus most likely be Merleau-Ponty (appearing as Pradelle in her *Mémoires*). See also Beauvoir's diary entry of June 29, 1927, in *Diary 1*, 294–297, and *Mémoires* 340–344; *Memoirs*, 245–248. For Zaza's love for Pradelle and her mother's initial reaction to it, see *Mémoires*, 461–467; *Memoirs*, 334.

35. Edward Caird, *The Critical Philosophy of Immanuel Kant*, 2 vols. (Glasgow: J. Maclehose and sons, 1909); Jean-Marie-Constant Duhamel, *Des méthodes dans les sciences de raisonnement* (Paris: Gauthier-Villars, 1878–1886).

36. Sylvie Le Bon de Beauvoir: La Maison des Amis des Livres was a bookstore-library, founded in 1915 by Adrienne Monnier at 7, rue de l'Odéon, that played an important role in literary life between the two world wars, and closed in 1951 (CJ 471).

37. Sylvie Le Bon de Beauvoir: This was *Enfants et meurtriers* (1926) by Herman Ungar (CJ 471). It was translated from the German, *Knaben und Morder*, into French by G. Fritsch-Estrangin (Paris: Editions de la Nouvelle Revue Française, 1926) and into English by Isabel Fargo Cole as *Boys and Murderers*. Beauvoir most likely read this book in French translation as she provided only the French title for it.

38. Benedetto Croce (1866–1952) was an Italian literary critic, historian, and philosopher greatly influenced by G. Vico and Hegel. He wrote *Ce qui est vivant et ce qui est mort de la philosophie de Hegel: étude critique suivie d'un essai de bibliographie Hégélienne*, translated from Italian into French by Henri Buriot (Paris: V. Giard and E. Brière, 1910) and translated into English by Douglas Ainslie under the title *What Is Living and What Is Dead in the Philosophy of Hegel* (New York: Russell and Russell, 1915).

39. Sylvie Le Bon de Beauvoir: Clemence Dane (1888–1965) was an English novelist and playwright who wrote *Legend* in 1919. Madala Grey is its heroine (CJ 472). At the beginning of Clemence Dane's *Legend*, Madala's friends and acquaintances learn that she has just died in childbirth while still in her twenties and after having written several novels of genius. The novel continues with flashbacks into Madala's life interspersed with discussions by the characters about the value of her novels, the way in which her novels represented or belied her true-life experiences, and the elusive quality of her nature. Of interest to Beauvoir's writings are discussions concerning love and marriage in which it is proposed that a woman would give up all fame and fortune to have a worthy man who loved her and whether or not this is admirable, and whether or not one should publish a person's posthumous private letters without that person's express permission. One quotation in *Legend* evokes Beauvoir's comments about never showing her real self to anyone, "Oh, can't you see? We've never seen the real Madala Grey. She gave—and became—to each of us—what we wanted most. She wrote down our dreams. She *was* our dreams" (197); What I have transcribed as "livre imparfait" and translated as "imperfect book," appears in the French edition as "bien imparfait," which would translate as "quite imperfect" (CJ 472).

40. The actual line in the English text *Legend* reads "I—I'd like to be married for myself, for my faults, for the bits I don't tell anyone. Kent would hate my faults. I'd have to hide my realest self. . . . If I'd not written Eden Walls would Anita have looked at me—or any of you?" (160–161).

41. Jean George Pierre Nicod (1893–1924) was a French philosopher and logician. The two books mentioned here have been published in English in one volume, *Geometry and Induction: Containing Geometry in the Sensible World and The Logical Problem of Induction* (Berkeley: University of California Press, 1970); Sylvie Le Bon de Beauvoir: Victor Basch was the author of the 1896 *Essai critique sur l'esthétique de Kant* [Critical essay on Kant's aesthetics] and became president of the Ligue des Droits de l'Homme [Human Rights League] in 1926 (CJ 473). Victor Basch (1863–1944), a French philosopher, specialist in German philosophy, and human-rights activist, was appointed as chair in the aesthetics and history of art in 1918 at the Sorbonne. Having been persecuted for his Jewishness as early as 1887, by 1907 he was active in the Ligue des Droits de l'Homme. He was later murdered along with his wife by the Vichy paramilitary for their Resistance activities. See Victor Basch, *For or against Dreyfus*.

42. Jacques Rivière (1886–1925) was a French author who founded the *Nouvelle revue française* (NRF). He exchanged a lengthy correspondence with his brother-in-law, Alain-Fournier, published in Rivière and Fournier, *Correspondance* (January 1905–July 1914), as well as with Claudel and Gide. Alain-Fournier (1886–1914) was the author of the novel that informs Beauvoir's early ideas on romantic love and life, *Le grand Meaulnes*. Rivière's writings include studies of Gide, Claudel, and Jammes among others; an account of his experiences as a prisoner during World War I, *L'allemand* (The German man); a novel, *Aimée*

(Beloved): and notes about his thoughts on Catholicism, *À la trace de Dieu* (Tracing God). For Mauriac, see note 17 above.

43. Jacques Rivière's novel *Aimée* made quite an impression on Simone de Beauvoir, who referred to it several times in *Diary 1* as well as in *Mémoires*. *Aimée* is the story of a young man named François, who although happily married to Marthe, his best female friend, falls madly and passionately in love with Aimée, the independent wife of his best male friend, Georges. François pursues Aimée throughout the entire novel but cannot bring himself to make a true pass at her due to his moral values and self-control. Upon learning that Aimée truly loves her husband but fears that he does not return her love, François realizes that true love means self-sacrifice and preferring the beloved to oneself, themes that are dear to Simone de Beauvoir in her diary and later novels. His realization causes him henceforth to devote all his energies to getting her husband to love her in return. Of interest to Simone de Beauvoir's development as a novelist is that all of Aimée's words, gestures, expressions, and actions are scrutinized much in the same way that Françoise, the protagonist, and other characters in Simone de Beauvoir's first novel, *L'invitée*, will analyze each of Xavière's moves and possible thoughts.

44. The standard translation for *angoisse* is "anxiety," according to the *Vocabulaire euro-péen des philosophes*, and I have translated *angoisse* as "anxiety" throughout both volumes of *Diary*.

45. See Beauvoir's *Mémoires* for her public version of this interaction with Stépha (397–398; *Memoirs*, 284–285).

46. In *Diary 1*, as in my approved transcription, Pontremoli's name appears with an acute accent over the "e" as "Pontrémoli." Henceforth in *Diary 2*, I have reproduced this name without an accent as "Pontremoli" to match the spelling provided in the French edition.

47. Perhaps Beauvoir is quoting from memory the part of Claudel's "La cantate à trois voix [Cantata for Three Voices]" when Laeta asks of what use is "a woman, if not for being a woman in the arms of a man" (342). Paul Claudel (1868–1955) was heavily influenced by two major experiences: his discovery of his faith in God and of the French poet Rimbaud. A playwright, lyricist, and theoretician, Claudel also had a career as a foreign diplomat, which led him to spend considerable time in America (1893–95), and in the Far East (1895–1909).

48. Francis Jammes (1868–1938) was a prolific writer of poetry and fiction. Initially a pro-tégé of Mallarmé and Gide, Jammes returned to Catholicism after befriending Paul Claudel.

49. Sylvie Le Bon de Beauvoir: This article appeared in the October 1928 issue (CJ 475). François Mauriac, "Souffrances du chrétien" *Nouvelle revue française*, 181 (October 1928). For mention of this work by Mauriac, see also *Mémoires*, 405; *Memoirs*, 290. See also notes 17 and 29 above above.

50. Sylvie Le Bon de Beauvoir: The most recent work of Romains in 1928 would have been *Le Dieu des corps* [Lord God of the flesh], the second part of the trilogy *Psyché* (CJ 475). Jules Romains (Louis Farigoule, 1885–1972), was a French writer and student of philosophy renowned for promulgating the literary theory of unanimism that posits a collective spirit or personality. Unanimism pervades his work *La vie unanime* (The unanimous life).

51. The Dôme, the Rotonde, and the Jockey are all restaurant-bars in Montparnasse.

52. Le petit Briard is "café Briard" according to Beauvoir's *Mémoires* (396).

53. Sylvie Le Bon de Beauvoir: *Commerce* was a quarterly literary journal founded in 1924 by Paul Valery, Léon-Paul Fargue, and Valéry Larbaud (CJ 476). It was published from 1924–

1932; Léon-Paul Fargue (1876–1947) was a French poet noted for his free verse and poetry in prose written with lyricism, imagination, and melancholy; Valéry Larbaud (1881–1957) was a French author widely traveled in Europe whose work dates from before 1935 when he became aphasic. At the time of writing her diaries from 1926–1930, Beauvoir probably would have had access to the following of his works: *Fermina Márquez* (*Fermina Marquez*), *A.O. Barnabooth* (*A.O. Barnabooth: His Diary*), *D'amants, heureux amants* (Of lovers, happy lovers) *Enfantines* (*Childish Things*), *Ce vice impuni* (This unpunished vice).

54. Sylvie Le Bon de Beauvoir: The science-fiction novel, *Le tunnel* (1913), by Bernhard Kellerman, was adapted for film in 1933. Jean Gabin and Madeleine Renaud were the main protagonists in the French version; there were also German and English versions. The novel and film are about the construction of a tunnel under the Atlantic Ocean that would link Europe and America (CJ 476).

55. Sylvie Le Bon de Beauvoir: *Métropolis* (1927) is the famous film by Fritz Lang (CJ 476). In this science fiction film, the German actress Brigitte Helm begins her career with the dual role of the pure maiden and the female robot in the futuristic city called Metropolis where the masters live in the upper world and the workers and slaves live in the uniform environment of the lower world.

56. Sylvie Le Bon de Beauvoir: The novel, *Mademoiselle Else*, was published in 1924 (CJ 476), and translated into English by F. H. Lyon as *Fräulein Else*. This novel is the story of the beautiful young girl Else who must obtain 50,000 florins in the 1920s to save her family from ruin. An elderly man proposes to give them to her in exchange for her company and favors. She first experiences disgust and refuses, but eventually she gives in to save her father's honor.

57. Sylvie Le Bon de Beauvoir: Thomas Mann's *La mort à Venise* was a novel published in 1912 (CJ 477). This novel is a short narrative about an aging and renowned author, Gustave Aschenbach, who goes to Venice on vacation where he falls madly in love with a handsome Polish teenage boy named Tadzio who is staying in his hotel. Although a cholera epidemic is threatening Venice, Aschenbach is so consumed by his passion that he is unable to leave the city or Tadzio.

58. Sylvie Le Bon de Beauvoir: This book is *La philosophie de Charles Renouvier* [The philosophy of Charles Renouvier] (1905) by Gabriel Séailles (CJ 477).

59. M.-P. is Maurice Merleau-Ponty; Sylvie Le Bon de Beauvoir: A *pneu* was a pneumatic message, a popular form of telecommunication during Beauvoir's youth. It consisted of a written message that took about 90 minutes from the time of its sending to the time of its reception and that traveled through tubes of compressed air circulating between post offices in Paris. This messaging system was in service between 1879 and 1984 (CJ 477).

60. Sylvie Le Bon de Beauvoir: Joaquim Nin (1879–1949) was a pianist and composer (CJ 477). He was also the Spanish-Cuban father of Anaïs Nin (1903–1977), the French writer.

61. Beauvoir quotes this same verse by Jammes from Elégie huitième, 76: "And your profound love which watches over my soul," September 1926, *Diary 1*, 92.

62. On October 3, 1927, Beauvoir writes about similar reminiscences concerning Jacques (*Diary 1*, 100–102).

63. Sylvie Le Bon de Beauvoir: Mauriac's *La vie de Racine* was published in 1928 (CJ 479).

64. Henri de Montherlant (1896–1972) was a French writer who depicted his ideal of a heroic life that excludes women. An analysis of his works figures heavily in Beauvoir's *Le deuxième sexe* (*The Second Sex*); Maurice Barrès (1862–1923), a symbolist French author,

was sometimes viewed as a dreamy rebel. In works that postdate the ones that Simone de Beauvoir mentions in this diary, Barrès is also sometimes viewed as paving the way for fascism because of his increasingly rigid right-wing views. In 1926 Simone de Beauvoir most often spoke of his *La trilogie du culte du moi* (Trilogy of self-worship), which was comprised of three different novels, *Sous l'oeil des barbares* (Under the surveillance of barbarians), *Un homme libre* (A free man), and *Le jardin de Bérénice* (The garden of Bérénice). Self-worship (*le culte du moi*) is the movement attributed to Barrès in which what's most important is to cultivate one's ego and to be true to oneself. In its most extreme form, his doctrine implies that all those who are not the self are barbarians. This concept is commonly translated as "self-worship," "egoism," "ego cultivation," or simply rendered in French as *le culte du moi*.

65. In her *Mémoires*, Beauvoir refers to the bookstore Picard's as "la librairie Picart" (324); Sylvie Le Bon de Beauvoir: Emil Ludwig's *Napoléon* was published in 1925 (CJ 479). Emil Ludwig (881–1948) was a German biographer originally named Emil Cohn. His books that Beauvoir might have read between 1926–1930 include *Goethe, Napoleon, Bismarck,* and *The Son of Man.*

66. Sylvie Le Bon de Beauvoir: Pierre Naville (1904–1993) was first a Communist and then-Trotskyist and the director of the journal *Clarté* (CJ 479). He was also a French writer and sociologist who founded *L'oeuf dur* (The tough egg), the avant-garde periodical with Philippe Soupault, F. Gérard, Max Jacob, Louis Aragon, and Blaise Cendrars in 1922. Between 1926 and 1928, he was a member of the French Communist Party for which he managed the publication *Clarté*. Books by him that Beauvoir might have read by 1928 include *Les reines de la main gauche* (Left-handed queens), 1924, and *La révolution et les intellectuels* (The revolution and the intellectuals), 1926. See Breton, *Manifestoes of Surrealism*, 147; What appears in the approved transcription as *Libres propos*, now shows in the French edition as "livres proposés," which would translate as "proposed books" (CJ 480). *Libres propos* was a paper, which featured the short essays called *Propos* that were written by Alain. Alain is the pseudonym of Emile-Auguste Chartier (1868–1951), a student of Lagneau and later a philosopher and essayist who hoped to make people view philosophy as a path to wisdom and to control of their passions. Beauvoir frequently refers to Alain in the 1927 portion of her diary.

67. Sylvie Le Bon de Beauvoir: There was a novel published in 1928 that was entitled *Nord, roman de l'Arctique* [North, novel of the Arctic] by Maximilien Heller (CJ 479).

68. *Critique* is most likely a reference to Kant's *Critique of Pure Reason.*

69. Sylvie Le Bon de Beauvoir: *L'homme au cheval gris* by Theodor Storm was published in 1927 (CJ 480). Theodor Woldsen Storm (1817–1888), originally named Schleswig-Holstein, was a German poet and novelist who first wrote novellas showing the joys of his childhood in the provinces. He later produced more realistic and melancholic novels, including *Der Schimmelreiter*, which was translated into French by Robert Pitrou in 1928 as *L'homme au cheval gris* (The Man on the Gray Horse) and by Raymond Dhaleine in 1945 as *L'homme au cheval blanc* (The Man on the White Horse). It was translated into English by Muriel Almon as *The Rider of the White Horse (The Dikegrave)*, by Denis Jackson as *The Dykemaster*, and by James Wright as *The Rider of the White Horse.*

70. Sylvie Le Bon de Beauvoir: Pierre Duhem was a chemist and a philosopher of the sciences and the author of *L'évolution de la mécanique* (1902) and of *Le système du monde, histoire des doctrines cosmologiques de Platon à Copernic* [The system of the world: a history of the cosmological doctrines from Pato to Copernicus] (1914) (CJ 480).

71. Michel Souriau, *Le jugement réfléchissant dans la philosophie critique de Kant* (Reflecting judgment in Kant's Critical Philosophy) (Paris: F. Alcan, 1926). Perhaps Auguste Valensin's *À travers la métaphysique* (Through Metaphysics) (Paris: Gabriel Beauchesne, 1925), a volume that includes a discussion of Kantian criticism, the theory of experience according to Kant, and the history of philosophy according to Hegel. See "Journals and New Books," 719–720.

72. Sylvie Le Bon de Beauvoir: Johann Paul Friedrich Richter is known as Jean Paul (1763–1825), and [*Leben des*] *Quintus Fixlein* was published in 1793 [*sic*] (CJ 481). Jean Paul was a German writer, heavily influenced by satirists Jonathan Swift and Laurence Stern, and known for his use in literature of the theme of the double in which one individual struggles with another to reconcile differences and similarities. *Vie de Quintus Fixlein*, often viewed as being one of Jean Paul's best works, was published in French by Stock in 1925.

73. Sylvie Le Bon de Beauvoir: At this moment, Simone de Beauvoir is returning to Belleville, to the Center of Social Aid associated with the *Équipes* (CJ 481). Clavel might be referring to the street that is known for its artisans, named after the general Pierre Clavel and located in the nineteenth district of Paris.

74. The name "Forrain" does not appear in the French edition (cf.: CJ 481).

75. What appears in the approved transcription as "très terne," which I have translated as "very drab," appears in the published French edition as "tristesse," which would be translated as "sadness" (cf.: CJ 481).

76. What appears in the approved transcription as "une belle exigence" and I have translated as "a great demand," the published French edition renders as "une telle exigence," which would be translated as "such a demand" (cf.: CJ 481).

77. The *Équipes Sociales* were study groups founded by the professor and philosopher Robert Garric to aid and educate the working classes in the eastern districts of Paris. Simone de Beauvoir met and admired him at the Institut Sainte-Marie in Neuilly in 1925. She continued to attend his lectures after completing her certificate. His influence caused her to get involved with the *Équipes Sociales*, an expression that literally translates as "Social Teams." Simone de Beauvoir volunteered to teach literature to young women for this association. Her particular group was located in Belleville. See *Mémoires*, 249–254; *Memoirs*, 179–184; Francis and Gontier, *Simone de Beauvoir*, 51–52; and Bair, *Simone de Beauvoir*, 9.

78. Gagnepan was one of the Lacoin's family homes.

79. Sylvie Le Bon de Beauvoir: Jean Richon was Titite's husband (CJ 482).

80. Preciosity and the salons became popular primarily among women but also some men during the 1620s as a literary and social reaction against the vulgarity of certain customs during the reign of Henri IV. It was stylish to recite poetry, present witty descriptions of others, and read upcoming plays aloud. The salons also began to lay claim to governing what was and was not in good taste. In 1659 Molière mocks preciosity and its supposed hold over defining good taste in his play, *Les précieuses ridicules* (*The Pretentious Young Ladies*). By 1665 salon life had lost its popularity (Favier, *Deux mille*, 459–460); Sylvie Le Bon de Beauvoir: Zon is Zaza's older sister (CJ 482).

81. For Rivière and Fournier, see note 42 above.

82. The portion of this sentence that I have translated "as the poet whose dream she carried, from whom she distanced herself by a strange mistake because she did not understand him," could also be translated "as the poet whose dream she carried, from which she distanced herself by a strange mistake because she did not understand it" (cf.: CJ 483).

83. Friedrich Nietzsche (1844–1900) was a German philosopher who challenged the foundations of Christianity and traditional morality.

84. Albert Einstein (1879–1955) was a German-born, American theoretical physicist known for the formulation of the theory of relativity. He received the 1921 Nobel Prize in Physics for his work in theoretical physics and wrote *Relativity: The Special and the General Theory*; Henri Bergson (1859–1941) was a French philosopher who taught at the Collège de France from 1900 to 1914 and whose philosophical works won him the 1929 Nobel Prize for literature. Hostile to Kant and to positivism, he argued for a conscious return to intuition and to a philosophy attentive to immediate experience. Bergson was very popular until World War II and influenced many French authors, including Henri Massis, Charles Péguy, and Marcel Proust, whose works Simone de Beauvoir refers to often in *Diary 1*. In August 1926, Simone de Beauvoir quotes several passages from Bergson's *Essai sur les donnés immédiates de la conscience* (*Time and Free Will*), *Diary 1*, 58–61; Becquerel may be Antoine Henri Becquerel, French physicist who, with Marie and Pierre Curie, was awarded the Nobel Prize for Physics in 1903 for his discovery of penetrating radiation coming from uranium salts, the first indicator of spontaneous radioactivity, or Jean Becquerel, author of *Le principe de relativité et la théorie de la gravitation. Leçons professées en 1921 et 1922 à L'École polytechnique et au Musée d'histoire naturelle* (The principle of relativity and the theory of gravity. Lessons professed in 1921 and 1922 at l'École polytechnique and at the Museum of Natural History), and of *Cours de physique à l'usage des élèves de l'enseignement supérieur et des ingénieurs* (Physics classes for graduate students and engineers); Henri Poincaré (1854–1912) was a French mathematician and author known for showing the application of math to physics. He is sometimes considered to have laid the preliminary groundwork for Einstein's theory of relativity. He firmly promoted the importance of intuition and developing a philosophy of science. His most influential work is *La science et l'hypothèse* (*Science and Hypothesis*); What appears in my approved transcription as "une belle journée d'été" and I have translated as "a beautiful summer day," the French edition shows as "une belle matinée d'été," which would translate as "a beautiful summer morning" (CJ 484).

85. Sylvie Le Bon de Beauvoir: *Lord Jim* is a novel published by Joseph Conrad in 1900 (CJ 484). Joseph Conrad (1857–1924) was an English novelist born of Polish parents in Russia. He is often viewed as one of the greatest novelists and prose stylists in English literature. Conrad is known for combining realism with high drama, and nautical backgrounds with high society and international politics. *Lord Jim* features the narrator Marlow's attempt to piece together and understand the story of Jim who goes to sea, quickly rises to fame, and then plummets to failure due to inexperience and poor decisions.

86. Sylvie Le Bon de Beauvoir: Joseph Delteil (1894–1978) was associated with surrealists (CJ 485). Joseph Delteil was also a controversial and prolific French writer who achieved fame upon the publication of his work, *Jeanne d'Arc* (1925), which won the Prix Fémina Vie heureuse. In 1923 and 1924, he also collaborated on a variety of journals including *La nouvelle revue française*, *La revue européenne*, *Littérature*, *Les feuilles libres*, *La révolution surréaliste*, *L'intransigeant*, *Paris journal* (Briatte).

87. Sylvie Le Bon de Beauvoir: The curtain, gong, and strikes are references to the Théâtre de l'Atelier (CJ 485).

88. Written in the manuscript is simply "m," which I understand to mean "maquereau" as is shown in the French edition (CJ 485), and which would translate as "pimp." To remain faithful to Beauvoir's writing of such a word by one letter, I have translated it as "p."

89. What appears in the approved transcription as "mêmes de Sorbonne" and which I have translated as "even from the Sorbonne," now appears in the French edition as "moeurs de Sorbonne," which would translate as "Sorbonne behaviors" (CJ 485).

90. Beauvoir recounts this event somewhat differently in her autobiography (*Mémoires*, 404; *Memoirs*, 289).

91. Although Beauvoir wrote *Colombe Béchard*, she is most likely referring to *Colombe Blanchet* by Alain-Fournier as the title appears in the French edition (CJ 486).

92. M.-P. is undoubtedly Merleau-Ponty. For *Nord*, see note 67.

93. What appears in the approved transcription as "tout à côté du lit," and I have translated as "right next to the bed," the French edition shows as "laid, à côté du lit," which would translate as "ugly next to the bed" (CJ 487).

94. For Josée Le Core, see note 27.

95. The exact verse from Robert Browning's "A Light Woman" reads "Yet think of my friend, and the burning coals / He played with for bits of stone." Beauvoir quotes this same verse and comments on it in October 1927 (*Diary 1*, 318).

96. What appears in the approved transcription as "court salut," which I have translated as "short greeting," the French edition renders as "seul salut," which I would translate as "sole greeting" (CJ 488).

97. Sylvie Le Bon de Beauvoir: Emile Meyerson (1859–1933) was a philosopher, who like Brunschvicg, represented French idealism (CJ 488). The reread book was Meyerson's *La déduction relativiste* (*The Relativistic Deduction*); For Duhem, see note 70 above; The book by Immanuel Kant is translated from German into French by Joseph Tissot under the title *Anthropologie d'un point de vue pragmatique ou de l'utilité* (Paris: Librairie Ladrange, 1863), 9–341. It is translated from German into English by Victor Lyle Dowdell under the title *Anthropology from a Pragmatic Point of View* (Carbondale: Southern Illinois University Press, 1978).

98. Sylvie Le Bon de Beauvoir: Heinrich Mann's *Mère Marie* was published in 1927; For Delteil, see note 86 above; Sylvie Le Bon de Beauvoir: *Le paradis à l'ombre des épées* (1924) is the *Première Olympique* [First Olympian] by Montherlant (CJ 488, 489). Henri de Montherlant's work, *Les olympiques* (The Olympians) (1924), combines a collection of essays, poems, and short stories that praise sports, physical effort, and the sense of solidarity and spirit involved in sports. In these writings, paradise is the stadium. Two published texts are linked by this title: *Première Olympique: Le paradis à l'ombre des épées* (First Olympian: Paradise in the shadow of swords) and *Deuxième Olympique: Les onze devant la porte dorée* (Second Olympian: The eleven before the golden door). See also note 64 above.

99. Sylvie Le Bon de Beauvoir: Siegfried is Giraudoux's 1922 *Siegfried et le Limousin* [Siegfried and the Limousin] (CJ 490).

100. For Jules Laforgue, see note 31 above.

101. David Hume (1711–1776) was a Scottish historian, man of letters, and philosopher known for being a great empiricist.

102. Léon Brunschvicg (1869–1944), was a French philosopher and a professor at the Sorbonne from 1909 to his death. His major works include *La modalité du jugement* (The modality of judgment); *Les étapes de la philosophie mathématiques* (Stages of mathematical philosophy); and *Le progrès de la conscience dans la philosophie occidentale* (The progress of consciousness in occidental philosophy). Brunschvicg would later direct Simone de Beauvoir's thesis on Leibniz. Brunschvicg's wife, Cécile Brunschvicg, was a prominent

feminist who fought to give girls access to the baccalauréat (Offen, "The Second Sex and the Baccalauréat," 266; cf.: Simons, "Beauvoir's Early Philosophy," 31); For Poincaré, see note 84 above; Sylvie Le Bon de Beauvoir: Sir Arthur Stanley Eddington (1882–1944) was a British astrophysicist interested in the theory of relativity, which his works helped to prove (CJ 490). Eddington was also known for his contributions to the study of the evolution, the motion and the internal constitution of stars, and for his study of the connection between physics and philosophy. His writings include *Mathematical Theory of Relativity* (1923), *The Internal Constitution of the Stars* (1926), and *Stars and Atoms* (1928).

103. The *agrégation* is the highest competitive exam for teachers in France.

104. Sylvie Le Bon de Beauvoir: Fernand Gérassi was a painter and Stépha's future husband (CJ 491).

105. "To be in high spirits" is equivalent to the French expression "avoir l'âme en fête," which would more literally translate as "to have one's soul in celebration."

106. Sylvie Le Bon de Beauvoir: In 1928–1929, the program for the *agrégation* included a written and oral part. The written part necessitated 1) in-depth knowledge of the Epicureans, the Stoics, the Skeptics, and the believers in probabilism (the doctrine stating that as certainty is impossible, probability suffices to govern faith and practice)—Hume and Kant, and 2) The methodology and philosophy of the sciences. The oral consisted of three parts. For the Greek section, expert knowledge of Plato's *Republic*, books VI and VII and Aristotle's *Nicomachean Ethics* were needed. The Latin section concerned Cicero's *De Fato* [*On Fate*] and Spinoza's *Ethica more geometrico demonstrata I* [*Ethics, Demonstrated in Geometrical Order*]. The French section tested knowledge of Rousseau's *Contrat social* [*The Social Contract*], Leibniz's *Nouveaux essais* [*New Essays on Human Understanding*], and Boutroux's *De la contingence des lois de la nature* [*The Contingency of the Laws of Nature*] (CJ 491).

107. Geneviève de Neuville, a daughter of close friends of Zaza's parents, became a good friend of Zaza. From Zaza's numerous letters to her it seems that they were approximately the same age and shared many similar traditional Catholic values (Lacoin, *Zaza*, 8, 126–130).

108. Sylvie Le Bon de Beauvoir: Philippe Soupault's *Le bar de l'amour* was published in 1925 (CJ 492). *Le bar de l'amour* tells the brief love story of Julien, a man who no longer desires to have any friends or habits, and Maud, a young married woman who is bored. Julien seduces her after meeting her husband, makes love to her once again rather brutally, and then decides to leave her although he might love her—above all, he seeks adventure.

109. Johann Wolfgang von Goethe (1749–1832), a German poet, dramatist, novelist, and scientist, is best known for his dramatic poem *Faust*.

110. What appears in the approved transcription as "c'est lui qui la soutint," which I have translated as "he was the one who supported her," the French edition shows as "c'est lui toujours qui la soutint," which would translate as "he was still the one who supported her" (CJ 493).

111. Sylvie Le Bon de Beauvoir: Jacques Wartelle was one of Simone's cousins from Arras (CJ 494).

112. What appears in the approved transcription as "un jour de fatigue," which I have translated as "a day of fatigue," CJ renders as "un peu de fatigue," which would translate as "a bit of fatigue" (CJ 494).

113. For Geneviève de Neuville, see note 107 above.

114. The French equivalent of the word, "very" (*très*) appears in the originally approved manuscript but does not appear in the French edition (CJ 495).

115. As previously stated, M.-P refers to Maurice Merleau-Ponty.

116. Sylvie Le Bon de Beauvoir: Simone was seven years old when she wrote *La famille Cornichon* (CJ 496). In *Mémoires*, Simone de Beauvoir describes three childhood stories that she wrote, *Les malheurs de Marguerite* (The misfortunes of Marguerite), her first aborted attempt, *La famille Fenouillard* (The Fenouillard family), and *La famille Cornichon* (*Mémoires*, 73; *Memoirs*, 53); Père Ubu (Father Ubu) is an allusion to the main character of the scandalous play by Alfred Jarry (1873–1907), *Ubu Roi* (*King Ubu*) (1896), written by Jarry at age fifteen to ridicule his teacher Hébert (originally Père Héb or Père Hébé), a stupid and selfish bourgeois. Père Ubu declares himself King of Poland, tortures and kills all around him, and eventually chases all out of Poland, eerily foreshadowing future events involving megalomania and genocide of the twentieth century (Esslin, *The Theater of the Absurd*, 356–360).

117. Sylvie Le Bon de Beauvoir: *Battling le ténébreux (ou la mue périlleuse)* [Battling the dark one (or the dangerous metamorphosis)] by Alexandre Vialatte was published in 1928 (CJ 496). Vialatte is a French author known above all for his French translations of Kafka's works. *Battling le ténébreux* is the story of three dreamy high school students who invent a supernatural and erotic world around Erna Schnorr, a young sculptress who has recently moved into their town. Battling loses himself in his efforts to seduce her and commits suicide by shooting himself in the chest.

118. Charles Baudelaire, (1821–1867) sometimes considered to be the precursor of all modern poetry, stands at the apex of the romantic revolt.

119. Gustave Flaubert (1821–80) was a French novelist renowned for producing realistic novels including *Madame Bovary* and *L'education sentimentale* (*Sentimental Education*).

120. Unlike in the approved transcription, the published French edition does not show the word "dear" (*cher*) repeated twice before "boulevard" (CJ 498).

121. Alain-Fournier's *Le grand Meaulnes* is the story of Meaulnes, the heroic adolescent adventurer who falls in love with Yvonne de Galais, marries her, gets her pregnant, and then decides that he must leave her in search of a greater good, that of reuniting a former love with her beloved. As in Beauvoir's *Diary 1*, recurring themes of this novel are that love involves suffering, that some men are adventurers, and that if a man truly loves a woman she might believe that it is her duty to make him happy, but she will ultimately learn that she is nothing more than a "poor woman like the others" (*Le grand Meaulnes*, 283); my translation.

122. Beauvoir was leaving the reading room of the Bibliothèque Nationale.

123. What appears on my approved transcription as "comme sa chambre" and translated as "like her room," the published French edition renders as "dans sa chambre," which would translate as "in her room" (CJ 499).

124. The Jockey and the Jungle are restaurants that Beauvoir frequented.

125. What appears in the approved transcription as "son sourire," which I have translated as "his smile," the published French edition records as "ton sourire," which would translate as "your smile" (CJ 499).

126. Sylvie Le Bon de Beauvoir: John Henry Newman (1801–1890) was an Anglican who converted to Catholicism and later became a Cardinal in the Roman Catholic Church. *Grammar of Assent* was one of his many influential works (CJ 499).

127. The exact source of this quotation is unknown; my translation. André Gide (1869–1951) was a French writer known for his unconventional views and his sense of adventure,

which permeate his writings. Simone de Beauvoir refers repeatedly to his works and views throughout *Diary 1*. She often contemplates trying to live by Gide's notion of availability (*disponibilité*), which states that to embrace novelty, individuals (usually young people) must give up home, family, and all places of rest including continuing affections, faithful love affairs, attachment to ideas, and anything that compromises justice (*Les nourritures terrestres* [*Fruits of the Earth*], 184–185).

128. Picard's refers to a bookstore often frequented by Beauvoir and her friends. See note 65 above; What appears in the approved transcription as "passent," which I have translated as "pass by," the published French edition renders as "pensent," which would translate as "think" (CJ 500).

129. What appears in the approved transcription as "tes mains," which I have translated as "your hands," the published French edition renders as the singular "ta main," which would translate as "your hand" (CJ 500).

130. The published French edition no longer includes the "sans doute" that exists in my approved transcription and that I have translated as "I daresay" (CJ 500).

131. Sylvie Le Bon de Beauvoir: Othon Friesz (1879–1949) was a French painter and designer (CJ 501).

132. The published French edition shows "together" (*ensemble*) for what appears in the approved transcription as "to work" (*travailler*) (CJ 501).

133. The French words, "un homme de chez nous," which I have literally translated as "a man from our hometown" might be a loose translation of a famous line from *Lord Jim*, "he is one of us (62)." Ann P. Messenger suggests that this phrase means that Jim is a moral being and cannot be tragically destroyed in her article, "One of Us," 129.

134. Sylvie Le Bon de Beauvoir: *L'idéalisme contemporain* was published in 1905 and *Les Étapes de la philosophie mathématiques* was published in 1912 (CJ 501).

135. Jacques de Lacretelle (1888–1985), a prolific French author, was elected to the Académie Française in 1936. His 1928 novel, *L'âme cachée*, retells the story of the Greek legend of Phèdre in a modern setting. In the published French edition, Lacretelle's title appears as *L'âme exclue* (The excluded soul) (CJ 502).

136. Sylvie Le Bon de Beauvoir's note indicates that the uninteresting book was by Jens Peter Jacobsen (1847–1885), a Danish writer (CJ 503).

137. Sylvie Le Bon de Beauvoir: *Dix-huitième année* was published in 1928 (CJ 503). Jean Prévost (1901–1944) was a French writer and Resistance fighter who studied at the lycée Henri IV in Paris under the philosopher Alain before 1919. He wrote numerous novels and essays including one of his earliest works, *Dix-huitième année*. His doctoral thesis, *La création chez Stendhal, essai sur le métier d'écrire et la psychologie de l'écrivain* (Creativity in Stendhal, Essay on the craft of writing and the psychology of the writer) won the grand prize for literature of the Académie Française in 1943.

138. Sylvie Le Bon de Beauvoir: *The Constant Nymph* is written by the English novelist, Margaret Kennedy (1896–1963), and was published in 1924 (CJ 503). *La nymphe au coeur fidèle* is Louis Guilloux's 1926 French translation of Margaret Kennedy's English novel, *The Constant Nymph*, published by Heinemann in England. It is the story of the teenage girl, Tessa, who loves the redheaded, impetuous, and talented young composer and conductor, Lewis Dodd, her father's protégé. Upon her father's sudden death, Charles Churchill, Tessa's uncle, arrives with his daughter, Florence, to take care of the family. Lewis is immediately taken with Florence and marries her despite his love for Tessa. As the story unfolds, *The Constant Nymph*

intertwines a variety of themes pertinent to the works and concerns of Beauvoir, including the rivalry between social classes, the struggle between the passions and the intellect, the meaning of art, jealousy in a love relationship, female and male sexuality, and the consequences of shunning societal norms. Of particular interest to Beauvoir's fiction in general and to *L'invitée* in particular is the love-hate triangle that forms among Lewis, Florence, and Tessa, and the way that it is resolved by the death of one of the females after each has struggled to impose her interpretation of the love triangle on the other. It is not the truth that wins but rather power and the determination to make others believe one's story. Some critics consider *The Constant Nymph* to be the first novel of the Bohemian genre and attribute its immediate popularity to its portrayal of what was considered to be shockingly explicit sexuality in the 1920s. It was later adapted to a play by Margaret Kennedy and Basil Dean and then by Giraudoux for the French theater as *Tessa*.

139. Sylvie Le Bon de Beauvoir: *Daphne Adeane* is written by the British novelist, poet, and journalist, Maurice Baring (1874–1945) and was published in 1926 (CJ 503). Baring wrote several books on Russia, novels, plays, and poetry after serving as a war correspondent in the Russo-Japanese war and as a staff officer in World War I.

140. The line, "He shows me reproductions of beautiful paintings seen in Germany," which translates "Il me montre des reproductions de beaux tableaux vus en Allemagne," appears in my approved transcription but does not appear in the published French edition.

141. Sylvie Le Bon de Beauvoir: The Greek villa is the villa Kérylos, built from 1902 to 1908 by the Hellenist Theodore Reinach, who called upon the architect Emmanuel Pontremoli, member of the Academy of the Fine Arts and winner of Rome's Grand Prix in 1890. It is still possible to visit this marvel (CJ 503).

142. Vieux Colombier is a cinema in the sixth district of Paris; Sylvie Le Bon de Beauvoir: *Underworld* is a 1927 film by Josef von Sternberg (CJ 504). This American thriller starring George Bancroft, Clive Brook, and Evelyn Brent features the story of a mob boss who befriends a failed lawyer and then falls in love with his partner.

143. Sylvie Le Bon de Beauvoir: *Variété* is a silent film by Ewald Andre Dupont (CJ 504). *Variété*, also known as *Variety* and *Jealousy* is the 1925 German silent movie starring a character named "Boss."

144. Sylvie Le Bon de Beauvoir: Henri Poincaré (1854–1912) is a mathematician, a philosopher of the sciences, and the author of *La science et l'hypothèse* [*Science and Hypothesis*] (1902) and *La valeur de la science* [*The Value of Science*] (1905) (CJ 505). See also note 84 above.

145. What my approved transcription shows as "aimons" (let's love) is published in the French edition as "suivons," which would translate as "let's follow" (CJ 505).

146. Marcel Arland (1899–1986), a French author attracted to dadaism and surrealism, often collaborated on the journal *Nouvelle revue française*. His writings manifest his interest in the complexities of the human soul. His works include *Monique, Terres étrangères* (Foreign lands), *Étienne, La route obscure* (Dark road), *Les âmes en peine* (Souls in pain), *Étapes* (Stages), and *L'ordre* (Order). In 1929 he won the Prix Goncourt for *L'ordre*. Beauvoir frequently refers to his writings in her 1926–1927 diary entries; For Jules Laforgue, see note 31 above.

147. For Meyerson, see note 97 above.

148. Sylvie Le Bon de Beauvoir: Cournot (1801–1877) was a mathematician, economist, and philosopher (CJ 506). Antoine Augustin Cournot was also renowned for developing

mathematical theories of chance and probability. In his book, *Researches into the Mathematical Principles of the Theory of Wealth*, he was among the first to apply mathematics to economic problems.

149. Sylvie Le Bon de Beauvoir: The full reference for Léon Brunschvicg's work is *L'expérience humaine et la causalité physique* [Human experience and physical causality] (Paris, Alcan, 1922) (CJ 506); The line, "where I always go in vain to look for the class schedule," is my translation for "où je vais toujours en vain chercher le programme," which appears in the approved transcription of the manuscript but does not appear in the French edition (CJ 506).

150. Sylvie Le Bon de Beauvoir: These are the children of Simone de Beauvoir's Aunt Lili, her mother's younger sister who married Alexis Quintin in 1920 (CJ 506).

151. *L'esprit des lois* by French author Montesquieu (1689–1755) compares three types of government—republic, monarchy, and despotism. Its principle theories state that climate and circumstances influence the form of governments and that the powers of government must be separated and balanced in order to safeguard the freedom of the individual. These ideas were instrumental in the later formation of the American Constitution.

152. The published French edition shows "son accomplissement," which would translate as "its accomplishment" instead of "un accomplissement" (an accomplishment), which appears in the approved manuscript (CJ 507).

153. In my approved transcription, the last legible word in this line is "à," which I have translated as "to" whereas the published French edition shows the last legible word as "si," which would translate as "if" (CJ 507).

154. Sylvie Le Bon de Beauvoir: This is Édouard Le Roy (1870–1954), the mathematician and philosopher (CJ 507).

155. The School of Chartres was an Episcopal school founded by Bishop Fulbert in 990, which became a center of renewal of interest in literary, philosophical, and scientific studies.

156. Chez Pocardi is a café frequented by Beauvoir and her friends. See also *Mémoires*, 419; *Memoirs*, 299.

157. Thomas Mann's *Death in Venice* is a short narrative about an aging and extremely renowned author, Gustave Aschenbach, who goes to Venice on vacation where he falls madly in love with an incredibly good-looking Polish teenage boy named Tadzio who is staying in his hotel. Although a cholera epidemic is threatening Venice, Aschenbach is so consumed by his passion that he is unable to leave the city or Tadzio.

158. *Hellade* was the name used for the islands and colonies of ancient Greece.

159. Charles Guérin (1875–1939), a French impressionist painter, was noted for his unusual and unique use of color, his paintings of nude and vampish women, and his illustration of several works by Colette. In 1923 he was one of the founders of the Salon des Tuileries in Paris. See the diary entry of November 11, 1926, for Beauvoir's description of one of her favorite paintings by Guérin (*Diary 1*, 172).

160. The most highly competitive exam, the *agrégation*, consisted of the writing of three essays during three specified time periods and one oral exam. The longest of the written essay exam periods lasted six hours during which the candidate had to write on an impromptu topic, whereas the other two written exams were more specialized questions dealing with questions studied for the program and lasted four hours each. For details on what was covered in the written and oral parts, see note 106 above. The oral exam included one question that had not been covered during course work, which the candidate had seven

hours to prepare before presenting a lengthy lesson (*la grande leçon*), and several shorter oral quizzes on philosophers that the jury picked at random—one in French, one in Latin, one in Greek, and one in English or German. Successful completion of the *agrégation* was required to teach in certain high schools (*lycées*) or in universities (*Facultés*). A candidate for the philosophy *agrégation* had to be ready to answer all questions on philosophy and philosophers, which is why it was a major feat to pass the exam. Passing the *agrégation* guaranteed a job for life as a civil servant in the French educational system. I am thankful to Sylvie Le Bon de Beauvoir for all of this information, which clarifies the information explaining the *agrégation* in note 129 for the year 1927 in *Diary 1*, 329.

161. Beauvoir recounts the meeting with Jacques when their relationship changes on October 3, 1926, in *Diary 1*, 100–101.

162. The French equivalent of "at top speed" is underlined in the French edition (CJ 510).

163. Sylvie Le Bon de Beauvoir: Sainte-Anne's is a psychiatric hospital where Beauvoir went to earn her certificate in psychology, which includes knowledge of psychopathology (CJ 512).

164. Sylvie Le Bon de Beauvoir: The word *diplôme* in this French context alludes to graduate studies that are the equivalent of today's Master's (*maîtrise*) in France (CJ 513). Following her success on the exams in ethics and psychology in the spring of 1928, Simone de Beauvoir met with Prof. Brunschvicg who approved her plan to begin work on her graduate thesis (henceforth *diplôme*) and suggested the topic, "The Concept in Leibniz," which she accepted (Beauvoir, *Mémoires* 369; *Memoirs* 266).

165. Sylvie Le Bon de Beauvoir: Maurice Blondel (1861–1949), was a French Catholic philosopher to whom Mademoiselle Mercier was very close (CJ 514). He was also a writer and university professor who reflected at length on the complex relationship between immanence and transcendence. Works by him that Beauvoir may have been reading between 1926 and 1930 include *L'action* (*Action*), *Lettre sur les exigences de la pensée contemporaine en matière d'apologétique et sur la méthode de la philosophie dans l'étude du problème religieux* (*Letter on Apologetics*), and *Histoire et dogme* (*History and Dogma*) to address the gap between Catholic thought and Modern philosophy and social existence. Blondel postulated that action alone could never satisfy the human yearning for the transfinite, which could be fulfilled only by God. He later also argued God's existence could be proved rationally. His other chief works were *La pensée* (*Thought*) (2 vol., 1934–1935) and *Le problème de la philosophie catholique* (The problem with Catholic philosophy) (1932). I am grateful to Gregory Sadler at Ball State University for much of this information.

166. For *Le grand Meaulnes*, see note 121 above; For Rivière, see note 42 above; Jacques Copeau (1879–1949) was a French actor, literary critic, stage director, and dramatic coach. He cofounded the *Nouvelle revue française* with André Gide, Jean Schlumberger, and others and coedited it for several years. Responsible for establishing the experimental Théâtre du Vieux Colombier in Paris, he is renowned for seeking a more direct performance style in which the focus was placed on the performing actor's interpretation of the role and symbolic scene design.

167. Edmund Husserl (1859–1938), the German philosopher, renowned for being the principal founder of phenomenology, a philosophy that promotes describing the lived experiences of consciousness. He examined objects of pure imagination with the same seriousness as data taken from the objective world and thus concluded that consciousness has no life apart from the objects it considers. This characteristic he calls "intentionality"

(object-directedness), following Brentano. The first edition of Husserl's work to appear in French was his 1931 *Cartesian Meditations: An Introduction to Phenomenology*, a revised version of two lectures presented in Paris in February 1929. Husserl's phenomenology was discussed in French texts as early as 1926, however, including Jean Hering's *Phénoménologie et philosophie religieuse* (Phenomenology and religious philosophy), and a text by Beauvoir's professor, Jean Baruzi, "Le problème du salut dans la pensée religieuse de Leibniz (The problem of salvation in the religious thought of Leibniz)." For further discussion of Baruzi, Husserl, and Beauvoir, see Margaret A. Simons, *Beauvoir and "The Second Sex,"* 197–202.

168. Sylvie Le Bon de Beauvoir: Lélette is Marie-Madeleine du Moulin de Labartète, the friend shared by the Lacoins and the Neuvilles (CJ 514).

169. Sylvie Le Bon de Beauvoir: Aunt Germaine is Jacques's mother (CJ 515).

170. The French equivalent of "see" is underlined in the transcription approved for translation, but not in the French edition.

171. Sylvie Le Bon de Beauvoir's note indicates the French equivalent of the Latin phrase (CJ 516). The Latin phrase "*Surgit amari aliquid,*" comes from a longer sentence in *De Rerum Natura* (*On the Nature of Things*) by the Latin author Lucretius:

—medio de fonte leporum

Surgit amari aliquid, quod in ipsis floribus angat. Lucr. iv. 1224.

From middle spring of sweets some bitter springs,

Which in the very flower smartly stings.

Montaigne also quoted this line in one of his essays. See Chapter 2.20, "We Taste Nothing Purely." I am grateful to Tamara O'Callaghan for this information.

172. Sylvie Le Bon de Beauvoir: *La puissance des ténèbres* is based on the 1886 realist drama by Leo Tolstoy (CJ 516).

173. Max Jacob (1876–1944) was the French poet often viewed as a precursor of surrealism. His poetry collection entitled *Le cornet à dés* (*Dice Cup*) reveals a mind tormented by mysteries and a spirit torn between its own contradictions; Marcel Schwob (1867–1905) was a French writer whose principle works include *Coeur double* (Double heart) (chronicles and short stories), *Le livre de Monelle* (*The book of Monelle*) (a symbolist vision of compassion that features the mysterious heroine Monelle and her adventures), and *Les vies imaginaires* (*Imaginary Lives*). As a child, Schwob fell in love with *Treasure Island* by Robert Louis Stevenson, and it influenced many of his later works. Often putting into play the question of why evil exists, Schwob leads readers to wonder whether he is writing fantasy or philosophy. He is also noted for French translations of English works such as *Hamlet*.

174. Sylvie Le Bon de Beauvoir: Lucien Fabre's *Rabevel, ou le mal des ardents* [Rabevel, or the ache of passion] was a novel that won the Prix Goncourt in 1924 (CJ 516); For Joseph Conrad, see note 85 above and Beauvoir's *Diary 1*, 70; 84; Sylvie Le Bon de Beauvoir: *Gaspar Ruiz* was published in 1927 (CJ 516).

175. The French edition shows "to invite" (*inviter*) for what is transcribed in the approved transcription of the manuscript as "écouter," which I have translated as "to hear" in this line (cf.: CJ 517).

176. Jacque Rivière's novel, *Aimée* is the reference for this quotation (173). Beauvoir is altering what François thinks to himself about his beloved Aimée, "My god," I added, "make me love you one day as I love this woman"; my translation.

177. For Beauvoir's autobiographical rendition using this same phrase, see *Mémoires*, 374; *Memoirs*, 270.

178. Sylvie Le Bon de Beauvoir: This is Léon Brunschvicg's *Le progrès de la conscience dans la philosophie occidentale* [The progress of consciousness in western philosophy] published in 1927 (CJ 519).

179. For Hamelin, see note 14 above; Beauvoir also wrote about Xavier du Moulin in September 1927 (*Diary 1*, 312). See also *Mémoires*, 355–357; *Memoirs*, 256–257; John Henry Newman (1801–1890), English churchman, cardinal of the Roman Catholic Church, was one of the founders of the Oxford movement, which wanted to renew the Anglican church by reviving certain Roman Catholic beliefs and traditions; St. Augustine of Hippo (354–430) was the great philosopher and theologian credited with describing the various states of the soul and the spiritual world. His best known works include *The Confessions*, in which he reveals and analyzes his heart; *The Retractions*, in which he explains and analyzes each activity in his life; and *The Letters*, in which his activity in the Church and his doctrine are the most apparent; Daniel-Rops is the pseudonym for Henri Jules Charles Petiot (1901–1965). His first book *Notre inquiétude* (Our worry) was published in 1926.

180. Sylvie Le Bon de Beauvoir: Albert Rivaud's classes on Plato were held at the Ulm street location (CJ 519).

181. Baruch Spinoza (1632–1677), the Dutch rationalist metaphysician believed in deduction, rationalism, and monism. He reworked Descartes to argue that mind and body are different parts of the same whole, which he referred to either as God or Nature.

182. Sylvie Le Bon de Beauvoir: Jacques Spitz's *Le vent du monde* was published in 1928 (CJ 519). Jacques Spitz (1896–1963) was a French engineer and author who wrote science fiction heavily influenced by surrealism.

183. Sylvie Le Bon de Beauvoir: Maurice Bedel, winner of the prix Goncourt in 1927, published *Molinoff, Indre et Loire* in 1928 (CJ 522).

184. Sylvie Le Bon de Beauvoir: Leo Tolstoy's play, *Le cadavre vivant* (1900), written in reaction to Chekhov's *Oncle Vania* [*Uncle Vanya*], was translated and staged by the Pitoëffs at the Théâtre des Arts (CJ 522); The French equivalent of "three men," which is in my approved transcription of the manuscript appears in the French published edition as the equivalent of "five men" (CJ 522).

185. Cicero (106 BC–46 BC) is often considered one of the greatest Roman orators, politicians, and philosophers. He is noted for translating the philosophy of others to make it accessible to a Roman audience and for constructing his own philosophical arguments to bring about his political goals.

186. Arthur Hannequin (1856–1905) is a philosopher who follows the thought of Leibniz to conclude that a preestablished harmony exists between any given reality and the modes of presentation proceeding from ourselves. Unlike Leibniz, Hannequin does not believe that the preestablished harmony is a given that remains static, but rather holds that it is continually being created by the living energy of the things involved (Benrubi, *Contemporary Thought of France*, 118); For Victor Delbos, see note 20 above; Harald Hoffding (1843–1931) was a Danish philosopher heavily influenced by Soren Kierkegaard. One of his best known works was translated from the German edition into English by B. E. Meyer as *History of Modern Philosophy*.

187. What is in my approved transcription as "ton coup de sonnette possible," and is translated as "your possible ringing of the doorbell," the French edition renders as "un coup de sonnette possible," which translates as "a possible ringing of the doorbell" (CJ 523).

188. Albert Rivaud (1876–1955) was the French philosopher and classical scholar who

314

succeeded Léon Brunschvicg as a professor of philosophy at the Sorbonne in 1927. Rivaud's works include *Le problème du devenir et la notion de la matière dans la philosophie grecque depuis les origines jusqu'à Théophraste* (The problem of becoming and the notion of matter in Greek philosophy from its origins to Theophrastus) and *Les notions d'essence et d'existence dans la philosophie de Spinoza* (The notions of essence and existence in the philosophy of Spinoza); Epicurius (341–270 BC) was a philosopher who opposed Platonism and held that the physical world was all there was, had always existed, and would last forever. He taught that there was no God and no purpose to life and that the senses rather than reason were the real test of truth; Lucretius (94–55 BC) was a Roman poet who wrote about the Epicurean system. Lucretius argues that the imperfection of the world proves that there is no God and that the world was formed by the chance collision of atoms and the subsequent life forms that developed from them and of which only the fittest survived (Bradshaw, "Epicurius").

189. Sylvie Le Bon de Beauvoir: Beucler's *Le mauvais sort* was published in 1928 (CJ 525). André Beucler (1898–1985) was the French author of numerous novels, narratives, scripts, and essays including the novels *La ville anonyme* (The anonymous town); *Gueule d'amour* (Lady killer), which Jean Grémillon produced as a film starring Jean Gabin in 1937; and *Le mauvais sort*. Born in Russia to a Russian mother and a French father, Beucler remained very attached to his origins, as his novels show, and also translated Russian works of other authors into French. In 1982 he won *Le grand prix de la société des gens de lettres* for the entirety of his work.

190. What appears in my approved transcription as "et toujours cela crée en moi cette lassitude" and translated as "and this always creates such lassitude in me," the published French edition renders as "et toujours cela crée en moi une lassitude," which would translate as "and this always creates lassitude in me" (CJ 525).

191. Sylvie Le Bon de Beauvoir: *Climats* was published in 1928 (CJ 526). André Maurois (1885–1967), a French historian, novelist, essayist, and humorist, wrote of his war memories in *Les silences du Colonel Bramble* (*The Silence of Colonel Bramble*) and left several traditionally fanciful novels treating wisdom without illusions, for example, *Ni ange ni bête* (*Neither Angel nor Beast*); *Climats*, which also has been published in English as *Climates*; *Whatever Gods May Be*; and *Atmosphere of Love*.

192. Pierre Duhem, *Le système du monde, histoire des doctrines cosmologiques de Platon à Copernic* (The system of the world: the history of cosmological doctrines from Plato to Copernicus). For Duhem, see note 70 above; Gottfried Leibniz (1646–1716), a German philosopher and mathematician, was the author of *Essais de Théodicée sur la bonté de Dieu, la liberté de l'homme et l'origine du mal* (*Theodicy*); *La monadologie* (*Monadology*); and *Nouveaux essais sur l'entendement humain* (*New Essays Concerning Human Understanding*), which is his view of Locke's *Essay Concerning Human Understanding*. Leibniz maintains that the universe is the result of a divine plan. Monads or simple substances each represent the universe from a different point of view and have perception or consciousness but cannot act. Only rational monads have apperception (self-consciousness). Beauvoir had begun working on a graduate thesis (*diplôme*) on Leibniz in the spring of 1928, when she approached Leon Brunschvicg about writing a graduate thesis at the same time as she prepared for the *agrégation* exam. He agreed and suggested as her topic, "The concept according to Leibniz," which she accepted. She appears to have studied Leibniz's view of sufficient reason, which claims that everything that happens is

explicable and every question has an answer, and his principle of the identity of indiscernibles, which states that if two things are alike in all ways they are the same object. So it must be the case that no two things are ever exactly alike or God would have had no reason for making two of them. See the discussion in Douglas Burnham's "Gottfried Wilhelm Leibniz." See also Beauvoir's *Diary 1*, 279–280.

193. Beauvoir's quotation comes from Friedrich Hölderlin. For a more literal translation, "It is a better age, that is what you seek, a more beautiful world," see "Hyperion or the Hermit," 54.

194. Gide, *Les nourritures terrestes*, 156; my translation. For a less literal translation, see Bussy's translation in *Fruits of the Earth*, 19. "A poignant existence" is an expression Beauvoir used as early as September 1926 (*Diary 1*, 93) and often repeated.

195. Beauvoir also comments on her "other self" in May 1927 (*Diary 1*, 250–252).

196. The Stryx is a bar that Beauvoir frequented. The French edition has corrected the spelling of "le Strix" found in my approved transcription to "le Stryx," which I have also adopted in the second volume of the translation of Beauvoir's 1926–1930 volume.

197. The name Jean Delrive that is in the approved transcription appears as Jean Debrix in the published French edition (CJ 528).

198. For Beauvoir's public autobiographical rendition of this same event, see *Mémoires*, 407–408; *Memoirs*, 291–292.

199. "You ask me why you and not another," a line by Laforgue, is repeated and paraphrased throughout Beauvoir's diary. This line is from untitled poem 9 in Laforgue, *Oeuvres complètes*, 2:178; my translation. See also Dale, trans., untitled poem 9, *Last Poems*, in *Poems*, 427. In November 1926, Beauvoir cites a more complete version of this poem and many others by Laforgue (*Diary 1*, 161–162). See also note 31 above.

200. What appears in my approved transcription as "les épreuves où s'essaierait leur force" (ordeals that would try their strength), the published French edition renders as "les épreuves où s'exercerait leur force," which would translate as "ordeals that would teach them strength" (CJ 529).

201. Jean Giraudoux (1882–1944) was a French novelist and a playwright. *Siegfried*, his adaptation of his earlier novel, *Siegfried et le Limousin*, was the debut of his theatrical career. See also notes 15 and 99 above.

202. The question, "What need to put everything into a system?" translates the French question, "Quel besoin de mettre en système?"

203. This is a paraphrase of Riquet's about Jacques. For Simone de Beauvoir's official public version of this episode, see *Mémoires* 407–408; *Memoirs* 291–292.

204. This paraphrase of Goethe is also quoted in Jean Cocteau, *Thomas l'imposteur*, which includes the subtext in which a young girl in love, Henriette, attributes the silences of her beloved (Gillaume Thomas) to the idea that either he does not love her and flees from her or he loves her and is trying to extinguish a flame to which he dared not aspire. Beauvoir reacts similarly to Jacques's lack of attention throughout most of her diary. In her autobiography, Beauvoir recounts that Jacques quoted this line, "I love you; does that concern you?" before their separation for the summer and after he has flunked his law exams, and that she, believing that it might be his hidden declaration of love, wrote him a long letter overtly stating her love for him. See *Mémoires*, 283; *Memoirs*, 205.

205. Sylvie Le Bon de Beauvoir: Louise was Simone de Beauvoir's maid during early childhood (CJ 532).

206. The exact French for what I have translated as "dear" is "*petit (e),*" which literally means "little," but which is used as a term of endearment in this context.

207. In my approved transcription, I deciphered "renouvelions," which would translate as "that we used to renew together" for this line. The published French edition renders the verb as the future tense "renouvellerons," which would translate as "that we will renew together" (CJ 534).

208. For Soupault's *Le bar de l'amour,* see note 108 above; For Giraudoux, see notes 15, 99, and 201 above; Ernst Bloch (1885–1977) was a German Marxist philosopher heavily influenced by Hegel and Marx and best known for his writings on utopianism, revolutionary ideology, liberation, and theology; Jean Cocteau (1889–1963) was a prolific French playwright, novelist, essayist, and artist. Of his voluminous work, the writings that Beauvoir most likely read or discussed with classmates between 1926 and 1930 include *Thomas l'imposteur (Thomas the Imposter), Le grand écart (The Great Divide), Le potomak (The Potomak), Les enfants terribles (The Holy Terrors), Orphée (Orpheus), Plain-chant (Plain Song), Opéra (Opera),* and *Le rappel à l'ordre (A call to order).* The latter contains the four essays "Le coq et l'arlequin (Cock and harlequin)," "Le secret professionnel (The professional secret)," "D'un ordre considéré comme une anarchie (Order considered as anarchy)," and "Picasso." In Beauvoir's *Diary 1,* there are frequent references to Cocteau; Louis Chadourne (1890–1925), a French poet and novelist, was the author of the poetry collection *Accords* (Harmonies), containing poems treating the relationship between self, time, and happiness, and of the novel *L'inquiète adolescence* (Restless adolescence); For Fournier, see note 42 above; For Gide, see note 127 above; Proust (1871–1922), was a French novelist best known for his depiction of time and memory and their relationship to internal and external reality in his sixteen-volume semiautobiographical cyclic novel, *À la recherche du temps perdu (In Search of Lost Time).* In it, Proust tells the story of a young hero's childhood, love affairs, and decision to become a writer.

209. The cock of Pythagoras is most likely a reference to Lucian's *Gallus,* in which Micyllus, a poor cobbler obsessed only with becoming rich is visited in a dream by Pythagoras, the master of transmigrations and reincarnations. He is in the shape of a cock who cures the cobbler of his desire for riches with the story of his own former unhappy existence as a powerful king—poisoned by his own son—and by showing him the wretched way of life of his rich neighbors. "Laërce" now appears in the published French edition, although "Lucian," is what the approved transcription shows. Sylvie Le Bon de Beauvoir: Diogenes Laertius (early third century) reports in his *Lives and Opinions of Eminent Philosophers* that Pythagoras forbade his disciples to kill and eat the white roosters because these birds were dedicated to Zeus and Apollo (CJ 535). For a fuller discussion of this variant, see Barbara Klaw's "Troublesome Translations and Elusive Allusions," 69–83.

210. See note 197 above.

211. The words "Oh! if only one, one fine evening would come . . ." are from untitled poem 9 in Laforgue, *Oeuvres complètes,* 2:178; my translation. According to my translation, the first two lines of this poem are "Oh! if only one by Herself, one fine evening would come/ No longer seeing anything but to drink from my lips or die!" See also notes 31 and 199 above.

212. For Simone de Beauvoir's official version of this conversation with Riquet, see *Mémoires,* 409; *Memoirs,* 292–293.

213. For more on this line by Goethe, "Does that concern you?" see note 204 above. See also the entry of August 21, 1926, for a larger discussion of this quote (*Diary 1,* 77).

214. My approved transcription shows "sans romantisme," which I translated as "without romanticism." The French edition shows "son romantisme," which would be translated as "his romanticism" (CJ 536).

215. My approved transcription shows "retrouve," which I translated as "rediscover." The French edition shows "trouve," which would be translated as "find" (CJ 537).

216. My approved transcription shows "don de moi," which I have translated as "gift of myself," whereas the French edition shows "don de soi," which would be translated as "gift of the self" (CJ 538).

217. "What is more necessary than oneself, there is only one victory, which is to make it the strongest forever!" is a slight rewording of the passage from Claudel's *Feuilles de saints*, 658–659, which Beauvoir quotes before the August 21, 1926, entry of her diary where she reflects on love (*Diary 1*, 75). I have provided a literal translation for Claudel's verse.

218. What my approved transcription records as "tant," which I have translated as "so much," the French edition renders as "tout," which would translate as "everything" in this line (CJ 538).

219. The word *diplôme* in French in this context refers to an essay that a student was required to write for a graduate degree comparable to a Master's degree in the United States. A student might also have attempted to pass the highly competitive *agrégation* and, if successful, write a *thèse d'état*, comparable to a doctoral dissertation in the United States.

220. Sylvie Le Bon de Beauvoir: The 1928 Salon d'Automne was held from November 4 to December 16 at the Grand Palais on the Champs-Elysées (CJ 539). The first Salon d'Automne was organized in 1903 to exhibit the innovative developments in painting and sculpture eschewed by the more conservative official Paris Salon. After World War I, the artistic works most frequently displayed in the Salon d'Automne included those of the Montparnasse painters Marc Chagall, Amedeo Modigliani, and Georges Braque, and the sculptors Constantin Brancusi, Aristide Maillol, Charles Despiau, and Ossip Zadkine. The glassworks of René Lalique and the architectural designs of Le Corbusier also figured in the exhibitions. See also the entries of November 3, 1926, and May 2, 1927, for references to the Salon d'Automne (*Diary 1*, 158; 244).

221. Sylvie Le Bon de Beauvoir: The painting viewed is André Favory's *La femme à la rose* [Woman with a rose] (CJ 539). André Favory (1888–1937), a classically trained artist, experimented for some years with cubism.

222. Sylvie Le Bon de Beauvoir: This painting is Paulemile-Pissarro's *L'épée à dragon* (CJ 539). Paulémile-Pissaro (1882–1974), the son and student of Camille Pissaro, was a watercolorist and pastel artist who frequented Delatousche, Ferjac, H. Martinet, Louis Moreau, and Maurice Savin and supported the anarchist group, Partisans. See "Delatousche," *Sans patrie ni frontières*.

223. Sylvie Le Bon de Beauvoir: Dimitri Mérinoff's painting is *Les saltimbanques* (CJ 539). Dmitri Mérinoff was a Russian expressionist painter who immigrated to the United States and eventually had a painting studio at Union Square in New York.

224. Sylvie Le Bon de Beauvoir: Robert Le Ricolais's painting is *Maisons à Corte* (CJ 539). Robert Le Ricolais (1894–1977) became a famous French architect who moved to Philadelphia and taught with Louis Kahn.

225. Sylvie Le Bon de Beauvoir: Gaston Vaudou's painting is *Maternité*. There is an indecipherable word after the French equivalent of "folds" (CJ 539). Vaudou (1891–1957), French artist who also painted *Nude Dressing Her Hair* (1919), exhibited at the Paris Salon and

was the 1919 Winner of the Silver Medal; Sylvie Le Bon de Beauvoir; Rodolphe Théophile Bosshard (1889–1960) was a Swiss painter (CJ 539). Bosshard was also known for painting *Couples* (1917).

226. Sylvie Le Bon de Beauvoir: Tamara de Lempicka is the Polish painter of *Portrait of Arlette Boucard* and *The Communicant* (CJ 539). Lempicka (1898–1960) studied art in Paris and became a well-known portrait painter. Her style, sometimes referred to as "soft cubism," uses formal and narrative elements in her portraits and nude studies that exude the forces of desire and seduction. After World War I, she became associated with lesbian and bisexual women in writing and artistic circles. See "Tamara de Lempicka," FulcrumGallery.com. http://www.fulcrumgallery.com/a34434/Tamara-De-Lempicka.htm (accessed March 9, 2017).

227. Sylvie Le Bon de Beauvoir: Osvaldo Medici's *Landscape* (CJ 539).

228. Sylvie Le Bon de Beauvoir: Ivan Babij is a Ukranian painter (CJ 539).

229. Sylvie Le Bon de Beauvoir: Jacqueline Marval's paintings are *Le rêve de la femme endormie* [The sleeping woman's dream], *La coupe fleurie* [The flowering cup], and *Les coquettes* [The coquettes] (CJ 539). Jacqueline Marval (1866–1932), a French painter, was a member of the Parisian avant-garde; What is deciphered as "disgusting" (*dégoûtantes*) in my approved transcription, the French edition renders as "dégouttantes," which I would translate as "flowers and women by Marval, dripping with tulle, whiteness, and toothpaste."

230. Sylvie Le Bon de Beauvoir: Jean Souverbie's painting is *Music* (CJ 539). Jean Souverbie (1891–1981) was a French artist heavily influenced by cubism and naturalism and is known for his creation of voluptuous, classical nudes.

231. Sylvie Le Bon de Beauvoir: This painting is Kees Van Dongen's *La charité* [Charity] (CJ 540).

232. Sylvie Le Bon de Beauvoir: This is Henry Ottman (1877–1927) (CJ 540).

233. Emile Othon Friesz (1879–1949) was a French painter heavily influenced by Camille Pissaro. Othon Friesz first informed his works with a nature-oriented concept and later with Fauvism. Critics view several of his earlier works as bold illustrations of Fauvism.

234. Henri Le Fauconnier (1881–1946) was a French cubist painter.

235. Sylvie Le Bon de Beauvoir: The painting by André Lhote (1885–1962) is *La brodeuse* [The embroiderer] (CJ 540).

236. Sylvie Le Bon de Beauvoir: This painting is Eugene Zak's *La grande soeur* [Big sister] (CJ 540). Eugene Zak (1884–1926) was a Polish painter who worked primarily in France. He was known as an exponent of Neo-Classicism and also for his link to the Warsaw-based group RYTM/RYTHM and to the École de Paris. Zak's paintings suggest the influence of Cézanne, Picasso, and Matisse.

237. Eugène Carrière (1849–1906) was a French symbolist painter known for his portraits of motherhood.

238. Sylvie Le Bon de Beauvoir: This painting is M. Asselins's *Portrait d'un vieux manoeuvre* [Portrait of an old maneuver] (CJ 540). Maurice Asselin (1882–1947) was an oil painter, watercolorist, and lithographer who produced landscapes, portraits, and genre scenes. He traveled frequently in Brittany. A friend of many authors, he also illustrated editions including *Mort de quelqu'un* (*The Death of a Nobody*) by Jules Romains.

239. Sylvie Le Bon de Beauvoir: These paintings are Yvonne Gilles's *Lilas* [Lilacs] and *Étang du bois de Boulogne* [Boulogne woods pond] (CJ 540).

240. Source of quotation unknown. She is perhaps referring to André Suarès (1868–1948), who was a French poet and one of the four mainstays of the *Nouvelle revue française*,

along with André Gide, Paul Claudel, and Paul Valéry. Or perhaps she is referring to Carlo Suarès (1892–1976), a French painter and Kabbalah writer who in 1928 published *Sur un orgue de barbarie* (On a barrel organ) in Paris.

241. Sylvie Le Bon de Beauvoir: *Topaze* is a play by Marcel Pagnol (1928), staged at the Theatre Variétés on the boulevard Montmarte. Pierre Bost's critique of this play is in the November 10 issue of *La revue hébdomadaire* (CJ 541); For *Siegfried*, see note 201 above.

242. Sylvie Le Bon de Beauvoir: Maurice Le Scouezec lived from 1881 to 1940 (CJ 541). He was a French Expressionist painter from Brittany.

243. In *Mémoires*, Beauvoir recasts this episode differently (408–409; *Memoirs* 292–93).

244. Beauvoir is perhaps referring to César Santellli's *La mystérieuse aventure* (The mysterious adventure) (Paris: Grasset, 1928); Georges Duhamel (1884–1966), poet, novelist, essayist, and playwright, wrote *La possession du monde* (*In Sight of the Promised Land*), which won the 1919 Prix Goncourt and develops the theme of a modern humanism denouncing the excesses of a mechanical civilization; René Arcos, the author of *L'île perdue, poème dramatique* (Lost island, dramatic poem) (Mercure de France, 1913), was also one of the group l'Abbaye, along with Charles Vildrac, Georges Duhamel, and other poets who worked to reinvent poetry as something concrete, fraternal, social, and humane.

245. The Bibliothèque Victor Cousin was the original library collection in what is now the Sorbonne library of the same name.

246. Sylvie Le Bon de Beauvoir: Savin was a student at the École Normale Supérieure (CJ 542).

247. For Gide (the author of *Les nourritures terrestres*), see note 127 above; For more on François Mauriac, see note 17 above; for more on his "Souffrances du chrétien," see note 49 above.

248. "Jacques, I do not have anything of much worth to say tonight" is my translation for the French sentence, "Jacques, je n'ai pas de monnaie ce soir," which ends the diary entry in the approved transcription of November 24, 1928 but does not appear in the French edition (cf.: CJ 542).

249. Sylvie Le Bon de Beauvoir: The 1920 silent film version of *The Mark of Zorro* was produced by Fred Niblo (CJ 543). *The Mark of Zorro* was a 1920 American silent film directed by Fred Niblo and Theodore Reed, and produced by Douglas Fairbanks, who plays Don Diego Vega and Señor Zorro in the film.

250. Beauvoir most likely meant Dr. Jekyll and Mr. Hyde when she wrote Dr. Jeckyll and Dr. Hyde. *Dr. Jekyll and Mr. Hyde* was a 1920 American silent horror film directed by John S. Robertson and starring John Barrymore. It was based on Robert Louis Stevenson's novella, *The Strange Case of Dr. Jekyll and Mr. Hyde*.

251. Sylvie Le Bon de Beauvoir: *La nuit tombe* is a 1928 novel by Henri Ardel (CJ 543).

252. The Latin words *amari aliquid* means "something bitter." See note 171 above.

253. *La Vie de St Alexis* is an eleventh-century French poem telling of an aristocratic son's choice to renounce his bride and social position to live as a hermit—first in the Orient, then in Rome. It was published in English by Holy Trinity Publications in 2006.

254. This description of her book refers to a currently unpublished novel, *Départ* (Departure), whose manuscript was sold by Sotheby to le Musée des Lettres et des Manuscrits de Paris and to the BNF in May 2008. Beauvoir began this novel in August 1927 and continued to develop it in 1928, during which she refers back to her 1926 and 1927 diary entries. She dedicated this novel to Zaza but eventually abandoned it due to her upcoming work for her

graduate thesis on Leibniz and her studies for the competitive *agrégation* exam (Le Bon de Beauvoir, *Beauvoir*, 41).

255. Sylvie Le Bon de Beauvoir: The staging is by Gaston Baty, a member of the Cartel of Four who went from the Montparnasse theater to the theater de l'Avenue (CJ 548).

256. Sylvie Le Bon de Beauvoir: Professor Laporte was in charge of a class on Hume (CJ 548).

257. Sylvie Le Bon de Beauvoir: Simone de Beauvoir's sister, Poupette, loves Merleau-Ponty (CJ 548).

258. What the approved transcription records as "autour d'une tasse de thé" and I have translated as "over a cup of tea," the published French edition shows as "autour d'une table de thé," which would translate as "around a tea table."

259. For Simone de Beauvoir's official public version of this same incident, see *Mémoires* 414–415; *Memoirs* 296–297.

260. "I don't care" (*Ça m'est égal*) appears only once in the approved transcription but is repeated twice in the published French edition (CJ 550).

261. Vieux-Colombier is a theater.

262. Alexander Pushkin (1799–1837) was a Russian poet considered to be among the greatest writers of his country. The most well-known animated puppet film created from his works is *The Tale of the Fisherman and the Fish;* Max Linder (1883–1925) was a French actor, director, screenwriter and producer whose real name was Gabriel-Maximilien Leuvielle. One of the least well-known silent comedy actors and filmmakers, he predates Charles Chaplin and Buster Keaton and is credited with having replaced surface burlesque with the creation of comedy that stems from movement instead of overacted mime. Beauvoir must have seen Linder's 1922 film, *The Three Must-Get-Theres*. See Thomas Staedeli, "Max Linder," and "Max Linder-Silent Movie St."

263. The words "s'a" are underlined in the French edition (CJ 552).

264. Sylvie Le Bon de Beauvoir: To pass the *agrégation*, it was mandatory to attend the lectures on pedagogy. These lectures were followed by a student-teaching internship (CJ 553).

265. Sylvie Le Bon de Beauvoir: *La vie inquiète de Jean Hermelin*, a novel by Jacques de Lacretelle was published in 1920 (CJ 553).

266. Sylvie Le Bon de Beauvoir: Charlotte is Simone de Beauvoir's cousin (CJ 553).

267. *The Gaucho* is an American adventure film released in 1927 in the United States. Douglas Fairbanks wrote the story for this film directed by F. Richard Jones. The actors include Douglas Fairbanks, Lupe Velez, Eve Southern, and Gustav von Seyffertitz.

268. Sylvie Le Bon de Beauvoir: Raymond Duncan (1874–1966) is the brother of dancer Isadora Duncan (CJ 554). An American dancer, artist, poet, craftsman, and philosopher, Raymond Duncan dressed in classical Greek attire and founded a school in Paris based on Plato's Academy with courses in dance, arts, and crafts. His philosophy of "actionalism" advocated a technique of living that synthesized labor and the arts through physical movement. His book, *Poèmes de parole torrentielle* (Torrential word poems), was published in 1927. "Raymond Duncan Collection." What appears in my approved transcription as "l'inquiétude d'être des choses," which I have thus translated as "the disquiet of being of things," is recorded in the French edition with quotation marks around the words "l'inquiétude d'être" followed by the words "des choses" without quotation marks (cf.: CJ 554). These particular words might also translate as "the disquiet of being things."

269. Sylvie Le Bon de Beauvoir: *Volpone ou le renard* [*Volpone or The Fox*], a comedy by Ben Jonson (1605), was adapted by Jules Romains and Stephan Zweig and staged in 1928 by Charles Dullin (CJ 554). *Volpone* is the story of a seventeenth-century Venetian noble-man named Volpone (Big Fox), who is an extravagant con artist; Mephisto (more commonly known as "Mephistopheles") is one of the seven chief devils and the tempter to whom Faust (of Goethe's *Faust*) sells his soul.

270. Perhaps Simon Gantillon's *Départs: spectacle en 15 tableaux* (Departures: a play in 15 scenes) (Paris: Société des spectacles, 1928), which was staged for the first time at Théâtre de l'Avenue on November 27, 1928.

271. What the French edition and the corrections on my approved transcription show as "que tout sera" (that everything will be), I deciphered as "que tout serve" (that everything is useful), which would logically continue the grammatical use of the subjunctive in this passage (CJ 556).

272. My approved transcription shows "lacets de tendresse," which I have translated as "snares of tenderness," whereas the French edition renders "lacs de tendresse," which would translate as "lakes of tenderness" (CJ 556).

273. Sylvie Le Bon de Beauvoir: *Opales* was published in 1928 (CJ 556). Marcel Jou-handeau (1888–1979), the author of *Opales*, was a prolific French writer known for the beauty and precision of his writing style, his homosexuality, and his torturous relationship with his wife Elise.

274. Sylvie Le Bon de Beauvoir: Jean Cocteau published *Le grand écart* [*The Great Divide*] in 1923 (CJ 557). See also note 208 above.

275. Pierre Mac Orlan (1883–1970) whose real name was Pierre Dumarchey, was a French writer known for his fiction, essays, poetry, songs, and radio broadcasts. Tormented by his sordid and dangerous past and fascinated by the representation of adventurers in novels, he demystifies and deromanticizes adventurers in his own novels as justifiably ridiculed and less than valuable citizens. See Cros, "PierreMac Orlan et le romantisme moderne."

276. What appears in my approved transcription as the French equivalent of Tuesday, is recorded as the French equivalent of Wednesday in the French edition (CJ 558).

277. Sylvie Le Bon de Beauvoir: Violaine and Jacques, Pensée and Orian, la France and St. Louis designate characters from the respective works by Claudel, *L'annonce faite à Marie* [*The Tidings Brought to Mary*] (1912) and from *Le père humilié* [*The Humiliation of the Father*] (1920) (CJ 558). For more on Paul Claudel, see note 47 above.

278. The Musée pédagogique (Museum of Pedagogy) was created in 1879 to gather and preserve artifacts and documents allowing for the writing of the history of teaching in France. In 1901 an Office of Information and Studies was also created for the collection of documents destined to promulgate information about public instruction abroad. In 1903 both of these creations merged into a single institution known as "Musée pédagogique, bibliothèque, office et musée, et l'enseignement public (Museum of Pedagogy, Library, Office, Museum and Public Teaching)," which extended to all levels of teaching. "Musée Pédagogique".

279. The words "dans cette écriture intelligente," which I have translated as "in this intelligent handwriting," are in my approved transcription but do not appear in the French edition (cf.: CJ 559).

280. See note 197 above.

281. I have chosen to translate "poirier" as a reference to the order of Spanish knights initiated in 1167; it might also be translated as "pear tree."

282. Sylvie Le Bon de Beauvoir: M. du Fraisaix is a classmate from the Cours Desir (CJ 560).

283. Sylvie Le Bon de Beauvoir: To have the right to participate in the competitive exams for the *agrégation* in philosophy, a student had to obtain a degree in science: either math (or physics, chemistry, and natural science) or general biology. Simone de Beauvoir had already gotten her degree in general mathematics in 1926 (CJ 561).

284. The "too" in the first part of this sentence translates an "aussi" that is in my approved transcription but does not appear in the French edition (cf.: CJ 561).

285. What appears as the French equivalent of "sadness" in my approved transcription appears as the French equivalent of "tenderness" in the French edition (CJ 563).

286. Plato's *Symposium, or The Drinking Party* is a debate between several participants at a dinner party concerning the meaning of love and the correct way to love. The topics discussed include the notion that each being is looking for its soulmate and that homosexuality is normal because in earliest times all human beings were either double men, double women, or a man-woman, each having two faces, four legs, four arms, and so forth, but their power angered the gods who split them asunder to diminish their strength. Other ideas of interest to Beauvoir's writings are that there are many forms of love that cause us to behave differently and that have different values. Love for beauty first encourages us to pursue the greatest number of beautiful bodies and eventually to procreate to escape our mortality. As we grow, we will progress from loving the surface beauty of individual bodies to loving the beauty of institutions, and then the beauty of learning, and finally the inner beauty of every soul. See Plato, *Symposium and Other Dialogues*, 21–24, 41, 45, 46; Plato's *Phaedrus* is a conversation between Socrates and Phaedrus that debates the virtues and faults of the lover and the non-lover to conclude that the love and friendship of a lover is always superior to that of a nonlover. See Plato's *Phaedrus*; Plato's "The Supremacy of Good," a chapter of *Republic*, uses the parable of a cave with prisoners who are suddenly unchained and brought outside into full sunlight to illustrate how education may change all of humanity for the good. It holds that those individuals who have discovered sunlight (true knowledge) have a moral duty to return to the cave to free all others so that they too may bask in sunlight. It warns that such goodness is rare, that most often those who enjoy sunlight work only to remain in the sun, and this means they seek their own gain by governing others. The truly good, however, should be forced to rule for they will always go back to the cave to liberate others. See Plato, "The Supremacy of Good," In *Republic*, 227–249.

287. *Tristan et Yseult* is a French poem written in octosyllabic couplets, whose oldest fragment appear to be the work of the poet Béroul composed in the last decades of the twelfth century. This poem tells the story of King Marc of Cornwall, who, wishing to ensure succession to his throne, sends his nephew Tristan to find the woman whose golden hairs have been brought to him by a swallow. Tristan succeeds in finding Yseult, daughter of the King of Ireland, and convinces her to accompany him to Cornwall to marry King Marc. On the journey back, Tristan unknowingly drinks of a love potion that was intended to make King Marc fall passionately in love with Yseult. Tristan and Yseult are thus drawn to each other through this magic force that they cannot resist. Yseult marries King Marc, but continues to meet with Tristan. The secret meetings of Tristan and Yseult are eventually discovered and they are condemned to be burned at the stake for adultery. They escape and hide together for three

years after which the effects of the love potion cease, and Tristan returns Yseult to King Marc. See C. W. Aspland, "Beroul: Tristan,"121–123.

288. What appears in my approved transcription as "ma" (my) before "Poupée" (Dolly), another nickname for Beauvoir's sister Hélène, is shown in the French edition as "la," which would translate as "the" (CJ 565).

289. Sylvie Le Bon de Beauvoir: *Elpénor* was published in 1926 (CJ 565) and published in English translation by Noonday Press in 1958. Jean Giraudoux's *Elpénor* is an amusing retelling of the adventures of Ulysses and a sailor named Elpenor. As the story progresses, the ability to manipulate and interpret language, literature, and especially the knowledge of mythology and poetry become increasingly important in the successes or failures of the two protagonists. Ulysses, due to his knowledge and wit, is able to escape from the Cyclops and the Sirens, whereas Elpenor turns to drugs and suicide. Ulysses brings Elpenor back to life by saying the right prayers to Zeus. Others soon mistake Elpenor for another man, and as he has no discernment, he soon believes in his newly attributed identity and is killed because of it. In contrast, Ulysses arrives safely home to learn about the adventures that others attribute to him. Some critics believe that the character Elpenor represents the lower class as a mass of mediocre and indifferent individuals. See Jean Yves Tadie, "Elpénor," 1511.

290. Sylvie Le Bon de Beauvoir: This describes a meeting to prepare for an *agrégation* student-teaching internship. The professor, Gustave Rodriguès, was its organizer. He was the President of the *Ligue des droits de l'homme* [Society for the Rights of Man], and committed suicide in 1940 when Germany occupied France (CJ 565).

291. For Proust, see note 208 above; Louis Aragon (1897–1982) was a French writer and one of the founders of surrealism, the movement in art and literature devoted to blurring dreams and reality in order to express the imagination without the conscious control of reason or convention; Rudyard Kipling (1865–1936) was an English author, known for his numerous works including *The Jungle Book, Gunga Din*, and *The Man Who Would Be King*; For Claudel, see note 47 above; André Breton (1896–1966) was a French surrealist writer and artist, who is often considered to be the main founder of surrealism. His best-known works include *Le manifeste du surréalisme* (*Manifesto of Surrealism*) and *Nadja*.

292. For Montherlant, see note 64 above; Paul Valéry (1871–1945), a French poet and novelist, was torn between intellectual narcissism and the detachment required to discern human possibilities. His crisis in Genoa one night in 1892 led him to abandon his first idols—love and poetry—and to distance himself from aestheticism and a search for pleasure. In their place, he glorified abstract reasoning.

293. For Nietzsche, see note 83 above; For Barrès, see note 64 above; For Spinoza, see note 181 above.

294. Père Ubu is the main protagonist in Alfred Jarry's 1896 play, *Ubu roi*, an obscene parody of *Macbeth* that caused a scandal in its time. Père Ubu is commonly viewed as the personification of all that is stupid and base in mankind. See also note 116 above.

295. The *khagneuses* are the female students in preparatory classes for the entrance exams for the École Normale Supérieure (ENS).

296. Sylvie Le Bon de Beauvoir: *La danse devant l'arche* is by Henri Franck, and was published in 1912 by the N.R.F. [*Nouvelle revue française*] with a preface by Anna de Noailles (CJ 242).

297. Sylvie Le Bon de Beauvoir: *Victor ou les enfants au pouvoir* [*Victor, or The Children Take Power*] was published in 1928 (CJ 569). Roger Vitrac (1899–1952) was a French poet

and dramatist, known for his surrealism, for cofounding dada, and in 1927, for establishing the Théâtre Alfred Jarry with Antonin Artaud where Vitrac's plays were performed. His plays include *Les mystères de l'amour* (The mysteries of love) (1927) and *Victor, ou les enfants au pouvoir* (1928), which tells the story of a spoiled, but very intelligent and manipulative nine-year-old boy; Sylvie Le Bon de Beauvoir: *La coquille et le clergyman* was a Germaine Dulac 1928 movie of surrealist inspiration and based on a scenario by Antonin Artaud, who felt betrayed by the film (CJ 569). *La coquille et le clergyman* was a 1928 black-and-white silent French film starring Alex Allin, Bataille, and Gerica Athanasiou. *La coquille et le clergyman* is now regarded as the first surrealist film (Louise Heck-Rabi, *La coquille et le clergyman*); The French equivalent of "on the cinema" appears in my approved transcription but does not appear in the French edition (cf.: CJ 569).

298. Sylvie Le Bon de Beauvoir: Aunt Marie is Jacques' grandmother (CJ 570).

299. Sylvie Le Bon de Beauvoir: George Moore (1852–1933) was an Irish writer (CJ 570); Colette (1873–1954) was the French novelist and performer, Sidonie Gabrielle Colette.

300. "The multiplicity of compossibles" is linked to the Leibnizian concept of compossible worlds. Although there are infinite possible substances, Leibniz called the finite number of substances that can exist together in the same world "compossible substances." Beauvoir refers to this same concept in her diary entry of July 22, 1927 (*Diary 1*, 289).

301. "The enclosed garden of Bérénice" refers to Maurice Barrès's novel *Le jardin de Bérénice*. See the end of Beauvoir's diary entry of December 2, 1926, for her use of a quote from this novel (*Diary 1*, 199). See also note 64 above.

302. Sylvie Le Bon de Beauvoir: René Béhaine (1880–1966) wrote *L'histoire d'une société* [*History of a Society*], a vast chronicle whose sixth volume was published in 1928 not as *Sous les yeux de l'esprit* [Under the gaze of the spirit] as Beauvoir states, but rather as *Avec les yeux de l'esprit* [With the eyes of the spirit]; George Moore's *Memoirs of My Dead Life* was published in 1906 and translated into French in 1922 (CJ 571). G. Jean Aubry translated the novel as *Mémoires de ma vie morte; galanteries, méditations, souvenirs, soliloquies et conseils aux amants avec des réflexions variés sur la vertu et le mérite* (Memoirs of my dead life: gallantries, meditations, memories, soliloquies, and advice to lovers with varied reflections on virtue and merit).

303. Sylvie Le Bon de Beauvoir: Merleau-Ponty's address was 24 rue de la Tour, Passy, Paris, in the sixteenth district (CJ 572).

304. Sylvie Le Bon de Beauvoir: Studio Diamant was a film studio installed by Henri Diamant-Berger (1895–1975) in the former Niépce and Setter factories in Billancourt (CJ 573).

305. Sylvie Le Bon de Beauvoir: *Crise* is a 1928 silent film by Pabst like the 1925 film *Rue sans joie*, which launched Greta Garbo. Brigitte Helm is the starring actress in Lang's 1926 *Metropolis*. Her career ended with the advent of talking films (CJ 573). *Crise* is the French title for the German film *Abwige/Begierde*, which is a psychological drama directed by G. W. Pabst starring Brigitte Helm and Gustave Diessel. It tells the story of a woman who normally loves her husband and who has never attempted to cheat on him; suddenly she has a crisis about her independence. *Rue sans joie* is the French title for the German film *Die Freudlose Gasse* directed by G. W. Pabst, based on the novel by Hugo Bettauer and starring Greta Garbo, Asta Nielsen, Marlene Dietrich, and Einar Hanson. This film tells the story of two women who choose different solutions during the costly times of postwar Vienna. Penniless Marie (played by Asta Nielsen) becomes a prostitute to raise money for the man she loves. Greta, the daughter of a rather poor middle-class bureaucrat, is able to resist prostitution to find success (Michael Koller, *The Joyless Street*).

306. George Meredith (1828–1909) was an English novelist and poet. His novel, *Beauchamp's Career*, was translated into French by Auguste Monod as *La carrière de Beauchamp*.

307. Sylvie Le Bon de Beauvoir: Maurice Barrès was the author of the 1922 novel *Un jardin sur l'Oronte* (CJ 574). In this novel the narrator, traveling in Syria, listens to a tale told to him by an Irishman in a garden overlooking the Orontes River.

308. The French equivalent of the word delightful (*délicieux*) appears in my approved transcription but is not in the French edition (cf.: CJ 577).

309. Sylvie Le Bon de Beauvoir: *Les liaisons dangereuses* (1782) is by Choderlos de Laclos (CJ 577).

310. Sylvie Le Bon de Beauvoir: Léon Robin is a Plato specialist (CJ 578).

311. Sylvie Le Bon de Beauvoir: "equal or unequal" is an allusion to the theory of knowledge exposed by Plato in his sixth book of *Republic* (CJ 578). What translates as "equal or unequal" was written in Greek by Beauvoir. Plato discusses equality and inequality in "Inner and Outer Morality" of *Republic* when he holds that all men are not equal and belong to certain social classes because their innate talents dictate their place in society. Of more interest to Beauvoir's later writings is the discussion in *Republic* Chapter 7, "Women, Children, and Warfare," in which it is argued that women are physically weaker than men, but equal in differing innate talents that would allow them to learn and perform the same task as men.

312. Sylvie Le Bon de Beauvoir: *Blèche* (1928) is by Drieu la Rochelle (CJ 578).

313. Sylvie Le Bon de Beauvoir: Vittorio Podrecca was on a big international tour with his *Teatro dei piccoli* [Children's theater] that was founded in Rome in 1914 (CJ 579).

314. Sylvie Le Bon de Beauvoir: *Le perroquet vert* (1924) is by the Princess Bibesco (CJ 579). *Le perroquet vert* (Paris: Grasset, 1924) was translated into English by Malcolm Cowley as *The Green Parrot* in 1928.

315. Sylvie Le Bon de Beauvoir: The book is Jean Guéhenno's 1927 *L'évangile éternel. Étude sur Michelet* [The eternal Gospel. Study on Michelet] (CJ 580).

316. For Hume, see note 101 above.

317. For Bergson, see note 84 above; Immanuel Kant (1724–1804), who argued that science, morality and religion are based on human understanding, is the central figure in modern philosophy.

318. Sylvie Le Bon de Beauvoir: Janson refers to the high school Janson-de-Sailly in the sixteenth district of Paris where Beauvoir would be doing her student teaching internship for the *agrégation* (CJ 581).

319. Sylvie Le Bon de Beauvoir: *Lonesome* is a 1928 silent film by Paul Fejos (CJ 582). *Lonesome*, starring Barbara Kent, Glenn Tryon, Fay Holderness, and Gustav Partos is an American silent film that depicts two people who fall in love during a day of vacation at Coney Island but are later separated and unable to find each other again; *La jalousie de barbouillé* by Cavalcanti is a French film released in 1929 based on Molière's play with the same title.

320. This is a slightly different translation than that presented in Klaw's *Le Paris de Beauvoir*, because after its publication Sylvie Le Bon de Beauvoir made changes in the transcription of the established manuscript (72).

321. For *Aimée*, see note 43 above.

322. For Spinoza, see note 181 above.

323. What I have transcribed as "Quelle vie pauvre chère!" and translated as "What a life, poor dear girl!" does not appear in the French edition (cf.: CJ 586).

324. What is in the approved transcription as "Eveski," the French edition renders as "Hévési."

325. The March 9 entry does not appear in my approved transcript but is in the French edition (CJ 587).

326. Sylvie Le Bon de Beauvoir: Borodin's *Le Prince Igor* [Prince Igor], interpreted by the Russian Opera, came to France under the direction of Serge de Diaghilev, with *Les danses polovtsiennes* [Polovstian dances], choreographed by Michel Fokine. This prestigious ballet troupe also included Pavlova and Nijinski, among others and invited Bakst and Picasso to design the sets (CJ 588).

327. Sylvie Le Bon de Beauvoir: Beauvoir's sister Henriette de Beauvoir made friends with Germaine Dubois (who is also known by the nickname Gégé) when they met in drawing class (CJ 588).

328. Sylvie Le Bon de Beauvoir: *Le malade imaginaire* is by Molière (CJ 588).

329. For *Le grand Meaulnes*, see note 121 above.

330. The words "bien-aimé, écris-moi," which I have translated as "beloved, write to me" do not appear in my approved transcription but do appear in the French edition (CJ 589).

331. Sylvie Le Bon de Beauvoir: *L'envoûté* was published in 1919 (CJ 590). Somerset Maugham's *The Moon and Sixpence* (London: Heinemann, 1919) was translated into French as *L'envouté* by Marie Christine Blanchet (Paris: Editions de France, 1928) and features the life and works of Paul Gauguin.

332. For Jammes, see note 48 above.

333. Sylvie Le Bon de Beauvoir: Nadine's father is Paul Landowski (1875–1961), a French sculptor and recipient of the Prix de Rome in 1900. In 1928 he realized the monument of *The Victory of the Ladies Way* and *Saint Genevieve* on the Pont de la Tournelle. He is also the father of the composer Marcel Landowski (CJ 591).

334. Sylvie Le Bon de Beauvoir: Alan Crosland's *The Jazz Singer* (1927), the first sound film with both speaking and singing featured Al Jolson at Aubert Palace.

335. Eugenio d'Ors y Roviro (1882–1954) was a Spanish art critic and essayist who wrote essays and philosophical novels.

336. Sylvie Le Bon de Beauvoir: *Le crime des justes*, the novel published in 1928 by André Chamson is the third part of *La suite cévenole* [Cevennes suite] (CJ 592) and was translated into English as *The Crime of the Just* by Van Wyck Brooks in 1930.

337. What appears in the approved manuscript as the French equivalent of eight o'clock is rendered as the French equivalent of six o'clock in the French edition (CJ 592).

338. Sylvie Le Bon de Beauvoir: *Hécate* was published in 1928 (CJ 592).

339. The seventh floor in the American system would be called the sixth floor in British English. Americans commonly call the ground floor the first floor.

340. For Simone de Beauvoir's public version of this meeting with Laporte, see *Mémoires*, 427; *Memoirs*, 304–305.

341. Sylvie Le Bon de Beauvoir: *L'effort* is a journal on literature, sociology, and art (CJ 593).

342. Sylvie Le Bon de Beauvoir: *Autour de L'argent* is a documentary on the filming of *L'argent*, the film by Marcel L'herbier, and *L'invitation au voyage* is from 1927 (CJ 593).

343. Sylvie Le Bon de Beauvoir: Zaza was leaving to care for one of her cousins. In reality, Zaza's mother wanted to distance her from Paris and from the influence of Simone de Beauvoir, and to start to limit the freedom that Zaza had enjoyed in Berlin. Zaza would be gone for two weeks (CJ 593).

344. In her diary entry of March 27, Beauvoir specifies that she is correcting articles for Stépha's Ukranian journal.

345. *Une vie secrète* by Henri-René Lenormand is a three-act play.

346. "Eugènes (Eugenes)" are rotund amorphous creatures with faces and clothing resembling those of humans that figure as some of the principal characters described and drawn in Cocteau's work *Le potomak* (1913–1914).

347. "Pétronille, la pauvre fille" (Pétronille, the poor girl) are lines from the refrain of the song "Pétronille-Java," that was popularized by Fernandel.

348. What appears in my approved transcription as "points," which I have translated as "dots" is recorded in the French edition as "ponts," which would translate as "bridges" (CJ 594).

349. There is no clear grammatical antecedent for the "him" referenced in this sentence. It is most likely Jacques as she refers to him earlier in this diary entry.

350. Sylvie Le Bon de Beauvoir: Marcel L'herbier's 1928 film *L'argent* was based on Zola (CJ 596).

351. Sylvie Le Bon de Beauvoir: *Moi, Juif, livre posthume* was published in 1928, and John Dos Passos's novel was published in 1925 (CJ 597).

352. What appears in my approved transcription as "nous goûtons," which I have translated as "we have the afternoon snack," is recorded in the French edition as "nous parlons," which would translate as "we talk" (cf.: CJ 597).

353. Sylvie Le Bon de Beauvoir: Charles Du Bos (1882–1939), who converted to Catholicism in 1927, kept a diary from 1908 on (CJ 598).

354. What appears in my approved transcription as "non-valeur," which I have translated as "worthlessness" is recorded in the French edition as "valeur," which would translate as "worth" (cf.: CJ 599).

355. Sylvie Le Bon de Beauvoir: Jean Renoir's *Catherine, ou Une vie sans joie* (1924, then 1927) features his wife, Catherine Hessling (CJ 600).

356. Sylvie Le Bon de Beauvoir: Fanchette may refer to the Charles Vayre film, *Au temps des cerises, ou Fanchette* [The time of the cherries, or Fanchette] (CJ 600).

357. Sylvie Le Bon de Beauvoir: Louise Marie Damien, known as Damia (1889–1978) was a realist singer (CJ 602).

358. Sylvie Le Bon de Beauvoir: Victor Sjöström's 1928 silent film, *The Wind*, starred Lillian Gish, and *Le rouge et le noir* was the 1928 Gennaro Righelli production (CJ 602, 603), based on Stendhal's novel of the same name.

359. Sylvie Le Bon de Beauvoir: Gide's *L'école de femmes* was published by the *Nouvelle revue française* in 1929 (CJ 604).

360. Sylvie Le Bon de Beauvoir: Henry David Thoreau (1871–1862) is the author of *Walden* (CJ 605).

361. Sylvie Le Bon de Beauvoir: Iris Storm is the heroine of Michael Arlen's 1924 *The Green Hat* (CJ 606).

362. *La fille du bédouin*, written by André Barde for the operetta, "Comte Obligado," was a 1927 song describing a bedouin's daughter who exchanged sexual favors to make a living. See Martin Pénet, *Mémoire de la chanson: 1200 chansons de 1920 à 1945* (Memoir of song: 1200 songs from 1920 to 1945) (Paris: Omnibus, 2004: 320–321).

363. Sylvie Le Bon de Beauvoir: Marie-Thérèse, also know as Zon, was Zaza's older sister who was marrying Albert de Vathaire (CJ 609).

364. Sylvie Le Bon de Beauvoir: Zaza was next on Madame Lacoin's marriage list (CJ 609).

365. Sylvie Le Bon de Beauvoir: *Femmes (Les sept soeurs)* [Women (The seven sisters)] is by Karin Michaëlis and was published in 1926 (CJ 609).

366. Sylvie Le Bon de Beauvoir: *Anny de Montparnasse*, is a 1929 film by Array. Anny Ondra (Ondrakova) was a Czech actress (CJ 611).

367. The French equivalent of this sentence about Poupette is in my approved transcription but does not appear in the French edition (cf.: CJ 611).

368. Sylvie Le Bon de Beauvoir: Barbette, whose real name is Vander Clyde, is a young American transvestite trapeze artist; he was discovered in 1923 by Cocteau who dedicated a collaborative work to him in 1926 with Man Ray (CJ 613).

369. Sylvie Le Bon de Beauvoir: Jacques Feyder's 1928 *Les nouveaux messieurs* was based on the plays by Robert de Flers (CJ 615).

370. Sylvie Le Bon de Beauvoir: Ludwig's *Goethe* was published in 1920 (CJ 615).

371. Sylvie Le Bon de Beauvoir: The friends not liked by Beauvoir are Sartre and Nizan (CJ 617).

372. For an explanation of the phrase that I have translated as "a man from our hometown," see note 133 above.

373. The end of this sentence, which I have translated as "in the sole immensity of his heart," might also be translated as "in the sole immensity of her heart."

374. In my approved transcription, this sentence begins with "Et moi," which I have translated as "And for me." In the French edition, the "Et moi," has been replaced by "Aussi," which would change my translation of this sentence to "It too is still something other than a love—much more" (cf.: CJ 620).

375. Sylvie Le Bon de Beauvoir: The name "Violante" is perhaps a reference to "Violante ou la mondanité [Violante or High Society]" (1892), from *Les plaisirs et les jours* [*Pleasures and Days*] by Proust; Thulé refers to "La ballade du roi de Thulé [The ballad of King Thulé]" in Goethe's *Faust* (1806) (CJ 621). See also note 150 in Beauvoir's *Diary 1*, 212.

376. What appears as the French equivalent of self (*soi*) in my approved transcription, is recorded as the French equivalent of night (*soir*) in the French edition; the translation of the beginning of this sentence would then be "Perhaps one day I will regret this quiet night so like oneself . . ." (. . . *pareil à soi-même* . . .) (cf.: CJ 622).

377. Sylvie Le Bon de Beauvoir: Siria was a dancer, a painter, and a friend of Kiki de Montparnasse (CJ 622).

378. Sylvie Le Bon de Beauvoir: *Les caves du Vatican* is a 1914 novel by Gide (CJ 622).

379. The approved transcription of "Eveski" in the French edition renders as "Hévési" (cf.: CJ 622).

380. Sylvie Le Bon de Beauvoir: *Cromeydre-le-vieil* is a 1920 play by Jules Romains (CJ 623).

381. The French equivalent of the words, "Tonight I said, 'No, not at all, it is really you and not an other,'" is in my approved transcription but do not appear in the French edition (cf.: CJ 624).

382. A "Mortimer" is a member of the inferior caste of Maheu's "eugenic cosmology" inspired by Jean Cocteau's *Le potomak*. For more on Cocteau, see note 208 above. For more on Cocteau's eugenics, see note 346 above.

383. Sylvie Le Bon de Beauvoir: *Rose d'ombre* is a film by Alexandre Arnoux (CJ 626).

384. "I needed this exhilaration to become a God again" refers back to the line from Chapter 6 of Barrès, *Sous l'oeil des barbares*, in *Romans et voyages*, 76. Beauvoir also quotes this line in October 1926 in *Diary 1*, 103. For the purposes of this notebook and for clarity, I have translated "ivresse" as "exhilaration" in this context instead of "intoxication" as in the 1926 diary. See also note 133 in Beauvoir's *Diary 1*, 211. For more on Maurice Barrès, see note 64 above.

385. Sylvie Le Bon de Beauvoir: This was the inauguration of the Monument to Mickiewicz. The consecration was for Bourdelle, who died in France later that year. In 1912 he had also sculpted the reliefs of the Théatre des Champs-Elysées (CJ 627).

386. Sylvie Le Bon de Beauvoir: Renoir is Pierre Renoir, Jean Renoir's brother, and Tessier is Valentine Tessier (CJ 627).

387. Sylvie Le Bon de Beauvoir: Maheu's "eugenic cosmology," inspired by *Le potomak*, places the Eugenes at the highest rank, the caste that includes Socrates and Descartes as well as Maheu, Sartre, and Nizan and relegates all of their other classmates to inferior categories: the Marrhanes, who float in Infinity; and the Mortimers, who float in the sea (CJ 628).

388. Sylvie Le Bon de Beauvoir: *La mort du père* is the sixth volume of the novels constituting *Les Thibault* [*The World of the Thibaults*] (1922–1940) (CJ 628). This seven-volume series was translated into English by Stuart Gilbert and published in a two-volume set called *The World of the Thibaults*, which includes *The Thibaults* and *Summer 1914*.

389. The date shown in my approved transcription of the manuscript is August 29; the date appearing in the French edition is August 23 (cf.: CJ 629).

390. See note 197 above.

391. Sylvie Le Bon de Beauvoir: Diane by Praxiteles is a copy of his statue found in Gabii, an ancient city of Latium (CJ 631).

392. The French equivalent of "and according to the beautiful Greek attribute" appears in my approved transcription, but it is absent from the French edition (cf.: CJ 632).

393. Sylvie Le Bon de Beauvoir: Colombe is Colombe Blanchet, the heroine of Alain-Fournier's second novel (CJ 634).

394. This quote is from the play by Jean Sarment, *Je suis trop grand pour moi, pièce en quatre actes* (I am too big for me).

395. P. J. Jouve is Pierre Jean Jouve (1887–1976), a French writer, novelist, and poet.

396. Sylvie Le Bon de Beauvoir: *Les silences du colonel Bramble* is a 1918 novel by André Maurois (CJ 636). For André Maurois, see also note 57 in *Diary 1*, 205.

397. Sylvie Le Bon de Beauvoir: This typist was typing Simone de Beauvoir's graduate thesis, or *diplôme* (CJ 637).

398. Beauvoir is repeating the earlier quote by Sarment. See note 394 above.

399. In my approved transcription, the French equivalent of the verb meaning to love is in the present tense; in the French edition, the same verb appears in the conditional, which would change the translation of the same question to "Why would she love him?" (cf.: CJ 644).

400. Sylvie Le Bon de Beauvoir: Uncle Pierre is Pierre Tresfort, the second husband of Jacques's mother, Germaine Fourier (CJ 646).

401. Sylvie Le Bon de Beauvoir: Claude is Jacques's half-brother (CJ 646).

402. Sylvie Le Bon de Beauvoir: Germaine is Zaza's younger 16-year-old sister (CJ 647).

403. What appears in the approved manuscript as "Maurice Ponty" is printed as "Merleau-Ponty" in the French edition (cf.: CJ 650).

404. Sylvie Le Bon de Beauvoir: Isadora Duncan (1877–1927) is an American dancer (CJ 650).

405. Sylvie Le Bon de Beauvoir: The five people are all cousins: Jeanne, Magdeleine and Robert, Simone de Beauvoir, and her sister (CJ 654).

406. Sylvie Le Bon de Beauvoir: Chardonne's *Les varais* was published in 1929 (CJ 654).

407. My translation.

408. Sylvie Le Bon de Beauvoir: *Enfantines* was published in 1918 (CJ 685).

409. Sylvie Le Bon de Beauvoir: *Bliss* is a 1920 work by Katherine Mansfield (CJ 656).

410. Sylvie Le Bon de Beauvoir: Jacqueline Marval (1866–1932) was a painter who is overall known as a Fauvist (CJ 656).

411. "The endless sky" translates "le ciel sans fin," which is the phrase in my approved transcription. The French edition shows "le ciel dans fin," which I believe is a misprint (CJ 658).

412. For more on the satirical tract against Bergson, see note 416 below; For more on Alain's *Libres propos*, see note 66 above.

413. I have translated the words "dans l'intervalle des chansons," which appear in my approved transcription, as "between songs." The French edition does not include the words "dans l'intervalle" (CJ 659).

414. Sylvie Le Bon de Beauvoir: *Moravagine* was published in 1926 (CJ 660).

415. Sylvie Le Bon de Beauvoir: Jacques Chardonne's *L'épithalame* was published in 1921 (CJ 660).

416. Sylvie Le Bon de Beauvoir: This tract is most probably George Politzer's *Le bergsonisme, une mystification philosophique* [Bergsonism, a philosophical mystification] (1926), written from a Marxist point of view (CJ 661).

417. Sylvie Le Bon de Beauvoir: *Les rois aveugles* was published in 1925 (CJ 662).

418. Sylvie Le Bon de Beauvoir: Abel Gance's masterpiece, *Napoléon*, first came out in 1927.

419. What the French edition renders as the French equivalent of "leaving" (*partant de*) in this sentence, my approved transcription shows as the French equivalent of "speaking of" (*parlant de*) (cf.: CJ 665).

420. For *The Constant Nymph*, see note 138 above; Sylvie Le Bon de Beauvoir: *The Mill on the Floss* (1860) is by George Eliot (CJ 665); For Eugenes and Mortimer, see notes 346 and 387 above.

421. Sylvie Le Bon de Beauvoir: Yvette is Aunt Lili's daughter (CJ 667).

422. Sylvie Le Bon de Beauvoir: Maurice de Vlaminck (1876–1958) was a painter and writer (CJ 667).

423. For Iris Storm, see note 361 above.

424. Sylvie Le Bon de Beauvoir: Charles Blondel is a French doctor and psychologist (1876–1939). The work cited is better known as *Introduction à la psychologie collective* [Introduction to Collective Psychology] and is from 1928 (CJ 673).

425. The French for this sentence, "Au milieu de ma vie libre, exaltée et puissante, le passage de ce maître terrible entre les mains de qui je suis une si petite fille, qui chasse ma vie d'un revers de main et tourne vers lui seul mon visage effrayé, mon visage comblé," appears in the approved transcription but does not appear in the French edition (cf.: CJ 679).

426. Sylvie Le Bon de Beauvoir: Rilke's book on Rodin is *Auguste Rodin* (1902–1907), and the novel *L'ordre* won the prix Goncourt in 1929 (CJ 679).

427. Sylvie Le Bon de Beauvoir: *Topaze* is a play by Marcel Pagnol at Variétés (CJ 680).

428. Sylvie Le Bon de Beauvoir: *Mon amie Nane* was published in 1905 (CJ 681).

429. Bagatelle is a rose garden in the Bois de Boulogne in Paris.

430. Sylvie Le Bon de Beauvoir: The Lacoin family had moved, and now lived near the Champs-Élysées at 5, bis, rue de Berri (CJ 686).

431. Sylvie Le Bon de Beauvoir: The idiots in question are members of *Action française* who came to disturb the meeting (CJ 687).

432. "You are a solitary consciousness" might also be translated as "You are a solitary conscience" or as "You are a solitary conscience and consciousness" because the French word "conscience" means both "conscience" and "consciousness."

433. These are from François Mauriac's *Adieu à l'adolescence*. Beauvoir refers to this lengthy poem frequently in her diaries. For more on Mauriac, see note 17 above.

434. This is an allusion to "True Love," in Song of Songs, 8.6. "For stern as death is love, relentless as the nether world is devotion; its flames are a blazing fire" (*The New American Bible*, Translated by members of the Catholic Biblical Association of America, New York: P. J. Kennedy & Sons, 1970, 917).

435. Source unknown. "He shut me out of the earth" translates the French, "Il m'a fermé la terre" (cf.: CJ 688).

436. Sylvie Le Bon de Beauvoir: Jeanne and Riri are her cousins; Riri is the son of her aunt Marguerite and her uncle Gaston (CJ 689).

437. Sylvie Le Bon de Beauvoir: Jean Epstein's *Finis terrae* is a silent movie filmed in Ouessant (CJ 689).

438. Sylvie Le Bon de Beauvoir: Les Ballets Russes was the famous company, founded in 1909 in Saint-Petersburg by Serge de Diaghilev, and later settled in Paris and Monte-Carlo as of 1917. *Petouchka* was created in 1911 (the choreography by Fokine, and the music by Stravinsky), *La chatte* in 1927 (Balanchine and Sauguet), *Apollon musagète* (Balanchine, Stravinsky). *Baba-Yaga* is a tale known by all Russian children (CJ 692).

439. Sylvie Le Bon de Beauvoir: Sartre doesn't like Gandillac much and "Le gonfalonnier de Parirac" is Sartre's spoonerism for Gandillac's entire last name, Le Patronnier de Gandillac (CJ 693).

440. There is no sexual connotation denoted by the word "castor," which translates into English as "beaver." To avoid the sexual connotation connected with the English word "beaver," all references to this word used as a nickname for Beauvoir will henceforth remain in the original French as "Castor."

441. Sylvie Le Bon de Beauvoir: Maheu's home is on Rue Cassette (CJ 694).

442. Gide, *Si le grain ne meurt*, 189.

443. Sylvie Le Bon de Beauvoir: Bernard is Zaza's younger 18-year-old brother (CJ 696).

444. The sea of Sargasses is a reference to Gide, *Le voyage d'Urien* (*Urien's Voyage*). See *Diary 1*, 154–155 for earlier references to this novel.

445. Sylvie Le Bon de Beauvoir: the first written exam, a lengthy essay, took six hours (CJ 698).

446. Sylvie Le Bon de Beauvoir: This was the topic of the second written exam, which took four hours (CJ 699).

447. Sylvie Le Bon de Beauvoir: This is the third essay exam to be written in four hours (CJ 700).

448. What appears as the French equivalent of "my" before *agrégation* in the approved transcription is published as the French equivalent of "his" in the French edition (cf.: CJ 703).

449. Henceforth, the term *petits camarades*, which refers to a specific group of close friends that includes Sartre, will be left in the French.

450. Sylvie Le Bon de Beauvoir: Simone de Beauvoir is borrowing these images from the physics of ancient stoicism: the history of the world is made of alternate periods, in one of which the supreme god or Zeus absorbs and reduces all things within himself whereas in another, he is deployed, animates, and governs an ordered real. The world as we know it is achieved by a universal conflagration that makes everything return to the divine substance, then it starts over, identical to itself, according to an eternal rigorous return (CJ 708).

451. What appears as the French equivalent of "no longer" in the approved transcription, is published as the French equivalent of "not" in the French edition (cf.: CJ 708).

452. Sylvie Le Bon de Beauvoir: Germaine is Zaza's younger sister (CJ 710).

453. Sylvie Le Bon de Beauvoir: *Caliban parle* was published in 1928 (CJ 712); The French equivalent of the words "with emotion" appears in the approved transcription of Beauvoir's handwritten diary but not in the French edition (cf.: CJ 712).

454. Sylvie Le Bon de Beauvoir: This is the end-of-the-year revue for the advertising academy that Henriette de Beauvoir (Poupette) attended; A *jean-bart* is a hat with an upraised brim (CJ 712).

455. Sylvie Le Bon de Beauvoir: Zaza's mother organized "interviews" where her daughters would meet an unknown young man and have to decide whether or not to marry him (CJ 714).

456. The words "and in the metro to her place" translate the words "et par le métro jusque chez elle," which appear in my approved transcription but not in the French edition (cf.: CJ 715).

457. Sylvie Le Bon de Beauvoir: *The Pilgrim* is a silent film from 1922 (CJ 716).

458. Sylvie Le Bon de Beauvoir: Boutroux's *De la contingence des lois de la nature* [*The contingency of the Laws of Nature*] was on the *agrégation* oral exam (CJ 717).

459. Sylvie Le Bon de Beauvoir: "Hat" (*Chapeau*) is Gérassi's nickname for Simone de Beauvoir (CJ 718).

460. The French equivalent of "very" appears in the approved transcription of Beauvoir's handwritten diary but not in the French edition (cf.: CJ 718).

461. Sylvie Le Bon de Beauvoir: The Grand-Duke is Paul Nizan (CJ 720).

462. Sylvie Le Bon de Beauvoir: They are studying a text by Plato (CJ 723).

463. The name, Lama, appears after the date in the French edition, but not in the approved transcription (CJ 723).

464. Sylvie Le Bon de Beauvoir: This text by Aristotle is among those on the oral exam (CJ 723).

465. Sylvie Le Bon de Beauvoir: Maheu had rented a hotel room for the rest of the competitive exam (CJ 723).

466. Sylvie Le Bon de Beauvoir: Arthur Hannequin was a commentator of Spinoza (CJ 724).

467. Sylvie Le Bon de Beauvoir: *Poussière* was published in 1927 (CJ 724).

468. Sylvie Le Bon de Beauvoir: Jean Buridan was a scholastic philosopher (1300–1358), the rector of l'Université de Paris, to whom one attributed the famous argument of "Buridan's ass" (CJ 724).

469. Sylvie Le Bon de Beauvoir: The phrase, "again concerning God, that He exists" comes from Descartes's fifth meditation (CJ 725).

470. Sylvie Le Bon de Beauvoir: Sophie Tucker is a famous American singer of Russian origin (1884–1966), "the queen of ragtime" from whom Sartre borrowed the tune "Some of these Days" in *La nausée* [*Nausea*]; Jack Hylton was very well-known in Europe between the two world wars for his foxtrot orchestra (CJ 726).

471. Sylvie Le Bon de Beauvoir: The song is the 1929 production "Listen to Dinah" [*sic*] by Coleman Hawkins (CJ 727).

472. The words "welcomed by the big blue armchair" translate the phrase in my approved transcription, "que recevait le grand fauteuil bleu." The French edition shows "qui" instead of "que," which would change the translation to "who got the big blue armchair" (CJ 729).

473. Her success means that she is eligible to sit for the oral exams.

474. Sylvie Le Bon de Beauvoir: Nizan's place is on rue Vavin and the painting is by Adolphe Mouron, known as Cassandre (1901–1968), a painter decorator, and poster designer. He contributed to creating a new advertising style, marked by graphic stylizations, for example, his posters for *Le Normandie*, Dubonnet, *L'Étoile du Nord*, and les Vins Nicolas (CJ 732).

475. The French equivalent of "so be it" appears in the approved transcription of Beauvoir's handwritten diary but not in the published French edition (cf.: CJ 733).

476. Sylvie Le Bon de Beauvoir: The "main lesson" without a program, on a subject drawn at random, had to be prepared within seven hours. It was supposed to represent an hourlong class that would be given to a student in the last year of an excellent high school. In reality, the level of this class had to be infinitely higher than this (CJ 733).

477. Sylvie Le Bon de Beauvoir: Jollivet is Simone Jollivet, known as Toulouse, the future companion of Charles Dullin (CJ 738).

478. Sylvie Le Bon de Beauvoir: *Er, l'arménien* is one of Sartre's writings (CJ 739).

479. Sylvie Le Bon de Beauvoir: Georges Politzer (1903–1942) was a Marxist philosopher, author of a satirical tract against Bergsonism, and a collaborator on *L'humanité* (CJ 741).

480. Sylvie Le Bon de Beauvoir: This song, composed and set to music by Sartre included the following verses: "Deign, deign to consider this: / De Gandillac, Le Patronnier [the pattern-maker], / Is the patron [boss/patron] of simpletons" (CJ 742). The word play based on Gandillac's official last name is unfortunately lost in translation.

481. "From you alone, I cannot wish to free myself" translates the French in my approved transcription, "C'est vous seul dont je ne peux vouloir me délivrer." The same sentence as provided by the French edition would be translated as, "From you alone, I can wish to free myself" (CJ 745).

482. Sylvie Le Bon de Beauvoir: Monseigneur Robert Hugh Benson is the author of *Le maître de la terre* [*Lord of the World*] (1907) and *Lettres spirituelles* [*Spiritual Letters*] (1928) (CJ 746).

483. Sylvie Le Bon de Beauvoir: A leprechaun is a mythical character taken from *The Crock of Gold*, the 1912 publication of the Irish writer James Stephens (1882–1950). The leprechaun is a gnome, who, crouched under tree roots, defies unhappiness, boredom, and doubt by making little shoes. Simone de Beauvoir and Sartre saw in this the incarnation

of the writer and got into the habit of calling the books that they would write, "their little shoes" (CJ 747).

484. Sylvie Le Bon de Beauvoir: Maggie Tulliver is the heroine of George Elliot's *The Mill on the Floss* (CJ 749).

485. What appears as "le Gandille" in the approved manuscript is published as "le Gandillac" in the French edition (CJ 750).

486. The words "my heart longed" are written in English in Beauvoir's handwritten diary (CJ 753).

487. Sylvie Le Bon de Beauvoir: Tom, for Maggie Tulliver, is the hero of George Eliot's *Mill on the Floss* (CJ 753).

488. Sylvie Le Bon de Beauvoir: Saint-Germain refers to the village Saint-Germain-les-Belles in this passage (CJ 754).

489. Sylvie Le Bon de Beauvoir: Madeleine Combes was an already aged author of serial novels when, in November 1925, she wanted to employ Sartre, who was then in his first year at École Normale Supérieure, as a ghostwriter for her works; she simultaneously tried to seduce him. Sartre has recounted the burlesque episodes of this story in the form of a long serial (CJ 755).

490. The words, "the sun was beating down terribly hard" translate the phrase, "où Mahomet tapait terriblement dur." Mahomet was used to refer to the sun in the early twentieth century. See, for example, the entry of May 18 in "Extraits des lettres Beaufort."

491. Sylvie Le Bon de Beauvoir: "Le Baladin [The Playboy]" was another writer's myth dear to Sartre at this time. It was borrowed from Synge. The Playboy was an eternal wanderer, who disguised the mediocrity of life with beautiful fabricated stories (CJ 755).

492. Sylvie Le Bon de Beauvoir: These are the notebooks that were given away as sales aids to promote Midy suppositories and ointment. Sartre used them to record his thoughts in alphabetical order on cinema, criticism, works read, things heard, poems, and all sorts of remarks. There are also some verses by Marot, an analysis of Conrad's *Lord Jim*, and judgments that amused him, such as, "This little work is tasty, irresistibly crisp, and sweet as a meringue" (CJ 756).

493. The approved transcription of the original handwritten manuscript includes two phrases that I have translated but which do not appear in the French edition, "cette assurance de son amour; cette peur de me faire du mal" (cf.: CJ 757).

494. I have translated the French clause found in my approved transcription of Beauvoir's handwritten diary, "il semblait possible qu'en face de moi toujours la même présence fût attendue." The French edition has replaced "attendue" (expected) with the word "possible" (possible), which would render the following translation, "it seemed possible that across from me that same presence was still possible" (CJ 758).

495. Sylvie Le Bon de Beauvoir: These words in Latin that mean, "All Gaul is divided," come from the beginning of Julius Caesar's *The Gallic Wars* (CJ 759).

496. Sylvie Le Bon de Beauvoir: This was one of the first times that Simone de Beauvoir had drunk wine (CJ 760).

497. Sylvie Le Bon de Beauvoir: La Pelouse is a big public meadow that runs along la Vézère (CJ 760).

498. For Grand Meaulnes, see note 121 above.

499. Sylvie Le Bon de Beauvoir: A tapir (literally a type of animal) is École Normale jargon for a student to whom one gives private lessons (CJ 766).

500. From "To do" through "Outfit purchased" just before the second final summary are diary pages that are included in my approved transcription but that do not appear in the French edition.

501. Sylvie Le Bon de Beauvoir: Sartre thought he was doing his military service in Versailles (CJ 771).

Bibliography

Alain-Fournier. *Le grand Meaulnes*. Paris: Emile-Paul, 1914. Translated by Françoise Delisle as *The Wanderer (Le grand Meaulnes)*. New York: New Directions, 1928.

Aspland, C. W. "Beroul: Tristan." In *A Medieval French Reader*. Oxford: Clarendon Press, 1979, 121–123.

Bair, Deirdre. *Simone de Beauvoir: A Biography*. New York: Summit Books, 1990.

Barbey, Bernard. *Le coeur gros*. Paris: B. Grasset, 1924.

Barrès, Maurice. *Le jardin de Bérénice*. In *Romans et voyages*.

——. *Romans et voyages*. Paris: Robert Laffont, 1994.

——. *Sous l'oeil des barbares*. In *Romans et voyages*.

——. *Un homme libre*. In *Romans et voyages*.

——. *Un jardin sur L'Oronte*. In *Romans et voyages*.

Basch, Victor. *For or against Dreyfus*. http://www.dreyfus.culture.fr/en/bio/bio-html-victor-basch.htm (accessed March 1, 2017).

Beauvoir, Simone de. *Cahiers de jeunesse*. Edited by Sylvie Le Bon de Beauvoir. Paris: Gallimard, 2008.

——. *Diary of a Philosophy Student*, vol. 1, 1926–27. Translated by Barbara Klaw. Edited by Barbara Klaw, Sylvie Le Bon de Beauvoir, and Margaret A. Simons with Marybeth Timmermann. Chicago: University of Illinois Press, 2006.

——. *La force de l'âge*. Paris: Gallimard, 1960. Translated by Peter Green as *The Prime of Life*. New York: The World Publishing Company, 1962.

———. *L'invitée*. Folio. Paris: Gallimard, 1943. Translated by Yvonne Moyse and Roger Senhouse as *She Came to Stay*. London: Fontana, 1984.

———. *Mémoires d'une jeune fille rangée*. Folio. Paris: Gallimard, 1958. Translated by James Kirkup as *Memoirs of a Dutiful Daughter*. New York: Harper and Row, 1959.

Benrubi, Isaac. *Contemporary Thought of France*. Redditch, U.K.: Read Books, Ltd., 2007.

Bergson, Henri. *L'évolution créatrice*. Paris: Alcan, 1914. Translated by A. Mitchell as *Creative Evolution*. New York: Modern Library, 1944.

Bradshaw, Rob I. "Epicurius" Early Church.org.uk: An Internet Resource for Studying the Early Church. http://www.earlychurch.org.uk/epicurius.php (accessed May 16, 2008).

Breton, André. *Manifestoes of Surrealism*. Translated by Richard Seaver and Helen R. Lane, University of Michigan Press, 1969, 147.

Briatte, R, Joseph Delteil, *Qui êtes-vous?* La Manufacture. http://josephdelteil.net/biographie.htm (accessed March 3, 2017).

Browning, Robert. "Light Woman." In *Dramatic Romances*. Edited by Anders Thulin, electronic edition version 1.1; 1994–09–15. http://eserver.org/poetry/dramatic-romances.txt (accessed November 2, 2001).

Brunschvicg, Léon. *Le progrès de la conscience dans la philosophie occidentale*. Paris: Felix Alcan, 2 vol., 1927, 807.

Burnham, Douglas. "Gottfried Wilhelm Leibniz." In *Internet Encyclopedia of Philosophy*. http://www.utm.edu/research/iep/l/leib-met.htm (accessed March 4, 2002).

Chadourne, Marc. *Vasco*. Paris: Plon, 1927.

Claudel, Paul. "La cantate à troix voix" in *Oeuvre poétique*, 342.

———. *Les feuilles de saints*. In *Oeuvre poétique*, 597–696.

———. *Oeuvre poétique*. Bibliothèque de la Pléiade. Paris: Gallimard, 1967.

———. "Saint Louis." In *Les feuilles de saints*, 651–662.

———. "Ténèbres." In *Images et signets entre les feuilles*. In *Oeuvre poétique*, 430. Translated by Joseph T. Shipley as "Shadows" in *Modern French Poetry*. New York: Greenburg, 1926, 72.

Cocteau, Jean. *Le Potomak*. Paris: Librairie Stock, 1950.

———. *Thomas l'imposteur*. Paris: Gallimard, 1923. Translated by Lewis Galantière as *Thomas the Imposter*. New York: Appleton, 1925.

Conrad, Joseph. *Lord Jim*. New York: Modern Library, 1931.

Crane, Brent. "The Virtues of Isolation," in *The Atlantic* (March 30, 2017). https://www.theatlantic.com/health/archive/2017/03/the-virtues-of-isolation/521100/ (accessed June 13, 2017).

Cros, Roger. "Pierre Mac Orlan et le romantisme moderne," *The French Review*, vol. 7, no. 6 (May 1934), 445–457.

Dane, Clemence. *Legend*. Westport, Conn.: Greenwood Press, 1978. Translated into French by Jeanne Scialtiel as *Légende*. Les Palmes, 8. Monaco: Éditions du Rocher, 1947.

Das, Subhamoy. "What Are the Upanishads to Indian Philosophy?" ThoughtCo. https://www.thoughtco.com/the-upanishads-basics-1770575 (accessed May 24, 2018).

"Delatousche," *Sans patrie ni frontières: Dictionnaire international des militants anarchistes*. http://militants-anarchistes.info/spip.php?article1133 (accessed on January 8, 2017).

Doidge, Norman. *The Brain That Changes Itself*. New York: Penguin Books, 2007.

Esslin, Martin. *The Theatre of the Absurd*. New York: Penguin Books, 1980. Third Edition.

"Extraits des Lettres Beaufort." In *Le petit écho* 40 (June 15, 1916). http://gallica.bnf.fr/ark:/12148/bpt6k6582327x/f1.textePage (accessed May 13, 2017).

Favier, Jean. *Paris: Deux mille ans d'histoire*. (Paris: Two Thousand Years of History). Paris: Fayard, 1997, 459–460.

Francis, Claude and Fernande Gontier. *Simone de Beauvoir*. Paris: Librairie académique Perrin, 1985. Translated by Lisa Nesselson as *Simone de Beauvoir: A Life, a Love Story*. New York: St. Martin's Press, 1987.

Gide, André. *Les nourritures terrestres*. In *Romans*. Translated by Dorothy Bussy as *Fruits of the Earth*. London: Secker and Warburg, 1962.

——. *L'immoraliste*. In *Romans*. Translated by David Watson as *The Immoralist*. New York: Penguin Books, 2001.

——. *Le voyage d'Urien*. In *Romans*. Translated by Wade Baskin as *Urien's Voyage*. New York: Citadel, 1964.

——. *Romans: récits et soties, oeuvres lyriques*. Bibliothèque de la Pléiade. Paris: Gallimard, 1958.

——. *Si le grain ne meurt*. Paris: Gallimard, 1928. Translated by Dorothy Bussy as *If It Die: An Autobiography/André Gide*. New York: Random House, 1957.

——. *Si le grain ne meurt*. Edition du groupe "Ebooks libres et gratuits," 1926, 189. http://www.ebooksgratuits.com/pdf/gide_si_le_grain_ne_meurt.pdf (accessed November 14, 2016).

Giraudoux, Jean. *Simon le pathéthique*. Paris: Grasset, 1926, 150.

Hicks, Esther and Jerry. *Ask and It Is Given*, London: Hay House, Inc., 2004.

Heck-Rabi, Louise. *La coquille et le clergyman*. http://www.filmreference.com/Films-Chr-Czl/La-Coquille-et-le-Clergyman.html (accessed January 14, 2017).

Hölderlin, Friedrich. "Hyperion or the Hermit" In *Hyperion and Selected Poems*. Edited by Eric L. Santner. New York: Bloomsbury Academic, 1990.

Issacharoff, Michael. *Discourse as Performance*. Palo Alto: Stanford University Press, 1989.

Jammes, Francis. "Elégie huitième." In *Le deuil des primevères*. In *Oeuvres complètes*, 76.

——. *Francis Jammes, Oeuvres complètes*, Geneva: Slatkine Reprints, 1978. Translation of selected prayers and elegies by William Alwyn as *Prayers and Elegies by Francis Jammes*. Youlgrave, England: Hub Publications, Ltd., 1978.

Jarry, Alfred. *Ubu Roi*. In *Tout Ubu*. Paris: Livre de Poche., Librairie Générale Française, 1962. Translated by Barbara Wright as *Ubu Roi: Drama in 5 Acts*. A New Directions book, 105; New Directions paperbook. Norfolk, Conn.: New Directions Pub. Corp, 1961.

"Journals and New Books," *Journal of Philosophy*, vol. 22, no. 26 (December 17, 1925), 719–720.

Klaw, Barbara. *Le Paris de Beauvoir/Beauvoir's Paris*. Paris: Syllepse, 1999.

——. "Simone de Beauvoir, Cousin Jacques du journal intime à l'autobiographie (Simone de Beauvoir, Cousin Jacques from her diary to her autobiography)." In *(Re) Découvrir l'oeuvre de Simone de Beauvoir* ((Re) Discover the Works of Simone de Beauvoir). Paris: Le Bord de l'Eau Éditions, 2008, 84–91.

——. "Simone de Beauvoir and Nelson Algren: Self-Creation, Self-Contradiction, and the Erotic, Exotic, Feminist Other." In *Contingent Loves*. Edited by Melanie Hawthorne. Charlottesville: University Press of Virginia, 2000, 117–152.

——. "The Literary and Historical Context of Beauvoir's Early Writings: 1926–27." In *Diary of a Philosophy Student*, 7–28.

——. "Troublesome Translations and Elusive Allusions in Beauvoir's Diary of a Philosophy Student," In *Proceedings of the 18th Conference of the Simone de Beauvoir Society: Yes-*

terday, Today, Tomorrow, Newcastle upon Tyne: Cambridge Scholars Publishing, 2017, 69–83.

Koller, Michael. *The Joyless Street*. http://www.sensesofcinema.com/contents/cteq/04/32/the_joyless_street.html (accessed January 14, 2017).

Lacoin, Elisabeth. *Zaza: Correspondance et carnets d'Elisabeth Lacoin 1914–1929*. Paris: Seuil, 1991.

Laforgue, Jules. "Ah! que d'Elle-même" (first line of poem "IX" without a title). In Laforgue, *Oeuvres complètes*, II, 177–178. Translated by Peter Dale as "If of her own accord," 425–427.

———. "Eclair de Gouffre" (A flash in the abyss). In *Le sanglot de la terre* (The sobbing of the earth), 53.

———. *Le sanglot de la terre*. In Laforgue, *Oeuvres complètes*, vol. 1.

———. "Marche funèbre." In *Le sanglot de la terre*, 25. Translated by Patricia Terry as "Funeral March" in *Poems of Jules Laforgue*, 19.

———. *Oeuvres complètes*, 2 vols. Genève: Slatkine Reprints, 1979 (reprint of 1922–30 edition). Partially translated by Peter Dale as *Poems: Bilingual Edition*. London: Anvil Press Poetry, 2001. Partially translated by Patricia Terry as *Poems of Jules Laforgue*. Los Angeles: University of California Press, 1958.

Lamb-Shapiro, Jessica. *Promise Land: My Journey through America's Self-Help Culture*. New York: Simon and Schuster, 2014.

La Rochelle, Drieu. *Plainte contre inconnu* (Complaint against the unknown).

Le Bon de Beauvoir, Sylvie. *Beauvoir*, L'Herne. Paris: Cahiers de L'Herne, 2012.

Léna, Marguerite. "Jeanne Mercier, lectrice de Maurice Blondel." In *Maurice Blondel et la quête du sens*. Edited by Marie-Jeanne Coutagne. Paris: Beauchesne, 1998, 109–117.

Lesbros, Dominique. *Paris en question(s): Histoire, culture, patrimoine, célébrités ou bizarreries*. Paris: Parigramme, 2008.

Lucretius. *De Rerum Natura* [*On the Nature of Things*], note 169. Notebook 6.

Mauriac, François. *L'adieu à l'adolescence: Poème*. Paris: Stock, 1911.

———. *La robe prétexte*.

———. *L'enfant chargé de chaines* (1913). Paris: Editions Gallimard, 1978. Translated by Gerard Hopkins as *Young Man in Chains*. London: Eyre and Spottiswoode, 1961.

———. "L'étudiant-départ II." In *Les mains jointes*. In *Oeuvres complètes*.

———. *Oeuvres complètes*, vol. 6. Paris: Fayard, 1951.

Messenger, Ann P. "'One of Us': A Biblical Allusion in Conrad's *Lord Jim*." *English Language Notes*, December 71 (9:2), 129.

Montaigne, Michel. "We Taste Nothing Purely," In the second volume of *The Essays of Michael Lord of Montaigne*, 1580, 1597. Translated by John Florio, 1603. World's Classics edition. 3 volumes, Vol. 2. London: Frowde, 1904. Ben R. Schneider Jr. "Materials for the Construction of SHAKESPEARE'S MORALS: The Stoic Legacy to the Renaissance." http://www.stoics.com/montaigne_2.html (accessed January 6, 2017).

"Musée Pédagogique: État général des fonds des Archives nationales (Pierrefitte-sur-Seine). Mise à jour 2012." http://www.archivesnationales.culture.gouv.fr/chan/chan/series/pdf/71AJ.pdf (accessed January 13, 2017).

Nietzche, Friedrich. *Ainsi parlait Zarathoustra = Also sprach Zarathustra* (German-French bilingual edition). Translated into French by Geneviève Bianquis. Paris: Aubier, 1992. Translated by R. J. Hollingdale as *Thus Spoke Zarathustra*. New York: Penguin, 1969.

Offen, Karen. "The Second Sex and the Baccalauréat in Republican France, 1880–1924." *French Historical Studies* XIII, no. 2 (Fall 1983), 252–286.

Plato. *Phaedrus*, Translated by W. G. Helmbold and G. Rabinowitz. Indianapolis: Bobbs-Merrill, 1956.

——. *Symposium and Other Dialogues*. Translated by Michael Joyce. New York: Everyman's Library, 1964, 21–24, 41, 45–46.

——. "The Supremacy of Good," *Republic*. Translated by Robin Waterfield. New York: Oxford University Press, 1993, 227–249.

Proust, Marcel. *À la recherche du temps perdu*. Bibliothèque de la Pléiade. 2 vols. Paris: Gallimard, 1954. Translated by C. K. Scott Moncrieff and Terence Kilmartin as *Remembrance of Things Past*. New York: Random House, 1981.

"Rabindranath Tagore—Biographical." Nobelprize.org. Nobel Media AB 2014. http://www.nobelprize.org/nobel_prizes/literature/laureates/1913/tagore-bio.html (accessed May 26, 2018).

"Raymond Duncan Collection: An Inventory of the Collection at Syracuse University," Special Collections Research Center, Syracuse University Library. http://library.syr.edu/digital/guides/d/duncan_r.htm (accessed January 13, 2017).

Rivière, Jacques. *Aimée*. Paris: Gallimard, 1993.

Rivière, Jacques, and Alain-Fournier. *Correspondance 1904–1914*, 2 vols. Paris: Gallimard, 1926.

Rochegude, Félix. *Promenades dans toutes les rues de Paris*. "VIIe arrondissment." Paris: Hachette, 1910.

Rodriguez, Tori. "Negative Emotions Are Key to Well-Being." *Scientific American* (May 1, 2013). https://www.scientificamerican.com/article/negative-emotions-key-well-being/ (accessed June 13, 2017).

Ruiz, Don Miguel. *The Four Agreements*. San Rafael, Calif.: Amber-Allen Publishing, 1997.

Sarment, Jean. *Je suis trop grand pour moi, pièce en quatre actes*, Comédie-Française. Paris: March 26, 1924.

Simons, Margaret A. *Beauvoir and "The Second Sex": Feminism, Race, and the Origins of Existentialism*. Lanham, Md.: Rowman and Littlefield, 1999.

——. "Beauvoir's Early Philosophy," in *Diary 1*.

Staedeli, Thomas. "Max Linder," http://www.cyranos.ch/linder-e.htm, and "Max Linder-Silent Movie St.," http://www.goldensilents.com/comedy/maxlinder.html (accessed January 13, 2017).

Tadie, Jean Yves. "Elpénor" in *Oeuvres romanesques complètes*, Pléiade, Paris: Gallimard, 1990, 1511.

Tagore, Rabindranath. *Gitanjali (Song Offerings)*. London: Macmillan, 1914: 23, 78. Translated by André Gide as *L'offrande lyrique*. Paris: Gallimard, 1963.

"Tamara de Lempicka," FulcrumGallery.com. http://www.fulcrumgallery.com/a34434/Tamara-De-Lempicka.htm (accessed March 9, 2017).

Tolle, Eckhart. *The Power of Now*. Novato, Calif.: New World Publishing, 1997.

Valéry, Paul. "Aurore." In *Charmes*.

——. "Cimetière marin." In *Charmes*. In *Oeuvres*. vol. 1, 147–151. Translated by David Paul as "The Graveyard by the Sea" in *Poems in the Collected Works of Paul Valéry, vol. 1*. Princeton, N.J.: Princeton University Press, 1971, 213–221.

——. *Oeuvres*. vol. 1, Bibliothèque de la Pléiade. Paris: Gallimard, 1957.

———. "Palme." In *Charmes*. In *Oeuvres*, I, 153–156. Translated by David Paul as "Palm" in *Poems in the Collected Works of Paul Valéry, vol. 1*. Princeton, N.J.: Princeton University Press, 1971, 229–235.

Verlaine, Paul. "Langueur." *Jadis et Naguère*. In Verlaine, *Oeuvres poétiques completes*, 370–71. Translated by C. F. MacIntyre under the title "Apathy," in *French Symbolist Poetry*. Berkeley: UCLA Press, 1964, 33. Translated by Norman R. Shapiro, under the title "Languor" in *One Hundred and One Poems by Paul Verlaine*. Chicago: University of Chicago Press, 1998, 134.

———. "La vie humble aux travaux ennuyeux et faciles." In *Sagesse*. In *Oeuvres*, 248.

———. *Oeuvres poétiques complètes*. Bibliothèque de la Pléiade. Paris: Gallimard, 1962.

Vocabulaire européen des philosophes: dictionnaire des intraduisibles. Paris: Seuil, 2004.

Whitman, Christy. *Art of Having It All*. Los Angeles: TVGuestpert Publishing, 2015.

———. *Quantum Success: Seven Essential Laws for a Thriving, Joyful, and Prosperous Relationship with Work and Money*. New York: Atria/Enliven Books, 2018.

Wilde, Oscar. *Intentions and The Soul of Man*. London: Methuen, 1969.

Index

About Money [*Autour de L'argent*]
(L'herbier), 134, 327n342

Action française, 332n431

Adieu à l'adolescence (Mauriac), 332n433

affirmations, 8, 18n14

agrégation: Beauvoir's preparation for, 46,
245, 248–49, 250–51, 252, 333n458;
Beauvoir's stress over, 258; Boivin
discusses, 189; colleagues preparing
for, 47, 62, 75, 227; Gandillac discusses, 47, 75, 122; Gandillac predicts
Beauvoir's success in, 111; information on, 307nn103,106, 311–12n160,
334n476; Maheu discusses, 216; and
Maheu's system, 162, 164; main lesson
presentations, 259, 334n476; Merleau-
Ponty changes science programs for,
107; Merleau-Ponty discusses, 246; oral
exams, 3, 260; pedagogy lectures for,
100, 321n264; *petits camarades* preparation for, 1, 234, 247, 248–49, 250–51,
333nn462,464,465; Schuler discusses,
62; science programs for, 323n283;
student-teaching internships, 110,
116, 125, 126, 139, 324n299, 326n318;
written exams for, 228–29, 230, 257,
332nn445–47, 334n473

Agriculteurs, 141, 233

Les Agriculteurs (cinema), 141, 233

Aimée (Rivière), 126–27, 219, 301n43,
313n176

Alain (Emile-Auguste Chartier), 37, 64, 90,
193, 303n66

Alain-Fournier, 300n42; Beauvoir discovers, 63; Beauvoir thinks of discussing
with Jacques, 51, 217, 221; *Colombe
Blanchet,* 42, 171, 306n91, 330n393;
Rivière on, 40

Alain-Fournier. *See also Le grand
Meaulnes*

Alcibiades, 187

A life without joy [*Catherine, ou Une vie sans joie*] (Renoir), 141, 328n355

L'âme cachée [The Hidden Soul] (Lacretelle), 56, 309n135

America: Day by Day (Beauvoir), 3

L'amitié (Foujita), 141

Amour [Love] (Praxiteles), 151

Anabase [*Anabasis*] (Perse), 251, 334n468

Anderson, Sherwood, 266

L'annonce faite à Marie [*The Tidings Brought to Mary*] (Claudel), 104, 322n277

Anny de Montparnasse [Anny from Montparnasse] (Array), 151, 329n366

Anthropology from a Pragmatic Point of View (Kant), 45, 306n97

Apollo (music hall), 25, 296n7

Apollon musagète (ballet), 223, 332n438

"L'après-midi d'un faune" [The afternoon of a faun] (Mallarmé), 296n11

À quoi penses-tu? (Passeur), 42

Aragon, Louis, 110, 324n291

Arcos, René, 90, 320n244

Ardel, Henri, 91, 320n251

L'argent [*Money*] (L'herbier), 137, 328n350

Aristotle: Beauvoir and Nizan translate, 258; Beauvoir studies, 91, 123; Beauvoir translates, 122; Gandillac discusses, 206; *petits camarades* study, 250, 251, 333n464; Riquet discusses, 85

Arland, Marcel, 59, 115, 212, 310n146, 331n426

Arlen, Michael, 146, 192, 201, 203, 206, 208, 225, 328n361

Arnoux, Alexandre, 329n383

Aron, 259, 287, 294

A Secret Life [*Une vie secrète*] (Lenormand), 135, 328n345

Assaraf, John, 18n14

Asselin, Maurice, 89, 319n238

Les atomes [*Atoms*] (Perrin), 90, 91

Audurand, Hélène, 153

Auguste Rodin (Rilke), 212, 213, 331n426

Augustine of Hippo, Saint, 71, 314n179

Au temps des cerises, ou Fanchette [The time of the cherries, or Fanchette] (Vayre), 141, 328n356

L'auto, 209, 213, 224

Autour de L'argent [*About Money*] (L'herbier), 134, 327n342

availability (*disponibilité*) (Gide), 309n127

Avdicovith, Stépha: affair with Eveski, 121, 125–26, 129, 133; bar outings with, 84–86, 92, 101, 105, 129, 143–44; Beauvoir compares to herself, 81–82; Beauvoir corrects articles for, 328n344; Beauvoir's correspondence with, 234; Beauvoir's fondness for, 38, 42–44, 46, 47, 48, 70, 76, 90, 98–99, 109, 113, 115, 215, 247; Beauvoir shows Zaza's letter to, 82; Beauvoir visits at home, 94, 100, 151; brief encounters with, 72; conversations with, 34; disappointed about Montparnasse outing, 117; discusses art, 90, 91; discusses Catholicism, 31, 32, 40; discusses Cocteau, 90, 103; discusses Goethe, 62; discusses Jacques, 121; discusses marriage, 53; discusses Merleau-Ponty, 110; discusses physical intimacy, 31–32, 33; discusses Poupette, 110; engagement of, 125–26, 131, 215; at *Équipes Sociales*, 56, 99; excited by Nietzsche, 49; on frivolity, 40–41; and future plans, 294; gatherings at home of, 59, 71, 76, 246; introduced to Merleau-Ponty, 47, 55, 61; Madame Lacoin on, 108–9; letter from home, 58; at library, 72, 109; life summaries on, 66, 285; loved by Romanian friend, 104, 121; Luxembourg Gardens outings with, 101; Maheu dislikes, 207; meets Pontrémoli, 70; memories of, 234–35; new year thoughts for, 119; outings with, 30, 42, 52, 54, 61, 66–67, 76, 110, 136, 138, 235, 243; outings with Beauvoir and Zaza, 47–48, 247; with Poupette and Beauvoir, 39; reading cards, 41, 70, 105; relationship with Fernand Gérassi, 48–49, 56, 66, 91; relationship with "German man," 43, 47, 50, 53, 55, 62; on salon culture, 39; theater outings with, 42, 73–74,

95, 99; visits Beauvoir at home, 108, 121; Zaza discusses, 59, 60; on Zaza's relationship with mother, 30
Avec les yeux de l'esprit [With the eyes of the spirit] (Béhaine), 115, 325n302

Baba-Yaga (ballet), 223, 332n438
Babij, Ivan, 88, 319n228
Bad fortune [*Le mauvais sort*] (Beucler), 75, 315n189
Bagatelle (rose garden), 217, 245, 332n429
Ballets Russes, 223, 332n438
Balzac, Honoré de, 63
Balzar, 266
Bandi. *See* Eveski
Barbette (trapeze artist), 153, 329n368
Barbier, 146
Barde, André, 147, 328n362
Le bar de l'amour (Soupault), 47, 85, 307n108
Baring, Maurice, 57, 310n139
Barrès, Maurice: Beauvoir cites, 115, 325n301; Beauvoir reads, 158, 160; Beauvoir's thoughts on, 231; Eveski discusses, 124; Galois discusses, 122–23; Galois reminds Beauvoir of, 39–40, 111; Gandillac discusses, 111, 199; identification of, 302–3n64, 326n307; as influence on Beauvoir, 3, 4n8, 57; Maheu discusses, 156, 227; Merleau-Ponty cites, 106, 118; Merleau-Ponty discusses, 37, 145; self-worship movement, 303n64
Baruzi, Jean, 4, 64, 65, 139, 154, 164, 193, 234
Basch, Victor, 31, 34, 38, 246, 300n41
Bateau Ivre, 167
Battling le ténébreux (ou la mue périlleuse) (Vialatte), 51, 308n117
Baudelaire, Charles, 52, 55, 57, 72, 159
Beauchamp's Career [*La carrière de Beauchamp*] (Meredith), 117, 326n306
Beauvoir, Françoise (Beauvoir's mother): Beauvoir feels sorry for, 66; cinema outings with, 141, 175; and death of grandfather, 188; discusses Zaza with Madame Lacoin, 108; goes out, 44; is

young, 37, 106; outings with, 41, 153; parlor gathering, 106; returns from Arras, 121; scolds Poupette, 108; Stépha reads cards for, 41; surprises Beauvoir and Sartre in meadow, 277; tells Beauvoir that Maheu stopped by, 234; theater outings with, 108, 153; walk from train station with, 139
Beauvoir, Georges de (Beauvoir's father): Beauvoir exasperated by, 66; Beauvoir picks up at train station, 144; and death of grandfather, 186, 188, 195; at family gathering for grandfather's memorial, 188; goes out, 44; hilarious conversation with Maheu, 234; is lighthearted, 106; likes Gandillac, 163; parlor gathering, 106; at Poupette's school party, 241; suprises Beauvoir and Sartre in meadow, 277; theater outings with, 230; to train station, 139; wants Beauvoir to marry country cousin, 197
Beauvoir, Henriette-Hélène Bertrand de (Poupette) (Beauvoir's sister): art gallery outings with, 191; attends Merleau-Ponty's party, 110–12; bar outings with, 78, 105, 130–31, 136–37, 167; Beauvoir's feelings about, 185; Beauvoir's fondness for, 38, 220; brief encounters with, 49, 216; Caveau de la Bolée outing, 151; chats with Stépha, 121; cinema outings with, 141; conversations with, 44, 52, 74; and death of grandfather, 186, 188; diary entries addressed to, 115; discusses art, 92; discusses Catholicism, 259; discusses Jacques, 242; discusses Maheu, 234; at *Équipes Sociales*, 99; Fontainebleau picnic with, 228; and future plans, 294; Gandillac discusses, 220, 233; Gandillac pays attention to, 228; identification of, 297n18; at Josée's home, 62, 153; life summaries on, 64, 65, 286; love for Merleau-Ponty, 96–97, 103, 108, 110, 180, 231, 321n257; Luxembourg Gardens outings with with, 141, 191; makes friends with Gégé, 327n327; Meyrignac vacation, 273, 278;

Beauvoir, Henriette-Hélène Bertrand de (Poupette) (Beauvoir's sister) (*continued*): need for approval of, 41; new year thoughts for, 119; outings with, 27, 54, 148, 159, 210, 223, 226–27; outings with Sartre, 264; outings with Sartre and Beauvoir, 264; paintings and drawings by, 51, 143, 160, 163, 243; party at school of, 241; at school event, 123; singing with, 166, 212, 213, 246; spends evening with Sartre, 242; Stépha discusses, 110; at Stépha's, 39, 59, 76, 246; theater outings with, 108; visits Madeleine Blomart, 230; visits Maheus, 225; visit to home of Madeleine Blomart, 230; working, 126

Beauvoir, Marguerite (Beauvoir's aunt), 28, 298n26

Beauvoir, Simone de: Castor nickname for, 288, 332n440; death of grandfather, 183, 186–87, 188, 195, 197; drinks alcohol for first time, 282, 335n496; future plans, 288–91, 294–95; life summaries, 62–66, 285–88, 291–94; return to Paris (1928), 23–26; Sartre supports, 257; vocation experience, 236–39; as Walkyrie, 248, 279, 280

Beauvoir as female scholar: Beauvoir's thoughts on, 75, 93, 111, 260; Gandillac on, 122; German man on, 54, 62; Maheu discusses, 208; Sartre on, 254; Zaza discusses, 209

Beauvoir's academic progress: *agrégation* oral exams, 3, 260; *agrégation* preparation, 46, 245, 248–49, 250–51, 252, 333n458; *agrégation* written exams, 228–29, 230, 257, 334n473; Gandillac on, 111, 150; general mathematics degree, 323n283; life summaries on, 63, 64, 65, 66, 286, 287, 288, 312n164; Merleau-Ponty on, 71; student-teaching internship, 125, 126, 139, 326n18

Beauvoir's academic progress. *See also diplôme*

Beauvoir's fiction: ideas for, 40, 93, 160, 180, 184, 191; as influence on Sartre, 2; influences on, 301n43, 310n138; plans

for writing, 186; and self-help as focus of Beauvoir's diary, 12

Beauvoir's fiction. *See also specific titles*

Becquerel (Antoine Henri or Jean), 41, 305n84

Bedel, Maurice, 73, 314n183

The bedouin's daughter [*Fille du bédouin*] (Barde), 147, 328n362

Béhaine, René, 115, 325n302

Being and Nothingness (Sartre), 2

Belleville. *See Équipes Sociales*

Benson, Robert Hugh, 270, 334n482

Bergson, Henri: Beauvoir studies, 41, 66, 67, 70; Eveski discusses, 124; Miquel discusses, 193; overview, 305n84; satirical tract against, 193, 195, 331n416

Le bergsonisme, une mystification philosophique [Bergsonism, a philosophical mystification] (Politzer), 193, 331n416

Besnard, Henri, 117, 123, 167

Beucler, André, 75, 315n189

Bibesco, Elizabeth, 123, 326n314

Bibichon, 67, 72, 73

Bible, 219, 332n434

Bibliothèque Ste. Geneviève, 70, 125, 134, 151, 154

Bibliothèque Victor Cousin, 70, 73, 90, 98, 320n245

"Le bien" [The Supremacy of Good] (Plato), 109, 323n286

Big sister [*La grande soeur*] (Zak), 89, 319n236

The Birth of Venus [*Naissance de Venus*] (Botticelli), 258

Blèche [Blech] (Rochelle), 122, 326n312

Blinded Kings [*Les rois aveugles*] (Kessel), 196

Bliss [*Félicité*] (Mansfield), 191, 205, 331n409

Bloch, Ernst, 85, 317n208

Blomart de Prandières, Madeleine: Beauvoir charmed by, 232; Beauvoir's correspondence with, 60; and Beauvoir's vocation experience, 238; brief encounters with, 242, 258; diary entries addressed to, 39; happiness of, 131,

132; husband of, 168; life summaries on, 64, 65, 287; and marriage, 219; on physical intimacy, 32; at Poupette's school party, 241; on Stépha's engagement, 125; visits to home of, 229–30, 264

Blondel, Charles, 206, 331n424

Blondel, Maurice, 66, 134, 312n165

Bobino, 148

Bohemian fiction, 310n138

Boigne, J., 35

Boismond, Renée, 182, 192

La Boîte à Musique, 264

Boivin, Leo, 71, 150, 155, 161, 162, 189, 215, 224

Le Bon Marché, 32, 41, 59, 263

Borne, 155, 169, 202, 215, 218, 260

Boschard, 191

Botticelli, Sandro, 258

Bouglé, Célestin Charles Alfred, 161, 202, 215

Boulenger, Elisabeth, 71, 232

Boulogne woods pond [Étang du bois de Boulogne] (Gilles), 89, 319n239

Boutroux, Émile, 225, 227, 245, 262, 263, 333n458

Boutroux, Pierre, 90, 113

Boys and Murderers [Enfants et meurtriers; Knaben und Morder] (Ungar), 30, 299n37

Brasserie Weber, 25, 296n10

Bréhier, Émile, 73, 76, 86, 122, 155, 163, 169, 223

Breton, André, 110, 324n291

Brochard, Victor, 206

La brodeuse [The embroiderer] (Lhôte), 89, 319n235

Browning, Robert, 306n95

Bruneau de Laborie, 241

Brunschvicg, Léon: on Beauvoir's diplôme, 223, 315n192; Beauvoir studies works by, 37, 46, 53, 55–56, 60, 61, 70, 260, 314n178; brings unexpected pleasures, 55–56; class of, 73, 76, 86, 97, 103, 122, 163, 205; dispute with Marcel, 193; Gandillac has discussion with,

163; gatherings with, 130, 156, 169, 286; Laporte on, 134; Merleau-Ponty discusses, 139; overview, 306–7n102; term paper to, 214

The Burial of Phocion [L'enterrement de Phocion] (Poussin), 50

Buridan, Jean, 251, 334n468

Burnouf, 205

Byron, Lord, 236

Le cadavre vivant [The Living Corpse] (Tolstoy), 73–74, 314n184

Caird, Edward, 26, 30, 31, 296n12, 299n35

Caliban parle [Caliban speaks] (Guéhenno), 241, 333n453

Canguilhem, Georges, 193

Le Carillon, 264

Carra, 85, 86, 101, 105

Carrière, Eugène, 89, 319n237

La carrière de Beauchamp [Beauchamp's Career] (Meredith), 117, 326n306

Cassandre, 258, 334n474

Castor nickname, 288, 332n440

Catherine, ou Une vie sans joie [A life without joy] (Renoir), 141, 328n355

Catholicism: Beauvoir argues with Poupette about, 259; Beauvoir's rejection of, 32, 62, 137, 164, 166, 259, 287; Josée discusses, 137; and self-help as focus of Beauvoir's diary, 6; Stépha discusses, 31, 32, 40

Cavalcanti, 125, 326n319

Caveau de la Bolée, 151

Les caves de Vatican [Lafcadio's Adventures] (Gide), 161, 329n378

Cazamian, Françoise, 62, 137

Cendrars, Blaise, 194

Cervantes, Miguel de, 166

Cézanne, Paul, 89, 152

Chadourne, Louis, 85, 317n208

La chair et le sang [Flesh and Blood] (Mauriac), 159

Champigneulles, Jacques: affair of, 7, 170–74, 175, 177, 178–79, 181, 182, 184, 219; Aunt Germaine reminds Beauvoir of, 67; Aunt Germaine speaks of, 68–69;

Champigneulles, Jacques (*continued*): Beauvoir compares Maheu to, 156, 203, 245; Beauvoir compares Merleau-Ponty to, 176; Beauvoir compares to Riquet, 85; Beauvoir considers telling Stépha about, 48; Beauvoir discusses with Merleau-Ponty, 106, 107; Beauvoir discusses with Riquet, 78–79, 85–86, 316n203; Beauvoir remembers love for, 199, 200; and Beauvoir's choice among loves, 280, 281, 283–84; Beauvoir's correspondence with, 100, 164, 173, 175; and Beauvoir's future plans, 294; Beauvoir's use of *tu* for, 27, 295n3, 296n8; and Beauvoir's vocation experience, 238, 239; Beauvoir thinks of discussing Alain-Fournier with, 51, 217, 221; Beauvoir wishes he would love Merleau-Ponty, 107, 108; Beauvoir worries about seeing, 275, 285; changed relationship with (1926), 63, 312n161; diary entries addressed to, 24, 26, 29, 46, 50, 53, 54–55, 59, 60, 61, 62, 67, 70, 72, 74, 75, 76, 82, 83, 84, 87, 90, 92, 93, 102, 105–6, 108, 117, 124, 127–28, 130, 131–32, 133, 145, 148–50, 159, 168–69, 198–99, 219, 220, 221, 235, 247, 267–68, 273; and *Équipes Sociales,* 39; in eugenic cosmology, 216; expressions of love for, 24, 25, 26, 30, 31, 35–36, 46, 49, 51–52, 69–70, 71, 77–78, 79–81, 88, 91, 95, 110, 118–19, 128–29, 143, 211, 220, 221, 316n204; and future plans, 294; identification of, 295n2; Lacretelle reminds Beauvoir of, 100; life summaries on, 63–64, 65, 285, 287, 292–93, 312n161; Maheu discusses, 234; marriage of, 4, 295n2; Merleau-Ponty discusses, 106, 107; Merleau-Ponty reminds Beauvoir of, 51; Monod discusses, 39; news of staff secretary job in South, 114; new year thoughts for, 118–19; Poupette discusses, 242; Riquet discusses, 78–79, 85–86, 316n203; and self-help as focus of Beauvoir's diary, 10–11;

Stépha discusses, 121; Zaza discusses, 174, 232, 243–44

Chamson, André, 134, 327n336

Le chanteur de jazz [*The Jazz Singer*] (Crosland), 133, 327n334

Chaplin, Charlie, 64, 244, 333n457

Chardonne, Jacques, 189–90, 194, 205, 331nn406, 415

La charité [Charity] (Van Dongen), 88, 319n231

Charles (Beauvoir's cousin), 66

Charlotte (Beauvoir's cousin), 100, 101–2, 275, 321n266

Chartier, Emile-Auguste. *See* Alain

Châtelet, 154

La chatte (ballet), 232, 332n438

Chekov, Anton, 152

Chevalier, Maurice de, 25, 116, 296n7

Chez André, 265

chez Chabin, 253, 263

chez Dupont, 255

Chez Lipp, 163, 230, 245

chez Monnier (bookstore). *See* La Maison des Amis des Livres

Chez Pocardi (café), 55, 61, 67, 145, 162, 170, 196, 207, 210, 213, 215, 225, 311n156

chez Pons, 231

chez Wepler, 265

Childish Things [*Enfantines*] (Larbaud), 190, 217, 331n408

Children's theater (*Teatro dei piccoli*), 123, 326n313

Cicero, 74, 314n185

Ciné-Latin, 91

cinema: *Anny de Montparnasse* [Anny from Montparnasse] (Array), 151, 329n366; *L'argent* [*Money*] (L'herbier), 137, 328n350; *Au temps des cerises, ou Fanchette* [The time of the cherries, or Fanchette], 141, 328n356; *Autour de L'argent* [*About Money*] (L'herbier), 134, 327n342; *Catherine, ou Une vie sans joie* [A life without joy] (Renoir), 141, 328n355; *Le chanteur de jazz* [*The Jazz Singer*] (Crosland), 133, 327n334;

Contrastes, Everest et amitié [Contrasts, Everest, and friendship], 164; *Crise* (Pabst), 116–17, 325n305; Damia singing, 143; *Dr. Jekyll and Mr. Hyde*, 91, 320n250; *Finis terrae* (Epstein), 220, 332n437; *Le gaucho* [The Gaucho], 100, 321n267; *L'invitation au voyage* [Invitation to a voyage] (Dulac), 134–35, 327n342; *La jalousie du barbouillé* [The jealousy of le barbouillé] (Cavalcanti), 125, 326n319; *Lonesome* (Fejos), 125, 326n319; *Mirage de Hollywood*, 220; *Napoléon* (Gance), 197, 331n418; *Nouveaux messieurs* [New gentlemen] (Feyder), 154, 329n369; *The Pilgrim* (Chaplin), 244, 333n457; *Rose d'ombre* [Shadow rose] (Arnoux), 164, 329n383; *Topaze* (Pagnol), 212, 332n427; le Tour de France, 249; *Underworld* [Les nuits de Chicago] (Sternberg), 158, 310n142

le Ciné Max-Lindor, 154

Claude (Jacques's half-brother), 182

Claudel, Paul: Beauvoir quotes from, 33, 87, 301n47, 318n217, 322n277; Beauvoir reads, 159, 270; Josée discusses, 104; on marriage, 195; Merleau-Ponty and Lévi-Strauss discuss, 110; on physical intimacy, 33

Climats [The Climates of Love] (Maurois), 76, 79, 315n191

Closerie des Lilas, 260, 264

Cocteau, Jean, 322n274; Bandi discusses, 135; Beauvoir reads, 158, 166; identification of, 317n208; Maheu discusses, 156; portrait of, 168; Riquet discusses, 85; on silence of the beloved, 316n204; Stépha discusses, 90, 103

Cocteau, Jean. *See* eugenic cosmology

Colette, Sidonie Gabrielle, 114, 325n299

Colin, Paul, 220

Colombe Blanchet (Alain-Fournier), 42, 171, 306n91, 330n393

Combes, Madeleine, 277, 335n489

Comédie des Champs-Elysées, 165

La comédie italienne (Watteau), 141

Commerce, 34, 301–2n53

Communauté Saint-François Xavier, 297n16

compossible worlds, 114, 325n300

Conrad, Joseph, 41, 57, 68, 81, 305n85, 309n133, 313n174

The Constant Nymph [La nymphe au coeur fidèle] (Kennedy), 57, 59, 199, 309–10n138

Contemporary idealism [*L'idéalisme contemporain*] (Brunschvicg), 55–56

The contingency of the Laws of Nature [De la contingence des lois de la nature] (Boutroux), 245, 333n458

Contrastes, Everest et amitié [Contrasts, Everest, and friendship], 164

Le contrat social [The Social Contract] (Rousseau), 252

Copeau, Jacques, 66, 312n166

Les coquettes (Marval), 88, 319n229

La coquille et le clergyman [The Seashell and the Clergyman] (Dulac), 114, 325n297

Cornuché, Eugene, 296n10

La coupe fleurie [The flowering cup] (Marval), 88, 319n229

Coupole, 234

Cournot, Antoine Augustin, 60, 61, 66, 310–11n148

Crane, Brent, 19n23

Crevel, René, 155

Le crime des justes [The Crime of the Just] (Chamson), 134, 327n336

Crise (Pabst), 116–17, 325n305

The Critical Philosophy of Immanuel Kant (Caird), 26, 30, 31, 296n12, 299n35

Critique of Pure Reason (Kant), 37

Croce, Benedetto, 3, 31, 300n38

Cromeydre-le-vieil (Romains), 161, 163, 329n380

Crosland, Alan, 327n334

le cult de moi (self-worship), 303n64

Damia (Louise Maria Damien), 143, 154, 193, 328n357

Dance at Le Moulin de la Galette [Le moulin de la galette] (Renoir), 152

The dance before the arch [*La danse devant l'arche*] (Franck), 112, 324n296

Dane, Clemence, 31, 300nn39–40

Dangerous Corner [*Tournant dangereux*] (Vlaminck), 201, 331n422

Dangerous Liaisons [*Les liaisons dangereuses*] (Laclos), 121, 326n309

Daniélou, Jean, 75, 111, 218

Daniel-Rops (Henri Jules Charles Petiot), 71, 314n179

La danse devant l'arche [The dance before the arch] (Franck), 112, 324n296

Daphne Adeane (Baring), 57, 310n139

The Dark Journey (*Léviathan*, Green), 142

da Vinci, Leonardo, 138, 142, 251

Davos, 146, 150, 202

Death in Venice (Mann), 35, 61, 302n57

Death of the father [*La mort du père*] (du Gard), 166, 330n388

Debrix, Jean. *See* Delrive, Jean

de Chamonix, 113

Degas, Edgar, 152

Le déjeuner [The lunch] (Monet), 152

De la contingence des lois de la nature [*The contingency of the Laws of Nature*] (Boutroux), 245, 333n458

Delbos, Victor, 27, 74

Delrive, Jean, 78, 85, 101, 105, 167, 172

Delteil, Joseph, 41, 45, 305n86

Départ [Departure] (Beauvoir), 93, 320–21n254

Départ [Departure] (Gantillon), 95, 101, 321n255

de Ravinel, M., 100, 144

De Rerum Natura [On the Nature of Things] (Lucretius), 313n171

Desnos, Robert, 27, 298n22

Desvallières, George, 89

Détective, 224, 251

Deux Magots (café), 202, 249, 255

Dialogue avec A. Gide [Dialogue with A. Gide] (Du Bos), 231, 233

Diary of a Philosophy Student (Beauvoir): diarist's markings in, 18n10; *Memoirs of a Dutiful Daughter* as rewrite of, 1–2, 18n8; translations of, 295n1; use of *tu* and *vous* in, 295n3, 296n8

Dieu et Mammon [*God and Mammon*] (Mauriac), 165–66

diplôme, 318n219; Beauvoir corrects, 189; Beauvoir dictates, 182; Beauvoir sits before without writing a word, 88; Beauvoir tackles, 161; Beauvoir works all day on, 160; Brunschvicg on, 223, 315n192; content of, 315–16n192; evening with, 222; exam for, 224; Gandillac discusses, 150; progress on, 125, 163; proposal accepted, 105; results for, 224, 288; timing of, 3; at typist, 174, 330n397

Dix-huitième année [Eighteenth year] (Prévost), 57, 309n137

do list, 288–91

Dôme (restaurant-bar), 78, 105, 153, 189, 235, 264, 267, 301n51

Dominique (Fromentin), 27, 297n19

Dominique's (café), 235

Don Quixote (Cervantes), 166

d'Ors y Roviro, Eugenio, 134, 327n335

dos Passos, John, 138, 247

Dr. Jekyll and Mr. Hyde, 91, 320n250

Dr. Jekyll and Mr. Hyde (film), 91, 320n250

Drouin, 127

Drucher, Monique, 38, 46

Dubois, Germaine (Gégé): bar outings with, 130–31, 136–37, 167; brief encounters with, 180; death of father, 189; identification of, 327n327; life summaries on, 286; outings with, 174, 191, 226; at Poupette's school party, 241; singing with, 212; visit to Stépha with, 246

Du Bos, Charles, 139, 140, 141, 231, 233, 234, 328n353

Ducassé, Alain, 71, 122, 153

Du côté de Guermantes, [*The Guermantes Way*] (Proust), 181

du Fraisaix, M., 106, 323n282

du Gard, Martin, 166, 330n388

Duhamel, Jean-Marie-Constant, 30, 84, 90, 299n35

Duhem, Pierre, 38, 45, 77, 303n70, 315n192

Dulac, Germaine, 114, 134–35, 197, 325n297, 327n342
Duncan, Isadora, 185, 331n404
Duncan, Raymond, 100, 321n268
Dunoyer De Segonzac, André, 88
Dupont, Ewald Andre, 310n144
Dürer, Albrecht, 50
Dusty Answer [Poussière] (Lehmann), 251, 333n467

The Ebb Tide (Stevenson), 26
L'école de femmes [The School for Wives.] (Gide), 144, 328n359
Eddington, Arthur Stanley, 46, 307n102
Eighteenth year [Dix-huitième année] (Prévost), 57, 309n137
Einstein, Albert, 41, 305n84
Eleven chapters on Plato [Onze chapitres sur Platon] (Alain), 90
Eliot, George, 199, 273, 276, 331n420, 335nn484, 487
Elpénor (Giraudoux), 110, 324n289
Eluard, Paul, 159
The embroiderer [La brodeuse] (Lhôtc), 89, 319n235
L'enfant chargé de chaines [Young Man in Chains] (Mauriac), 27, 297n17
Enfantines [Childish Things] (Larbaud), 190, 217, 331n408
Enfants et meurtriers [Knaben und Morder; Boys and Murderers] (Ungar), 30, 299n37
L'enterrement de Phocion [The Burial of Phocion] (Poussin), 50
L'envoûté [The Moon and Sixpence] (Maugham), 132, 327n331
L'épée à dragon (Paulémile-Pissaro), 88, 318n222
Epicurus, 75, 260, 315n188
L'épithalame [Wedding song] (Chardonne), 194, 205, 331n415
Epstein, Jean, 220, 332n437
Équipes Sociales: action committee, 46, 59, 105; Action française disruption, 332n431; Beauvoir's introduction to, 63; meeting for, 218; overview, 304n77

Équipes Sociales. See Équipes Sociales study group (Belleville)
Équipes Sociales study group (Belleville): Beauvoir reads Tristan et Yseult, 109; discussion on Foch's burial, 139; friends accompany to, 56, 99; life summaries on, 64, 65; Monod at, 76, 121; reminds Beauvoir of Jacques, 39
Er, l'Arménien [Er, the Armenian] (Sartre), 264
L'esprit des lois [The Spirit of the Laws] (Montesquieu), 60, 311n151
Étang du bois de Boulogne [Boulogne woods pond] (Gilles), 89, 319n239
Les Étapes de la philosophie mathématiques [Stages of Mathematical Philosophy] (Brunschvicg), 55–56
The eternal Gospel. Study on Michelet [L'évangile éternel. Étude sur Michelet] (Guéhenno), 124, 326n315
L'éthique à Nicomaque [Nicomachean Ethics] (Aristotle), 250, 333n464
"L'étoile de mer" [Starfish] (Desnos), 27
Eugenes. See eugenic cosmology
eugenic cosmology (Maheu): Beauvoir cites, 163, 234; Beauvoir's thoughts on, 216; drawing Eugenes, 135, 224; elements of, 328n346, 329n382; Gandillac discusses, 199; Jacques in, 216; Maheu discusses, 206, 208–9, 249; overview, 330n387; Sartre discusses, 249
Européen, 147, 153, 193
Européen (bar), 147, 153, 193
L'évangile éternel. Étude sur Michelet [The eternal Gospel. Study on Michelet] (Guéhenno), 124, 326n315
Evelynes (restaurant), 209, 223, 245
Eveski (the Hungarian) (Bandi): affair with Stépha, 121, 125–26, 129, 133; conversation with, 124–25, 135; interest in Beauvoir, 113; at library, 113, 124, 161; life summaries on, 286; reads his novel to Beauvoir, 145; theater outings with, 123; thesis on melodrama of, 207

L'évolution de la mécanique [*The Evolution of Mechanics*] (Duhem), 38, 45, 303n70

L'expérience humaine [Human experience] (Brunschvicg), 60

Extraits d'un journal [Excerpts from a diary] (Du Bos), 139, 140, 328n353

Fabre, Lucien, 68, 313n174

Falstaff, 257

La famille cornichon [The pickle family] (Beauvoir), 51, 308n116

Fargue, Léon-Paul, 34, 151, 302n53

Fauconnet, Guy-Pierre, 88

Faust (Goethe), 329n375

Favory, André, 88, 318n221

Favre, Ch., 231

Fejos, Paul, 326n319

Félicité [*Bliss*] (Mansfield), 191, 205, 331n409

The female traveler [*La voyageuse*] (Picasso), 142

La femme à la rose [Woman with a rose] (Favory), 88, 318n221

La femme nue [The nude woman] (Renoir), 152

Femmes (Les sept soeurs) [Women (The seven sisters)] (Michaëlis), 149, 329n365

Fernandez, Ramón, 65, 115, 139, 234

Le feutre vert [*The Green Hat*] (Arlen), 328n361; Beauvoir cites, 146, 192; Beauvoir lends to Maheu, 201, 203, 206; Maheu discusses, 208; Maheu wants to buy for wife, 225

Feyder, Jacques, 154, 329n369

Fille du bédouin [The bedouin's daughter] (Barde), 147, 328n362

films seen. *See* cinema

Finis terrae (Epstein), 220, 332n437

Flandrin, Jean-Hippolyte, 88

Flaubert, Gustave, 52

Flesh and Blood [*La chair et le sang*] (Mauriac), 159

La Fleur de Lys (restaurant), 164, 234

The flowering cup [*La coupe fleurie*] (Marval), 88, 319n229

Foch, Ferdinand, 139

Fontainebleau, 228

Force of Circumstance (Beauvoir), 2

Forrain, Mademoiselle, 46

Foujita, Tsuguharu, 91, 131, 141, 232, 236

The Four Agreements (Ruiz), 14

Fourier, Germaine (Beauvoir's aunt), 67, 68–69, 70, 181, 182, 313n169

Fournier, Henri-Alban. *See* Alain-Fournier

Fragonard, Jean-Honoré, 141–42

France, Anatole, 246

Franck, Henri, 112, 324n296

Fromentin, Eugène, 27, 297n19

Fruits of the Earth [*Les nourritures terrestres*] (Gide), 90

Gaius Marius, 187

Galais, Franck de, 188

Galois, Daniel: attends Gandillac's party, 182; attends Merleau-Ponty's party, 111–12; Beauvoir's feelings about, 156, 206, 241; Beauvoir's infatuation with, 112, 113–14, 115, 116, 130, 183–84, 190; brief encounters with, 55, 110, 132, 207, 260; *diplôme*, 223; discusses Barrès, 122–23; discusses Gandillac, 114; discusses life, 198; discusses Merleau-Ponty, 114; does not arrive, 115; enjoys Guéhenno, 241; at *Équipes Sociales* meeting, 218; Josée discusses, 192; at library, 122; life summaries on, 286; Maheu dislikes, 207; Merleau-Ponty discusses, 246; new year thoughts for, 119; reminds Beauvoir of Barrès, 39–40, 111; visits Beauvoir at home, 126; Zaza admires, 222

Galois, Évariste, 202

Galsworthy, John, 122

Gamochaud, 71

Gance, Abel, 197, 331n418

Gandillac, Mademoiselle, 111

Gandillac, Maurice de: art gallery outings with, 236; attends Merleau-Ponty's party, 111, 112; with Beauvoir and Maheu, 206–7, 213; Beauvoir compares to Maheu, 206; Beauvoir compares to Merleau-Ponty, 174; Beauvoir dreams about, 163–64; Beauvoir feels distance from, 217, 218, 233, 239; on Beauvoir's academic progress, 111, 150; Beauvoir's father likes, 163; Beauvoir's feelings about, 75, 77, 79, 84, 93, 147, 156, 183, 184, 188; Beauvoir's fondness for, 155, 164; brief encounters with, 129, 134; in class, 73, 76, 82, 99, 104, 154, 155, 163, 195, 201, 204, 205, 215; conversations with, 72, 154, 161, 163, 174, 189, 195, 198–99, 202, 206–7, 210, 220, 223; discusses *agrégation*, 47, 75, 122; discusses Beauvoir's *diplôme*, 150; discusses eugenic cosmology, 199; discusses Giraudoux, 71, 180; discusses Jacques's affair, 178–79, 181; discusses literature, 103; discusses marriage, 93, 94, 163, 170, 198, 223; discusses Plato, 109, 122; discusses Poupette, 220, 233; discussess Davos, 202; at *Équipes Sociales* meeting, 218; essays by, 196, 198; Fontainebleau picnic with, 228; and future plans, 294; Galois discusses, 114; humility of, 165; Josée discusses, 49, 192; lake evening with, 250; at library, 70, 74, 83, 110, 112–13, 160, 181, 185, 194, 216, 220; life summaries on, 285, 286, 287; Luxembourg Gardens outings with, 148; Maheu discusses, 207; Merleau-Ponty discusses, 233; new year thoughts for, 115, 119; *Les nouvelles littéraires* interview with, 90; outings with, 130, 226–27, 267; Palais Royal Gardens outings with, 196, 198, 204, 210; party at home of, 182; pays attention to Poupette, 228; at Poupette's school party, 241; relationship with Monique Merleau-Ponty, 179–80, 258; Sartre's nickname for, 224, 332n439; Sartre's song about, 266, 334n480; speaks of Beauvoir to Sartre, 198, 213; stays for dinner, 163; visits Beauvoir at home, 126; visits Beauvoir in Meyrignac, 273; and written *agrégation* exams, 229; Zaza discusses, 169–70, 180, 231

Gantillon, Simon, 95, 101, 321n255

The garden of Berenice [*Le jardin de Bérénice*] (Barrès), 115, 325n301
Garric, Robert, 63–64, 118, 218, 304n77
Gaspar Ruiz (Conrad), 68, 313n174
Le gaucho [*The Gaucho*], 100, 321n267
Gégé. *See* Dubois, Germaine
Geometry and Induction: Containing Geometry in the Sensible World and The Logical Problem of Induction (Nicod), 31, 34, 300n41
Gérassi, Fernand: bar outings with, 92; Beauvoir's fondness for, 113, 122, 151; Beauvoir's initial impressions of, 47; Beauvoir visits at home, 94, 100, 137, 151; brief encounters with, 47; discusses Alain-Fournier, 94; discusses art, 90, 91; engagement to Stépha, 125–26, 131, 215; gathering at home of, 246; gives Poupette advice on paintings, 143; identification of, 307n104; memories of, 235; nickname for Beauvoir ("Hat"), 246, 333n459; paintings by, 243; relationship with Stépha, 48–49, 56, 66, 91
Germaine, Aunt. *See* Fourier, Germaine
Gide, André, 329n378; Beauvoir finds solace in, 173; Beauvoir lends to Maheu, 161; Beauvoir quotes from, 54, 77, 226, 316n194, 332nn442,444; Beauvoir studies, 140, 144, 159; Du Bos on, 231, 233; Gandillac discusses, 90; on individualism, 231; as influence on Beauvoir, 308–9n127; Maheu discusses, 162; on Montaigne, 138; Pontrémoli discusses, 70; Riquet discusses, 85; as spiritual stimulant, 140
Gilles, Yvonne, 89, 319n239
Gilles (Watteau), 141
Giraudoux, Jean, 324n289; Beauvoir compares herself to character from, 79; Beauvoir emotional about, 212; Beauvoir loves novels of, 90, 98, 110; Beauvoir reads, 161, 212; dream inspired by, 26; Gandillac discusses, 71, 180; identification of, 316n201; on marriage, 296–97n15; Riquet discusses, 85; Stépha reads, 46

Gluckmann, Grigory, 89, 141

Goblot, Edmond, 215

God and Mammon [*Dieu et Mammon*] (Mauriac), 165–66

Godard, Jean-Luc, 251

Goethe, Johann Wolfgang von: Beauvoir quotes from, 81, 85, 160, 316n204, 317n213, 329n375; Beauvoir studies, 154–55; on love, 158; Ludwig on, 154, 329n370; Merleau-Ponty discusses, 161; Stépha discusses, 62

Goethe (Ludwig), 154, 329n370

La grammaire de l'assentiment [*Grammar of Assent*] (Newman), 54, 308n126

Grand Duke. *See* Nizan, Paul

Le grand écart [*The Great Divide*] (Cocteau), 103, 322n274

La grande soeur [Big sister] (Zak), 89, 319n236

Le grand Meaulnes [*The Wanderer*] (Alain-Fournier): Beauvoir compares paintings to, 141, 152; Beauvoir dreams of, 53; Beauvoir reads, 131; Beauvoir thinks about, 192; Gandillac discusses, 93, 198, 199; Fernand Gérassi discusses, 94; Mathieu and Vauthé discuss, 66; men remind Beauvoir of, 283; Riquet discusses, 85; as spiritual stimulant, 140; themes in, 308n121

The Great Divide [*Le grand écar*], (Cocteau), 103, 322n274

Green, Julien, 142, 145

The Green Hat [*Le feutre vert*] (Arlen). *See Le feutre vert*

The Green Parrot [*Le perroquet vert*] (Bibesco), 123, 326n314

Guéhenno, Jean, 124, 218, 241, 246, 326n315, 333n453

Guérin, Charles, 62, 88, 311n159

The Guermantes Way [*Du côté de Guermantes*] (Proust), 181

Hamelin, Octave, 26, 70, 71, 134, 296n14

Hannequin, Arthur, 74, 251, 314n186, 333n466

Hawkins, Coleman, 253, 334n471

Hawthorne, Nathaniel, 145

Hécate (Jouve), 134, 327n338

Hegel, G. W. F., 3, 31

Hélène (Beauvoir's aunt), 186

Heller, Maximilien, 37, 42, 47, 55

Helm, Brigitte, 137

L'herbier, Marcel, 134, 137, 327n342, 328n350

Hévési. *See* Eveski

The Hidden Soul [*L'âme cachée*] (Lacretelle), 56, 309n135

Hippolyte, Jean: Beauvoir feels positive about, 162; brief encounters with, 150, 155; in class, 71, 122, 153; conversation with, 195; discusses Romains, 161; joking about, 169, 215; and written *agrégation* exams, 229

Höffding, Harald, 74, 314n186

Hölderlin, Friedrich, 316n193

Homer, 168, 169, 176, 178

L'homme au cheval gris [*The Man with the Gray Horse*] (Storm), 38, 303n69

Hugo, Victor, 122, 152

Human Experience [*L'expérience humaine*] (Brunschvicg), 60

Hume, David: Beauvoir finds boring, 51; Beauvoir finds skepticism interesting, 134; Beauvoir studies, 46, 47, 49, 53, 54, 124, 125, 202, 224; LaPorte on, 134; Maheu discusses, 214, 224

The Humiliation of the Father [*Le père humilié*] (Claudel), 104, 322n277

the Hungarian. *See* Eveski

la Huppa, 193

Hura, John, 88

Husserl, Edmund, 66, 312–13n167

Hylton, Jack, 253, 334n470

L'idéal du mathématicien [The mathematician's ideal] (Boutroux), 90, 113

L'idéalisme contemporain [Contemporary idealism] (Brunschvicg), 55–56

The Imaginary Invalid [*Le malade imaginaire*] (Molière), 131, 327n328 individualism: Beauvoir on Maheu's profession of, 214, 219, 221; Beauvoir's homework paper on, 162; Beauvoir's profession of, 222, 291; and Du Bos, 231; Gandillac discusses, 174; Gide on, 231; Maheu discusses, 156, 164, 216, 222, 249; Miquel discusses, 193

Institut Catholique, 28, 63, 70–71, 74, 83, 91, 92, 125, 145

Institut Sainte-Marie (Neuilly), 63–64, 65, 297n16, 304n77

In the South Seas (Stevenson), 26, 296n11

Introduction à la psychologie collective [sociale] [Introduction to Collective (Social) Psychology], (Blondel), 206, 331n424

les Invalids, 191

L'invitation au voyage [Invitation to a voyage] (Dulac), 134–35, 327n342

L'invitée (Beauvoir), 301n43, 310n138

Jacob, Max, 68, 313n173

Jacobsen, Jens Peter, 57, 309n136

Jacquemont, Mademoiselle, 46, 72

Jacques. See Champigneulles, Jacques

La jalousie du barbouillé [The jealousy of le barbouillé] (Cavalcanti), 125, 326n319

Jammes, Francis, 33, 133, 301n48, 302n61, 327n332

Janson-de-Sailly (high school), 125, 326n318

Le jardin de Bérénice [The garden of Berenice] (Barrès), 115, 325n301

Jardin des Plantes, 201

Un jardin sur l'Oronte (Barrès), 118, 326n307

Jarry, Alfred, 51, 308n116, 324n294

The jealousy of le barbouillé [La jalousie du barbouillé] (Cavalcanti), 125, 326n319

Jean de la Lune [Jean from the moon], 165, 167, 173, 330n386

Jeanne (Beauvoir's cousin), 161, 175, 188, 220, 229, 273, 331n405

Jeanne d'Arc [Joan of Arc] (Delteil), 41, 45, 305n86

Jean Paul, 38, 304n72

Jockey (restaurant-bar), 77, 78, 106, 129, 136–37, 144, 167, 301n51

Jollivet, Simone (Toulouse), 263, 334n477

Jonson, Ben, 101, 108, 322n269

Josée. See Le Cor, Josée

Jouhandeau, Marcel, 103, 322n273

Jouve, Pierre Jean, 134, 172, 330n395

Jungle (bar), 94, 118, 130–31

Kalli, 88

Kant, Immanuel: Basch on, 31, 34, 38, 300n41; Beauvoir studies, 29, 35, 37, 45, 82, 100, 103, 125, 129, 224, 306n97; Beauvoir studies ardently, 39; Boutroux on, 225, 227; Brunschvicg on, 37; Caird on, 26, 30, 31, 296n12, 299n35; Delbos on, 27; Eveski discusses, 124; Maheu discusses, 214, 216; Maheu's notes on, 224; Nabert on, 37; overview, 326n317; Souriau on, 38, 304n71; Stépha and Josée discuss, 52; Valensin on, 38, 304n71

Kant's philosophy [La philosophie de Kant] (Delbos), 27

Keaton, Buster, 68, 249

Kellermann, Bernhard, 34, 302n54

Kennedy, Margaret, 57, 59, 199, 309–10n138

Kessel, Joseph, 196

King Ubu (Ubu Roi, Jarry), 51, 308n116, 324n294

Kipling, Rudyard, 110, 173, 324n291

Klaw, Barbara, 18n8

Knaben und Morder [Enfants et meurtriers; Boys and Murderers] (Ungar), 30, 299n37

Knam (café), 104, 122, 125, 193, 264, 265

Koulak, 257

Labartète, Marie-Madeleine du Moulin de (Lèlette), 67, 313n168

Laclos, Choderlos de, 121, 326n309

Lacoin, Bernard, 226, 227, 332n443

Lacoin, Elisabeth (Zaza): admires Galois, 222; art gallery outing with, 151–52; Beauvoir's correspondence with, 36, 76, 82, 101, 108, 115, 235, 242; Beauvoir's expressions of affection for, 24, 28; and Beauvoir's stress over *agrégation,* 258; and Beauvoir's vocation experience, 238; brief encounters with, 145; cinema outings with, 134–35; conversation with, 223; death of, 4; *Départ* dedicated to, 320n254; dinner at home of, 160; discusses Gandillac, 169–70, 180, 231; discusses Jacques, 174, 232, 243–44; discusses Maheu, 209; discusses Merleau-Ponty, 170, 227–28, 229; discusses Stépha, 59, 60; at *Équipes Sociales* meeting, 218; Fontainebleau picnic with, 228; and future plans, 294; gathering at home of, 71; identification of, 295n5; at library, 247; life summaries on, 63, 64, 65, 66, 285, 286, 288; Luxembourg Gardens outings with, 201, 239, 243; *Memoirs of a Dutiful Daughter* written for girls like, 2; Merleau-Ponty discusses, 246; mother's marriage plans for, 149, 240, 329n364, 333n455; new home of, 332n430; new year thoughts for, 119; outings with, 51, 56, 61–62, 72, 183, 191–92, 226–27, 239; outings with Beauvoir and Stépha, 47–48, 247; outings with Merleau-Ponty and Beauvoir, 218–19, 258; and physical gestures of affection, 33; quotes Tagore, 29, 298–99n30; relationship with Merleau-Ponty, 51, 229, 231–32, 233, 256, 259, 299n34; relationship with mother, 30, 108–9; returns from Bayonne, 144; returns from Germany, 129, 131; sent away to remove from Beauvoir's influence, 135, 327n343; sister's wedding, 149, 328n363; on spiritual awakening, 222–23; on Stépha's engagement, 125; at Stépha's gatherings, 59; study of Baudelaire, 52, 55, 72; supports Beauvoir's academic progress, 3; theater outings with, 130; Tuileries Gardens outings with, 197, 222, 251; visits Beauvoir at home, 163; writes about Merleau-Ponty, 115; and written *agrégation* exams, 229

Lacoin, Germaine (Zaza's sister), 183, 239, 330n402

Lacoin, Madame (Zaza's mother), 30, 108–9, 240, 299n32, 327n343, 329n364, 333n455

Lacoin, Marie-Thérèse (Zon; Zaza's sister), 149, 240, 328n363

Lacombe, 218

Lacretelle, Jacques de, 56, 100, 309n135, 321n265

Lafcadio's Adventures [*Les caves de Vatican*] (Gide), 161, 329n378

Laforgue, Jules: Beauvoir quotes from, 79, 316n199, 317n211; Galois discusses, 111; identification of, 299n31; Josée discusses, 59; Palais Royal Gardens remind Beauvoir of, 30; Riquet discusses, 92; Stépha discusses, 46

Lalande, 134, 145, 153, 166, 175, 197, 225, 229

Lama. *See* Maheu, René

Lambert, Mademoiselle (*Mémoires*). *See* Mercier, Jeanne

Lamb Shapiro, Jessica, 17n4

Lancret, Nicolas, 141

Landowski, Nadine, 133, 163

Landowski, Paul, 133, 327n333

Landscape (Médici), 88, 319n227

Lang, Fritz, 302n55

Lapin Agile, 159

Laporte: Beauvoir finds boring, 82, 95; Beauvoir finds interesting, 103, 124; Beauvoir meets with, 134, 138, 154; class of, 74, 82, 109, 134, 161, 178, 204; consultation with, 134, 178; dream about, 194; identification of, 321n256

Larbaud, Valéry, 34, 190, 217, 302n53, 331n408

Lautmann, 64, 65, 76, 223

Law of Attraction, 7

Layton and Johnstone (piano duo), 192, 225, 253

Le Baladin [The Playboy], 278, 279, 335n491

Lecas, 71

Lecoin, Jeanne, 157

Leçons [Lessons] (Cournot), 160

Leçons de métaphysiques [Lectures on Metaphysics] (Kant), 37

Le Cor, Josée: admires Beauvoir, 198; Beauvoir's fondness for, 49–50, 102, 192; brief encounters with, 28, 44; in class, 82, 86, 155, 163, 205; conversation with, 223; discusses Beauvoir's friendship, 210–11; discusses Catholicism, 137; discusses Claudel, 104; discusses Galois, 192; discusses Gandillac, 49, 192; discusses Jacques's affair, 174, 180; discusses Maheu, 210; discusses Merleau-Ponty, 192, 241–42; discusses Valéry, 202; and future plans, 294; gatherings at home of, 62, 153; identification of, 298n27; life summaries on, 65, 285, 287, 288; love for Merleau-Ponty, 95–97, 102, 103, 106–7, 108, 109, 126, 129, 158, 175–76, 180, 241–42; Luxembourg Gardens outings with, 196, 211, 222; Maheu gives drawing to, 215; outings with, 52, 137, 226–27, 228, 245; at Poupette's school party, 241; reproaches Beauvoir for being "social," 223; sadness of, 109, 126, 129; at Stépha's gatherings, 59; theater outings with, 131; at Zaza's home, 71

Lectures on Metaphysics [Leçons de métaphysiques] (Kant), 37

Le Fauconnier, Henri, 89, 319n234

Legend (Dane), 31, 300nn39–40

Lehmann, Rosamund, 251, 333n467

Leibniz, Gottfried Wilhelm: Beauvoir explicates, 264; Beauvoir's diplôme on, 3, 315–16n192; Beauvoir studies, 145, 151, 153, 154; on compossible worlds, 114, 325n300; Mercier's dissertation on, 77; Mercier writes dissertation on, 77; Nizan draws, 197, 248; petits camarades study, 1, 234, 247, 248

Lempicka, Tamara de, 88, 319n226

Lenormand, Henri-René, 135, 328n345

leprechaun image, 271, 277, 278, 334–35n483

Le Ricolais, Robert, 88, 318n224

Le Roy, LaPorte on, 134

Le Scouezec, Maurice, 90, 320n242

Lessons (Leçons, Cournot), 160

Léviathan [The Dark Journey] (Green), 142

Levinsky: bar outings with, 84–85, 86, 101, 105; Beauvoir's fondness for, 113; love for Beauvoir, 122; outings with, 113, 235; at Stépha's home, 94

Lévi-Strauss, Claude: brief encounters with, 132; in class, 71; discusses surrealism, 125; at library, 135; outings with, 130; and student-teaching internships, 110, 116, 126, 127, 286

Lévy, Georgette: agrégation preparation, 62; on Beauvoir's diplôme, 223; Beauvoir's friendship with, 64; Beauvoir's hostility toward, 215; on career ambition, 140; condemns Beauvoir, 195; envies Beauvoir, 230; Maheu discusses, 170, 207; malicious gossip of, 163; Merleau-Ponty refuses to discuss, 176; sudden chill with, 65

Lhôte, André, 89, 319n235

Les liaisons dangereuses [Dangerous Liaisons] (Laclos), 121, 326n309

Libres propos (Alain), 37, 193, 303n66

la libriairie Picart (Mémoires). See Picard's

Life of Goya [Vie de Goya] (d'Ors y Roviro), 134, 327n335

Life of Quintus Fixlein [Vie de Quintus Fixlein] (Jean Paul), 38, 304n72

The Life of St. Alexis [La vie de Saint Alexis], 93, 320n253

life summaries, 62–66, 285–88, 291–94

Lilacs [Lilas] (Gilles), 89, 319n239

Lili (Beauvoir's aunt), 25, 46, 251, 331n421

Linder, Max, 99, 321n262

The Living Corpse [Le cadavre vivant] (Tolstoy), 73–74, 314n184

Locke, John, 145, 148

Lonesome (Fejos), 125, 326n319

Lord Jim (Conrad), 41, 57, 305n85, 309n133

Losson, M., 144–45

Louise (Beauvoir's childhood maid), 82

Louvre, 50, 151–52

love, Alain-Fournier on, 308n121

Love [*Amour*] (Praxiteles), 151

love: Beauvoir's thoughts on, 199–201, 217, 221; Dane on, 300n39; vs. disgust, 44; Fromentin on, 297n19; Mauriac on, 297n17; Rivière on, 301n43; and self-help as focus of Beauvoir's diary, 10–12

love. *See* Champigneulles, Jacques, Beauvoir's expressions of love for; marriage; *specific people*

Lucian, 85, 317n209

Lucien Leuwen (Stendahl), 216

Lucretius, 75, 313n171, 315n188

Ludwig, Emil, 37, 154, 303n65, 329n370

The Lunch [*Le déjeuner*] (Monet), 152

Luxembourg Gardens: beauty in, 24, 34–35, 215, 234; Beauvoir reads alone in, 97, 133, 144, 145, 154, 155, 159, 160, 195, 234; Beauvoir spends time alone in, 205, 225–26; Beauvoir talks to Sardinian in, 166; Beauvoir walks anguished in, 164; group outings in, 229; outings with cousins, 175; outings with Gandillac, 148; outings with Josée, 196, 211, 222; outings with Marie-Louise, 201; outings with Merleau-Ponty, 100, 145, 199, 246, 261; outings with Miquel, 209; outings with Poupette, 141, 191; outings with Sartre, 259, 260, 263, 264; outings with Stépha, 101; outings with Zaza, 201, 239, 243; Sartre argument in, 2–3, 259; watching a child at dusk in, 164

Mabille, Elisabeth (*Mémoires*). *See* Lacoin, Elisabeth

Mac Orlan, Pierre, 103, 322n275

Madame Nizan, 249

Mademoiselle Else (Schnitzler), 34, 302n56

Madonna [*La vierge*] (da Vinci), 142

Magda, 170–74, 175, 177, 181, 219. *See also* Champigneulles, Jacques, affair of

Magdeleine (Beauvoir's cousin): art gallery outings with, 88; brief encounters with, 72; dinner at Aunt Marguerite's with, 161; at family gathering for grandfather's memorial, 187; identification of, 331n405; lunch with, 73; Meyrignac vacation, 270, 274, 278; outings with, 159, 175

Maheu, Inès (wife of René Maheu), 200, 214, 219, 220, 221, 225, 242, 243, 261, 264

Maheu, René: accepts Merleau-Ponty, 207; admires Beauvoir's openness, 208, 210; *agrégation* preparation, 227, 234, 248–49, 250–51, 333n465; Beauvoir compares to Gandillac, 206; Beauvoir compares to Jacques, 156, 203, 245; Beauvoir compares to Sartre, 257, 260; Beauvoir lends Arlen book to, 201, 203, 206; Beauvoir lends Gide book to, 161; Beauvoir on individualism of, 214, 219, 221; and Beauvoir's choice among loves, 262, 268, 271–73, 274–75, 280, 281, 283–84; Beauvoir's correspondence with, 258, 262; Beauvoir's desire for, 199–200, 201–3, 206–7, 212–14, 216–17, 241, 255, 256, 261–62, 263–64, 269; Beauvoir's father has hilarious conversation with, 234; Beauvoir's feelings about, 156–57, 162–63, 183, 195–96; Beauvoir's fondness for, 145, 155, 170; Beauvoir's initial impressions of, 135; Beauvoir's intimacy with, 268; and Beauvoir's relationship with Sartre, 254–55, 256, 261, 262; and Beauvoir's vocation experience, 238; Boivin quotes, 189; brief encounters with, 160, 180; and Castor nickname, 288, 332n440; in class, 214, 215; conversations with, 217–18, 227; diary entries addressed to, 161, 212–13, 252, 274; *diplôme*, 224; discusses Beauvoir's friendship, 207–8; discusses Beauvoir's homework, 163; discusses eugenic cosmology, 206, 208–9, 249; discusses individualism, 156, 164,

216, 222, 249; discusses Jacques, 234; discusses marriage, 162, 222; discusses Merleau-Ponty, 157; discusses Sartre, 249, 282; dislikes Galois, 207; dislikes Stépha, 207; distance from Riquet, 167; explicates text in Brunschvicg's class, 122; flunks *agrégation* written exams, 257; and future plans, 294; individualism of, 214, 216, 219, 221, 222; Inèz wife of, 243; Josée discusses, 210; leaves for vacation, 262; lectures by, 185; at library, 181, 215; life summaries on, 286–87; memories of, 214–15; Meyrignac visit, 281–82; outings with, 196–97, 216, 224–25, 244–45, 249; Palais Royal Gardens outings with, 164, 174, 213, 224, 234; *petits camarades* outings, 252, 253–56; Poupette discusses, 234; reading recommended by, 289; at Sartre's gathering, 253; system of, 162, 164; takes bus with Beauvoir, 150; on values, 198; visit to home of, 225, 332n441; wants to introduce Sartre to Beauvoir, 196–97, 234, 247; wife of, 200, 214, 219, 220, 221, 225, 242, 243, 261, 264; wife's jealousy, 261; and written *agrégation* exams, 228–29, 230; Zaza discusses, 209

Maheu, René. *See* eugenic cosmology

Maillet, 153

Maillol, Aristide, 89

La Maison des Amis des Livres (chez Monnier), 30, 89, 110, 114, 117, 138, 151, 168, 189, 211, 222, 299n36

Maisons à Corte (Le Ricolais), 88, 318n224

Le malade imaginaire [*The Imaginary Invalid*] (Molière), 131, 327n328

Mallarmé, Stéphane, 26, 296n11

Mallutée, C., 100

Manceron, Geneviève, 63

Manet, Édouard, 152

Manhattan Transfer (dos Passos), 138, 247

Mann, Heinrich, 45, 306n98

Mann, Thomas, 26, 31, 35, 61, 296n13, 302n57

Man Ray, 27, 28, 298n27

Mansfield, Katherine, 191, 205, 331n409

The Man with the Gray Horse [*L'homme au cheval gris*] (Storm), 38, 303n69

Marcel, Gabriel, 139, 193, 234

Marguerite (Beauvoir's aunt), 161, 175, 188

Marie, Aunt (Jacques's grandmother), 114

Marie-Louise, 50, 53, 60, 67, 95, 123, 170, 201, 234

The Mark of Zorro [*Le signe de Zorro*], 91, 320n249

marriage: Beauvoir's thoughts on, 72, 193, 195, 211, 219; Dane on, 300n39; Gandillac discusses, 93, 94, 163, 170, 198, 223; Giraudoux on, 296–97n15; Maheu discusses, 162, 222; Merleau-Ponty discusses, 97–98, 176; Sartre discusses, 266; Stépha discusses, 53

Marval, Jacqueline, 88, 191, 319n229, 331, 331n410

Maternité (Vaudou), 88, 318n225

The mathematician's ideal [*L'idéal du mathématicien*] (Boutroux), 90, 113

Mathieu, Thérèse, 66

Matin de chasse [Morning hunt] (Flandrin), 88

Matisse, Henri, 55, 89, 191

Mauguë, 65, 76, 127, 222

Mauriac, François: Beauvoir finds humane, 36; Beauvoir finds weak and distressing, 27; Beauvoir intoxicated by, 159; Beauvoir quotes from, 219, 297n17, 332n433; Beauvoir reads, 29, 142, 165–66; Gandillac discusses, 90, 180; Merleau-Ponty discusses, 37, 145; on physical intimacy, 33; Pontrémoli discusses, 70; Stépha discusses, 32; on systems, 298n29

Maurois, André, 76, 79, 315n191, 330n396

Maurras, Charles-Marie-Photius, 124, 246

Le mauvais sort [Bad fortune] (Beucler), 75, 315n189

Ma vie [*My Life*] (Duncan), 185

Maxence, Edgard, 218

Maxim's (bistro), 25, 296n10

Max Linder cinema, 244

Médici, Osvaldo, 88, 319n227

Mémoires d'une jeune fille rangée [*Memoirs of a Dutiful Daughter*] (Beauvoir), 1, 2, 18n8, 295n2. *See also specific pseudonyms*

Memoirs of My Dead Life [*Mémoires de ma vie morte*] (Moore), 115, 325n302

Mercier, Jeanne: Beauvoir's correspondence with, 117, 235; Beauvoir sees as imprisoned, 230; Beauvoir visits, 28–29; dissertation on Leibniz, 77; identification of, 297n16; invitation from, 26–27; life summaries on, 63, 64, 65

Meredith, George, 117, 326n306

Mère Marie [*Mother Mary*] (Mann), 45, 306n98

Mérinoff, Dmitri, 318n223

Merleau-Ponty, Maurice: accompanies Beauvoir to l'École Normale, 105; address of, 325n303; attends Gandillac's party, 182; bar outings with, 106; Beauvoir compares to Gandillac, 174; Beauvoir compares to Jacques, 176; Beauvoir discusses Maheu with, 157; Beauvoir finds of no great interest, 247; Beauvoir's companionship with, 36–37, 76–77; Beauvoir's correspondence with, 35, 45, 125, 144, 145, 185, 200, 225, 241; Beauvoir's feelings about, 73, 75, 79, 103–4, 147, 156, 161, 175–76, 183, 184, 204, 226; Beauvoir's fondness for, 130, 135; Beauvoir shows Zaza's letter to, 82; and Beauvoir's stress over *agrégation*, 258; Beauvoir's thoughts of, 59; Beauvoir studies Plato with, 252; and Beauvoir's vocation experience, 238; Beauvoir wishes Jacques would love, 107, 108; brief encounters with, 99, 151, 222, 257, 260, 264; changes science programs for *agrégation*, 107; in class, 104, 223; conversations with, 202, 223; diary entries addressed to, 82–83, 107, 116, 226; *diplôme*, 223, 224; discusses Galois, 246; discusses Gandillac, 233; discusses Jacques, 106, 107; discusses literature, 100; discusses marriage, 97–98, 176; discusses Zaza, 246; at *Équipes Sociales*

meeting, 218; exam preparation, 239; Fontainebleau picnic with, 228; Galois discusses, 114; introduced to Stépha, 47, 55, 61; Josée discusses, 192, 241–42; Josée's love for, 95–97, 102, 103, 106–7, 108, 109, 126, 129, 158, 175–76, 180, 241–42; lake evening with, 250; lectures by, 86; at library, 74, 83; life summaries on, 64, 65, 285, 286, 287, 288, 293; Luxembourg Gardens outings with, 145, 148, 199, 246, 261; Maheu accepts, 207; Maheu discusses, 157; and *Nord*, 42, 47; outings with, 122, 138, 152, 226–27; outings with Zaza and Beauvoir, 218–19, 258; party at home of, 110–12; on physical intimacy, 32; Poupette's love for, 96–97, 103, 108, 110, 180, 231, 321n257; relationship with Zaza, 51, 229, 231–32, 233, 256, 259, 299n34; reminds Beauvoir of Jacques, 51; sister of, 130; socializing with Stépha, 55; Stépha discusses, 110; at Stépha's gatherings, 76; and student-teaching internships, 110, 116, 126–27, 139, 286; supports Beauvoir's academic progress, 3, 71; unrequited love for Beauvoir, 197; visits Beauvoir at home, 126, 163, 194; and written *agrégation* exams, 229; Zaza discusses, 170, 227–28, 229; Zaza writes about, 115

Merleau-Ponty, Monique, 111, 179, 241, 246, 258

Messenger, Ann P., 309n133

Métropolis (Lang), 34, 302n55

Meyerson, Emile, 45, 59, 306n97

Michaëlis, Karin, 149, 329n365

Michel, 78, 85, 86, 92, 105

Michelangelo, 251

Michelet, Jules, 124, 326n315

Milhaud, Gaston, 26

Miller, Hans, 117

The Mill on the Floss (Eliot), 199, 273, 276, 331n420, 335n487, 335nn484, 487

Miquel: bar outings with, 101, 105; Beauvoir's correspondence with, 105, 117; Beauvoir's feelings about, 156, 193–94; Beauvoir's fondness for, 82,

90, 143; brief encounters with, 100, 258; conversations with, 64, 156, 193; life summaries on, 285; new year thoughts for, 119; outings with, 89–90, 154, 209; theater outings with, 123

Mirabeau, 290

Mirage de Hollywood, 220

Modigliani, Amedeo, 91

Moi, Juif [My Jewish self] (Schwob), 138, 328n351

Molinoff, Indre et Loire [*Molinoff or The Count in the Kitchen*] (Bedel), 73, 314n183

Mon amie Nane [My friend Nane] (Toulet), 213, 332n428

Monet, Claude, 152

Money [*L'argent*] (L'herbier), 137, 328n350

Monnier, Adrienne. *See* La Maison des Amis des Livres

Monod, Germaine, 38, 39, 59, 76, 99, 121

Montaigne, 138, 313n171

Montesquieu, 60, 66, 311n151

Montherlant, Henri de, 37, 45, 111, 302n64, 306n98

Monument to Mickiewicz, 165, 330n385

The Moon and Sixpence (*L'envoûté*, Maugham), 132, 327n331

Moore, George, 114, 325, 325nn299, 302

Moravagine (Cendrars), 194

Morel, Madame, 265, 267

Morning Hunt [*Matin de chasse*] (Flandrin), 88

Morris columns, 25, 296n9

La mort du père [Death of the father] (du Gard), 166, 330n388

Mortimers. *See* eugenic cosmology

Mother Mary [*Mère Marie*] (Mann), 45, 306n98

Moulin, Edgard du, 149

Moulin, Xavier du, 65, 71, 111

Le moulin de la galette [*Dance at Le Moulin de la Galette*] (Renoir), 152

Moulin Rouge, 136, 153

Moulin Rouge (cabaret), 136, 153

Musée Carnavalet, 141

Musée du jeu de Paume, 141–42

Musée pédagogique (Museum of Pedagogy), 104, 322n278

Music (Souverbie), 88, 319n230

My friend Nane [*Mon amie Nane*] (Toulet), 213, 332n428

My Jewish self [*Moi, Juif*] (Schwob), 138, 328n351

My Life [*Ma vie*] (Duncan), 185

"Mystère en pleine lumière" ("Mystery in full light"), 160

La mystérieuse aventure [The mysterious adventure] (Santelli), 90, 320n244

Nabert, 37

Naissance de Venus [*The Birth of Venus*] (Botticelli), 258

Napoléon (Gance), 197, 331n418

Napoléon (Ludwig), 37, 303n65

Naville, Pierre, 37, 303n66

Neuville, Geneviève de: Beauvoir bored at home of, 66–67; Beauvoir chooses book for, 61; bored at home of, 66–67; Fontainebleau picnic with, 228; identification of, 307n107; at Marie-Thérèse Lacoin's wedding, 149; with Zaza, 223; Zaza discusses, 47, 49

Neuville, Jacques de, 149

New gentlemen [*Nouveaux messieurs*] (Feyder), 154, 329n369

Newman, John Henry, 54, 55, 56, 71, 308n126, 314n179

Nicod, Jean George Pierre, 31, 34, 300n41

Nicomachean Ethics [*L'éthique à Nico-maque*] (Aristotle), 250, 333n464

Nietzsche, Friedrich, 40, 44, 49, 111, 305n83

Night is falling [*La nuit tombe*] (Ardel), 91, 320n251

Nizan, Paul: *agrégation* preparation, 234, 248–49, 250–51; on Beauvoir's *agrégation* academic progress, 257; Beauvoir's dislike for, 329n371; Beauvoir studies with, 260; in class, 161; discusses Marxism, 258; drawings by, 197, 248, 251; and future plans, 294; Grand Duke nickname of, 333n461; life summaries on, 287;

Nizan, Paul (*continued*): with Maheu, 214; Maheu discusses, 162, 249; Maheu sees, 216; marriage of, 211; Meyrignac visit, 282; outings with, 155; *petits camarades* outings, 252, 255, 264–65; on right to love, 94; at Sartre's gathering, 253; wife of, 248, 249–50, 252, 261, 264–65; work at home of, 259

Nolad, 193

Nord (Heller), 37, 42, 47, 55

Les nourritures terrestres [*Fruits of the Earth*] (Gide), 90

Nouveaux messieurs [New gentlemen] (Feyder), 154, 329n369

La nouvelle revue française, 95, 115, 168

Les nouvelles littéraires, 90, 100, 160

The nude woman [*La femme nue*] (Renoir), 152

La nuit tombe [Night is falling] (Ardel), 91, 320n251

Nymphéas [Water lilies] (Monet), 152

La nymphe au coeur fidèle [*The Constant Nymph*] (Kennedy), 57, 59, 199, 309–10n138

The Odyssey (Homer), 168, 176

L'offrande lyrique [*Song Offerings*] (Tagore), 29, 298–99n30

Ohanna, 151, 153

Olga, 101, 105

Olympia (Manet), 152

Les olympiques (Montherlant), 306n98

On the Nature of Things [*De Rerum Natura*] (Lucretius), 313n171

Onze chapitres sur Platon [Eleven chapters on Plato] (Alain), 90

Opales [Opals] (Jouhandeau), 103, 322n273

L'ordre [The order] (Arland), 212, 331n426

Othon Friesz, Emile, 55, 88–89, 309n131, 319n233

Ottman, Henry, 88, 319n232

Pabst, G. W., 325n305

Pagnol, Marcel, 89, 212, 320n241, 332n427

Palais Royal Gardens: Beauvoir lunches alone in, 29, 47, 135, 139, 161, 181; Beauvoir reads at, 181; mysterious scenes at, 28; outings with Eveski in, 207; outings with Gandillac in, 196, 198, 204, 210; outings with Maheu in, 164, 174, 213, 224, 234; reminds Beauvoir of Laforgue, 30

Panthéon, 180

Le paradis à l'ombre des épées [Paradise in the shadow of swords] (Montherlant), 306n98

Paris, locations in: Les Agriculteurs (cinema), 141, 233; Apollo (music hall), 25, 296n7; Bagatelle (rose garden), 217, 245, 332n429; Balzar, 266; Bateau Ivre, 167; Bibliothèque Ste. Geneviève, 70, 125, 134, 151, 154; Bibliothèque Victor Cousin, 70, 73, 90, 98, 320n245; Bobino, 148; La Boîte à Musique, 264; Le Bon Marché, 32, 41, 59, 263; Brasserie Weber, 25, 296n10; Le Carillon, 264; Caveau de la Bolée, 151; Châtelet, 154; Chez André, 265; chez Chabin, 253, 263; chez Dupont, 255; Chez Lipp, 163, 230, 245; Chez Pocardi (café), 55, 61, 67, 145, 162, 170, 196, 207, 210, 213, 215, 225, 311n156; chez Pons, 231; chez Wepler, 265; Ciné-Latin, 91; le Ciné Max-Lindor, 154; Closerie des Lilas, 260, 264; Coupole, 234; Deux Magots (café), 202, 249, 255; Dôme, 264; Dôme (restaurant-bar), 78, 105, 153, 189, 235, 264, 267, 301n51; Dominique's (café), 235; Européen (bar), 147, 153, 193; Evelynes (restaurant), 209, 223, 245; Falstaff, 257; La Fleur de Lys (restaurant), 164, 234; Fontainebleau, 228; Institut Catholique, 28, 63, 70–71, 74, 83, 91, 92, 125, 145; Janson-de-Sailly (high school), 125, 326n318; Jardin des Plantes, 201; Jockey (bar), 77, 78, 106, 129, 136–37, 144, 167, 301n51; Jungle (bar), 94, 118, 130–31; Knam (café), 104, 122, 125, 193, 264, 265; Koulak, 257; Lapin Agile, 159; Louvre, 50, 151–52; La

Maison des Amis des Livres (chez Monnier), 30, 89, 110, 114, 117, 138, 151, 168, 189, 211, 222, 299n36; Maxim's (bistro), 25, 296n10; Max Linder cinema, 244; Monument to Mickiewicz, 165, 330n385; Morris columns, 25, 296n9; Moulin Rouge (cabaret), 136, 153; Musée Carnavalet, 141; Musée du jeu de Paume, 141–42; Musée pédagogique (Museum of Pedagogy), 104, 322n278; Panthéon, 180; Père-Lachaise Cemetery, 188; Picard's (bookstore), 37, 54, 68, 100, 142, 303n65, 309n128; Place de l'Alma, 165; Rotonde (restaurant-bar), 86, 102, 262, 301n51; Rumpelmayer's, 232; Stryx (bar), 77, 78, 84–85, 92, 101, 105, 170–71, 190, 316n196; Studio des Ursulines (cinema), 27, 164, 298n21; Studio Diamant, 116–17, 325n304; Tuileries, 161; Vieux Colombier (cinema), 58, 98–99, 163, 310n142

Paris, locations in. See Luxembourg Gardens; Palais Royal Gardens; Tuileries Gardens

Pascal, Blaise, 62, 155

Passeur, Steve, 42

Pater, Jean-Baptiste, 141

Paulémile-Pissaro, 88, 318n222

Péguy, Charles, 63, 118

Le père humilié [The Humiliation of the Father] (Claudel), 104, 322n277

Père-Lachaise Cemetery, 188

Perrin, Jean, 90, 91

Le perroquet vert [The Green Parrot] (Bibesco), 123, 326n314

Perse, J., 251, 334n468

petits camarades, 333n449; agrégation preparation, 1, 234, 247, 248–49, 250–51, 333nn462,464–65; Beauvoir's thoughts on, 270, 279, 284; gatherings of, 253, 261; life summaries on, 288; outings, 252, 253–56, 264–65

petits camarades. See Maheu, René; Nizan, Paul; Sartre, Jean-Paul

Petouchka (ballet), 223, 332n438

Phaedrus [Phèdre] (Plato), 109, 323n286

phenomenology, 4

La philosophie de Charles Renouvier [The philosophy of Charles Renouvier] (Séailles), 35, 302n58

La philosophie de Kant [Kant's philosophy] (Delbos), 27

physical intimacy: Beauvoir experiences, 268, 277–79; Beauvoir longs for, 194–95; Beauvoir's discomfort with thought of, 32–34, 136; Gandillac discusses, 179

physics, Beauvoir's study of, 41, 42, 305n84, 307n102

Picard's (bookstore), 37, 54, 68, 100, 142, 303n65, 309n128

Picasso, Pablo, 142

The pickle family [La famille cornichon] (Beauvoir), 51, 308n116

The Pilgrim (Chaplin), 244, 333n457

Place de l'Alma, 165

Les plaisirs et les jours [Pleasures and Days] (Proust), 329n375

Plato, 323n286; Alain on, 90; Beauvoir and Merleau-Ponty study, 252; Beauvoir studies, 84, 91, 97, 129, 243, 256; Beauvoir studies with Merleau-Ponty, 252; Beauvoir studies with Sartre, 258; classes on, 314n180; on equality, 326n311; Gandillac discusses, 109, 122; Riquet discusses, 85; on sex differences, 326n311; study with petits camarades, 250, 255, 333n462

The Playboy (Le Baladin), 278, 279, 335n491

Playboy concept, 278, 279, 335n491

plays seen. See theater

Pleasures and Days [Les plaisirs et les jours] (Proust), 329n375

pneumatic messages, 35, 103, 117, 239, 302n59

Poe, Edgar Allen, 26, 296n11

Poincaré, Henri, 41, 46, 56, 58, 305n84, 310n144

Poliakoff, Monina, 37–38

Politzer, George, 193, 265, 267, 287, 331n416, 334n479

Pontremoli, Emmanuel, 310n141

Pontrémoli, Michel: art gallery outings with, 160; Beauvoir's correspondence with, 35, 36, 54, 60, 70, 117, 235; Beauvoir's thoughts of, 59, 60; brief encounters with, 72, 222; in class, 76; at library, 70; life summaries on, 64, 65; loans books to Beauvoir, 61; new year thoughts for, 119; on physical intimacy, 32; visits to, 57–58, 245–46

Ponty, Madame, 111

Portrait d'un vieux manoeuvre [Portrait of an old maneuver] (Asselin), 89, 319n238

Le potomak (Cocteau), 166, 328n346, 329n382, 330n387. *See also* eugenic cosmology

Poupette. *See* Beauvoir, Henriette-Hélène Bertrand de

Poussière [*Dusty Answer*] (Lehmann), 251, 333n467

Poussin, Nicolas, 50

The Power of Darkness [*La puissance des ténèbres*], 68, 313n172

The Power of Now (Tolle), 19n21

Pradelle (*Mémoires*). *See* Merleau-Ponty, Maurice

Prandières, Madeleine de. *See* Blomart de Prandières, Madeleine

Praxiteles, 151

Prévost, Jean, 57, 114, 309n137

Le Prince Igor (Borodin), 130, 327n326

Le progrès de la conscience [The progress of consciousness in western philosophy] (Brunschvicg), 70, 314n178

Proust, Marcel: Beauvoir aspires to emulate, 185; Beauvoir quotes from, 160, 329n375; Beauvoir reads, 140, 181, 241; Beauvoir studies, 140; identification of, 317n208; Merleau-Ponty and Lévi-Strauss discuss, 110; Pontremoli discusses, 57; Riquet discusses, 85; as spiritual stimulant, 140

La puissance des ténèbres [*The Power of Darkness*], 68, 313n172

Pushkin, Alexander, 99, 115–16, 321n262

Puvis de Chavannes, Pierre, 180

Pythagorus, 85, 317n209

Quantum Success (Whitman), 17–18n5

Quermadec, Lisa (*Mémoires*). *See* Le Cor, Josée

Quintin, Lili (Beauvoir's aunt), 311n150

Rabevel, ou le mal des ardents [Rabevel, or the ache of passion] (Fabre), 68, 313n174

racism, 3

Ramuz, Charles Ferdinand, 299n33

Raphaël, 151

The Red and the Black [*Le rouge et le noir*] (Righelli), 143, 328n358

religion. *See* Catholicism

Renaud, Mademoiselle, 205

Renoir, Jean, 141, 328n355

Renoir, Pierre-Auguste, 88, 141, 152

Renouvier, Charles, 26, 29, 35, 296nn12, 14

Renouvier (Milhaud), 26

Renouvier's system [*Le système de Renouvier*] (Hamelin), 26

The Republic (Plato), 84, 326n311

Le rêve de la femme endormie [The sleeping woman's dream] (Marval), 88, 319n229

Les Revellers, 253

Richard, Mademoiselle: Beauvoir is indifferent to, 201; brief encounters with, 150; at Brunschvicg's, 156; in class, 180; discusses Maheu, 214; kindness of, 205; outings with, 146, 157; resignation of, 132; unhappiness of, 162

Richon, Jean, 39

Righelli, Gennaro, 328n358

Rilke, Rainer Maria, 94, 212, 213, 331n426

Rimbaud, Arthur, 92

Riquet: bar outings with, 85, 92, 101, 170, 171; Beauvoir compares to Jacques, 85; Beauvoir discusses Jacques with, 78–79, 85–86, 316n203; Beauvoir's correspondence with, 117; Beauvoir's feelings about, 79, 83, 93, 106, 172; Beauvoir's fondness for, 90; discusses cinema, 92; distance from Maheu, 167; does not greet at bar, 105; new year thoughts for, 119

Riri (Beauvoir's cousin), 220, 332n436

Rivaud, Albert, 71, 75, 92, 148, 202, 314–15nn180, 188

Rivière, Jacques: on Alain-Fournier, 40; Beauvoir discovers, 63; Beauvoir quotes from, 69, 313n176; Beauvoir thinks of discussing with Jacques, 51, 217, 221; identification of, 300–301n42; as influence on Beauvoir, 301n43; on love, 219; Mathieu and Vauthé discusses, 66; Merleau-Ponty reads aloud from, 126–27; as spiritual stimulant, 140; Stépha discusses, 32

La robe prétexte [The Stuff of Youth] (Mauriac), 29, 298n29

Robert (Beauvoir's cousin), 186, 189, 331n405

Robin, Léon: Beauvoir analyzes Sextus Empiricus with, 223; Beauvoir finds deadly, 154; Beauvoir finds insipid, 93; Beauvoir presents in class of, 122; Beauvoir sleeps in class of, 149; brief encounters with, 150; class of, 72, 76, 150, 154, 178, 195, 204, 205; identification of, 326n310; joking about, 155, 252; laughter in class of, 126; lectures painful to follow, 86

Rochelle, Drieu la, 122, 326n312

Rodin, Auguste, 212, 213, 331n426

Rodriguès, Gustave, 110, 126, 130, 324n299

Rodriguez, Tori, 19n24

Les rois aveugles [Blinded Kings] (Kessel), 196

Romains, Jules, 33, 161, 163, 193, 301n50

Ronsard, Pierre de, 63

Rose d'ombre [Shadow rose] (Arnoux), 164, 329n383

Rotonde (restaurant-bar), 86, 102, 262, 301n51

Le rouge et le noir [The Red and the Black] (Righelli), 143, 328n358

Rousseau, Jean-Jacques, 151, 153, 154, 252, 263, 264

Roussel, Mademoiselle, 215

Roustand, 100

Roy, Édouard Le, 61, 311n154

Ruiz, Don Miguel, 14

Rumpelmayer's, 232

Sainte Anne [The Virgin and Child with St. Anne] (da Vinci), 142

Sainte-Anne's, 65, 312n163

Salacrou, Armand, 161

Sallust, 166

salon culture, 39, 304n80

Salon d'Automne, 88–89, 90, 318n220

Les saltimbanques (Mérinoff), 88, 318n223

Le sang des autres (Beauvoir), 64

Santelli, César, 90, 320n244

Sarment, Jean, 172, 175, 330n394

Sartre, Jean-Paul: affectionate conversation with, 259; agrégation preparation, 1, 234; argument at Luxembourg Gardens, 2–3, 259; on Beauvoir as female scholar, 254; and Beauvoir as Walkyrie, 248, 279, 280; Beauvoir compares to Maheu, 257, 260; Beauvoir intoxicated with, 263; Beauvoir reads works by, 264; on Beauvoir's agrégation written exam success, 257; and Beauvoir's choice among loves, 262, 268, 271–73, 274–75, 280, 281, 283–84; Beauvoir's correspondence with at Meyrignac, 273, 275; Beauvoir's dislike for, 329n371; Beauvoir's intimacy with, 277–79; Beauvoir studies Plato with, 258; beginning of relationship with Beauvoir, 1, 248–49, 250–51, 252, 253–56, 257–58, 259–61; brief encounters with, 185; cinema outings with, 260, 265–66, 267; and Combes, 277, 335n489; conversations with, 155; discusses eugenic cosmology, 249; discusses Rousseau, 252; drawings by, 251; explication by, 76; and future plans, 294, 336n501; Gandillac speaks of Beauvoir to, 198, 213; gathering at home of, 253; influence on Beauvoir of, 259–60; as leprechaun, 271, 277, 278, 279, 334–35n483; life summaries on, 287, 288;

Sartre, Jean-Paul (*continued*): Luxembourg Gardens outings with, 259, 260, 263, 264; with Maheu, 195, 214; Maheu discusses, 249, 282; Maheu sees, 216; Maheu wants to introduce to Beauvoir, 196–97, 234, 247; *Memoirs of a Dutiful Daughter* on, 1, 2–3; Meyrignac visit, 276–80; music by, 265, 334n480; nickname for Gandillac, 224, 332n439; outings with, 258, 260–61, 262–63, 265, 266–67; *petits camarades* outings, 252, 253–56, 264–65; and Playboy concept, 278, 279, 335n491; Poupette spends evening with, 242; reading recommended by, 289; song about Gandillac, 266, 334n480; tells Beauvoir about herself, 257; "that's when everything started," 1, 248

Savin, 90, 104, 155–56, 180, 193, 205, 320n246

Schmit, 71

Schnitzler, Arthur, 34, 302n56

The School for Wives [*L'école de femmes*] (Gide), 144, 328n359

Schuler, Mademoiselle, 62, 137

Schwob, Marcel, 68, 313n173

Schwob, René, 138, 328n351

Schwob, 150, 155, 161, 162, 180, 182, 215

Séailles, Gabriel, 35, 302n58

The Seashell and the Clergyman [*La coquille et le clergyman*] (Dulac), 114, 325n297

The Second Sex (Beauvoir), 2

self: and Beauvoir's vocation experience, 236–39; revealing, 31, 300nn39–40

Self-Help (Smiles), 5–6

self-help as focus of Beauvoir's diary, 5–17; on attitudes towards others, 10–11; on emotion, 14–16, 19n24; on goal-setting, 8–9; on gratitude, 6–7; on Law of Attraction, 7; on present moment, 12–17, 19n21; on self-analysis, 7–8; and self-help tradition, 5–6, 17–18nn4–5, 19n21; on self-love, 7, 8, 9, 10; universality of, 6, 18n9; and written meditations, 9–10, 18n17

self-worship [*le cult de moi*], 303n64

Séverini, Gino, 191

Sextus Empiricus, 76, 182, 223

Shadow Rose [*Rose d'ombre*] (Arnoux), 164, 329n383

She Came to Stay (Beauvoir), 2

Siegfried et le Limousin [*Siegfried and the Limousin*] (Giraudoux), 46, 79, 89, 90, 316n201

Le signe de Zorro [*The Mark of Zorro*], 91, 320n249

Si le grain ne meurt (Gide), 226, 332n442

The Silence of Colonel Bramble [*Les silences du colonel Bramble*] (Maurois), 173, 330n396

Les silences du colonel Bramble [*The Silence of Colonel Bramble*] (Maurois), 173, 330n396

Simon le pathéthique (Giraudoux), 26, 296–97n15

Siria, 160, 329n377

The sleeping woman's dream [*Le rêve de la femme endormie*] (Marval), 88, 319n229

Smiles, Samuel, 5–6

The Social Contract [*Le contrat social*] (Rousseau), 252

Song Offerings [*L'offrande lyrique*] (Tagore), 29, 298–99n30

Song of Songs, 332n434

"Souffrances du chrétien" [The Christian's Suffering] (Mauriac), 33, 90

Soupault, Philippe, 47, 85, 92, 307n108

Souriau, Michel, 38, 304n71

Soutine, Chaim, 91

Souverbie, Jean, 88, 319n230

Spinoza, Baruch: Beauvoir's love for, 128, 138; Beauvoir studies, 71, 72; Gandillac discusses, 111; Hannequin on, 251, 333n466; identification of, 314n181; Laporte on, 134; Maheu studies, 161; Merleau-Ponty and Lévi-Strauss argue about, 127

Spinoza, LaPorte on, 134

The Spirit of the Laws [*L'esprit des lois*] (Montesquieu), 60, 311n151

Spitz, Jacques, 71, 314n182
Stages of Mathematical Philosophy [*Les Étapes de la philosophie mathématiques*] (Brunschvicg), 55–56
Stendhal, 124, 126, 162, 193, 216, 238, 290
Stépha. *See* Avdicovith, Stépha
Sternberg, Josef von, 58, 158, 310n142
Stevenson, Robert Louis, 26, 95, 296n11
stoicism, 237, 333n450
Storm, Theodor, 38, 303n69
Strindberg, August, 145, 152
Stryx (bar), 77, 78, 84–85, 92, 101, 105, 170–71, 190, 316n196
Studio des Ursulines (cinema), 27, 164, 298n21
Studio Diamant, 116–17, 325n304
The Stuff of Youth [*La robe prétexte*] (Mauriac), 29, 298n29
Suarès, André, 89, 319–20n240
Suarès, Carlo, 89, 320n240
Sylla, 187
Symposium, or The Drinking Party [*Le banquet*] (Plato), 109, 323n286
Le système de Renouvier [Renouvier's system] (Hamelin), 26
Le système du monde, histoire des doctrines cosmologiques de Platon à Copernic [The system of the world: the history of cosmological doctrines from Plato to Copernicus] (Duhem), 77, 315n192
The system of the world: the history of cosmological doctrines from Plato to Copernicus [*Le système du monde, histoire des doctrines cosmologiques de Platon à Copernic*] (Duhem), 77, 315n192

Tagore, Rabindranath, 6, 29, 298–99n30
The Tale of the Fisherman and the Fish (Pushkin), 99, 321n262
Tallemant des Réaux, Gideon, 290
Teatro dei piccoli (Children's theater), 123, 326n313
theater: *À quoi penses-tu?* (Passeur), 42; Barbette (trapeze artist), 153, 329n368; *Le cadavre vivant* [*The Living Corpse*] (Tolstoy), 73–74, 314n184; *Départ (Departure)* (Gantillon), 95, 101, 322n270; *Jean de la Lune* [Jean from the moon], 165, 167, 173, 330n386; *Le malade imaginaire* [*The Imaginary Invalid*] (Molière), 131, 327n328; *Le Prince Igor* (Borodin), 130, 327n326; *The Tale of the Fisherman and the Fish* (Pushkin), 99, 321n262; *Teatro dei piccoli* (Children's theater), 123, 326n313; Théâtre de Dix Heures, 230; *The Three Must-Get-Theres* (Linder), 99, 321n262; *Volpone ou le renard* [*Volpone or The Fox*] (Jonson), 101, 108, 322n269
Théâtre de Dix Heures, 230
Thérèse Desqueyroux (Mauriac), 142
Thomas l'imposteur (Cocteau), 316n204
Thoreau, Henry David, 145, 328n360
The Three Must-Get-Theres (Linder), 99, 321n262
The Tidings Brought to Mary [*L'annonce faite à Marie*] (Claudel), 104, 322n277
The time of the cherries, or Fanchette [*Au temps des cerises, ou Fanchette*] (Vayre), 141, 328n356
Tolle, Eckhart, 19n21
Tolstoy, Leo, 73–74, 314n184
Topaze (Pagnol), 89, 212, 320n241, 332n427
Toulet, Paul-Jean, 213, 242, 332n428
le Tour de France, 249
Tournant dangereux [*Dangerous Corner*] (Vlaminck), 201, 331n422
Tresfort, Pierre, 182, 330n400
Tresfort, Pierre (Beauvoir's uncle), 182, 330n400
Triky, 154
La trilogie du culte du moi [Trilogy of self-worship] (Barrès), 303n64
Tristan (Mann), 26, 296n13
Tristan et Yseult, 109, 323–24n287
The troubled life of Jean Hermelin [*La vie inquiète de Jean Hermelin*] (Lacretelle), 100, 321n265
Troussel, Charlot, 191
Tucker, Sophie, 253, 264, 334n470

Tuileries, 30, 161, 197, 222, 224, 228, 251, 257, 267; outings with Maheu at, 224

Tuileries Gardens: art gallery outing in, 191; Beauvoir reads alone in, 161, 228; outings with Gandillac in, 258; outings with Maheu in, 224; outings with Sartre in, 257, 267; outings with Stépha in, 30; outings with Zaza in, 197, 222, 251

Le tunnel (Kellermann), 34, 302n54

Ubu Roi [King Ubu] (Jarry), 51, 308n116, 324n294

unaminism, 301n50

Underworld [Les nuits de Chicago] (Sternberg), 158, 310n142

Ungar, Herman, 30, 299n37

Upanishads, 5, 6

Urien's Voyage [Le voyage d'Urien] (Gide), 226, 332n444

Valensin, Auguste, 38, 304n71

Valentine (Beauvoir's aunt), 102

Valéry, Paul, 111, 115, 138, 202, 324n292

Vallotton, Félix, 89

Van Dongen, Kees, 88, 91, 225, 319n231

Vanetti, A., 100, 144–45

Les varais (Chardonne), 189–90, 331n406

Variété [Variety] (Dupont), 58, 310n144

Vathaire, Pierre de, 145, 149

Vaudou, Gaston, 88, 318–19n225

Vauthé, Annie, 66

Vayre, Charles, 141, 328n356

Le vent [The Wind] (Sjöström), 143, 328n358

Le vent du monde [The world's wind] (Spitz), 71, 314n182

Vialatte, Alexandre, 51, 308n117

Victor ou les enfants au pouvoir [Victor, or The Children Take Power] (Vitrac), 114, 324–25n297

Vie de Goya [Life of Goya] (d'Ors y Roviro), 134, 327n335

Vie de Quintus Fixlein [Life of Quintus Fixlein] (Jean Paul), 38, 304n72

La vie de Racine (Mauriac), 36

La vie de Saint Alexis [The Life of St. Alexis], 93, 320n253

La vie inquiète de Jean Hermelin [The troubled life of Jean Hermelin] (Lacretelle), 100, 321n265

La vierge [Madonna] (da Vinci), 142

Une vie secrète [A secret life] (Lenormand), 135, 328n345

Vieux Colombier (cinema), 58, 98–99, 163, 310n142

The Virgin and Child with St. Anne [Sainte Anne] (da Vinci), 142

Vitrac, Roger, 114, 324–25n297

Vlaminck, Maurice de, 201, 331n422

Volpone ou le renard [Volpone or The Fox] (Jonson), 101, 108, 322n269

Le voyage d'Urien [Urien's Voyage] (Gide), 226, 332n444

La voyageuse [The female traveler] (Picasso), 142

Wagner, 111

Wagner, Mademoiselle, 111, 182

Wagner, Richard, 246

Walkyrie nickname, 248, 279, 280

Waroquier, Henry de, 89

Wartelle, Jacques, 49, 307n111

Water lilies [Nymphéas] (Monet), 152

Watteau, Jean-Antoine, 141

Wedding song [L'épithalame] (Chardonne), 194, 205, 331n415

Weil, Simone, 104–5, 112

When Things of the Spirit Come First (Beauvoir), 3

Whitman, Christy, 17–18nn5, 14, 17

Wilde, Oscar, 193

The Wind [Le vent] (Sjöström), 143, 328n358

With the eyes of the spirit [Avec les yeux de l'esprit] (Béhaine), 115, 325n302

Woman with a rose [La femme à la rose] (Favory), 88, 318n221

Women (The seven sisters) [Femmes (Les sept soeurs)] (Michaëlis), 149, 329n365

working-class life, 146–47

The world's wind [*Le vent du monde*] (Spitz), 71, 314n182

Wright, Richard, 3

Young Man in Chains [*L'enfant chargé de chaines*] (Mauriac), 27, 297n17

Yvette (Beauvoir's cousin), 201, 331n421

Zak, Eugène, 89, 319n236

Zaza. *See* Lacoin, Elisabeth

Zuorro, Marc, 253

Zweig, Stephan, 122

Errata for the Hardcover Edition of
Diary of a Philosophy Student,
Volume 1, 1926–27

1926 (SECOND NOTEBOOK)

p. 83, line 18: "because of Cocteau" should read "and Cocteau's precepts."

p. 101, line 22: "irritate him" should read "invite him over."

p. 119, line 26: insert "(p. 60)" before "All right."

p. 144, line 3: "dead people" should read "maestros."

p. 150, line 13: "Luxembourg Gardens" should read "Musée du Luxembourg."

p. 154, line 9: "intoxicated" should read "thrilled."

p. 158, line 36: "intoxications" should read "raptures."

p. 160, line 33: "self-intoxication" should read "exhilaration with myself."

p. 167, line 9: "The Self" should read "Evening."

p. 169, line 1: "youthful" might also be translated as "childish."

p. 175, line 10: "I was astonished to savor" should read "I marveled at savoring."

p. 177, line 6: "(oh, gallery 143)" should read "(oh, the gallery of Jacque's home)."

p. 184, line 30: "faciès" should read "facies."

p. 184, line 32: "apellant" should read "appelant."

p. 184, n. *, line 1: "letters" should read "words."

p. 187, line 28: "intoxication" should read "exhilaration" both times.

p. 187, line 33: "daughter" should read "lady."

p. 195, line 6: "love" should read "comfort."

p. 199, n. 2, line 6: "published as *Études* [*Studies*]" should read "among others."

p. 200, n. 4: the first sentence should read "This quotation is a modified version of 'Qu'un cri sorte de là,' from Charles Ferninand Ramuz's *Adieu à beaucoup de personnages* (1924); my translation."

p. 201, n. 19: the first two sentences should be deleted.

p. 203, n. 42: "play" should read "dialogue."

p. 210, n. 121, line 1: "most likely refers to" should read "might refer to."

p. 210, n. 121, lines 5–8: "One might ... 204" should read "Jacques might also be the friend in question. See *Mémoires*, 83–85, 168–169, 125–131, 274–282; *Memoirs*, 60–61, 91–96, 120–122, 198–204."

p. 211, n. 125: "Hélène" should read "Henriette;" after "sister"; insert "Henriette became known years later as the painter by the name of Hélène de Beauvoir."

p. 220, n. 276, line 13: "Bertrande" should read "Bertrand;" delete "or Hélène."

p. 222, n. 301, line 4: "and student of" should read "well-versed in."

p. 222, n. 311: "Hegel's notion ... 532" should read "Félix Ravaisson's *Essai sur la Métaphysique d'Aristote*, vol. 1, p. 462 (first published in 1837 and later reprinted in philosophy textbooks such as Nicolas Joseph Schwartz's *Manuel de l'histoire de la philosophe ancienne*, p. 13). Ravaisson writes 'Avec la réciprocité d'affection, l'amitié exige donc entre les amis la réciprocité absolue et comme l'identité de conscience.' (Correspondence of February 15, 2011, from Toril Moi to Margaret Simons)."

p. 223, n. 324: after "word." insert, "It was later determined that beatitude [*béatitude*] was the correct deciphering of this word."

1927 (FOURTH NOTEBOOK)

p. 230, lines 16 and 17: "self-important" should read "autonomous."

p. 230, line 29: "young girl" should read "young woman."

p. 233, line 20: "Are the barbarians right" should read "Would the barbarians be right?"

p. 234, line 19: After "Équipes Sociales," insert the following note: "The Château de Malmaison was formerly the residence of Empress Joséphine de Beauharnais."

p. 236, lines 12 and 13: "the gathering of any dream leaves in the dreamer's heart" should read, "and without heartbreak leaves the harvesting of a dream to the heart that stole it."

p. 239, line 19: "drunkenness" should read "euphoria."

p. 239, line 22: "a snack" should read "the afternoon snack."

p. 243, line 6: "verses" should read "worms."

p. 245, line 27: "girls who go to l'École Normale" should read "*Normaliennes* [female Normalians]."

p. 245, line 33: "lemonade again" should read "another lemon squeezed dry."

p. 247, line 22: "charitable work" should read "social work."

p. 251, n. *, line 2: "only the life of the real exists because" should read "only life is real since."

p. 255, line 21: "But arrive where?" should be in standard font.

p. 266, line 20: "thesis" should read "*diplôme*."

p. 268, line 19: "woods" should read "Bois de Boulogne park."

p. 273, line 2: "a snack" should read "the afternoon snack."

p. 276, line 25: "will sacrifice" should read "would sacrifice."

p. 279, line 35: delete "it" after "perceive."

p. 287, line 1: "imagine" should read "represent."

p. 287, line 23: "near to" should read "then about."

p. 287, line 30: "dirty, poorly kept" should read "dirty students in need of bathing."

p. 289, line 21: "questions (for the *agrégation*)" should read "subjects to be presented during the *agrégation* oral exams."

p. 290, line 10: " . . . and you want a discreet heart . . ." should not be surrounded by quotation marks.

p. 291, line 33: "students" should read "students in middle or high school."

p. 298, line 21: "lacking" should read "failed."

p. 301, line 20: the heading "August 4" should read "August 3."

p. 303, line 1: the heading "Thursday, August 5" should read "Thursday, August 4."

p. 306, line 30: "The letter I wrote in response is there" should read "The letter I wrote is there and the response."

p. 307, line 5: "more feverish" should read "no longer feverish."

p. 312, line 29: "I compare a life weary of being to this painful return where a sole person kept going" should read "I compare it to this distressing return where one person alone maintained a life weary of being."

p. 313, line 8: "assignments" should read "essays."

p. 314, line 2: "at twilight every day" should read "with the passing of time."

p. 315, line 14: "study groups" should read "*Équipes Sociales*."

p. 315, line 21: "chatted seriously" should read "had a serious discussion."

p. 316, line 6: "some of them in this home of mine" should read "definitely; in this home of mine."

p. 317, line 10: "girlfriend" should read "friend."

p. 317, line 11: "on a lakeside bench" should read "on a bench in the Bois de Boulogne park."

p. 317, line 13–14: "sensitivity" should read "finesse."

p. 318, line 2: "Nyu" should read "Nju."

p. 318, line 18: "woods" should read "Bois de Boulogne park."

p. 322, n. 33: "From Mallarmé's 'Apparition,' trans. Lewisohn. Beauvoir also quoted this poem on October 6, 1926" should read "From Mallarmé's 'Apparition.' See note 132 in Beauvoir's 1926 diary."

p. 328, n. 115: "*Critique de la raison pure* [*Critique of Pure Reason*]" should read "*Critique de la raison pratique* [*Critique of Practical Reason*]."

p. 329, n. 129, should read as follows: The *diplôme*, or *Diplôme d'études supérieures* (DES), refers to a graduate thesis equivalent to today's Masters (*maîtrise*) in France (CJ 513). Following her success on the exams in ethics and psychology in the spring of 1928, Simone de Beauvoir met with Prof. Brunschvicg who suggested for her *diplôme* topic, "The Concept in Leibniz" (Beauvoir, *Mémoires* 369; *Memoirs* 266). The highly competitive exam, the *agrégation*, consisted of three essays written during three specified time periods, and one oral exam. The longest of the written exams was a six-hour essay written on a previously unannounced topic. The other two written exams were each four hours long and from subjects announced in advance. The oral exam included one lengthy lesson, on a topic not covered in coursework, for which the student had seven hours to prepare [*la grande leçon*], and several shorter oral quizzes on philosophers selected at random by the jury, including one each in French, Latin, Greek, and either English or German. Successful completion of the *agrégation* was required to teach in certain high schools [*lycées*] or in universities [*Facultés*] and guaranteed a job for life in the national French educational system (email correspondence between Sylvie Le Bon de Beauvoir and Barbara Klaw of July 16 and 19, 2007).

p. 330, n. 134: From "In 1925" through "Simone de Beauvoir, 49)," should read "The historic educational reforms of 1924 permitted women for the first time to attend the École Normale Supérieure on rue d'Ulm and to take all of the *agrégation* exams and *certificats* previously reserved for men."

p. 330, n. 144: "José Le Core" should read "José Le Corre."

p. 331, n. 150, line 8: "thesis" should read "*diplôme.*"

p. 332, n. 173: delete entire note.

p. 333, n. 189, line 3: "French" should read "Swiss."

p. 334, n. 192, line 1: "epitaph" should read "epigraph."

p. 334, n. 196, line 7: "two years of memorization" should read "years of intensive training in precise methods of intelligent thinking and working."

p. 334, n. 207: delete entire note.

p. 335, n. 219, line 6: "infante" should read "infante défunte."

Contributors

SIMONE DE BEAUVOIR (1908–86) was a French existentialist philosopher. Her works include *The Ethics of Ambiguity* (1947) and *The Second Sex* (1949).

BARBARA KLAW is a professor emerita of French at Northern Kentucky University. She is the translator of *Diary of a Philosophy Student: Volume 1, 1926–27*, and author of *Le Paris de Beauvoir*.

SYLVIE LE BON DE BEAUVOIR, adopted daughter and literary executor of Simone de Beauvoir, is the editor of *Lettres à Sartre* and other works by Beauvoir.

MARGARET A. SIMONS is Distinguished Research Professor Emerita at Southern Illinois University Edwardsville and the author of *Beauvoir and "The Second Sex": Feminism, Race, and the Origins of Existentialism*. Klaw, Le Bon de Beauvoir, and Simons coedited *Diary of a Philosophy Student: Volume 1, 1926–27*

MARYBETH TIMMERMANN is a contributing translator and editor of Beauvoir's *Philosophical Writings*, *"The Useless Mouths" and Other Literary Writings*, *Political Writings*, and *Feminist Writings*.

BOOKS IN THE BEAUVOIR SERIES

Series edited by Margaret A. Simons and
Sylvie Le Bon de Beauvoir

Philosophical Writings
    Edited by Margaret A. Simons
    with Marybeth Timmermann
    and Mary Beth Mader
    Foreword by
    Sylvie Le Bon de Beauvoir

Diary of a Philosophy Student:
Volume 1, 1926–27
    Edited by Barbara Klaw,
    Sylvie Le Bon de Beauvoir,
    and Margaret A. Simons,
    with Marybeth Timmermann
    Translation and Notes
    by Barbara Klaw
    Foreword by
    Sylvie Le Bon de Beauvoir

Wartime Diary
    Edited by Margaret A. Simons
    and Sylvie Le Bon de Beauvoir
    Translation and Notes
    by Anne Deing Cordero
    Foreword by
    Sylvie Le Bon de Beauvoir

"The Useless Mouths" and Other
Literary Writings
    Edited by Margaret A. Simons
    and Marybeth Timmermann
    and Foreword by
    Sylvie Le Bon de Beauvoir

Political Writings
    Edited by Margaret A. Simons
    and Marybeth Timmermann
    and Foreword by
    Sylvie Le Bon de Beauvoir

Feminist Writings
    Edited by Margaret A. Simons
    and Marybeth Timmermann
    Foreword by
    Sylvie Le Bon de Beauvoir

Diary of a Philosophy Student:
Volume 2, 1928–29
    Edited by Barbara Klaw,
    Sylvie Le Bon de Beauvoir,
    Margaret A. Simons,
    and Marybeth Timmermann
    Translation and Notes by
    Barbara Klaw
    Foreword by
    Sylvie Le Bon de Beauvoir

The University of Illinois Press
is a founding member of the
Association of University Presses.

UNIVERSITY OF ILLINOIS PRESS
1325 South Oak Street   Champaign, IL 61820-6903
www.press.uillinois.edu